1998

Managing
Business Ethics

Straight Talk About
How To Do It Right

ACQUISITIONS EDITOR   Tim Kent
ASSISTANT EDITOR   Ellen Ford
MARKETING MANAGER   Debra Riegert
PRODUCTION EDITOR   Christine S. Walsh
DESIGN DIRECTION   Karin Gerdes Kincheloe
COVER ILLUSTRATION   Randy Lyhus
COVER AND TEXT DESIGN   Nancy Field
MANUFACTURING COORDINATOR   Dorothy Sinclair
ILLUSTRATION COORDINATOR   Jaime Perea

This book was set in Janson Text by Publishing Synthesis, Ltd. and
printed and bound by Courier Stoughton. The cover was printed by Phoenix.

Recognizing the importance of preserving what has been written, it is a
policy of John Wiley & Sons, Inc. to have books of enduring value published
in the United States printed on acid-free paper, and we exert our best
efforts to that end.

Library of Congress Cataloging in Publication Data:
Treviño, Linda Klebe.
   Managing business ethics : straight talk about how to do it right
/ Linda Klebe Treviño, Katherine A. Nelson.
      p.   cm.
   Includes bibliographical references.
   ISBN 0-471-59848-8 (pbk.)
   1. Business ethics   2. Business ethics—Case studies.
I. Nelson, Katherine A., 1948–   . II. Title.
HF5387.T734 1995
174′ .4—dc20   94-42380
                                                          CIP

Printed in the United States of America

10 9 8 7 6 5 4 3 2 1

Contents

SECTION III
Ethics and the Manager   109

SECTION IV
Ethics and the Organization   171

A NOTE TO STUDENTS

This book was written for you. We have listened to your complaints and your wishlists and have tried to pare this complicated subject down to a digestible size. The cases that appear in this book all happened to people just like you, who were not as prepared to deal with the dilemmas as you will be after taking this course. Before you get into this, we have one suggestion: know that regardless of how large an organization you find yourself in, you're not some little cog in a giant wheel. You have the power to change, not only your own behavior and knowledge of ethics, but also the behavior and knowledge of the people you work with. Use that power: the job you save may be your own.

ACKNOWLEDGEMENTS

It takes a lot of work by a lot of people to make a project like this come together. We would like to begin with some joint thank-you's. Then, because this process has been so meaningful for each of us, we would like to separately share our more personal thanks.

We both offer our heartfelt appreciation to the executives—Harry Birkeruth, Kent Druyvesteyn, Lawrence Foster, Joe Paterno, Shirley Peterson, Vin Sarni, and Carl Skooglund—who agreed to share their valuable time and advice, some of them on multiple occasions. Their wisdom can be found throughout this book, and not just in the pages explicitly devoted to them. They helped bring the subject of managing business ethics to life.

We also wish to thank Ruby Shepherd (secretary to the Department of Management at Penn State) for typing interview manuscripts, Gary Weaver (University of Delaware and formerly Penn State doctoral student) for being our philosophy advisor, Nancy McDonnell (Penn State faculty member) for providing insight from an international business perspective, Dennis Gioia (Penn State faculty member and dear friend) for sharing his Pinto Fire Case and especially his reflections, and Richard Daley and Scott Hibbard (University of Montana) for contributing the Manville case.

John Wiley & Sons, Inc. is a fine publisher with a superb team. These people encouraged, nudged, wined, dined, housed, laughed, nudged, and nudged again. We have so many Wiley people to thank for making this project a success: Tim Kent, our editor; Ellen Ford, our main contact and source of moral support; Christine Walsh, our production editor; and Karin Kincheloe, our design coordinator.

The book's reviewers also contributed significantly to making this a better book. Our thanks go to Steve Brenner (Portland State University), Donald L. McCabe (Rutgers University), Jerald Greenberg (Ohio State University), Phyllis (Pat) Rettew (Vanderbilt University), Jack M. Hires (Valparaiso University), Peggy Sue Heath (University of Washington), Ralph Braithwaite (University of Hartford),

Justin Tan (University of Central Florida), Bill Rupp (University of Georgia), and John Dobson (California Polytechnic University).

We also want to thank our students and particularly the Penn State MBA classes of 1995 and 1996 who actually read some of the chapters in manuscript form and provided us with excellent feedback and advice.

We especially want to thank Liz Watkins at the Hazleton campus of Penn State University, who graciously allowed us to use conference room facilities on multiple occasions when we would rendezvous midway between New York and State College for all-day writing and discussion sessions.

SPECIAL ACKNOWLEDGEMENTS— LINDA K. TREVIÑO

Many special people have helped along the path that brought me to the writing of this book. I'd like to begin by thanking my mentors in the doctoral program at Texas A&M University's management department. Many thanks to Stuart Young-blood (now at Texas Christian University), Don Hellriegel, Richard Woodman, Dick Daft (now at Vanderbilt University), and Mary Zey (Sociology Department), who encouraged my early theorizing and research in business ethics. They told me to go with my gut and to do what was important—and they supported my every step.

Shortly after becoming a faculty member at Penn State, I had the good fortune to meet my friend and co-author, Kate Nelson. I was intrigued by a brief Wall Street Journal article about Kate's work at Citibank (you'll read more about that later). We met and became fast friends, who (believe it or not) loved talking about business ethics. We decided to write an article together and the rest, as Kate says, is history. Kate brought the real world into this book in a way that I couldn't have done. She was also willing to tell me when I was getting too academic (not her words exactly). It became more and more clear to me that we were supposed to write this book together, and I'm very glad we did. Thanks, Kate!

The article became a book proposal that we shared with publishers at the Academy of Management meeting in 1992. Shortly thereafter, Bill Oldsey (formerly publisher at John Wiley, Inc.) showed up in my office at Penn State. His enthusiasm for the book was immediate and infectious. I want to thank Bill for the special part he played in this incredible journey.

Finally, I want to thank the light of my life, Dan, for the inspiration, love, and support he provides every day of my life, and for being one of the most ethical human beings I know. And I want to thank family members (especially my father, brother, and uncle), colleagues, and many dear friends for not only cheering me on (as usual), but for their many contributions to this book. They have served as readers and interviewees. They have provided clipping services, and offered ideas for cases. They were there when I was overwhelmed. I can't thank them enough.

SPECIAL ACKNOWLEDGEMENTS—
KATHERINE A. NELSON

You can't write a book about something if you don't have an abiding interest in the subject matter. I began to care about ethics and integrity as a very young child, and as part of a family where "doing it right" was the only way to do something. So, my biggest debt is to my parents, Harry R. and Benadette Prendergast Nelson, and my brother, James V. Nelson. My parents worked tirelessly to carefully and lovingly set me on the right path. Jim's generosity and enthusiastic support of his older sister has encouraged me not only to teach ethics, but also to write this book. I'm grateful to Jim's wife, Susan, for her many encouraging words of support when I was ready to tear my hair out. My extended family has also done much to hone my sense of right and kindness—my grandparents, my aunts, uncles, cousins—and I am grateful to them.

Thanks also to my dear friend and business partner, Jonathan H. Mann, who is continually a source of encouragement, intelligence, and humor. A heartfelt thanks goes to my inner circle of friends, who provided valuable encouragement, advice, and moral support: Sally Nelson, Ann and John Hedberg, Carol Dygert, Jan Tunney, Anja Reid, Gregory MacKay, George Hensinger, Joe Karam, Alice and Randy Bogar, Marie Hameline, and John Grozier.

Many thanks to my friends in the academic community. Thanks go first to Wharton, where I'm a senior fellow, and particularly to Dr. Thomas W. Dunfee, who's not only my manager there and a world-class ethicist, but who's also a superior human being and a cherished friend. Thanks to Dr. Thomas Donaldson of Georgetown, another world-class ethicist, for his encouragement and friendship. Thanks also to Lauretta Tomasco of Wharton and to Pat Rettew, who is retired from Vanderbilt University's faculty, who have both contributed to this effort with their advice, moral support, and friendship.

Thanks also go to the many managers who, each in his or her own way, taught me that business ethics needn't be an oxymoron: Cal Asher, formerly of the Utica (NY) Observer-Dispatch; Charlie Fohlin, formerly of Honeywell Information Systems in Wellesley, MA; Tom Brown, formerly of Merrill Lynch in White Plains, NY; and Christopher York, Don Armiger, Peter Thorp, Judith Fullmer, Henry Morales, Jerry Lieberman, Michael Brooks, Michael Silverman, Peter Carey, and Jane Shannon—all currently or formerly with Citibank in New York City.

A special thank you goes to Stephen—an honorable man if there ever was one— who has provided thoughtful advice, encouragement, friendship, the no–so–occasional nudge when I needed one, and, most important, his love. And thanks to Del, who raised him to be so special.

Of course, a final thank you goes to my co–author, Linda Treviño, for her dear, dear friendship, and for working with me to produce this book in what was—in comparison to accounts from other writing teams—an almost painless experience.

SECTION I

Introduction to Business Ethics

CHAPTER ONE

Introducing Straight Talk About Managing Business Ethics: Where We're Going and Why

Tʜɪs ʙᴏᴏᴋ ʙᴇɢᴀɴ with a fortuitous phone call back in 1987 that resulted in a friendship. Linda Treviño, associate professor of organizational behavior at Penn State University, noticed a small article on the front page of the *Wall Street Journal.* The piece described a game to teach business ethics that had been developed at Citicorp, the nation's largest commercial bank. As someone who teaches ethics to business students, and who cares deeply about preparing students to think about ethics and manage their conduct in corporations, she decided to find out more about Citicorp's game. She called the game's developer, Kate Nelson, a vice president and head of human resources communications at Citicorp. The rest, as they say, is history.

We began a dialogue and over time discovered that we had a lot in common. We had both learned that many students—whether on a campus or in a corporation—felt intimidated and turned off by the subject of ethics. We had both listened to their frustrations: "Why does this have to be so mysterious? This is hopeless; there's nothing we can do about the behavior of people who report to us. Give us some guidance. Tell us what we should be doing. Don't frame business ethics in terms of Aristotle. Tell us what will be expected of us at General Electric, Ford, and Bank of America. Advise us on what to do when something goes wrong, and how to prevent that from happening." In many ways, this book is a response to those concerns.

But, before writing the book we had to make several decisions. First, would such a big undertaking be a worthwhile effort? Could we take the mystery out of business ethics? Could we address the cynicism that seemed so widespread? Did we have something unique to say? Would it make any difference? We became convinced that we could write a book that would teach something unique and that we could do it in a fun and practical way.

Taking Away the Mystery

We want to take the mystery out of business ethics. In other situations (romance, for example?) mystery may stimulate interest. But mystery only serves to make ethics inaccessible to most students or managers. For most people, the word "ethics" means something esoteric, impractical and far-removed from reality. But, organizational ethics isn't mysterious. It's about **us**—people making decisions in actual organizations every day. All of us belong to organizations. We're members of schools, fraternities, sororities, clubs, sports teams, religious organizations, and work organizations. As members of these organizations, we frequently find ourselves facing ethical dilemmas—*situations concerning right and wrong where values are in conflict.*

As a student, you may have observed a friend cheating and wondered what to do. Which is the more important value—sticking by a friend, or complying with the honor code that requires you to turn in a cheater? In a work setting, perhaps you've been tempted to do something you believe is wrong (i.e., lie to a customer about a delivery date) because your boss encourages you to focus on short-term financial results. Which is more important—honesty or adhering to your boss's expectations? Loyalty is an important value for most of us. But, what happens when one of your employees (a good friend) hasn't been meeting agreed-on performance expectations for some time? Which is more important—loyalty to the organization or loyalty to your friend? All of these examples represent values in conflict. All are ethical dilemmas.

Until about ten years ago, we knew so little about the topic of organizational ethics that a book like this probably couldn't have been written. With rare exceptions, our knowledge was limited to a few surveys saying that, yes, ethics is a problem. But, in recent years, researchers have begun to rigorously study organizational ethics. Although there's much left to learn, we're beginning to understand the factors that influence ethical decisions in organizations. That's the kind of information we'll share with you so that you'll understand yourself and others better and you'll be a better manager by being able to influence others' behavior in an ethical direction.

MOVING BEYOND CYNICISM

Cynicism has become epidemic throughout society and is manifested in a "contemptuous mistrust" of scientists, politicians, religious and business leaders.[2] Irving Kristol, writer, educator, and editor, said, "One of the reasons the large corporations find it so difficult to persuade the public of anything is that the public always suspects them of engaging in clever public relations instead of simply telling the truth."[2]

Unfortunately, this cynicism extends to managers themselves. Since the classic studies of business ethics conducted in the 1960s and 1970s,[3] managers have repeatedly reported their own cynicism—the pressure they feel to compromise their personal ethical standards on the job, and they're even more cynical about their peers' ethics than their own.[4] They blame business' preoccupation with gain, the lack of reinforcement of ethical behavior, competition, the existence of generally accepted unethical practices in certain industries, a sense that only results are important to superiors, and the ineffective enforcement of ethics codes. Among all managers, those at lower levels have reported feeling the most pressure to compromise their ethics.[5] And, because students expect to compromise their values, they say they'll do whatever it takes to be successful in the business community—because unfortunately many of them perceive that business expects them to compromise their values.[6]

Many of our readers are business school students, the future managers of business enterprises. After years of teaching business ethics, we're concerned that cynicism may be particularly acute in this group. Surveys suggest that many business students believe that they'll be expected to check their ethics at the corporate door. Whether accurate or not, students are cynical about practicing managers' ethics.[7] And, as future managers, they're anticipating that they will be pressured to compromise their own ethical standards in order to succeed.[8]

Perhaps we can blame the media for undergraduate students' cynical view of American business. However, how can we explain the cynical attitudes of MBA students who typically enter a graduate business program after several years of work experience? Amitai Etzioni, a renowned sociologist, was a visiting professor at the Harvard Business School from 1987 to 1989. He concluded that, in his attempts to teach business ethics, "by and large, I clearly had not found a way to help classes full of MBAs see that there is more to life than money, power, fame and self-interest."[9] This wasn't a case of simple anticipation or speculation because most of these students had returned for the MBA degree after working in the business community for several years. These students' attitudes were shaped by real work experience, suggesting that business itself may be reinforcing this cynical message.

We want to move beyond bemoaning the current cynical state of affairs and help our readers overcome cynicism by doing two things: 1) by empowering current and future managers with the tools they need to address ethical problems and manage for ethical behavior and 2) by providing positive examples of people and organizations who are "doing things right."

Tools to Manage Unethical Behavior

With so much focus on negative events, people can become cynical because they feel helpless to influence these events. They feel overwhelmed by the pressures they perceive to be pushing them and others inexorably toward self-interested behavior at the expense of their higher aspirations. The "mystery" of organizational ethics contributes to this feeling of helplessness. How can we do anything about something we don't understand? We hope to dispel this feeling of helplessness, and simultaneously reduce the cynicism by offering conceptual and practical tools for managing ethics.

Focus on the Positive and the Ethical

We'd also like to focus on the positive and the ethical in people and in organizations. We're not Pollyannas: we see plenty of real- world examples to inspire us to keep ourselves and our organizations moving in a positive and ethical direction.

Ethical conduct is alive and well at work. In a recent *Industry Week* survey, three out of four respondents claimed that their company's code of ethics, or ethics in general, actually means something to them in their day-to-day work, and that figure is up from an earlier survey.[10] Employees are clearly looking for positive guidance from their organizations so that they can feel good about the work they do every day.

Many organizations are acknowledging that they're not islands, isolated from the larger communities that surround them. In fact, they know that they function best within healthy communities. The leaders of these organizations have been referred to as "enlightened capitalists."[11] They reject the notion, dominant in the 1980s, that business' sole responsibility is to maximize profits. Although they're true believers in the free market system, these "enlightened capitalists" acknowledge that the free market system can also produce negative side effects such as pollution and "poverty-amid-plenty."[12] They believe that it's better for business to voluntarily help solve these problems than be forced to do so by the government. One corporate lawyer estimated that a new law results in 200 to 300 pages of regulations—all of which have to be followed by the corporations affected by the law. Furthermore, they argue that business has a responsibility to address certain social problems because of its unique abilities, and because a healthy social environment is a prerequisite for a healthy business environment. Therefore, they maintain that a business that serves its multiple stakeholders best (i.e., customers, employees, the community—essentially, any party who has a *stake* in what the organization does and how it performs), also serves its shareholders best in the long run.[13]

ISN'T BUSINESS ETHICS JUST A FAD?

Obviously, before taking on the task of writing this book, we had to be convinced that business ethics wasn't just a fad that would die out while the book was still on our hard drives.

Management researchers began to study business ethics during the 1960s by conducting surveys of managers' attitudes toward business ethics.[14] Some thought that business ethics was just a fad then (related to media attention to the burgeoning consumer rights movement, for example)—that interest in the topic would quickly fade. But, interest has climbed for at least 30 years, fueled by regular media coverage of ethical lapses in the business community. Examples include the federal savings and loan disaster, Wall Street insider trading scandals, the Exxon Valdez oil spill, Beech-Nut's sale of a chemical concoction as pure apple juice, Dow Corning's attempts to cover up the health problems associated with breast implants, and the tobacco industry's refusal to admit that cigarettes are a health hazard.

Ethical lapses aren't limited to business; ethical problems affect every institution of our society. For example, in the 1970s, the Watergate scandal focused attention on ethical lapses in government. This focus continued with questions about the faulty decision making that led to the Challenger disaster, check-writing scandals in Congress, Irangate, Tailhook, and Nannygate.

Religious, educational, philanthropic, and sports organizations haven't been immune. Catholic priests have sexually abused children, students have cheated on exams and plagiarized papers, philanthropic organizations have spent contributors' funds irresponsibly, and student athletes have run afoul of National Collegiate Athletic Association (NCAA) rules. Ethics is a "hot" topic in newspapers, magazines, and on television news magazines such as "60 Minutes." Although we don't want to leave it to the media to define ethical business practice, the media's continuing interest in business ethics issues suggests that ethics isn't just a fad.

Articles and books have also proliferated in the academic and professional press, suggesting that these communities are becoming increasingly interested in ethics as well. And, organizations of every kind are addressing the "ethics problem" in a number of ways. Many of them are establishing high-level ethics committees, drafting codes of ethical conduct, and conducting ethics training programs.

The wider American community also seems very interested in ethics and values these days. Perhaps the best example of their interest is that, as of June 1994, about 1 million copies of William Bennett's (former Education Secretary under Ronald Reagan) *Book of Virtues* were in print in hard cover.[15] So, in addition to focusing on the negative—the ethical lapses—there seems to be a need in our society to also focus on the positive—models of positive ethical behavior in private and public life.

So, why do some still attach the "fad" label to business ethics? To qualify as a fad, interest in business ethics should have been exaggerated and short term. But, as we've seen, the interest in ethics reflects the reality of life in all sectors of our society, and it has continued to grow over the past 30 years. Perhaps some prefer to label the ethics issue as a "fad" because fads go away and we truly wish ethics problems would simply disappear like the hula hoop, a bona fide fad that came and went with the 1960s. But ethical lapses occur regularly in all areas of our lives and they're a part of human behavior that's here to stay. That's one reason why we wrote this book. If the ethics "problem" isn't just a fad, then managers have an ongoing concern that they must anticipate, understand, and manage. We also believe that the interest in ethics as a positive force hasn't been adequately tapped in the business world. Although they do not get as much media attention, there are many positive examples of business people doing good and doing well. We want to share those too.

CAN BUSINESS ETHICS BE TAUGHT?

Before launching a book writing effort, we also needed to be convinced that we could actually teach our readers something. Despite growing interest in ethics and ethics training, dissenters from both the business and academic communities[16] have raised serious questions about whether ethics can or should be taught. Felix Rohatyn, a noted New York investment banker, said that ethics can't be taught past the age of 10. Lester Thurow, former Dean of the Massachusetts Institute of Technology's Sloan School of Management, echoed this view when he stated that business schools can do little if students haven't already learned ethics from their families, clergy, previous schools, or employers.[17]

In the wake of the insider trading scandals of the 1980s, Mr. Thurow and a chief operating officer of a large Wall Street investment firm claimed on a television news program that educational institutions or business organizations could have done little about the unethical individuals who participated in insider trading. These people just hadn't been raised with the proper values.

If they're correct, ethics education is a waste of time and money. Bad apples are just tainted people who can't be trained or rehabilitated. Therefore, resources should be devoted to identifying and discarding bad apples, not educating them.

Aren't Bad Apples the Cause of Ethical Problems in Organizations?

In part, the belief that ethics can't be taught is driven by the assumption that ethical problems are caused by "bad apples" and that unethical behavior in organizations can be traced to a few "bad apples" that spoil it for the rest of us. According to this belief, people come to organizations as either good or bad and organizations can do little to change them. All they can do is attempt to hire people of good character and get rid of the bad ones.

This "bad apple" idea[18] is appealing because unethical behavior can then be blamed on the bad individual. Although it's unpleasant to fire people, it's relatively easier to discard a "bad apple" than to search for some organizational problem that caused the apple to rot.

Garry Trudeau's (1987) Doonesbury cartoon treatment of Dennis Levine, who was convicted of insider trading, reflects the bad apple view. In the cartoon, Levine is totally unresponsive to an ethics counselor's attempts to appeal to his sense of morality.

Scot, Ethics Counselor: ". . . and since everyone else was doing it, you figured using insider information was okay?"
Levine: "Yeah, like the golden rule says."
Scot: "Uh, the golden rule? Which golden rule is that?
Levine: "Do unto others before they do it unto you first."
Scot: "Okay, ethically, you seem to be a little rusty . . . Why don't we review a few basic moral questions, okay? What's the opposite of wrong?"
Levine: "Poor."

Trudeau portrays Levine as a "bad apple" who is totally unresponsive to the counselor's attempt to appeal to some basic understanding of right and wrong. Levine, the "bad apple," just doesn't "get it."

Despite the appeal of the "bad apple" idea, character is a poorly defined concept, and when people talk about it, they rarely define what they mean. They're probably referring to a complex combination of traits that are thought to guide individual behavior in ethical dilemma situations. If character guides ethical conduct, training shouldn't make much difference because character is thought to be relatively stable, meaning that it's difficult to change, persists over time, and guides behavior across different contexts. Character develops slowly as a result of upbringing and the accumulation of values that are transmitted by schools, families, friends, and religious organizations. Therefore, people come to educational institutions or work organizations with an already defined good or poor character. Good apples will be good and bad apples will be bad.

In fact, people do have predispositions to behave ethically or unethically (we'll talk about these in Chapter 5). And sociopaths can certainly slip into organizations with the sole intent of helping themselves to the organization's resources, cheating customers, and feathering their own nests at the expense of others. They have little interest in "doing the right thing." When this type of individual shows up in your organization, the best thing to do is to discard the bad apple, making an example of the incident to those who remain.

But, discarding "bad apples" won't necessarily solve an organization's problem with unethical behavior. The organization must also scrutinize itself to deterimine if there's something rotten in the system that's spoiling the apples. You'll learn in this book that most people aren't guided by a strict and consistent internal moral compass. Rather, they look outside themselves for cues about how to behave, particularly when the circumstances are ambiguous or unclear as they are in many ethical dilemma situations. At work, the organizational culture transmits many of these cues. Norms, role models, reward systems, and many other components of the organizational culture combine to let people know what they're expected to do. Although much more subtle, this is as much an educational process as explicit ethics training.

An organization that's serious about supporting ethical behavior and preventing misconduct must delve deeply into its own cultural norms and practices to search for systemic causes of unethical behavior. If ethics problems are rooted in the organization's culture, discarding a few "bad apples," without changing the culture that supported their activities, isn't going to solve the problem. An effective and lasting solution will rely upon systematic attention to all aspects of the organization's culture and what it is explicitly or implicitly "teaching" organizational members.

Shouldn't Employees Already Know the Difference between Right and Wrong?

A belief associated with the good/bad apple idea is that any individual of good character should already know right from wrong and should be able to be ethical without special training. You probably think of yourself as an individual of good character. So, think about the following real dilemma.

> You're the VP of a medium-sized organization that uses chemicals in its production processes. In good faith, you've hired a highly competent person to ensure that your company complies with all environmental laws and safety regulations. This individual informs you that a chemical the company now uses in some quantity is not yet on the approved EPA list, although it's undergoing review and is scheduled to be placed on the approved list in about three months because it's been found to be safe. You can't produce your product without this chemical, yet you're not supposed to use the chemical until it's approved. Waiting for approval would require shutting down the plant for three months, putting hundreds of people out of work, and threatening the company's very survival. What should you do?

The solution isn't clear cut and good character isn't enough to guide decision making in this case. As with most ethical dilemmas, values are in conflict here— obeying the letter of the law versus keeping the plant open and saving jobs. The decision is complicated by the fact that the chemical has been found to be safe and is going to be approved in a matter of months. As in many of today's business decisions, this complex issue requires the development of occupation-specific skills and abilities. For example, some knowledge in the area of chemistry, worker safety, and environmental laws and regulations would be essential. Basic good intentions aren't enough.

James Rest, a scholar in the areas of professional ethics and ethics education, argued convincingly that "to assume that any 20-year-old of good general character can function ethically in professional situations is no more warranted than assuming that any logical 20-year-old can function as a lawyer without special education."[19] Good general character (whatever that means) doesn't prepare an individual to deal with the very special ethical problems that are likely to arise in one's career. Individuals must be trained to recognize and solve the unique ethical problems of their particular occupation. That's why many professional schools (business, law, medicine and others) have added ethics courses to their curricula.

So, although individual characteristics are a factor in determining ethical behavior, good character alone simply doesn't prepare people for the special ethical problems they're likely to face in their jobs or professions. Education can prepare them to anticipate these problems, recognize ethical dilemmas when they see them, and provide them with frameworks for thinking about ethical issues in the context of their unique organizations.

Aren't Adults' Ethics Fully Formed and Unchangeable?

Another false assumption guiding the view that business ethics can't be taught is the belief that one's ethics are fully formed and unchangeable by the time one is old enough to enter college or a job. However, moral psychology research has found that this is definitely not the case.[20] Moral judgment develops throughout childhood and young adulthood in a complex process of social interaction with peers, parents, and other significant persons, and this development continues at least through young adulthood. In fact, young adults in their twenties and thirties in moral development educational programs have been found to advance in moral reasoning even more than younger individuals.[21] Given that most people enter professional education programs and corporations during young adulthood, the opportunity to influence their moral reasoning clearly exists.

Business school students may need ethics training more than most. Research has found that students in business ranked lower in moral reasoning than students in philosophy, political science, law, medicine, and dentistry.[22] And undergraduate business students and those aiming for a business career have been found to be more likely to engage in academic cheating (test cheating, plagiarism, etc.) than students in other majors or those headed toward other careers.[23]

It should be clear from the above arguments that *ethics can be taught*. Ethical behavior relies on more than good character. Although good upbringing may provide a kind of moral compass that can help the individual determine the right direction and then follow through on a decision to do the right thing, it's certainly not the only factor determining ethical conduct. In today's highly complex organizations, individuals need additional guidance. They can be helped to recognize the ethical dilemmas that are likely to arise in their jobs; the rules, laws, and norms that apply in that context; reasoning strategies that can be used to arrive at the best decision; and an understanding of the complexities of organizational life that can conflict with one's desire to do the right thing. For example, businesses that do defense-related work are expected to comply with a multitude of laws and regulations that go way beyond what the average person can be expected to know.

The question of whether ethics *should* be taught remains. Many still believe that ethics is a personal issue that should be left to individuals to struggle with themselves. Similar to attempts to proselytize about religion, they see attempts to teach ethics as inappropriate efforts to impose certain values and to control behavior.

Defining Ethics.   Some of the controversy about whether ethics should be taught may stem from disagreement about what we mean by ethics. Ethics can be defined as "a set of moral principles or values," a definition that portrays ethics as highly personal and relative. I have my moral principles, you have yours, and neither of us should try to impose our ethics on each other.

But, we believe that a better definition of ethics may be *the principles, norms, and standards of conduct governing an individual or group.* We expect work organizations to govern work-related conduct. They prescribe all kinds of behavior including what time to arrive and leave the workplace, whether smoking is allowed on the premises, how customers are to be treated, and how quickly work should be done. Prescriptions about ethical conduct aren't much different. Work organizations prescribe how employees should fill out expense reports and they define what they consider to be a conflict of interest or bribe. If we use this definition, ethics becomes an extension of good management. Leaders identify appropriate and inappropriate conduct and they convey their expectations to employees through ethics codes, training programs, and other communication mechanisms.

In most cases, individual employees will agree with the prescriptions. For example, who would disagree that it's wrong to steal company property, lie to customers, dump cancerous chemicals in the local stream, or comply with regulations on defense contracts? However, at times, an employee may find the organization's standards inconsistent with his or her own moral values or principles. For example, a highly religious employee of a health maintenance organization may object to offering abortion as an alternative when providing genetic counseling to pregnant women. Or, a highly devoted environmentalist may believe that his or her organization should go beyond the minimum standards of environmental law when making decisions about how much to spend on new technology or on environmental clean-up efforts. These individuals may be able to influence their organizations' policies. Otherwise, the person's only recourse may be to leave the organization for one that is a better values match.

Good Control or Bad Control?   Whether we prefer to admit it or not, our ethical conduct is influenced (and, to a large degree, controlled) by our environment. In work settings, leaders, managers, and the entire cultural context are an important source of this influence and guidance. If, as managers, we allow organizational members to drift along without our guidance, we're unintentionally allowing them to be "controlled" by others. If this happens, we're contributing to the creation of "loose cannons" who can put the entire organization at risk. And ethics training is an important aspect of controlling employee behavior. It can provide essential guidance regarding organizational rules and policies and behavior that's considered appropriate or inappropriate in a variety of situations.

But, should organizations be "controlling" their employees? B.F. Skinner,[24] the renowned late psychologist, argued that it's all right, even preferable, to intentionally control behavior. He believed that all behavior was controlled, intentionally or unintentionally. Therefore, what was needed was more intentional control, not less. Similarly, ethical and unethical behavior in organizations is already being controlled explicitly or implicitly by the existing organizational culture. Therefore, organizations that neglect to teach their members "ethical" behavior, may be tacitly encouraging "unethical behavior" through benign neglect. It's the organization's responsibility to provide guidance through explicit training and through the support of the organization's formal and informal cultural systems. The supervisor who attempts to influence the ethical behavior of subordinates shouldn't be viewed as a meddler, but as a part of the natural management process.

To summarize, we believe that educational institutions and work organizations should teach people about ethics and guide them in an ethical direction. Adults are open to, and often welcome, this type of guidance. Ethical problems are not caused entirely by "bad apples." They're also the product of organizational systems that either encourage unethical behavior or, at least, allow it to occur. Making ethical decisions in today's complex organizations isn't a simple task. Good intentions and a good upbringing aren't enough. The special knowledge and skill required to make good ethical decisions in a particular job may be different from what's needed to resolve personal ethical dilemmas, and this knowledge and skill must be taught and cultivated.

THIS BOOK IS ABOUT MANAGING ETHICS—NOT ABOUT PHILOSOPHY

Now that we've (hopefully) convinced you that ethics is a worthwhile topic that can be taught, we need to discuss our somewhat unique approach to teaching business ethics. We'll begin by telling you what this book isn't. It's not a conventional business ethics text, most of which have a primarily normative, prescriptive, and theoretical focus. These texts are typically written by philosophers. They describe a number of normative ethical theories and they then apply these theories to business ethics cases. The main goal is to provide the reader with tools for *deciding what's right* in ethical dilemma situations. Business people know that deciding what's right represents an essential part of organizational ethics, but some might argue that it's actually the easier part. In organizations, *doing what's right* is often more challenging because individuals and groups have to make decisions in a highly complex context where roles and norms, authority and power relationships, competitive pressures, profit motives, and organizational structures all come into play.

In this book, we present ethics from a different perspective—one that emphasizes a managerial focus. Between us, we have many years of experience in management and in management teaching and research. We believe that the more practical and managerial side of business ethics has been neglected in business ethics texts. We also believe that the majority of students and business people are more interested in ethics practice. That's why we took a more practical tack in this book.

Our approach is based on very different assumptions than those of our philosopher colleagues. We assume that ethics is essentially about human behavior, and that if we understand human behavior in an organizational context, we can better understand and manage our own and others' ethical behavior. Kent Druyvesteyn, Vice President for Ethics at General Dynamics from 1985 to 1993 has made a clear distinction between philosophy and management in his many talks with students and executives over the years. As he puts it, "I am not a philosopher and I am not here to talk about philosophy. Ethics is about conduct."

We agree with Mr. Druyvesteyn. After years of study and experience, we're convinced that most people need a *management approach* to help them deal with organizational ethics. As with any other management problem, managers are seeking to understand why people behave the way they do so that they can influence this behavior. Most managers want the people with whom they work to be productive, to produce high quality products, to treat customers well, and to do all of this in a highly ethical manner. They also want and need help accomplishing these goals.

Therefore, we rely on a managerial approach to understanding organizational ethics. We introduce concepts that can be used to guide managers who want to understand their own ethical behavior and the behavior of others in the organization. And, we provide practical guidance to those who wish to lead their department or organization in an ethical direction.

Consider this diagram:

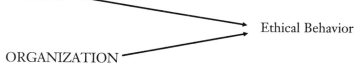

First, we're defining ethical behavior in business as *behavior that is consistent with the principles, norms and standards of business practice that have been agreed on by society.* We propose that ethical behavior is influenced by two types of factors: characteristics of the individual and the characteristics of the organization in which the individual finds himself or herself.

Traditional ethics texts focus more on ethics as an individual-level phenomenon. They provide the normative ethical theories that can help individuals analyze the ethics of a given situation—to decide what's right. The idea is that ethical behavior will improve if people acquire these conceptual tools that can help them make sound ethical decisions.

We also believe that these ethical theories are important and we introduce some of the most important and practical ones in Chapter 4. But we believe that acquiring these conceptual tools provides only a small part of the knowledge needed to manage business ethics. Cognitive limitations and biases (see Chapter 5) often limit our ability to make the best decision. Furthermore, even when people know the right thing to do, they find it difficult to do the right thing because of group or organizational pressures. Therefore, our approach focuses more on the individual *in the organizational context* and on ways to manage your own conduct and the conduct of other people in the organization, especially those who report to you (Chapter 7 covers group and organizational influences and Chapter 9 emphasizes the role of organizational culture).

So you'll notice from the diagram that we believe both individual factors and organizational factors affect ethical behavior. But organizational factors (in capital letters) are emphasized in the book because they are the factors managers can influence.

BRINGING ETHICS DOWN TO SIZE

Another difference between this book and other, more conventional texts is found in the mix of examples we've used. Most ethics texts focus almost exclusively on "big" dilemmas that reflect a corporate position: "Should the company market this product or do business in China? Are executive compensation plans fair and equitable?" We include corporate-level examples, too, because they're important. But, this book is also loaded with examples that reflect the ethical dilemmas facing individual employees and managers at all levels (see especially Chapters 3 and 6). "Should you blow the whistle on your employer? Should you accept a gift from a supplier? Should you hire your spouse's company to provide an important service to your firm?"

ETHICS AND THE LAW

You'll find many references to the law in the pages that follow. By including these references, we certainly don't mean to imply that the only guiding principle for deciding what's right should be whatever is legal. Perhaps the easiest way to think about the relationship between business ethics and the law is in terms of a Venn diagram. If we think of the law as reflecting society's *minimum* norms and standards of business conduct, we can see that there is a great deal of overlap between what's legal and what's ethical. Generally speaking, most people believe that law-abiding behavior is also ethical behavior. But, there are many standards of conduct agreed upon by society that are not codified in law. For example, conflicts of interest may not be illegal, but they are generally considered to be unethical in our society and are commonly covered in codes of ethics. So, the domain of ethics includes the legal domain, but extends beyond it to include the ethical standards and issues that the law does not address. Finally, there are times when you might encounter a law that you believe is unethical. For example, not too long ago racial discrimination was legal in the United States. Therefore, the legal and ethical domains certainly overlap to a large degree, but not completely. It is conceivable to think of something as being legal and unethical, or unethical but not covered by any law.

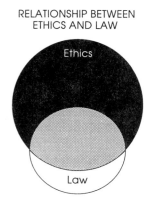

RELATIONSHIP BETWEEN
ETHICS AND LAW

LEARNING ABOUT ETHICS CAN BE FUN

Most of you probably think ethics is about as enjoyable as a trip to the dentist's office. It's good for you, you know you should do it, but it's certainly not going to be fun. Unfortunately, many of us have had experiences in our schools and work organizations that have only reinforced the perception of ethics as preachy, dull, and BORING.

We think we can change this perception of ethics as boring because our experience tells us that 1) people are interested in controversial ethical issues, 2) they want to know what others think, and 3) given the right environment and support, learning about organizational ethics can actually be fun.

In *The Republic*, Book VII, Plato said, "No compulsory learning can remain in the soul . . . teaching children, train them by a kind of game, and you will be able to see more clearly the natural bent of each." Math games, geography games, certainly—but ethics games? Yes!

Think about the popular parlor game, Scruples. In Scruples, players debate everyday moral questions, challenge each others' sincerity, and have lively discussions about questions such as whether they would leave their name if they dented a car in the mall parking lot. If you've played the game you know that it's fun. At the same time, you learn something about how you and your friends think about everyday ethical dilemmas. A number of large corporations are using a similar concept to enliven their ethics training programs.

Katherine Nelson, coauthor of this book, created the first corporate ethics game while she was head of human resources communications at Citicorp. (Since leaving Citicorp in 1991, she has developed a generic game which she has brought to a wide variety of corporations, universities, and government agencies.) The Citicorp exercise is entitled, "The Work Ethic: An Exercise in Integrity." "The Work Ethic" has been used widely within Citicorp—over 40,000 employees have participated in sessions in over 60 countries. Additionally, it has been translated into seven languages besides English: French, Italian, Spanish, Portuguese, Flemish,

Japanese, and German. And additional cases have been developed for various job disciplines, businesses, and geographic locations.

The game works like this: a group of employees is divided into teams, which encounter a series of ethical dilemmas. A facilitator conducts the game and positions the exercise with the following messages:

> "We're playing a game about ethics because we want to make sure we get your attention."

> "We want to make sure you know integrity is important here."

> "This is an opportunity for you to practice making ethical decisions in a risk-free environment."

> "We're doing this to give you an overview of corporate policy and how things are done here."

> "We're also going to outline all of the resources available to you if you think you'd like some help or advice if you're faced with an ethical dilemma."

The teams consider a range of ethical issues—sexual harassment, reporting ethical concerns, responsibilities to customers, the need for confidentiality, and conflicts of interest (see the end of the chapter for a sample question). The mix of issues is decided by the organization. The teams take a few minutes to discuss each issue. Then, based on a consensus among team members, they vote for one of four courses of action. Once the teams vote, the facilitator plays devil's advocate and questions the entire group on why they voted the way they did. The discussion can get very heated with participants loudly defending their positions. The facilitator then reveals the scores (scores are predetermined preferably by the management of the organization where the game is being played). If the participants disagree with the scores, they can appeal them to an appeals board of senior managers.

The senior management appeals board is one of the most important aspects of the ethics game. The very presence of senior managers for 90 minutes or so sends a strong message that integrity and ethics must be important in this company or all these executives wouldn't be spending so much time talking about it. In addition, when discussing an appeal, the appeals board often communicates messages about company standards and expectations better than anything else.

Since the game usually raises more questions than it answers, it's critical to have a debriefing. At the end of the game, the facilitator gives advice on how to solve ethical dilemmas, and outlines the resources that are available to help people if they find themselves in need of advice.

In the process of discussing possible answers, participants are engaged because it's fun to discuss these controversial issues and to learn what others think. At the same time, they learn about relevant laws, company policies, and what their peers and appeals board members think about the issue. Most important, it gets people talking about ethics. The experience is always lively and educational.

Although some may view an ethics game as heresy, those who have seen these training programs in action are quickly convinced of their effectiveness and the idea has become "hot" in ethics training. "Work Ethic" type questions are dispersed throughout the book and are offered for discussion at the end of several chapters, including this one.

HOW THE BOOK IS STRUCTURED

When we first sat down together to plan this book, we made a list of all the cynical things about ethics our students had ever said to us. That list served as the starting point for the book's organization.

Chapter 2 begins with (and attempts to answer) the question many students ask, "Why Be Ethical?" We attempt to counter some of their natural cynicism by describing concrete examples showing that business people really do care about ethics, and that your success can depend on how well you can manage ethics.

The second section of the book focuses on ethics from an individual perspective. Chapter 3 categorizes the common ethical problems individuals face in organizational settings. Chapter 4 presents the reader with an overview of some basic philosophical theories that have formed the underpinning for the traditional study of business ethics. It also suggests a list of practical decision-making steps individuals can follow to evaluate an ethical dilemma and decide upon a course of action. Chapter 5 presents a more psychological approach to individual ethical decision making. It provides a kind of "reality check" for Chapter 4, suggesting that human cognitive limitations and biases can interfere with the ideal decision-making process. Chapter 5 also suggests that people do have predispositions to behave in certain ways when faced with ethical dilemma situations.

In Section III, we begin to develop our management perspective on business ethics. Chapter 6 presents common ethical problems managers face when dealing with their subordinates, their superiors, and their peers and provides advice on what factors to consider when you're confronted with one of them. In addition, the chapter gives managers and employees advice on how to manage their relationships with the people they work with, work for, and direct. Chapter 7, "Managing for Ethical Conduct," introduces management concepts that can help explain why people behave ethically or unethically. And we provide practical advice for managers about how to use these management concepts to encourage ethical conduct and discourage unethical conduct in their employees.

Section IV is entitled, "Ethics and the Organization." It begins with a chapter entitled, "Ethical Problems of Organizations." Although some people question whether corporations are moral entities, there are clearly ethical issues that can be classified as organizational level rather than managerial level. This chapter classifies those and provides examples of them. Chapter 9 focuses on business ethics as an organizational culture phenomenon. It provides a comprehensive overview of how an organization can build a culture that reflects a concern for ethics, and how it can change its culture to be more supportive of ethical conduct. Chapter 10 follows with practical advice on how organizations can design an ethics infrastructure, and effective communications and training programs. It also includes examples of successful programs various companies have implemented to encourage ethical conduct among their employees. Many of these examples resulted from interviews we conducted with top managers in these companies.

Section V wraps up the book with a chapter on international business ethics and a chapter that provides an overview of our interviews with executives. Chapter 11 extends our discussion of business ethics to the global business environment. Although there are global examples throughout the book, this is an important enough issue to warrant its own chapter. Finally, Chapter 12 provides advice from the firing line—from executives who have spent time developing their own organizations' ethics efforts. Their advice pulls together many of the themes of the book and we think they're enjoyable to read.

We hope that reading this book gives you a better understanding of how you can promote ethical behavior in yourself and others. An understanding of ethics is critical to all of us because good ethics represents the very essence of a civilized society. Ethics is the bedrock upon which all of our relationships are built; it's about how we relate to our employers, our employees, our co-workers, our customers, our communities, our suppliers, and one another. Ethics is not about the connection we have to other beings—we are all connected—rather, it's about the quality of that connection. That's the real bottom line.

DISCUSSION QUESTIONS

1. Before reading this chapter, did you think of ethics as "just a fad?" Why or why not? What do you think now? Why?

2. Have you been cynical about business and its leaders? Why or why not? (See cynicism exercise that follows.) How does cynicism affect you, as a business student or as a manager?

3. Apply the "bad apple" idea to your own experience by citing an example of unethical conduct you observed. Was it the fault of a bad apple, was there "something rotten" in the barrel that contributed to the problem, or was it a combination of the two?

4. Cite an example of a situation you're familiar with where the "right" answer just wasn't obvious. What would a decision maker need to know in order to arrive at an acceptable solution?

5. Are you convinced that business ethics can and should be taught? Why or why not?

IN-CLASS EXERCISE

Following is a "Work Ethic" Question. Your professor will divide the class into groups and will ask the groups to come to consensus about the "right" answer.

Question: A well-liked member of your staff with an excellent record confides in you that he has AIDS. Although his illness has not affected his performance, you're concerned about his future health and about the reactions of his co-workers.
   You:

a) tell him to keep you informed about his health and say nothing to his co-workers.

b) arrange for him to transfer to an area of the organization where he can work alone.

c) hold a staff meeting to inform his co-workers and ask them how they feel about his continued presence on your team.

d) consult your human resources officer on how to proceed.

Homework   Based on your own work experience, create an ethical dilemma question like the "Work Ethic" one to use as the basis for class discussion.

EXERCISE

Your Cynicism Quotient

Answer the following questions as honestly as you can. Circle the number between 1 and 5 that best represents your own beliefs about business.

	Strongly Disagree				Strongly Agree
1. Financial gain is all that counts in business.	1	2	3	4	5
2. Ethical standards must be compromised in business practice.	1	2	3	4	5
3. The more financially successful the business person, the more unethical the behavior.	1	2	3	4	5
4. Moral values are irrelevant in business.	1	2	3	4	5
5. The business world has its own rules.	1	2	3	4	5
6. Business persons care only about making profit.	1	2	3	4	5
7. Business is like a game - one plays to win.	1	2	3	4	5

	Strongly Disagree				Strongly Agree
8. In business, people will do anything to further their own interest.	1	2	3	4	5
9. Competition forces business managers to resort to shady practices.	1	2	3	4	5
10. The profit motive pressures managers to compromise their ethical concerns.	1	2	3	4	5

Add the total number of points. The maximum is 50 points. Total _____

The higher your score, the more cynical you are about ethical business practice. Think about the reasons for your responses. Be prepared to discuss them in class.

NOTES

[1]O'Toole, J. 1991. Do good, do well: The business enterprise trust awards. *California Management Review:* Spring, 9–24.

[2]Olasky, M. N. 1985, 1986. Ministers or panderers: Issues raised by the public relations society code of standards. *Journal of Mass Media Ethics*, 1, no. 1.

[3]Baumhart, R. C. 1961. How ethical are businessmen? *Harvard Business Review*, 39 (4): 6–8.

Brenner, S. N. & Molander, E. A. 1977. Is the ethics of business changing? Harvard Business Review, 55: 57–71.

[4]Carroll, A. B. 1975. Linking business ethics to behavior in organizations. *S. A. M. Advanced Management Journal*, 43: 3, 4–11.

Jones, T. M. & Gautschi, F. H. 1988. Will the ethics of business change? A survey of future executives. *Journal of Business Ethics*, 7: 231–248.

Lincoln, D. J., Pressley, M. M., & Little, T. 1982. Ethical beliefs and personal values of top level executives. *Journal of Business Research*, 10: 475–487.

Posner, B. Z. & Schmidt, W. H. 1987. Ethics in American companies; A managerial perspective. *Journal of Business Ethics*, 6: 383–391.

Posner, B. Z. & Schmidt, W. H. 1992. Values and the American manager. *California Management Review*, Spring: 80–94

[5]Baumhart, R. C. 1961. How ethical are businessmen? *Harvard Business Review*, 39 (4): 6–8.

Baumhart, R. C. 1968. *An honest profit: What businessmen say about ethics in business.* New York: Holt, Rinehart and Winston.

Brenner, S. N. & Molander, E. A. 1977. Is the ethics of business changing? Harvard Business Review, 55: 57–71.

[6]Wood, J. A., Longenecker, J. G., McKinney, J. A., & Moore, C. W. 1988. Ethical attitudes

of students and business professionals: A study of moral reasoning. *Journal of Business Ethics*, 7: 249–257.

[7]DeSalvia, D. N. & Gemmill, G. R. 1971. An exploratory study of the personal value systems of college students and managers. *Academy of Management Journal*, 14: 227–238.

Lane, M. S., Schaupp, D., & Parsons, B. 1988. Pygmalion effect. *Journal of Business Ethics*, 7: 223–229.

[8]Fulmer, R. M. 1968. Business ethics: A view from the campus. *Personnel Administrator*, 45 (2): 31–39.

Jones, T. M. & Gautschi, F. H. 1988. Will the ethics of business change? A survey of future executives. *Journal of Business Ethics*, 7, 231–248.

[9]Etzioni, A. 1989. Money, power, and fame. *Newsweek*, Sept. 18: 10.

[10]Benson, T. E. 1991. Industry ethics edge upward. *Industry Week*, Sept. 16: 18,20.

[11]O'Toole, J. 1991. Do good, do well: The business enterprise trust awards. *California Management Reviews*, Spring: 9–24.

[12]Ibid.

[13]Ibid.

[14]Baumhart, R. C. 1961. How ethical are businessmen? *Harvard Business Review*, 39 (4): 6–8.

[15]Fineman, J. 1994. Virtuecrats. *Newsweek*, June 13: 31–36.

[16]Levin, M. 1990, Ethics courses: Useless. *New York Times*, November 25.

[17]Hanson, K. O. 1988, Why we teach ethics in business school. *Stanford Business School Magazine*, February: 14–16.

[18]Trevino, L. K. & Youngblood, A. 1990. Bad apples in bad barrels: A causal analysis of ethical decision-making behavior. *Journal of Applied Psychology*, 75 (4): 378–385.

[19]Rest, J. R. 1988. Can ethics be taught in professional schools? The psychological research. *Easier Said Than Done*, Winter.

[20]Ibid.

[21]Rest, J. R. & Thoma, S. J. 1986. Educational programs and interventions. In *Moral development: Advances in research and theory*. J. Rest, ed. New York: Praeger, 59–88.

[22]Rest, J. R. 1987. Moral judgement: An interesting variable for higher education research. Paper for the Annual Convention for the Association for the Study of Higher Education, Baltimore, MD: November 21.

[23]McCabe, D. & Trevino, L. K. 1993. Academic dishonesty: Honor codes and other situational influences. *Journal of Higher Education*, 64: 522–538.

[24]Skinner, B. F. 1971. *Beyond freedom and dignity*. New York: Knopf.

CHAPTER TWO

Why Be Ethical?
(Why Bother? Who Cares?)

INTRODUCTION

IT'S IMPOSSIBLE to know what John might have accomplished if he had lived. Since he was a brilliant young tax lawyer, he might have helped you structure your finances or defended you in court. He surely would have been the friendly, decent kind of neighbor you leave your key with when you leave town. Unfortunately, we'll never know.

We haven't created John, or made him up. He was a son, a brother, a husband, and he became a father one month after he died in 1978. He was 32 years old. He died because some people who worked for a leading corporation never thought about how their product could affect him—or if they did think about it, they didn't care enough.

John unloaded sheets of asbestos during the summer between college and law school. Ten years later, asbestos particles killed him. The manufacturer knew before John was born that asbestos could cause fatal lung diseases and cancers in workers who handled it. But for decades they warned no one. And John, along with ship builders, brake repairers, and others, paid a terrible price—their lives.

Why be ethical? Why bother? Who cares? As individuals we must care about ethics because people like John will no longer contribute to our society; because our toddlers have sipped apple juice that contained no apples; our sisters have had birth control devices that maimed them; our coastlines have been scarred by oil spills (see Chapter 8 for more information on these cases).

As workers we care about ethics because most of us prefer to work for ethical organizations. We want to feel good about ourselves and the work we do. As managers, we must be concerned about the ethics of the people who report to us. More than just our jobs depend on this concern—recent legislation has made managers liable for the criminal activities of their subordinates.

Organizations must care about ethics because their members depend on them to help define the boundaries of acceptable and unacceptable behavior. Also, ethical lapses can cost an organization dearly, in shattered customer confidence, increased government regulation, and huge fines.

Finally, no matter what our role, we must bother about ethics because we're people first. We live in a world community—we're all inextricably connected to each other and to the environment and our future depends upon our caring enough.

WHY BOTHER? WHO CARES?

The Motivation to Be Ethical

Classical economists assume that practically all human behavior, including altruism, is motivated solely by self-interest—that humans are purely rational economic actors who make choices solely on the basis of cold cost/benefit analyses. But, there is much evidence to suggest that people also act for altruistic or moral purposes that seem to have little to do with cost/benefit analyses.[1] For example, people will:

- mail back lost wallets to strangers, cash and all
- help strangers in distress
- donate blood marrow for strangers, or a kidney to a family member

In his book, *The Moral Dimension*, Etzioni[2] cites many more examples and research evidence to document his claim that human action has two distinct sources: the pursuit of pleasure or self-interest, *and* moral commitments. Accordingly, most human decisions are based on ethical and emotional considerations as well as rational economic self-interest. They're motivated by both economic *and* moral concerns.

Therefore, we begin this chapter with an important assumption—that, as members of society, all of us have moral and ethical concerns as well as economic self-interested concerns. You will see in this chapter that people and organizations care about ethics for reasons that stem from both of these sources. For example, organizations may be interested in being ethical in order to avoid criminal liability or a bad reputation or they may be interested in being ethical just because they believe it's the right thing to do.

Media Focus on Ethics
and Corporate Reputation

If you believe that the media focus attention on issues people care about, then lots of people must care about ethics. In recent years, the media spotlight has focused on the problem of serious ethical lapses in every type of organization—business, government, educational, religious, sports, and others. We've all heard about insider traders, businesses that overcharge the government, government employees who steal or misuse funds, academics who falsify their research results, students who cheat, ministers who steal from their congregations, athletes who take bribes, and more.

Hollywood, society's most powerful image maker, has generally portrayed business people as sleazy, greedy, and heartless. Who can forget J.R. Ewing, who "slithered across the TV screen as the vile head of Ewing Oil" on the TV series "Dallas," or Michael Douglas as Gordon Gecko, the unscrupulous corporate raider who corrupted a young stockbroker in the film *Wall Street*?[3] Charles Brown, former chairman of AT&T asked, "When was the last time you watched a TV sitcom in which a businessperson was the hero?"[4]

Can the media really influence an organization's image? The answer is yes. Since 1982, *Fortune* magazine has conducted an annual "most admired corporations" survey, based on ratings provided by senior executives, outside directors and financial analysts. Using these survey data along with additional data, a recent academic study investigated the relationship between media coverage and change in corporate image or reputation.[5] Overall, more positive media coverage meant a more positive corporate reputation. And, for companies that began with poor reputations, positive media exposure was associated with significant image improvements.

But, does reputation really matter? According to *Business Week*, "business has a huge stake in the way the rest of society perceives its ethical standards." On the negative side, scandals give business "a black eye"[6] and cost money. For example, in response to media reports that raised questions about Dow Corning's breast implants, the stock of Corning, Inc., one of the two corporate parents, declined by about 15%, despite the fact that the implants represented only around 1% of Dow Corning's business, and insurance coverage seemed adequate to cover potential lawsuits.[7] Similarly, Exxon has undergone years of negative media scrutiny since the Exxon Valdez oil spill.

Business isn't the only kind of organization that can be negatively affected by media exposure and a bad reputation. Since the 1940s, the United Way has been the "blue chip of charities." In 1992, the United Way's reputation as a trusted community philanthropic organization was severely damaged when the extravagances of its leader were aired in the press. President William Aramony resigned amid charges of nepotism and misuse of agency funds to support his lavish lifestyle. For the United Way, reputation translates into dollars contributed to its funding coffers. Since the scandal, the organization (both at national and community levels) has been struggling to regain its lost public trust. Reports suggest that the United Way network raised $66 million less in 1992 than in 1991. In attempts to regain the public trust, United Way has appointed a new president, and implemented new cost controls and accountability measures. For United Way, "doing business differently" is now seen as a matter of the organization's survival.[8]

On a more positive note, a favorable corporate reputation "may enable firms to charge premium prices, attract better applicants, enhance their access to capital markets, and attract investors."[9] In a speech to the 1993 Conference Board meeting on business ethics, Arnold Hiatt, retired chairman of Stride Rite Corporation, spoke about the benefits produced by a positive corporate reputation. Stride Rite invests 5% of pretax earnings in the Stride Rite Foundation, and is considered to be a leader in designing programs for children in the Boston community. The firm was named one of the 10 best companies by *Money Magazine* and one of the top U.S. companies for employees by *Working Mother* magazine. According to Hiatt, their reputation has allowed the firm to attract and retain the best employees, keeping absenteeism and turnover at Stride Rite low, and employee pride high. This is an important bottom line issue because the Conference Board estimates that it costs $21,000 to recruit, attract, and train a new employee and to bring his or her productivity level up to par with existing employees.

The positive impact of the favorable publicity is enormous. In just one year, Hiatt appeared on network television numerous times, including the Phil Donahue show and nightly news programs. Articles appeared in 300 magazines and newspapers including the front page of the Washington Post and the New York Times, reaching over 100 million readers. This free publicity is considered to be worth ten times what paid advertising is worth because of its credibility and readability. In 1991, the company estimated that it received free advertising worth $22 million.

The media generally ignores the millions of routine but ethical transactions that must occur every day if society is to function effectively. However, the media spotlight does shine on those particularly positive or negative events that are considered to be newsworthy. Organizations that find themselves in the media spotlight will find their reputations either enhanced or sullied by this media attention.

Managers Care About Ethics

Managers care about ethics in part because they face the thorny problem of how to prevent and manage unethical behavior in their ranks. Ask any manager for examples and be prepared to spend the day. As just one example of self-interested unethical behavior, the U.S. Chamber of Commerce estimates that workplace theft costs U.S. businesses up to $40 *billion* each year and employees are thought to be responsible for much of it.[10] In addition to self-interested behavior, employees may engage in unethical behavior because they think (rightly or wrongly) that it's expected. Or, they simply may not know that they are doing something that's considered to be unethical.[11]

Whatever its source, subordinates' unethical behavior is a management problem that won't go away. It may become even more of a challenge as downsizing reduces management layers, leaving fewer managers to supervise more workers.

Some estimate that the manager's traditional span of control of 7 workers may increase to as much as 21. With so many workers to supervise, the manager can't directly observe behavior. Downsizing is also increasing the number of part-time or contingency workers. These workers are likely to feel less loyalty to the organization and may be more prone to engage in unethical behaviors such as theft.

Furthermore, more workers may cross the ethical/unethical behavior line during tough economic times. Employees may believe that they can help the company survive by fudging sales figures, abusing competitors, or shortchanging customers. Those who are potential layoff candidates are also more likely to flirt with impropriety.[12] Many perceive the message to be "reaching objectives is what matters and how you get there isn't that important."[13] Therefore, today's managers may have to work even harder to communicate that ethical conduct is expected, even in tough times.

Business Leaders Care About Ethics

Many business leaders care about ethics and about business' image in society. John Akers, former Chairman of the Board of IBM, wrote that "No society anywhere will compete very long or successfully with people stabbing each other in the back; with people trying to steal from each other; with everything requiring notarized confirmation because you can't trust the other fellow; with every little squabble ending in litigation; and with government writing reams of regulatory legislation, tying business hand and foot to keep it honest . . . There is no escaping this fact; the greater the measure of mutual trust and confidence in the ethics of a society, the greater its economic strength."[14]

Robert D. Haas, chairman and CEO of Levi Strauss & Co., discussed the importance of company values this way:

> Levi has always treated people fairly and cared about their welfare. The usual term is "paternalism." But it is more than paternalism, really—a genuine concern for people and a recognition that people make this business successful.
>
> In the past, however, that tradition was viewed as something separate from how we ran the business. We always talked about the "hard stuff" and the "soft stuff." The soft stuff was the company's commitment to our work force. And the hard stuff was what really mattered; getting pants out the door.
>
> What we've learned is that the soft stuff and the hard stuff are becoming increasingly intertwined. A company's values—what it stands for, what it's people believe in—are crucial to its competitive success. Indeed, values drive the business . . . Values are where the hard stuff and the soft stuff come together . . . .[15]

We believe that, although intertwined with the "hard stuff," organizational ethics is a distinct managerial concern that must be addressed by management at all levels of the organization. Top management's role is particularly important. The leaders of America's business organizations don't "leap from bed in the morning in order to maximize the risk-adjusted present value of streams of future cash flows." Their role is "not simply financial and administrative, but social, political, and moral."[16] This book will provide insight into this moral leadership role and its importance in creating and maintaining the organization's ethical culture (see Chapter 9).

Employees Care About Ethics— Employee Attraction and Commitment

Organizations are concerned about their ability to hire and retain the best workers. The evidence suggests that employees are more attracted to and more committed to ethical organizations. "People who know that they are working for something larger with a more noble purpose can be expected to be loyal and dependable, and, at a minimum, more inspired."[17]

Recent studies confirm that it may be important to consider how potential and current employees are affected by the organization's ethics. In a survey conducted by *Working Woman* magazine, "a strong majority of those polled said that they would not work for a company with a history of environmental accidents, insider trading or worker accidents, or a law firm that defends known racketeers."[18] In another survey conducted by a national opinion research firm, ethical corporate behavior, honest company communications, and respectful treatment ranked among employees' five top-ranked goals, before good pay, which was eleventh on the list, and job security, ranked fourteenth. Ethical corporate behavior was ranked so high because "workers translate the ethics of the company into how they're personally treated." People "want to be proud of where they work." They "don't want to work for bandits, and when companies get negative publicity for their activities, workers suffer."[19]

In an academic study, researchers[20] found that workers were more committed to organizations that had a "benevolent" ethical climate (that focused on the welfare of individuals and organization members), while organizational commitment was lower in an "egoistic" climate (based on self-interest and people being out for themselves). Yet another survey found that managers who found their senior management to be credible (i.e., honest and competent) reported positive attachments to their organization.[21]

Does Society Care? Business and Social Responsibility

Most of this book is about ethics inside organizations. But, we also need to consider business' role in society and whether business has social as well as financial responsibilities. *Corporate social responsibility* (CSR) has been conceptualized as a pyramid constituting of four kinds of responsibility that must be considered simultaneously: economic, legal, ethical, and philanthropic[22] (See Figure 1.)

Economic responsibilities   Economic responsibilities refer to business' primary function as a producer of goods and services that consumers need and want, while making an acceptable profit. This responsibility is considered to be primary, because without financial viability the other responsibilities become moot issues.

FIGURE 1 Corporate Social Responsibility Pyramid
(Reprinted, by permission, from the Foundation for the School of Business
at Indiana University, *Business Horizons*, July/August, 1991.)

Milton Friedman is the most outspoken proponent of the argument that management's sole responsibility is to maximize profits for shareholders. Yet, even he states that management should "make as much money as possible *while conforming to the basic rules of society, both those embodied in the law and those embodied in ethical custom.*"[23] Interestingly, this statement tacitly embraces two of the three additional components of the corporate social responsibility pyramid: legal and ethical responsibility.

Legal responsibilities.   In addition to its economic responsibilities, business is expected to carry out its work in accordance with the law. The law guiding business practice can be viewed as a fundamental precept of the free enterprise system and as coexisting with economic responsibilities.

Ethical responsibilities.   Obviously, not every societal expectation has been codified into law. Therefore, ethical responsibilities encompass the more general responsibility to do what's right and avoid harm. For example, in PPG Industries, Inc.'s *Worldwide Code of Ethics*, the Chairman's letter states, "In all of our dealings, whether internal or external, it is not enough to simply say that our conduct is lawful. The law is the floor; compliance with it is the absolute minimum expected of a PPG associate, no matter where he or she works. Our ethics go beyond the legal code. They require us to behave in a manner which is not only lawful but also morally acceptable to all of the constituencies with whom we have dealings."

In 1993, when GM claimed that its sidesaddle fuel tank design (placed outside the truck frame in order to carry more fuel) met all federal regulations, a Georgia jury apparently wasn't convinced that the company had met its *ethical* obligation to avoid harm. In the case of a 17-year old who was killed when his pickup truck's gas tank exploded, the jury found the company negligent and awarded the boy's parents over $100 million in punitive damages.

Given its problematic history (more than 150,000 lawsuits alleging health problems from exposure to asbestos), the Manville Corporation (formerly Johns-Manville) now goes above and beyond its legal responsibilities with regard to product safety. In addition to complying with U.S. law by placing warning labels on all of its fiberglass products, Manville puts warning labels on fiberglass products being shipped to Japan. The company did this despite the fact that such warnings are not required by local law, and despite the fact that the company was advised against it by the Japanese government because the warnings might result in cancer fears. Tom Stephens, chairman, president, and Chief Executive Officer (CEO) said, "But a human being in Japan is no different from a human being in the U.S. We told them we had a policy. We had to have a label." Although the company lost 40% of its sales to Japan in one year, it was later able to rebuild its Japanese business.[24]

Thus, the ethical responsibility category frequently interacts with the legal category, pushing the expansion of legal responsibilities, and placing expectations on business persons to function at a level above the law. Business ethics involves how business organizations manage both their legal and ethical obligations.

Philanthropic responsibilities. Finally, philanthropic responsibilities involve the corporation's active involvement in activities that promote human welfare or goodwill. This generally includes donations of time and money, such as donations to the United Way, or mentoring programs for disadvantaged youth. Because philanthropy is considered to be a voluntary or discretionary aspect of corporate social responsibility, failure to be philanthropic is not considered to be *unethical*.

Is Socially Reponsible Business Good Business?

The answer to this question is, we're not sure. There's ample anecdotal evidence on both sides. For example, many of today's blue chip companies were created at the turn of the century "under circumstances approaching securities fraud. The robber barons who promoted them enjoyed great material rewards at the time—and their fortunes survived several generations."[25] And we can probably all name individuals who have "gotten ahead" the unethical way. Despite our desire to believe otherwise, unethical managers can be successful, and unethical organizations can be profitable, even in the long term.

On the other hand, one can point to highly ethical organizations that have been extremely profitable. In an attempt to demonstrate a positive link between good ethics and firm financial performance, James Burke, former CEO of Johnson & Johnson, compiled a list of major companies with a reputation for ethics and social responsibility. The group, including such recognized names as J&J, Coca-Cola, Gerber, IBM, Deere, 3M, Xerox, J.C. Penney, and Pitney Bowes, grew at a rate of 11.3% annually from 1950 to 1990 while the growth rate for Dow Jones industrials as a whole was only 6.2% for the same period.[26] Similarly, Stride Rite Corporation (discussed earlier) was one of the top financial performers on the New York Stock Exchange, number 12 out of 1000 in 1989, 1990, and 1991. Its earnings have increased each year since it started its social programs almost 20 years ago.

Many business leaders argue that ethics pays in the long term. For example, Norman Augustine, chairman and CEO of Martin Marietta, a large defense contractor, recounted a situation when the company's ethics were on the line. When competing on a government contract, the company received a brown paper bag containing their competitor's bid. They immediately turned it over to the U.S. government and told the competitor about it. Martin Marietta lost the contract, employees lost jobs, and shareholders lost money—huge short-term losses. But, Augustine is convinced that the loss was only short term. "We helped establish a reputation that, in the long run, will draw us business. . . it always pays off in the long term."

Consistent with the anecdotal evidence on both sides, academic studies have shown both positive and negative relationships between corporate social responsibility and financial performance.[27] When positive correlations are found, it isn't clear whether social responsibility leads to increased financial performance or whether higher financial performance provides firms with more slack resources that they can then devote to social performance. A recent study suggested that both may be true.[28] The positive relationships found in recent research suggest that being socially responsible certainly doesn't harm the firm's bottom line as some economists have suggested in the past.

According to Vogel, "Ethics are certainly not a barrier to financial success, but neither are they a prerequisite to it."[29] This statement is consistent with our earlier statement that the motivation to be ethical is moral as well as financial. An organization shouldn't necessarily expect financial returns for doing the "right" thing.

So why do most business people do the right thing most of the time, and why do they persist in believing that "good ethics is good business?" Because they're people first, who value their good reputations and the opinion of their friends, family, and the community. They're guided by a moral compass that points them in an ethical direction, as well as a financial compass that points them toward consideration of the costs and benefits of a decision. As one business person put it, "I can only really speak for myself, and to me, my word is the most important thing in my life and my credibility as an individual is paramount. All the other success we have had is secondary."[30]

Michael Josephson clearly separated good ethics from good business when he said:

> Goodness does not guarantee winning. And unless we can teach that to people, they are always going to look for the angle. . . . But ethics [is a] separate, independent evaluation of conduct . . . Ethics is like your skin—it goes with you everywhere. Ethics is a moral perspective that asks you to judge your conduct in terms of what's right and wrong, what's decent, what's good, what's honest, what's honorable. The reason to be ethical is simply that it's the right thing to do.[31]

Socially responsible investors.   A new breed of shareholder cares about both the financial and social bottom line of business. One of the fastest growing shareholder groups consists of "socially responsible" investors who insist that their investments meet ethical as well as financial criteria. They "put their cash where their conscience is." Although the social criteria vary, many shun certain types of industries, such as nuclear energy, weapons, and tobacco, while they support companies that use energy wisely, protect the environment, and market safe products and services. They may also consider the firm's human resource practices such as female and minority advancement, day care, or profit-sharing. Books such as *The Better World Investment Guide*[32] provide ethical investors with specific company evaluations based upon ethical criteria. A number of brokers, financial planners, and mutual funds are also now serving these investors' needs. A trade association, the Social Investment Forum, reported that socially responsible investing grew from $40 billion in 1984 to over $500 billion in 1990. The impressive financial results of socially responsible mutual funds suggest that profitability and principles can go hand in hand. What does all of this mean for business ethics? It means that, at least for this growing group of investors, shareholders' interests are no longer distinct from employee, customer, and community interests. They're all interconnected[33]

Social responsibility rewarded—The Business Enterprise Trust.   The Business Enterprise Trust (BET) is an organization established to acknowledge the hundreds of individuals and business organizations exhibiting "courage, integrity and social vision" in their work. The first BET award nominations in 1990 focused on socially responsible products, philanthropic projects, enlightened personnel practices, and more:

- Pelligrino Porraro of Prudential Insurance who bucked the system and the bureaucracy to create "living benefits" for terminally ill life insurance policy holders who can now access their "death benefits" while still alive.
- The aging owners of the Orchard Corporation who passed up lucrative acquisition offers until they found a buyer who pledged not to sell off assets to finance the acquisition, and who was willing to let the company continue its people-oriented "open communications policy."[34]

Others have been nominated for providing community services that go way beyond traditional philanthropy. A prime example is GE Plastics' (a division of General Electric) "Share to Gain" program, implemented for the first time at the company's division meetings in 1989. GE had recently acquired Borg-Warner Chemicals and company representatives decided that some kind of team-building activity was needed to help Borg Warner attendees get to know GE employees and their culture. Forsaking the usual annual meeting events (golf, fishing, and sailing) GE Plastics planned something entirely new—an opportunity for people to get to know each other by "sharing a hard day's work for a good cause." Five community sites in San Diego, California, were chosen based on their desperate need for repair. After meticulous planning, hundreds of people worked together to totally renovate each facility in a single eight-hour day. The events were a tremendous success by all accounts. The facilities were renovated, the participants built new friendships and working relationships, and felt good about what they had accomplished together.

Trust and the benefits of self-governance.   A more elusive benefit of ethics in organizations is trust. Many in the business community believe that, although difficult to document, trust has both economic and moral value. The introductory statement to the Disney code of ethics states that, "[The] public trust, above all else, is the basis for the remarkable success of the Disney organization." John Shad, former chair of the Securities and Exchange Commission, claimed that brokers annually trade $40 trillion in securities on the telephone, in a highly efficient system with almost no fraud or cheating.[35]

Individuals and organizations build trust accounts that work something like a bank account.[36] You make deposits and build your trust reserve by being honest and by keeping commitments. You can draw on this account and even make mistakes as long as the reserve is maintained. Having a trust reserve allows the individual or organization the flexibility and freedom to act without scrutiny, saving a great deal of time and energy in all types of relationships. Imagine a marriage that is based on trust. The partners go about their daily business without feeling any need to check up on each other or to hire private detectives to confirm the other's whereabouts.[37] The same is true of trust-based business relationships where a handshake seals a deal, and a business partner's word is considered to be a contract. Corporations also build trust with their customers. Johnson & Johnson made a huge contribution to its trust account when it recalled all Tylenol from store shelves after the poisoning crisis in 1982 (a situation discussed in more detail in Chapter 8). Despite no recall requirement and huge recall costs, the company put its customers first.

However, trust accounts are easily overdrawn. And when they are, all flexibility disappears. Every word and action is carefully checked and double checked for signs of dishonesty. In organizations, lawyers are hired, contracts are drawn up and signed, and CYA (cover your "you know what") memos fly. Ethics scandals have breached the public's trust in a number of institutions, including business. When trust is breached, the public typically calls for more government intervention and punishment of rule violators. Government intervention means less self-governance and more government control; interference that organizations view as costly.

In 1988, Gary Edwards, executive director of the Ethics Resource Center, testified before the Armed Services Committee of the U.S. House of Representatives on the topic of self-governance in the defense industry. He made the following link between trust and self-governance.

> Ideally, self-governance sets and achieves ethical standards higher than the requirements of the law and, in so doing, draws on and nourishes a moral force in its employees altogether different from the spirit of grudging compliance with—or adversarial evasion of—externally imposed legal requirements. When self-governance is effective, public trust is merited and secured, When self-governance fails, a measure of economic freedom is lost as government moves to protect the public interest and re-establish its trust.[38]

Avoiding the Costs of Criminal Liability

In addition to all of the other reasons for being ethical, the law now presents a crystal clear cost-based reason.[39] Until recently, criminal law focused on the individual defendant rather than the corporation and fines on corporations were relatively modest. However, since the mid-1980s the trend has been toward increasing fines for both individuals and organizations convicted of felony crimes. The U.S. Congress created the U.S. Sentencing Commission in 1984 in response to criticism of judicial discretion in sentencing, and perceived disparities between sentences for "white-collar" and other types of crimes. In 1987, the Commission imposed Federal Sentencing Guidelines for individual offenders. These guidelines limited judicial sentencing discretion and mandated some incarceration for virtually every felony offender.

In 1991, the Commission issued its new sentencing guidelines for *organizations* convicted of federal crimes. The organization can be convicted even if only one employee is caught breaking the law. The guidelines cover most federal crimes including fraud, antitrust, securities, tax, bribery, and money-laundering offenses and they impose a schedule of mandatory fines. "Virtually without exception, the Guidelines require a convicted organization to make restitution and to pay a substantial fine (which is not tax deductible)."[40] The guidelines also include a provision calling for a "corporate death penalty." The provision was recently used by federal prosecutors in the case of American Precision Components Inc., a Farmingdale, N.Y., company that sold ordinary nuts and bolts to government contractors as highly tested space components.[41] The company has agreed to divest all of its assets.

Perhaps most important for our discussion, fines and other sanctions can vary widely depending on whether management reports itself and cooperates with investigative authorities and depending on whether the company has a program in place to prevent and detect illegal behavior. Therefore, the same crime can be subject to a wide range of penalties. The minimum fine under the Guidelines is $250 and the maximum is $290 million or even more if the crime meets certain criteria. (For more specific information about how fines are determined, see the tables at the end of the chapter.) The Guidelines also provide that a defendant organization that doesn't have an effective compliance program should be put on *corporate probation*. Some of the recommended conditions of probation include requiring that the organization: publicize (at its own expense and as directed by the court) the fact of its conviction, and the nature of the punishment; periodically report to the court regarding financial condition and operating results; submit to periodic, unannounced reviews of books and records, and interrogation of employees by court appointed experts (paid by the organization); and inform the court of any material adverse change in business conditions or prospects.

Clearly, organizations now have an incentive to develop an effective legal compliance program. Although these programs vary somewhat, the framework provided by the Sentencing Guidelines has guided their development. The requirements include making legal compliance the responsibility of high-level officers, communicating rules through written materials and training, establishing monitoring and reporting systems, and disciplining offenders and those responsible for not detecting offenses (among other requirements). (See Table 1 for the full list of requirements.)

TABLE 1   Seven Requirements for Due Diligence and an Effective Compliance Program

1) Establishing compliance standards reasonably capable of preventing criminal conduct

2) Assigning specific high-level individuals with responsibility to oversee those compliance standards

3) Exercising due care to ensure that discretionary authority is not delegated to individuals with a propensity to engage in illegality

4) Taking necessary steps to communicate compliance standards and procedures to all employees, with a special emphasis on training and the dissemination of manuals

5) Taking reasonable steps to achieve compliance with written standards through monitoring, auditing, and other systems designed to detect criminal conduct, including a reporting system free of retribution to employees who report criminal conduct

6) Consistently enforcing the organization's written standards through appropriate disciplinary mechanism, including, as appropriate, discipline of individuals responsible for failure to detect an offense

7) After an offense is detected, taking all reasonable steps to respond and to prevent future similar conduct

It should be clear by now that the misconduct of a single employee can put an entire organization at risk, and that the development of an effective compliance program can help an organization prevent trouble with the law. However, problems can arise if an organization's "ethics" program focuses exclusively on legal compliance. Employees often view compliance programs as symbols of management's mistrust or of management's attempt to cover itself at employees' expense. Employees are more likely to accept a compliance program if it is part of an organization's more positive focus on ethics and values. We will talk more about specific organizations' ethics and compliance programs in Chapter 11.

ETHICS AND THE NEW ORGANIZATIONAL PARADIGM

The old joke that business ethics is an oxymoron may be outmoded. The concepts of *business* and *ethics* may be more compatible today than some might think. The emerging business paradigm encompasses individual and group empowerment, responsibility, removal of distinctions between workers and managers, harmony, cooperation, teamwork, trust, honesty, and integrity.[42]

Paradigm shift.   The word "paradigm" comes from the Greek word for "pattern." In this context, the word paradigm refers to *the pattern we use for looking at and un-*

derstanding the world—our shared, fundamental assumptions about the nature of work and business and their place in society.

The old business paradigm is mechanistic and analytical, and is represented by traditional ideas about hierarchy, control, scientific management, assembly lines, and the primacy of quantitative analysis. In the best selling book, *In Search of Excellence*, Tom Peters attacked the old model and touched a nerve. The old model wasn't flexible enough to adapt quickly to the speed of information and changes in the environment. American business was conducted like a football game, where players follow calls from the sidelines.

According to Noel Tichy of the University of Michigan business school, a better model may be a rugby game that "requires tremendous communication, continuous adjustment to an uncertain environment, and problem solving without using hierarchy."[43] The old paradigm no longer works in an age of global knowledge enterprises, instant communication, and ecological limits. When the old paradigm no longer works, paradigm shift occurs.

Paradigm shift isn't about simple reform—a change within the existing paradigm that retains its old assumptions. Rather, it's about a complete transformation of these underlying assumptions and their replacement by new ones.[44] According to a recent Fortune magazine article, the new paradigm "takes ideas from quantum physics, cybernetics, chaos theory, cognitive science, and Eastern and Western spiritual traditions to form a world view in which everything is interconnected . . . ."[45]

The new business paradigm—people and work.   The twin focus of the new paradigm is on people and interconnectedness. Work organizations are viewed as communities, and employees are members of these communities. People spend many of their waking hours in the work setting and devote much of their energy to work-related activities. This means that work is an important source of meaning in people's lives.[46] In these new corporate communities, intuition and spiritual values are valued alongside analytical skills. Network structures that place customers and employees at their centers are replacing the rigid hierarchies of the past. Business is no longer just about products and bottom line profits. The words products and profits join with words like meaning and values.

If all of this sounds a bit far fetched, note that some of America's most successful CEOs have not only bought these ideas, they're selling them. Herman Miller, CEO of Max DePree, in his best-selling book, *Leadership is an Art*, wrote of a "covenant" (not a contract) between company and employee. According to DePree, this covenant helps employees feel part of a community and provides the basis for superior managment.[47]

Robert Haas, CEO of Levi Strauss has expressed it this way: "We are not doing this [values-based strategy] because it makes us feel good—although it does. We are not doing this because it is politically correct. We are doing this because we believe in the interconnectedness between liberating the talents of our people and business success."[48]

Jack Welch, the hard-driving CEO of General Electric, has expressed his belief in the new paradigm by saing that he wants GE employees to feel "rewarded in both the pocketbook and the soul."[49] He has also said, "Every organization needs values, but a lean organization needs them even more . . . we're all working harder and faster. But unless we're also having more fun, the transformation doesn't work. Values are what enable people to guide themselves through that kind of change . . . Trust is enormously powerful in a corporation. People won't do their best unless they believe they'll be treated fairly . . . The only way I know to create that kind of trust is by laying out your values and then walking the talk."[50]

Jan Carlzon, president and CEO of Scandinavian Airlines System since 1981, has talked about the power of respect, trust, and *love* (yes, love) in management. He believes that if employees are treated with love, respect, and trust they will contribute to the firm's success in their 50,000 "moments of truth" with customers each day. If love, respect, and trust are used to motivate people, they will dare to take risks, even to make mistakes. If fear is the motivator, they won't. The implications for organization ethics are profound. In the new paradigm, individuals are assumed to be whole systems. Therefore, they're not only allowed to take their values to work, they *must* do so.

The new business paradigm—interconnectedness. Similarly, organizations are viewed as integral parts of an interconnected world community and ecosystem. In an ecosystem, one doesn't exploit workers, customers, or the environment, because the negative effects of exploitation are tacitly understood. They harm everyone.

The sense that corporations are part of the broader community and ecosystem has manifested itself in the expansion of social responsibility beyond an individual organization's boundaries. For example, Sears has said that it won't import forced-labor products from China. Dow Chemical asks its international suppliers to conform to U.S. standards on pollution and safety that are frequently tougher than local laws. Levi Strauss & Co. has ditched some suppliers that didn't measure up to its tough conduct standards, and has exacted reforms from many others. Home Depot distributed a questionnaire to its worldwide suppliers, asking whether any factory in the supply chain employs children or prison convicts.[51]

The new paradigm has clearly shifted perceptions of social responsibility beyond the corporation's front door—to its suppliers and their suppliers both here and abroad. Each corporation is viewed as part of an expanded network of organizations that can affect all of the people and environments that are directly or indirectly touched by its activities.

CONCLUSION

This chapter was designed to pique your interest in business ethics. Hopefully, we have convinced you that lots of people care about it, and that it's worth bothering about. The remainder of the book aims to help you understand ethics from a managerial perspective, explaining how this aspect of the organizational world actually works and what you can do to manage it. It will also provide practical decision-making guidance for facing your own ethical decisions and for helping others do the same.

DISCUSSION QUESTIONS

1. Do you think business ethics is important? Why or why not?

2. Identify reasons why an organization would be interested in being ethical and then classify those reasons in terms of whether they represent moral motivation or economic motivation.

3. Do you agree with the corporate social responsibility pyramid? Why or why not? What are the implications of stopping at a particular pyramid level? For example, would it be all right if a company took its sole responsibility to be financial responsibility to its shareholders? Financial responsibility and legal responsibility?

4. Think about the television programs and films you've seen recently in which business was portrayed in some way. How were business and business people portrayed? Is there anything business could or should do to improve its media image?

5. Do you believe that employees are more attracted and committed to ethical organizations? Are you? Why or why not? Make a list of the companies you would prefer to work for and the reasons why. Are there also companies that you would refuse to work for? Why? Are there ethically "neutral" companies that don't belong on either list?

6. Do you think organizations should be concerned about the new sentencing guidelines? Should they be doing anything differently because of them?

7. Discuss the new organizational paradigm. Have you seen examples of it? Counterexamples?

CASE

River Blindness[52]

Merck & Co.   Headquartered in New Jersey, Merck & Co. is one of the largest pharmaceutical companies in the world. In 1978, Merck was about to lose patent protection on its two best-selling prescription drugs. These medications had been a significant part of Merck's $2 billion in annual sales. Because of this, Merck decided to pour millions into research to develop new medications. During just three years in the 1970s, the company invested over $1 billion in research, and was rewarded with the discovery of four powerful medications. Profits, however, were never all that Merck cared about. The son of the founder of Merck, George W. Merck, said, "We try never to forget that medicine is for people. It is not for the profits. The profits follow, and if we have remembered that, they have never failed to appear.

The better we have remembered that, the larger they have been." This philosophy was at the core of Merck & Co.'s value system.

River blindness. The disease onchocerciasis, known as "river blindness," is caused by parasitic worms that live in the small black flies that breed in and about fast-moving rivers in developing countries in the Middle East, Africa, and Latin America. When a person is bitten by a fly (and some people are bitten thousands of times a day), the larvae of the worm can enter the person's body. The worms can grow to almost two feet long and can cause grotesque growths on an infected person. The real trouble comes, however, when the worms begin to reproduce and release millions of microscopic baby worms into a person's system. The itching is so intense that some infected persons have committed suicide. As time passes, the larvae continue to cause severe problems, including blindness. In 1978, the World Health Organization estimated that more than 300,000 people were blind because of the disease, and another 18 million were infected. In 1978, the disease had no safe cure. There were two drugs that could kill the parasite, but both had serious, even fatal, side effects. The only measure being taken to combat river blindness was the spraying of infected rivers with insecticides in the hope of killing the flies. However, even this wasn't effective since the flies had built up an immunity to the chemicals.

Merck's ethical quandry. Since it takes $200 million in research and 12 years to bring the average drug to market, the decision to pursue research is a complex one. Since resources are finite, dollars and time have to go to projects which hold the most promise, both in terms of making money so a company can continue to exist and in alleviating human suffering. This is an especially delicate issue when it comes to rare diseases, when a drug company's investment could probably never be recouped because the number of people who would buy the drug is so small. The problem with developing a drug to combat river blindness was the flip side of the "orphan" drug dilemma. There were certainly enough people suffering from the disease to justify the research, but since it was a disease afflicting people in some of the poorest parts of the word, those suffering from the disease were too poor to purchase the medication.

In 1978, Merck was testing a drug for animals called "ivermectin" to see if it could effectively kill parasites and worms. During this clinical testing, Merck discovered that the drug killed a parasite in horses that was very similar to the worm that caused river blindness in humans. This, therefore was Merck's dilemma: company scientists were encouraging the firm to invest in further research to determine if the drug could be adapted for safe use with humans.

Case-Based Questions

1. Think about the definition of stakeholders from Chapter 1—any parties with a stake in the organization's actions or performance. Who are the stakeholders in this situation?

2. What are the potential costs and benefits of such an investment?

3. If a safe and effective drug could be developed, the prospect of Merck recouping its investment was almost zero. Could Merck justify such an investment to shareholders and the financial community?

4. If Merck decided not to conduct further research, how would they justify such a decision to their scientists? How might the decision to develop the drug, or not to develop the drug, affect employee loyalty?

5. How would the media treat a decision to develop the drug? Not to develop the drug? How might either decision affect Merck's reputation?

6. Think about the decision in terms of the corporate social responsibility pyramid. Did Merck have an ethical obligation to proceed with development of the drug? Would it matter if the drug had only a small chance to cure river blindness? Or, does this decision become a question of philanthropy?

7. How does Merck's value system fit into this decision?

If you were the senior executive of Merck, what would you do?

How Fines Are Determined Under the U.S. Sentencing Guidelines

Exact penalties are based on a base fine and the "culpability score" assigned by the court. The base fine is the greatest of the following: the pretax gain from the crime, the amount of intentional loss inflicted on the victim(s), an amount based on the Sentencing Commission's ranking of the seriousness of the crime (ranging from $5,000 to $72.5 million). This amount is then multiplied by a number that depends on the culpability score. The culpability score ranges from 0 to 10 and the multipliers range from .05 to 4 (see Table 1).

Every defendant starts at a culpability score of 5 and can move up or down depending upon aggravating or mitigating factors (see Table 2 for these factors). The presence of aggravating factors can cause the culpability score to increase. These aggravating factors include 1) organizational size, combined with the degree of participation, tolerance, or disregard for the criminal conduct by high level personnel or substantial authority personnel in the firm, 2) prior history of similar criminal conduct, and 3) obstructing or impeding an investigation.

However, the presence of mitigating factors can cause the culpability score to drop. In order to decrease the culpability score, the organization must have in place an "effective program to prevent and detect violations of the law." If the court determines that the organization has such a program, 3 points can be removed from the base culpability score of 5. Besides having an effective compliance program in place, the culpability score can be substantially reduced if the organization reports the criminal conduct promptly after becoming aware of the offense and before imminent government investigation. According to the Guidelines, an organization that reports its own misconduct, cooperates with authorities, and accepts responsi-

TABLE 1 Method for Determining Minimum and Maximum Fines

Culpability score	Mimumum multiplier	Maximum multiplier
10 or more	2.00	4.00
9	1.80	3.60
8	1.60	3.20
7	1.40	2.80
6	1.20	2.40
5	1.00	2.00
4	0.80	1.60
3	0.60	1.20
2	0.40	0.80
1	0.20	0.40
0 or less	0.05	0.20

TABLE 2 Aggravating and Mitigating Factors That Can Increase or Decrease Culpability Scores

Aggravating Factors—result in an increase to the base level of 5

1. The size of the organization coupled with the degree of participation, tolerance, or disregard for the criminal conduct by "high level personnel" or "substantial authority personnel." In a firm with greater than 5000 employees, this factor can result in an increase of as much as 5 points.

2. Prior history: Organizations that have been either civilly or criminally adjudicated to have committed similar conduct within the past five years can have as many as 2 points added.

3. Obstructing, impeding, (or attempting to obstruct or impede) during the investigation, prosecution, or sentencing can result in 3 points added.

Mitigating Factors—result in downward departures from the base level of 5

1. Having an effective program to prevent and detect violations of the law can result in a downward departure of 3 points.

2. Self-reporting, cooperating, and accepting responsibility for the criminal conduct can result in a downward departure of 5 points.

bility can have as many as 5 points subtracted from the base culpability level of 5 (see mitigating factor no. 2).

The mitigating factors that reduce the culpability score have important implications for the way companies manage ethical conduct. For example, many believe that overseeing an "effective" program for preventing and detecting legal violations is a full-time job for at least one person. It would likely involve the development of a conduct code, training programs, scrutiny of reward systems, the development of communication systems, detection systems, etc. Practical information about how organizations are actually implementing ethics programs will be discussed in more detail in Chapter 10.

NOTES

[1]Etzioni, A. 1988. *The moral dimension: Toward a new economics*. New York: Free Press.

[2]Ibid.

[3]Grover, R. 1988. Bad guys wear pinstripes. *Business Week*, October 21: 61–63.

[4]Fusco, M. A. C. 1988. Ethics game plan: Taking the offensive. *Business Week Careers*, Spring/Summer:51.

[5]Wartick, S. L. 1992. The relationship between intense media exposure and change in corporate reputation. Spring: 33–49.

[6]Yes, business and ethics do go together. 1988, *Business Week*, February 15: 118.

[7]Labich, K. 1992. The new crisis in business ethics. *Fortune*, April 20: 167–176.

[8]Segal, T & Del Valle, C. 1993. They didn't even give at the office. *Business Week*, January 25: 68–69.

[9]Fombrun, C. & Shanley, M. 1990. What's in a name? Reputation building and corporate strategy. *Academy of Management Journal*, 333: 233–256.

[10]Zemke, R. 1986 Employee theft. How to cut your losses. *Training*, May: 74–78.

[11]Collins, J. 1990. Why bad things happen to good companies and what can be done. *Business Horizons*, November–December: 18–22.

[12]Hager, B. 1991. What's behind business' sudden fervor for ethics. *Business Week*, September 23: 65.

[13]Labich, K. 1992. The new crisis in business ethics. *Fortune*, April 20: 167–176.

[14]Akers, J. F. 1989. Ethics and competitiveness—putting first things first. *Sloan Management Review*, Winter: 69–71.

[15]Howard, R. 1987. Values make the company: An interview with Robert Haas. In *Leaders on leadership*. W. Bennis, ed. Boston: Harvard Business School, 33–54.

[16]Badaracco, J. L., Jr. 1992. Business ethics: Four spheres of executive responsibility. *California Management Review*, Spring: 64–79.

[17]Channon, J. 1992. Creating esprit de corps. In *New traditions in business*. J. Renesch. San Francisco: Berrett-Koehler Publishers. 53–68.

[18]Sandroff, R. 1990. How ethical is American business? *Working Woman Magazine*, September: 113–116.

[19]Kleiman, C. 1989. Heading the list of worker wishes isn't more money! *The Morning Call*, October 2: B10.

[20]Cullen, J. B. & Victor, B. 1993. The effects of ethical climates on organizational commitment: A multilevel analysis. Unpublished manuscript.

[21]Posner, B. Z. & Schimdt, W. H. 1992. Values and the American manager. *California Management Review*, Spring: 80–94.

[22]Carroll, A. B. 1991. The pyramid of corporate social responsibility: Toward the moral management of organizational stakeholders. *Business Horizons*, 34 (4): 39–48.

[23]Friedman, M. 1970. The social responsibility of business is to increase its profits. *New York Times*, September 13: 122–126.

[24]Singer, A. W. 1993. Can a company be too ethical? *Across the Board*, April: 17–22.

[25]Bhide, A. & Stevenson, H. H. 1990. Why be honest if honesty doesn't pay. *Harvard Business Review*, September–October: 121–129.

[26]Labich, K. 1992. The new crisis in business ethics. *Fortune*, April 20: 167–176.

[27]Aupperle, K. E. Carroll, A. B. & Hatfield, J. D. 1985. An empirical examination of the relationship between corporate social responsibility and profitability. *Academy of Management Journal*, 28: 449–459.

McGuire, J. B., Sundgren, A. & Scheeweis, T. 1988. Corporate social responsibility and firm financial performance. *Academy of Management Journal*, 31: 854–872.

Ullman, A. H. 1985. Data in search of a theory. a critical examination of the relationships among social performance, social disclosure, and economic performance of U.S. firms. *Academy of Management Review*, 10: 3, 540–447.

[28]Waddock, S. A. & Graves, S. B. 1994. The corporate social performance–financial performance link. Paper presented at the Academy of Management meeting, August, Dallas.

[29]Vogel, D. 1988. Ethics and profits don't always go hand in hand. *Los Angeles Times*, December 28:7.

[30]Bhide, A. & Stevenson, H. H. 1990. Why be honest if honesty doesn't pay. *Harvard Business Review*, September-October: 121–129.

[31]Josephson, Michaael S. 1989. Ethics in a legalistic society. *Exchange*, Fall: 3–7.

[32]Alperson, M., Marlin, A. T., Schorsch, J. & Will, R. 1991. *The better world investment guide*. New York: Prentice-Hall.

[33]Warner, J. 1990. Putting your cash where your conscience is. *Business Week*, December 24: 74–75.

[34]O'Toole, J. 1991. Do good, do well: The business enterprise trust awards. *California Management Review*, Spring, 9–24.

[35]Kuhn, J. W. 1992. Ethics in business: What managers practice that economists ignore. *Business Ethics Quarterly*, 2 (3): 304–315.

[36]Covey, S. R. 1989. *The 7 habits of highly effective people*. New York: Simon & Schuster.

[37]Ibid.

[38]Center Director Testifies Before Congress Report.

[39]Adapted from a speech given by attorney Steven Alan Reiss, 1992.

[40]Reiss, S. A. 1992. Speech given at the Conference Board meeting on Business Ethics, 1992.

[41]*United States* v. *American Precision Components Inc.*, 93–450.

[42]Rose, F. 1990. A new age for business? *Fortune*, October 8: 156–164.

[43]Ibid.

[44]Garfield, C. 1992. Second to none: Business in the ecological age. *Noetic Sciences Review*, Winter: 15–19.

[45]Rose, F. 1990. A new age for business? *Fortune*, October 8: 156–164.

[46]Badaracco, J. L., Jr. 1992. Business ethics: Four spheres of executive responsibility. *California Management Review*, Spring: 64–79.

[47]Miller, H. 1991. Should your company save your soul? *Fortune*, January 14: 33.

[48]Haas, R. 1994. Managing by values. *Fortune*, August 1: 46–52.

[49]Rose, F. 1990. A new age for business? *Fortune*, October 8: 156–164.

[50]Welch, J. 1993. Jack Welch's lessons for success. *Fortune*, January 25: 86–93.

[51]McCormick, J. & Levinson, M. 1993. The supply police. *Newsweek*, February 15: 48–49.

[52]Bollier, D. 1991. Merck & company. Stanford, CA: The Business Enterprise Trust.

SECTION II

Ethics and the Individual

CHAPTER THREE

Common Ethical Problems

INTRODUCTION

THE BAD NEWS about business ethics is: your career can be irrevocably damaged if you mishandle an ethical dilemma. But there's also good news: many ethical dilemmas in business are quite predictable. You can be fairly certain that during the course of your career, you'll run into myriad ethical dilemmas such as an unreasonable customer, or the appropriate use of corporate resources, or discrimination of one sort or another. Since ethical dilemmas are somewhat predictable, you have a better chance of dealing appropriately with ethical problems if you think about what's likely to happen before it occurs.

Before we get into a discussion of ethical dilemmas, however, it's important to look at the relationship that exists between you and your employer. Although most people don't sign a contract the day they join a company or organization, there is a contractual relationship of sorts between workers and employers. Both parties have expectations, and rights, and offer consideration to the other. Your employer pays you in salary and benefits to perform a job and your organization expects you to behave in a certain way; you have a responsibility to be "part of the family" and exhibit loyalty and other corporate "virtues" and to refrain from other, less desirable behaviors. On the other hand, you expect not only a salary for the work you perform, but also you expect a certain modicum of fairness, too. Most people expect employers to treat them decently and to provide an appropriate work environment. Whenever we discuss the employer/employee contract in this chapter, it's this complicated set of expectations that we're referring to.

So what are some typical ethical dilemmas? We've compiled some of the more obvious dilemmas and have divided them into broad categories including human resources issues, conflicts of interest, customer confidence issues, and the use of corporate resources. We will address a number of specific topics under each broad category. To make it easy to follow, each topic contains the following information:

- What is it?—a definition of the issue.
- Why is it an ethical problem?
- Professional costs—possible penalties for ethical or legal transgressions.
- Special notes—some topics may include important information related to the topic.

HUMAN RESOURCES ISSUES

It's difficult to overstate how important it is for a company to effectively manage its people. Human resources—the employees who make up an organization—are any corporation's most important and expensive investment, and are the underpinning of an organization's success or failure. Barbara Toffler[1] found that 66% of the ethical issues encountered by the managers she interviewed involved managing human resources or internal organizational processes. In addition, the widest legal exposure for many companies may involve violations or perceived violations of the employer–employee contract.

Although it may be difficult in times of high unemployment to imagine a shortage of qualified workers, all projections point to just such a shortage by the end of the 1990s. In the United States, this translates not into a shortage of workers, but into a shortage of workers with the skills necessary to fill highly skilled jobs. As a result, corporations are actively designing programs to attract, motivate, and retain qualified employees.

Probably the most effective way to retain qualified employees is to create a working environment where people feel appreciated. People who like to come to work may be significantly more productive than workers who feel their efforts are unappreciated, their management doesn't care about them, or their ideas don't count. Productivity, which is at the very heart of competitiveness, can exist only when employees are respected by management and when employees are encouraged to respect one another.

We use the term "human resources issues" to describe the problems that occur when people work together. They can include discrimination, sexual or other types of harassment, performance evaluation, hiring, firing, or simply "how people get along." (Performance evaluation—including appraisals, discipline, hiring, firing, and layoffs—will be discussed in Chapter 6.)

The word to remember when considering human resources issues is fairness, and most corporate policy is constructed to build fairness into the system. When we talk about fairness, we mean equity, reciprocity and impartiality—the way most people have thought about what "fair" means since they were children.[2] Something is said to be fair and equitable when something is divided between two people according to the worth and gains of the two individuals: "If they received equal shares, did they work equally hard?" Most people think it's unfair when two people have performed the same duty and they receive a different share of the reward. Another measure of fairness is reciprocity, or the fairness of exchanges: "You did this for me and I'll do that for you." Most people perceive it as being unfair if one person fails to hold up his or her part of a bargain. The third measure of fairness is impartiality: "Is the person who's going to listen to my story biased in some way, or has he or she prejudged the situation?" Not surprisingly, most people think of fairness as being completely inconsistent with prejudice and bias.

Most protective legislation and corporate human resources policy tries to incorporate those elements. The goal is to hire, treat, promote, appraise, and layoff or fire employees based solely on their qualifications and not on factors like sex, race, or age. The goal is to level the playing field and create a fair environment where performance is the only factor that counts (equity), where employer–employee expectations are understood and met (reciprocity), and where prejudice and bias are not factors (impartiality).

Discrimination

You're interviewing candidates for a job as chief engineer on a new power plant that will be located near a major metropolitan area. The job will place significant emotional and physical demands on the person selected to run the project. The senior vice president who will serve as the chief engineer's manager says that whoever is selected as chief engineer will have to commit to at least two years to the job and that the demands of the job will allow for no vacations. It's a big commitment for whoever gets the job, but the rewards will be substantial if the project is a success. The leading candidate for the position—an engineer with an outstanding track record during her 12-year career at your company—tells you that she just discovered she's pregnant. Do you recommend her for the job?

Since discrimination by race, religion, national origin, sex, and age is prohibited by federal law in the United States, many companies have defined policies prohibiting any kind of discrimination. Unfortunately, there can be quite a gulf between where corporate policy leaves off and reality begins. When people from various backgrounds get together to provide a service or manufacture a product, there surely will be people who have conscious or unconscious biases toward various groups, and others who are simply ignorant of the effect their behavior has on others.

What Is it?

Discrimination occurs whenever something other than qualifications affect how an employee is treated. Unequal treatment—usually unfavorable—can take many forms. Older workers who suddenly find themselves reporting to younger ones can be resentful since they feel younger workers lack experience. Younger employees can be tempted to ignore advice from older workers, who they feel are "out of touch." The attitudes toward age will most likely become increasingly important over the next decade as the general population grows older.

Racial, ethnic, religious, or sexual stereotypes can creep into the behavior of even the most sophisticated individuals. The importance of being able to manage different types of people can't be overstated. In the United States, ethnic and racial minorities are growing faster than the population as a whole. By the year 2000, almost 85% of the new entrants into the work force will be women, minorities, or immigrants.[3]

In the case involving the leading candidate for chief engineer, her pregnancy could result in discrimination. Although pregnant employees are protected by law (see "Why is it an ethical problem?" which follows), in this case any time away from the job would be viewed as a liability. Would the interviewer and the senior vice president be discriminating against the pregnant employee if they denied her this job because of her pregnancy? What would the ramifications be if a worker accepted the job, and later became pregnant? Would she be allowed to continue in the job, or would she be replaced? Could an employer justify limiting applications for this job to men or single women? Is the employer justified in demanding a two-year commitment with no time off? Can an employer ever predict an employee's attendance? What if a man accepts the job and is later hit by a truck or suffers a heart attack? Could the woman's time away from her job be built into the project—could she accomplish some work while at home after delivery and have an assistant manager stand in for her on site? How smart is it to have just one person manage a project of this magnitude?

Discrimination can be a subtle or not-so-subtle factor not only in working relationships, but also in hiring, promotions, and layoff decisions. People who don't fit a "corporate profile" may be passed over for advancement because they're female, or a member of a minority group, or for other reasons that may or may not be covered in protectionist legislation. Surely there are many ceilings in the workplace—not just the glass ceiling that refers to barriers to female advancement. There probably are also ceilings for people who are over 50 years old, or who have medical problems, or who are short, disabled, overweight, bearded, balding, or homosexual—any quality that varies from the "norm." And some employers create job requirements—as in those for the chief engineer—which could automatically eliminate certain employees, not because of their qualifications, but because of personal circumstances.

Why Is It an Ethical Problem?

Discrimination is an ethical issue—beyond any legal protections—because it's at the core of fairness in the workplace. Fairness, according to Sheppard, Lewicki, and Minton,[4] is a critical commodity because it's viewed in the United States as an "inalienable" right. As we said earlier in this chapter, two factors inherent in the concept are equity and impartiality, and discrimination gnaws at the soul of fairness. Even our government has attempted to ensure fairness and justice; the word "trust" is on every piece of currency and the Pledge of Allegiance declares "with liberty and justice for all." In addition, our entire legal system has justice and the protection of individual rights as its cornerstone. Consequently, people expect fairness from organizations in general, but specifically from their employers.

Costs

Victims of discrimination can file under Title VII of the Civil Rights Act of 1964 with the Equal Employment Opportunity Commission (EEOC), or bring suit under tort or contract law. This legislation specifically prohibits discrimination based on race, religion, sex, color, and national origin. Groups specifically protected by Title VII include women, African-Americans, Hispanics, Native Americans, and Asian-Pacific Islanders. (Also, some states and local communities have added more protections—like sexual orientation and marital status—to that list.) The Pregnancy Discrimination Act of 1978 prohibits discrimination against pregnant women. The 1967 Age Discrimination in Employment Act extends protection to people 40 years of age and older. The 1973 Rehabilitation Act was the first federal legislation to protect disabled Americans against discrimination by federal, state, local governments, agencies, and contractors. The Americans with Disabilities Act (ADA) of 1990 extends protection to the private sector by requiring all companies with more than 15 employees to make reasonable accommodations in order to employ workers with disabilities. Although the law doesn't list conditions or diseases that are protected—since people react so differently to disease, and some may be disabled and some may not—some conditions are specifically included or excluded. HIV infection, for example, is considered a disability and people who have it are protected by the ADA law.

Discrimination lawsuits can be costly for employers not simply in terms of legal fees and damages and media coverage. The effect on the morale of the victims (and often their co-workers) can decrease productivity and increase absenteeism and turnover. Alexander and Ruderman[5] found that employees' perception of fairness is strongly tied to job satisfaction, lower conflict, harmony, increased trust in management, and less intention to leave the company.

If you're an individual accused of discriminating against another employee, the least you'll endure is an investigation. If you're found guilty, you'll probably be penalized or even fired. If you're found innocent, you or your accuser will most likely be counseled about your behavior and its effects, and one or both of you may be transferred to another area. If you manage someone who has been accused of discrimination, expect a lot of questions concerning why you were unaware of it or tolerated it. If you were aware of it and didn't do anything about it, be prepared for disciplinary action, particularly if a lawsuit results.

Special Note

The many programs that train employees to "value diversity" can seem to be at odds with the efforts to assimilate various groups and especially with the laws and policies that prohibit discrimination. Learning to appreciate differences flies in the face of what many of us are taught from the time we're children—we should "fit in." Not only are many of us taught to downplay our own uniqueness in an effort to blend in, but also we're taught to ignore differences in other people. We usually are taught "not to notice" different colors, religions, accents, ways of dressing, and physical disabilities or abilities. Even sexual differences, which can be hard to ignore, have been played down in the not-too-distant past. (Remember when many women felt the need to wear pin-striped suits and silk bow ties?)

Valuing diversity means treating people equally while incorporating their diverse ideas. Discrimination means treating people unequally because they are, or appear to be, different. Valuing diversity is a positive action, while discrimination is a negative action. Valuing diversity tries to incorporate more fairness into the system, while discrimination incorporates unfairness into the system. The key to valuing diversity is understanding that different doesn't mean deficient and it doesn't mean less. Different means different.

Harassment—Sexual and Otherwise

The U.S. Senate confirmation hearings of Clarence Thomas' nomination to the Supreme Court focused American business and workers on the issue of sexual harassment like nothing else ever has. One result of that incident was an overnight increase in the number of corporations offering sexual harassment training to sensitize employees to the issue. Another result was a growing apprehension on the part of employees—especially men—toward workers of the opposite sex. Sometimes the line between friendly and offensive is blurry.

> One of your co-workers is Joanne, a computer whiz with an offbeat style and a great sense of humor. Two of Joanne's favorite "targets" are you and Bill, another co-worker who tends to be quite standoffish in his business relationships. Joanne is the department clown and is forever goading you and Bill—you, because you're a great audience and clearly think she's hilarious; Bill, because she likes to try to get him to be more approachable. Joanne frequently alludes to sexual subjects and has called both you and Bill "little alley cats" and "studs." While Joanne's behavior doesn't offend you at all, you're surprised when Bill approaches you in the men's room and bitterly complains about Joanne's constant teasing.

What Is it?

Federal law has defined two types of sexual harassment: Quid Pro Quo and Hostile Work Environment.

Quid Pro Quo means that sexual favors are a requirement—or appear to be a requirement—for advancement in the workplace.

Hostile Work Environment means that a worker has been made to feel uncomfortable because of unwelcome actions or comments relating to sexuality. This type of sexual harassment is especially murky because sexual harassment of this type is like beauty: it's in the eye of the beholder. What constitutes sexual harassment for one person, may not for another. Putting your arm around a person's shoulder may feel like harassment to one individual, whereas someone else may be comfortable with such a gesture. This type of sexual harassment includes not only physical gestures, but also can include remarks of a sexual nature—even compliments—and displays of sexually provocative material, like nude or revealing photographs displayed in an office.

In both types of sexual harassment, the decision about whether the behavior constitutes sexual harassment is determined from the point of view of a "reasonable" person and the harasser's intentions aren't considered, which is why sexual harassment issues can be confusing. Since sexual harassment is determined by the reaction of the victim, you have to consider—not what you mean by your comments or actions—but how they might be interpreted by the other person.

Most people will readily agree that kissing someone or patting someone on their rear end could be construed by some as being sexual harassment. But are you sexually harassing someone if you compliment her appearance, or touch his arm, or make jokes of a sexual nature?

In Joanne's case, she hasn't done a very good job of considering exactly who her audience is and how each of her two co-workers might react to her jokes. While you might think it's funny to be called a little stud, Joanne probably should think more carefully about how someone like Bill might react to being called a name with sexual connotations. Is Joanne out of line? Is Bill overreacting? According to the law, it doesn't matter if you and Joanne think Bill is overreacting. The yardstick used to determine whether sexual harassment occurred will be Bill's feelings of discomfort and not Joanne's intentions.

Why Is It an Ethical Problem?

Harassment (sexual or otherwise) is a form of discrimination and is therefore an ethical issue because it unfairly focuses job satisfaction, advancement, or retention on a factor other than the ability to do the job. Most instances of sexual harassment have nothing to do with romance and everything to do with power and fairness.

Costs

Victims of sexual harassment can file under Title VII of the Civil Rights Act of 1964 with the Equal Employment Opportunity Commission (EEOC), or bring suit under tort or contract law. An employer can be held liable for an employee's sexual harassment activities if the employer has knowledge of the conduct and has done nothing to correct it. As a result, most companies take a sexual harassment charge very seriously.

Most companies will launch an immediate investigation if someone is accused of sexually harassing another employee. If this is a first-time event and the incident that prompted it is not determined to be lewd or an assault—think of the scenario featuring Joanne that was discussed earlier—the employee may be warned, disciplined, or transferred to another area. (However, in some major companies a first-time offense is enough to get someone fired.) If the behavior is judged to be lewd or forceful, or if there's evidence that the employee has demonstrated a pattern of behavior, the employee will most likely be fired, and often very quickly. (One corporation was able to conduct an investigation, find evidence of a pattern, and terminate the harasser in less than 48 hours.) If the accused is found innocent, or if it's determined that a misunderstanding exists between the two parties, the accused and the accuser will probably be counseled by human resources professionals and, if necessary, one of them may be transferred to another area.

The manager of a sexual harasser can expect a lot of questions concerning why he or she was unaware of it. If the manager was aware of it and didn't do anything about it, he or she should be prepared for disciplinary action, particularly if a lawsuit results. Sexual harassment lawsuits are very expensive for corporations. Awards to victims have been substantial as is the toll such charges can take on co-workers' morale and on the ability to hire qualified candidates.

CONFLICTS OF INTEREST

People and corporations are naturally involved in a tangle of relationships—both personal and professional. Your personal reputation, and the reputation of your company, are inextricably tied to how well you handle relationships with other employees, customers, consultants, vendors, family, and friends. Your ability to act impartially, and *look* as if you are acting impartially, are key to your fulfilling your end of the employer–employee contract.

Your daughter is applying to a prestigious Ivy League university. Since admission to the school is difficult, your daughter has planned the process carefully. She has consistently achieved high marks, taken preparatory courses for entrance exams, and has participated in various extracurricular activities. When you tell one of your best customers about her activities, he offers to write her a letter of recommendation. He's an alumnus of the school and is one of its most active fund raisers. Although he's a customer, you also regularly play golf together and your families have socialized together on occasion.

What Is It?

A conflict of interest occurs when your judgment or objectivity is compromised. The appearance of a conflict of interest—when a third party could think your judgment has been compromised—is generally considered to be just as damaging as an actual conflict.

In the case of a customer offering to do a favor for you—or your daughter or other member of your family—some of the questions you'll need to ask yourself include: Would your customer's offer influence your business relationship? Could someone think your business judgment has been compromised by accepting your customer's offer? Is your relationship more than just a business one, so that accepting an offer could be interpreted as a simple act of friendship?

Some corporations have policy that permits the acceptance of favors from customers or vendors if there's also a friendship present; and "friendship" is usually defined by these companies as a long-standing relationship that's well-known in the community. For example, in small towns where everyone knows everyone else, many customers will be friends and it's unrealistic to expect anything else. Other companies would discourage accepting a favor like this one under any circumstances. Things to consider when making your decision in this case include: how long you've been friends with your customer, how well-known the relationship is in your community, his knowledge of your daughter's qualifications, and whether your customer expects anything in return for his recommendation or if the letter is simply a gesture of friendship with no strings attached. How would his recommendation be perceived by others?

Almost every business situation can involve conflicts of interest. A conflict can occur when a vendor lavishly entertains you or when you entertain a customer—if the object is influence. Both situations could prompt an observer to think that a special deal or advantageous terms are part of the relationship. Conflicts of interest can occur when people who report to you observe that you have an especially close friendship with one of their co-workers. Conflicts can occur when you're asked to judge the creditworthiness of your neighbor or if you perform consulting work for your employer's competitor. They can involve accepting hand-tooled cowboy boots from an advertising agency, being sponsored for membership in an exclusive private club by a consulting company, or allowing a supplier to give you a discount on equipment for your home when you place an order for your office.

Common conflicts of interest include:

- **Overt bribes or kickbacks**—Anything that could be considered a bribe or kickback is a clear conflict of interest. It doesn't matter whether the bribe or kickback is in the form of money or something else of substantial value that is offered in exchange for access to specific products, services, or influence.
- **Subtle "bribes"**—These can be interpreted to include gifts and entertainment. Most corporate policy places a ceiling of $25–$100 on the gifts employees can accept from, or give to, customers or vendors. Reciprocity is one yardstick used for determining whether entertainment is acceptable. If you can't reciprocate with the same kind of entertainment being offered to you, it's probably inappropriate to accept it. For example, if a vendor offers you tickets to the Super Bowl, or a weekend of golf, or dinner for four at a $200-

per-person restaurant, it's probably inappropriate for you to accept under any circumstances. The emphasis on reciprocity is to maintain a fair, even playing field for all vendors, so that you (as a purchaser) will be unbiased when making a decision about a vendor. As mentioned earlier, both reciprocity and impartiality are elements of fairness.

Accepting discounts on personal items from a vendor will also be interpreted as a conflict. The formula to use when determining whether to accept a discount is simple: if it's a formal arrangement between your company and a supplier and is offered to all employees, it's probably acceptable; if the discount is being extended only to you, it's not acceptable.

- **Influence**—Your relationship with someone by itself can constitute a conflict of interest. For example, if you're in charge of purchasing corporate advertising and your cousin or neighbor or college friend owns an advertising agency, it will be considered a conflict if you make the decision to hire that firm. That doesn't preclude the firm from bidding, but it does preclude you from making the decision. If a decision involves anyone with whom you have a personal relationship, you should ask someone else to make it. Another way to avoid the appearance of a conflict in a situation like this one, which is charged with issues of partiality, is to arrange for a "blind" competition, where the identity of various bidders is known only by someone not involved in the decision-making process. However, since any decision made by you in such a case will be suspect—even in blind evaluations—you should include other employees in the decision-making process.

- **Privileged information**—As an employee, you're naturally privy to information that would be valuable to your employer's competitors. That's why it's generally considered a conflict of interest if you hold a full-time job for ABC Bank and decide to do some consulting work for XYZ Bank. There are certainly exceptions to this rule of thumb: if you're a computer programmer at Green's Restaurant, it probably isn't a conflict to wait on tables at Red's Restaurant. Two factors could make such a situation acceptable: if the work you perform at your second job doesn't compromise the work you do at your first one, and if both employers are aware of your activities.

  In addition, it can appear as if you're involved in a conflict if you and a close relative or friend work for competitors or if one of you works for an organization—such as a media company—which might have a particular interest in your company's activities. One good way to handle this is to let your manager know where your close relatives and friends work—full disclosure removes substantial risk from the situation.

Why Is It an Ethical Problem?

The basis of every personal and corporate relationship is trust and it exists only when individuals and corporations feel as if they're being treated fairly, openly, and on the same terms as everyone else. Conflicts of interest erode trust by making it look as if special favors will be extended for special friends and that attitude can enhance one relationship, but at the expense of all others.

Costs

Depending on the offense, myriad federal and state laws cover conflicts of interest. Certain professions, such as banking, accounting, law, religion, and medicine, have special obligations—often spelled out in professional codes of ethics—commonly referred to as "fiduciary" responsibilities. Fiduciary responsibilities result from relationships that have their basis in faith, trust, and confidence.

If you're suspected of a conflict of interest, the least you can expect is an investigation by your company. If it determines that your behavior demonstrates a conflict or the appearance of a conflict, you may be warned, disciplined, or even fired depending on the nature of your behavior. If you've accepted a bribe or kickback, you could face termination and even arrest. Being involved in a conflict of interest means that your judgment has been compromised and it can severely damage your professional reputation.

CUSTOMER CONFIDENCE ISSUES

We've all heard the saying, "The customer is always right," and companies like Wal-Mart have benefited by weaving that slogan into the fabric of their corporate cultures. But excellent customer service is more than being able to return a defective refrigerator or having cheerful customer service representatives (although that helps). Excellent customer service also means providing a quality product or service at a fair price, honestly representing the product or service, and protecting the customer's privacy.

You work for a financial services organization in Atlanta. Your team has recently completed an analysis of Big Co. including financial projections for the next five years. You're working late one night when you receive a call from an executive vice president at Big Co. in Los Angeles, who asks you to immediately fax her a summary of your team's report. When you locate the report, you discover that your team leader has stamped "For internal use only" on the report cover. Your team leader is on a hiking vacation and you know it would be impossible to locate him. Big Co. has a long-standing relationship with your company and has paid substantial fees for your company's services.

What Is It?

Customer confidence issues include a range of topics including confidentiality, product safety and effectiveness, truth in advertising, and special fiduciary responsibilities.

- **Confidentiality**—Privacy is a basic customer right. Privacy and the obligation to keep customer information in confidence often goes beyond protecting financial information. It can also mean keeping in strict confidence information concerning acquisitions, mergers, relocations, layoffs, or an executive's health or marital problems. In some industries, confidentiality is so important an issue that companies prohibit their employees from publicly acknowledging a customer relationship. In the financial services industry, for example, it's common practice to refuse to divulge that XYZ Company is even a customer.

    In the case involving Big Co., an executive is demanding access to a confidential report. First, are you absolutely certain that the caller is indeed a Big Co. executive? If you have verified her identity, do you know whether she has clearance from Big Co. to examine your team's report? If she does have clearance, is your team's report in a format that your company wants to share with Big Co., or does it need revision? Whenever you see "For internal use only," that's what it means, and it can be enormously risky to release the report to anyone—including the customer—without permission. In a case like this one, you should track down someone who's in a position of authority in your company—your manager's manager perhaps—before you override the warning on the report and release any information.

    On occasion, third parties may ask for customer information. For example, a reporter or a client may ask you about customer trends. It's never acceptable to discuss specific companies or individuals with a third party, or provide any information that might enable a third party to identify a specific customer. If you want to provide information, you can offer aggregate data from a number of companies, as long as the data provided doesn't allow any one customer to be identified.

- **Product safety**—Another basic customer right is product safety and there's probably no issue that will more seriously affect a corporate reputation. Not only is it imperative to care about customer safety, but a company must also actively demonstrate its concern for customer well-being. In 1994, a large financial firm was excoriated for selling shares in questionable partnerships to individual investors, who later lost substantial sums on their investments in the partnerships. The firm not only suffered repeated lashings in the press, but it paid enormous fines as well, and its reputation has suffered greatly. Although this may not be the kind of situation we ordinarily think of when we consider product safety, people have suffered because a firm overstated the soundness of its "product." In this case the product was advice, and the public, the press, and the courts deemed once again that the "safety" of a product or service is an important consumer right.

- **Truth in advertising**—Imagine that your financial firm is offering a new issue—a corporate bond with an expected yield of 7–7.5%. In the past, offerings like this one have generally been good investments for clients, and you have sold the issue to dozens of large and small clients. You're leaving on a two-week vacation and only have a few hours left in the office, when your firm announces that the yield for the bond has been reduced; the high end will now be no more than 7%. The last day of the issue will be next week, while you're way on vacation. What should you do?

  The fact is that your customers have been misled (albeit unintentionally) about the yield on that particular bond, and now you are under an obligation to tell the truth about the instrument before the issue closes. Why? Because another basic consumer right is to be told the truth about the products and services purchased. Failure to tell the truth about a product can be devastating for an organization and it also can cause big problems for the company employees who are involved in perpetuating the false information.

- **Special fiduciary responsibilities**—As discussed earlier in this chapter, certain professions, such as banking, accounting, law, religion, and medicine, have special confidentiality obligations to customers. These professions are widely know as "trust" professions, meaning that these practitioners have been entrusted with sensitive, confidential information about their clients. The law and the judicial system have recognized these special obligations, and they are spelled out in the codes of ethics for those professions.

Why Is It an Ethical Problem?

We use the term "customer confidence issues" as an umbrella to address the wide range of topics that can affect your relationship with your customer. These are ethical issues because they revolve around fairness, honesty, and respect for others and customer relationships can't survive without those basics of trust.

Costs

There are severe corporate and individual penalties regarding truth in advertising and product safety, and more may be on the way. In addition to fines and imprisonment, the publicity in cases where product safety is a factor is generally staggering, as is the public's reaction. Even if a company is exonerated in the long run, the publicity generated by these situations can be seriously damaging and it can take years for a company to recover, especially if there's evidence of wrongdoing and consumers feel that the organization has violated a public trust.

The fastest way to lose a customer or client is to violate their basic rights to honesty, a quality product or service, or confidentiality. And, obviously, losing customers will short circuit any career. In addition, if you belong to a profession with special fiduciary responsibilities, violating customer trust or confidentiality can result in disciplinary action or censure.

USE OF CORPORATE RESOURCES

As discussed in the introduction, you and your employer have a special relationship, and each owes the other a modicum of loyalty based on that relationship. In addition, since you're a corporate representative, you're considered an "agent" of your company. This means that your actions can be considered as actions of the corporation. This section of the chapter presents the flip side of an earlier section on Human Resources Issues—your employer's responsibilities to you are described in that section and your responsibilities to your employer are described here.

> A young woman who works for you is moving with her husband to another city, where she'll be looking for a new job. She's an excellent worker and when she asks you for a reference, you're glad to do it for her. She specifically asks for a written recommendation on your corporate letterhead.

What Is It?

The use of corporate resources involves your fulfilling your end of the employer–employee "contract." It means being truthful with your employer and management, and being responsible in the use of corporate resources, including its finances and reputation.

- **Use of corporate reputation**—Whenever you identify yourself as an employee of your company, people can infer that you are speaking on behalf of it, which is why you have to be careful how you link yourself to your company. For example, if you use corporate letterhead to write a recommendation for someone or to simply complain to the telephone company, it can be construed as a "corporate" position. Consequently, corporate letterhead should be used only for corporate business. If, as in the case of the recommendation, you need to identify yourself as an employee, use your personal stationery and attach your business card. The objective is to differentiate between your personal opinions and any official stance of your organization.
  Recommendations, in particular, present a challenge for employers and individuals. Many companies attempt to check with former employers when hiring someone. This can present a problem since most companies prohibit their personnel from officially supplying this type of information because of lawsuits that have resulted from employer-supplied recommendations. (Many employers will supply only the following information concerning former em-

ployees: name, date of employment, and job title. And most employers will require your written consent before they supply any salary information to a third party.)

Similarly, if you're asked to make a speech, write an article, serve on the board of a nonprofit organization, or participate in any activity that would identify you (and your personal opinions) with your company, be sure to get permission from your manager, the legal department, or human resources. You may unwittingly be supporting a position or organization with which your company may not wish to be associated. For example, while it might seem like a great idea for you to serve on the board of your local ASPCA, if you work for a pharmaceutical company that tests drugs on animals, you may be placing your employer in an embarrassing position. Of course, you can serve on the board as a private citizen, but not as an employee of XYZ Drug Company unless you've received corporate authorization.

Also, if you are contacted by the press, immediately contact your company's public relations department. Unless you're trained to answer press inquiries and receive authorization to do it, you should *never* comment to the press. It's easy to innocently supply confidential information or cast a negative light on your company when you're untrained to deal with probing or ambiguous questions posed by a skilled journalist.

- **Corporate financial resources**—In a game entitled, "Where Do You Draw the Line—An Ethics Game," produced by Simile II, players explore the differences between taking $10 worth of pencils from their company and distributing them to poor children, making $10 worth of personal long distance calls at work, and taking $10 from their company's petty cash drawer. Is there a difference among these scenarios or are they pretty much the same thing? Most people eventually conclude that all of them, regardless of the employee's intentions, involve stealing $10 worth of corporate resources. The bottom line is that corporate equipment and services should be used only for company business. Whether it involves making personal phone calls, completing expense reports, appropriating office supplies, sending personal mail through the company mail room, or using copy equipment to print a flyer for your scout troop, personal or inappropriate use of corporate resources is unethical and violates most corporate policy.

- **Providing honest information**—Another key issue concerns truth. Although everyone will agree that telling the truth is important, someday you may have a manager who says something like, "These numbers look too negative—let's readjust them so it looks better to senior management." Many managers feel it necessary to put a positive spin on financials before submitting them up through the ranks. As a result, some companies have suffered serious financial penalties because their numbers have been positively spun on so many succeeding levels, they bear no resemblance to reality by the time they reach the top. "Fudging" numbers can have serious consequences since senior management may make crucial decisions based on flawed data. (Corporations are fined by regulators if inaccurate financial information is submitted to regulators or incorporated into formal financial statements.) If you're asked to skew any kind of corporate information, you may want to consult with someone outside of your chain of command such as the legal, human resources, or audit department.

Why Is It an Ethical Problem?

Your use of corporate resources is an ethical issue because it represents fulfilling your end of the employer–employee contract—and its roots are in fairness and honesty.

Costs

Obviously, if you've stolen corporate assets or filed an inflated expense report, you'll almost certainly be fired, and you may be arrested. If you have divulged confidential information to another corporation (as in supplying a recommendation for a former employee), your company may be placed at risk for a lawsuit.

If you fail to uphold your end of the employer–employee loyalty contract, your career at your company can be short circuited. Most corporate cultures place tremendous importance on honesty, loyalty, and teamwork. Generally, successful corporations are communities, where a sense of family has been encouraged. Just as family members try to protect one another and keep family information private, the company community tries to encourage the same behavior. Individuals who violate the "family" trust by squandering resources, being dishonest, or misusing the "family" reputation, are frequently isolated or even banished.

CONCLUSION

This chapter has highlighted some of the most common ethical dilemmas you might encounter during your career. Although ethical dilemmas can be very difficult to evaluate, it can be easier to decide what to do when you've spent some time thinking about them ahead of time—*before* they happen. In the next two chapters, we'll examine tools you can use to help you evaluate dilemmas, and decide what to do.

DISCUSSION CASES

Human Resources Issue   Your division has formed a committee of employees to examine suggestions and create a strategy for how to reward good employee ideas. You are the only minority member of the committee, which has five other members. You're pleased to be part of this effort since appointments to committees such as this one are viewed generally as a positive reflection on job performance. At the first meeting, tasks are assigned and all the other committee members think you should survey minority members for their input. During the weeks that follow, you discover that several committee meetings have been held without your knowledge. When you ask why you weren't notified, two committee members tell you that survey information wasn't needed at the meetings and you'd be notified when a general meeting was scheduled. When you visit one committee member in his office, you spot a report on the suggestion program that you've never seen before. When you ask about it, he says it's just a draft he and two others have produced. How would you handle this?

Conflicts of Interest Issue   You've just cemented a deal between a $100 million pension fund and Green Company, a large regional money manager. You and your staff put in long hours and a lot of effort to close the deal and are feeling very good about it. You and three of your direct reports are having lunch in a fancy restaurant to celebrate a promotion, when the waiter brings you a phone. A senior account executive from Green is on the phone and wants to buy you lunch in gratitude for all your efforts. "I'll leave my credit card number with the restaurant owner, he says. "You and your team have a great time on me." Describe three courses of action you might take and the pros and cons of each.

Customer Confidence Issue   You're the vice president of finance for a small computer company, which has shown a small profit during the last three years. Your company is planning a stock offering, and positive earnings forecasts are essential to its success. While you're preparing the forecasts, a friend tells you in confidence that his company—the major chip supplier to your company—is experiencing serious manufacturing difficulties. He says that, although it won't be announced for several weeks, chips will be in short supply for at least a year. He estimates that your company's supplies may be cut by as much as 25%. Your earnings forecast is scheduled to be issued two weeks before the announcement from the chip supplier. Should you consider this information in preparing for the stock offering?

Use of Corporate Resources Issue   You work for Red Co. You and a colleague, Pat Brown, are asked by your manager to attend a week-long conference in Los Angeles. At least 25 other employees from Red Co. are attending, as well as many customers and competitors from other institutions. At the conference, you attend every session and see many of the Red Co. people, but you never run into Pat. Although you've left several phone messages for her, her schedule doesn't appear to allow room for a meeting. However, when you get back to the office, the department secretary, who's coordinating expense reports, mentions to you that your dinner in L.A. must have been quite the affair. When you ask, "What dinner?", she describes a dinner with 20 customers and Red Co. employees that Pat paid for at a posh L.A. restaurant. When you explain that you didn't attend, she shows you the expense report with your name prominently listed as one of the attendees. Describe at least two ways in which you could handle this situation.

DISCUSSION QUESTIONS

1. Have antidiscrimination laws helped or hurt the fair treatment of workers?

2. Is diversity management an ethical issue?

3. Is sexual harassment as important an issue for men as it is for women?

4. What conditions would make accepting a gift from a vendor or a client acceptable? Would the conditions change outside the United States?

5. Describe the conditions under which you could hire a college friend.

6. Why do certain professions—bankers, accountants, lawyers, physicians, clergymen and women—have fiduciary responsibilities?

7. Do employers have a responsibility to alert other employers to an employee's wrong-doing by supplying an unfavorable reference? Discuss the nature of community responsibility and self-protection.

NOTES

[1]Toffler, B. 1986. *Tough choices: Managers talk ethics.* New York: John Wiley & Sons, 12.

[2]Wilson, J. Q. 1993. *The moral sense.* New York: The Free Press, 55–78.

[3]Rice, F. 1994. How to make diversity pay. *Fortune*, August 8: 79.

[4]Sheppard, B., Lewicki, R., and Minton, J. W. 1992. *Organizational justice: The search for fairness in the workplace.* New York: Lexington Books.

[5]Alexander, S. and Ruderman, M. 1987. The role of procedural and distributive justice in organizational behavior. *Social Justice Research*, 177–198.

CHAPTER FOUR

Deciding What's Right:
A Prescriptive Approach

INTRODUCTION

THERE ARE TWO ways to think about individual ethical decision making—a prescriptive approach and a descriptive approach. The *prescriptive* approach, derived from philosophy, offers decision-making tools (ways of thinking about ethical choices) that prescribe what decision you *should* make as a "conscientious moral agent"[1] who thinks carefully about moral choices. They're designed to help you make the best possible ethical decision. In this chapter we'll introduce some of these and explain how you can integrate them and use them in a practical way.

However, we know that people don't always make the best decision. Prescriptions aren't always followed. So, it's helpful to understand how people's minds really work—how people really make decisions. The *psychological* approach, discussed in the next chapter, relies on psychological research and describes how people actually make ethical decisions. It focuses in particular on the cognitive biases and limitations that often keep us from making the best possible decisions. Hopefully, if we understand both approaches, we can improve our ethical decision making.

Many ethical choices are clear-cut enough for us to be able to decide what to do rather quickly because they pit "right" against "wrong." Is deciding whether to embezzle corporate funds a tough ethical dilemma? Not really, because embezzling is stealing and it's wrong, period. There's not much of a dilemma there. But things can get pretty murky in situations where two or more important values, rights, or obligations conflict and we have to choose between equally unpleasant alternatives. Consider the following dilemma.

The Layoff

You're the plant manager in one of ABC Company's five plants. You've worked for the company for 15 years, working your way up from the factory floor after the company sent you to college. Your boss just told you in complete confidence that the company will have to lay off 200 workers. Luckily, your job won't be affected. But, a rumor is now circulating in the plant and one of your workers (an old friend who now works for you) asks the question, "Well, Pat, what's the word? Is the plant closing? Am I going to lose my job? I've got a kid in college. I need to know!" What will you say?

This is a true ethical dilemma because two values are in conflict. Two "right" values that can create significant conflict are truth and loyalty. As illustrated in the case, telling the truth to your friend means that you may have to break your promise to be loyal to the company that has treated you so well. In this chapter, we'll introduce conceptual tools that are designed to help you think through ethical dilemmas from multiple perspectives. None of the approaches is perfect. In fact, they may lead to different conclusions. The point of using them is to get you to think carefully and avoid falling into a solution by accident.

PRESCRIPTIVE APPROACHES TO ETHICAL DECISION MAKING APPLIED TO BUSINESS ETHICS

Philosophers have been wrestling with ethical decision making for centuries. We certainly don't intend to provide a philosophy course here, but we can distill some important principles that can guide you in your ethical decision making. In this section, we'll outline some of the major contemporary approaches that we think can provide you with the most practical assistance.[2] We'll then incorporate them into a series of steps that you can use to evaluate ethical dilemmas, and we'll apply these steps to the short layoff case.

Focus on Consequences (Consequentialist Theories)

One set of philosophical theories is categorized as *consequentialist* (sometimes referred to as teleological, from the Greek telos or goal). When you're attempting to decide what's right or wrong, consequentialist theories focus attention on the results or *consequences* of the decision or action.

Utilitarianism is probably the best known consequentialist theory. According to the principle of utility, an ethical decision should maximize benefits to society and minimize harms. What matters is the net balance of good consequences over bad.

A utilitarian would approach an ethical dilemma by identifying the alternative actions and their consequences. For example, what would be the consequences (societal harms and benefits) of my telling my friend what I know about the layoff? What would be the consequences (societal harms and benefits) of not sharing what I know? This would be followed by a kind of mental calculation of all the costs and benefits of these consequences. For example, one cost of telling my friend would be that s/he might tell others and send the plant into chaos. A potential benefit might be that I would retain the trust of a valued friend. The "best" decision would be the one that yielded the greatest net benefits and the "worst" decision would be the one that yielded the greatest net harms. So, if more people would be ultimately hurt than helped if Pat informs her friend of the impending layoff, a utilitarian would conclude that Pat shouldn't tell.

The utilitarian approach can be extremely helpful in thinking through an ethical dilemma. Don't we generally look at the consequences of our own and others' actions in trying to decide what's right? And, don't we consider who will benefit and who will be harmed? When the state decides to build a new highway through your property, aren't they using a utilitarian rationale when they argue that the benefits to the community (increased development, reduced traffic, fewer accidents, etc.) outweigh the harms to the few property holders who will be inconvenienced by an eyesore in their back yard?

But, a challenge of using a strictly consequentialist approach is that it is often difficult to obtain the information required to evaluate all of the consequences for all individuals who may be directly or indirectly affected by an action or decision. When, in business, do we have ALL of the facts? And even if you have all of the information, it can be extremely cumbersome to have to calculate all of the harms and benefits every time you encounter a new ethical dilemma. Try it. Can you list all of the potential harms and benefits for all of those who may be directly or indirectly involved in the layoff situation described above?

Another difficulty with this type of approach is that the rights of a minority group can easily be sacrificed for the benefit of the majority. For example, slave holders in the old South argued that the greatest good would be served by maintaining the system of slavery.

Nevertheless, the utilitarian approach remains particularly important to ethical decision making in business for a variety of reasons. First, utilitarian thinking—through its descendant, utility theory—underlies much of the business and economics literature. Second, on the face of it, most of us would admit that considering the consequences of one's decisions or actions is extremely important to good ethical decision making. In fact, studies of ethical decision making in business have found that business managers generally rely upon a utilitarian approach.[3] So, the remaining question is whether other kinds of considerations are also important.

Focus on Duties, Obligations, and Principles (Deontological Theories)

The word "deontological" comes from the Greek *deon* or duty. Rather than focusing on consequences, deontological approaches would ask, "what is Pat's duty now that she knows about the layoff?" Deontologists base their decisions about what's right on broad, abstract universal principles such as honesty, promise keeping, fairness, rights (to safety, privacy, etc.), justice, and respect for persons and property. According to some deontological approaches, some moral principles are binding, regardless of the consequences. Therefore, some actions would be considered wrong even if the consequences of the actions were good. In other words, a deontologist focuses on doing what is "right" (based on moral principles such as honesty) whereas a utilitarian focuses on doing what will maximize societal welfare. An auditor taking a deontological approach would insist on telling the truth about a company's financial difficulties even if doing so might cause more harm than good and risk putting the company out of business, while a utilitarian auditor would weigh the societal harms and benefits before deciding what to do.

Some deontological theories focus on rights rather than duties or principles. The concept of rights goes back to classical Greek notions of "natural rights" that emerge from "natural law." Rights can be thought of as "negative rights" such as the limits on government interference with citizens' right to privacy or the pursuit of happiness. Or, rights can be thought of in more positive terms, such as the individual's rights to health and safety. The rights of one party are generally related to the duties of another. So, if we agreed that workers have the right to a safe working environment, businesses would have the duty to protect that right.

So, how does a deontologist determine what rule, principle, or right to follow? Some rely on western biblical tradition or moral intuition for guidance. For example, the Golden Rule, familiar to many of us, provides an important deontological guide: "Do unto others as you would have them do unto you." In our layoff situation, the Golden Rule would suggest that Pat should tell her friend what she knows because she would want her friend to do the same for her if the situation were reversed.

The German philosopher, Emmanuel Kant, provides a particular mode of deontological thinking about ethical choices through his "categorical imperative": "Act as if the maxim of thy action were to become by thy will a universal law of nature." This mode of thinking asks whether the rationale for your action is suitable to become a universal law or principle for everyone to follow. For example, if you break a promise, the categorical imperative asks, "is promise breaking a principle everyone should follow?" No, if everyone did this, promises would become meaningless. In fact, they would cease to exist.

A practical deontological question to ask yourself might be, "what kind of world would this be if everyone behaved this way or made this kind of decision in this type of situation?" What kind of world would this be if everyone broke promises at will?

In a further application of the categorical imperative, think about the following example. A number of physicians are recruited to participate in a large scale multicenter study to investigate the survival rates of breast cancer victims who are being treated with a new drug. Strict rules are developed regarding inclusion of patients into the study. Only those who have had surgery within the last three months can be included. Dr. Smith has a patient who hears about the study and wants very much to participate. Because Dr. Smith thinks that the drug could really help this patient, he agrees to include her even though her surgery took place six months ago. He changes the dates on her charts to conform with the study requirements and reasons that this one little change shouldn't affect the study results.

According to the categorical imperative, we must ask whether the rationale for Dr. Smith's action (helping his patient by breaking the study rules) is suitable to become a principle for all to follow. The answer is no. What if a number of other doctors did the same thing as Dr. Smith? What if those involved in medical research followed their own preferences or motives rather than the rules guiding the study? Society would be unable to rely on the results of medical research. What kind of a world would it be if researchers were routinely dishonest? One where we simply couldn't rely on the integrity of scientific research and most of us would deem that kind of world unacceptable.

A major challenge of deontological approaches is deciding which duty, obligation, right, or principle takes precedence because, as we said earlier, ethical dilemmas often pit these against each other. What does the deontologist do if one binding moral rule clashes with another? Can it be determined which is the more important right or principle? Because the U.S. Constitution is based on a rights approach, many U.S. public policy debates revolve around questions such as these. For example, the abortion debate rests on the question of whether the rights of the mother or the fetus should take precedence.

Another difficulty of deontological approaches involves the difficulty of arguing for a rule or principle that, if followed in a particular situation, will have devastating consequences. That's where consequentialist and deontological approaches conflict. For example, what if Pat determines that telling her friend what she knows (in accordance with the principles of honesty and respect for her friend as a person) could have devastating consequences for the company as a whole? In response to this concern, some philosophers argue that deontological principles (i.e., truth telling, promise keeping) don't have to be regarded as absolute. For example, one could violate a rule or principle for a good reason (according to Kant, a reason that you would be willing to accept for anyone in the same position).[4]

Focus on Integrity (Virtue Ethics)

The virtue ethics approach focuses more on the integrity of the moral actor than it does on the moral act itself. Although virtue ethics as a philosophical tradition began with Aristotle, a number of contemporary ethicists (including business ethicists) have brought it back to the forefront of ethical thinking.[5]

A virtue ethics perspective considers primarily the actor's character, motivations, and intentions. This doesn't mean that principles, rules, or consequences aren't considered at all, but they're considered in the context of assessing the actor's character and integrity. For example, one's character may be assessed in terms of principles such as honesty, in terms of rule following (did this actor follow his profession's ethics code?) or in terms of consequences (as in the physician's agreement to, above all, do no harm).

In virtue ethics, character is very much defined by one's community. Therefore, it's important to think about the community or communities within which business people operate. Think about yourself. What community or communities would you look to for help in deciding whether you were a business person of integrity? Your professional association? Your church? Your family? Your peers within your company? Would the communities you identify be different if you were evaluating your nonwork self?

Virtue ethics may be particularly useful in determining the ethics of an individual who works within a professional community that has well-developed norms and standards of conduct. For example, the accounting profession has developed a code of conduct for professional accountants. Being a virtuous accountant would mean abiding by that code of professional responsibility. The same goes for financial consultants who are certified and who agree to abide by specific professional rules and standards.

The advantage of a virtue ethics approach is it allows the decision maker to rely on relevant community standards without going through the complex process of trying to decide what's right in every situation using deontological or consequentialist approaches. The assumption is that the community has already done this type of thinking. However, what if the community hasn't done this type of thinking? Or, what if the community is just wrong? Furthermore, the usefulness of virtue ethics in business may be limited because in many areas of business there is limited agreement about what the standards are. There is no universal code of conduct for all business managers to follow.

These are just a few of the philosophical approaches that may be applied in ethical dilemma situations. We've introduced the ones we feel have the most practical benefit to business managers and, admittedly, we've introduced them in a rather general way, without many of the nuances developed by philosophers over the years. We've suggested that all of the approaches have limitations. No one of them, by itself, provides perfect guidance in every situation. Obviously, if all of the approaches lead to the same solution, the decision is a relatively easy one. The tough ones are when the approaches conflict.

We don't have a perfect solution. We certainly won't resolve the academic controversies over the "best" philosophical approach here. But we believe that all of the approaches we've presented suggest important factors to keep in mind in making business ethics decisions. Therefore, we offer the following eight steps that rely on all of the types of analysis just discussed.[6] Before presenting them, we'd like to offer a caveat. The eight steps suggest a linear decision-making process that is necessarily inaccurate. Ethical decision making is often not linear. But it will be helpful to cover all of these points, even if not in this particular sequence.

EIGHT STEPS TO SOUND ETHICAL DECISION MAKING IN BUSINESS

1. Gather the Facts

The philosophical approaches don't tell us to gather the facts. But they seem to assume that we'll complete this important step. You might be surprised at how many people jump to solutions without having the facts. Ask yourself, "How did the situation occur? Are there historical facts that I should know? Are there facts concerning the current situation that I should know?"[7]

Fact gathering is often easier said than done. Many ethical choices are particularly difficult because of the uncertainty involved in them. Facts may simply be unavailable. For example, in our layoff case, Pat may not have good information about the legal requirements on informing workers about layoffs. Also, she may not have enough information to determine how long it would take these 200 workers to find new jobs. But, recognizing these limitations, you should attempt to assemble the facts that are available to you before proceeding.

2. Define the Ethical Issues

Many of us have knee-jerk responses to ethical dilemmas. We jump to a solution without really thinking through the issues and the reasons for our response (we'll talk more about why in Chapter 5). For example, in the layoff case, one person might say, "Oh, that's easy. Pat has to keep her promise to her boss and protect her job." Another person might say, "Pat just has to tell the truth to her friend."

So, our second recommendation is, don't jump to solutions without first identifying the issues or points of conflict in the dilemma. The issues often go back to the deontological, or principle-based, theories we just discussed. In the case above, one issue has to do with the workers' right to know about the plant closing in advance. How much advance notice is appropriate? What does the law say? Another issue has to do with the company's right to keep the information private. What is the company's obligation to its workers in this regard? At a more personal level, there are the issues related to honesty, loyalty, and promise keeping. Is it more important to be honest with a friend or to keep a promise to one's boss? Does one owe more loyalty to a friend or to one's boss? Points of conflict may go back to the conflict between consequentialist and deontological approaches. For example, if I tell the truth (consistent with the principle of promise keeping) bad things will happen (negative consequences).

Also, our inclination is to stop with the first ethical issue that comes to mind. For example, in our layoff case, we might be inclined to stop with the issue of loyalty to a friend. Challenge yourself to think of as many issues as you possibly can. Here's where talking about the problem with others can help. Present the dilemma to co-workers, to your spouse or to friends you respect. Ask them whether they see other issues that you may have missed.

3. Identify the Affected Parties

Consequentialist and deontological thinking both involve the ability to identify the parties affected by the decision. The consequentialist will want to identify all those who are going to experience harms and benefits. The deontologist might want to know whose rights are involved and who has a duty to act in the situation.

Being able to see the situation through others' eyes is a key moral reasoning skill. Lawrence Kohlberg called this skill *role taking*. Frequently, you have to think beyond the facts provided in a case in order to identify all affected parties. It often helps to begin with the individuals in the case who are immediately affected (e.g., Pat, the worker, Pat's boss) and then to progressively broaden your thinking to incorporate larger groups. For example, in this case, you might include the other workers, the local community, the rest of the company, and society in general. As you think of more and more affected parties, additional issues will probably come to mind. For example, think about the local community. If this is a small town with few other employers, fairness to the entire community becomes an issue. Shouldn't they have as much time as possible to plan for the impact of this plant closing? Try to put yourself in their shoes. How would they argue their case? How would they feel?

In Chapter 1, we introduced the concept of *stakeholders*, all of those who have a *stake* in what the organization does and how it performs. Stakeholders can include owners, managers, customers, employees, suppliers, the community, the government, the natural environment and, of course, stockholders. In the context of ethical decision making in business, we should identify the stakeholders affected by the decision and ask how they are affected. Try to make your thinking as broad as possible here. Some of the stakeholders affected by the decision may not even be born yet. The best concrete example of unborn stakeholders might be "DES daughters." In the 1940s, DES, a synthetic estrogen, was prescribed for pregnant women who seemed to be in danger of miscarrying. By 1971, it became clear that DES produced a birth defect in the daughters of these women. Because of the birth defect, DES daughters were more likely to develop vaginal cancer, especially between the ages of 15 and 22. They also had a higher than normal rate of cervical cancer.[8]

Once stakeholders are identified, role-playing can help you to see the issue from different stakeholder perspectives. In your classroom or your department, get individuals to seriously play the relevant roles. You may be surprised at how perspectives change based upon this simple exercise. What decision would you reach if you were someone else in the situation? This step incorporates the Golden Rule: Treat others as you would like others to treat you. Imagine yourself as each of the players in a decision situation. What decision would they reach and why?

Another consideration may be to ask whether you can "test" a potential decision with affected parties before your prospective course of action is made final. The objective is to gauge how various audiences will react, and to be able to adjust or fine-tune a decision along the way.[9] One question you could ask yourself is, how would this or that stakeholder react if this decision were made public? For example, imagine that ABC Co. (in our layoff case) had another thriving plant in another location. However, in the decision-making process, it was assumed that employees wouldn't want to relocate because of their ties to the local community. Wouldn't it be best to ask them their preferences than to assume what they would want to do?

4. Identify the Consequences

After identifying the affected parties, think about the potential consequences for each of these parties. This step is obviously derived from the consequentialist approaches. It isn't necessary to identify every possible consequence. But, you should try to identify consequences that have a relatively high probability of occurring and those that would have particularly negative consequences if they did occur (even if the probability of occurrence is low). Who would be harmed by a particular decision or action? For example, in our case, telling the truth to the worker might cause Pat to lose her job, which would have negative consequences for her entire family (especially if she's a single mother). However, it would give her worker (and presumably others who would be told) the benefit of more time to look for a new job, perhaps saving many families from negative financial consequences. Can you determine which solution would accomplish the most net good? A popular version of utilitarianism asks the question, "which decision or action will produce the greatest good for the greatest number of people?" Would telling a lie to your friend benefit the most people? Or would it be better for all affected parties if you tell the truth?

Long-term versus short-term consequences. In business decisions, it's particularly important to think in terms of short-term AND long-term consequences. Are you confident that your position will be as valid over a long period of time, even if circumstances or people change? In this case, is the long-term health of the company and the people who will remain employed more important than the short-term consequences to the 200 workers who will be laid off?

Symbolic consequences. In business, it's also extremely important to think about the potential *symbolic* consequences of an action. Every decision and action sends a message; it stands for something. What message will be sent by a particular decision or action? What will it mean if it is misunderstood? For example, if Pat doesn't tell her worker the truth, and he finds out later that she knew, what will the symbolic message be to this worker and the others who work for Pat—that she's more interested in saving her own hide than in taking care of them?

Consequences of secrecy. If a decision is made in private in order to avoid some negative reaction, think about the potential consequences if the decision were to become public. For example, the public has been outraged by the fact that tobacco companies may have hidden their knowledge of the negative health effects of cigarette smoking.[10]

5. Identify the Obligations

Identify the obligations involved and the reasons for each. For example, consider Pat's obligation toward the affected parties. When identifying Pat's various obligations, be sure to state the reasons *why* she has this duty or obligation. Think in terms of values, principles, character, or outcomes. For example, if you're considering Pat's obligation to keep her promise to her boss, your reasoning might go like this: "Pat shouldn't break her promise to her boss. If she does, the trust between them will be broken. Promise-keeping and trust are important values in superior/subordinate relationships."

This step, and the obligations you identify, may vary depending on the people involved and the roles they play. For example, our faith in our financial system depends in part upon auditors' obligation to tell the truth about a company's financial difficulties. Similarly, our faith in science as an institution depends on the integrity of the scientific data and how scientists report it. So, the auditor and the scientist have a particularly strong obligation to tell the truth.

6. Consider Your Character and Integrity

In thinking about what you should do in an ethical dilemma, it may also be useful to consider what your relevant community would consider to be the kind of decision that an individual of integrity would make in the situation. You have to begin by identifying the relevant community. Then, you have to determine how community members would evaluate the decision or action you're considering.

A method that can help you with this process is known as *the disclosure rule*. It asks whether you would feel comfortable if your activities were disclosed in the light of day in a public forum like *The New York Times* or some other medium. Obviously, *The New York Times* assumes a general community standard. It's important for you to determine which medium is the appropriate one in your situation. But, in general, if you don't want to read about it in *The New York Times*, you probably shouldn't be doing it. If you would be embarrassed to have someone read about your activities in the newspaper—or if you'd be uncomfortable telling your parents, children, spouse, or clergy about your decision—you probably should rethink it.

Boris Yavitz, the former dean of Columbia University's Graduate School of Business, offered another version of the test for New Yorkers: "Unless you would do it in Macy's department store window at high noon, don't do it." And Thomas Jefferson expressed it like this: "Never suffer a thought to be harbored in your mind which you would not avow openly. When tempted to do anything in secret, ask yourself if you would do it in public. If you would not, be sure it is wrong."

This kind of approach can be especially valuable when a decision needs to be made quickly. Suppose someone in your organization asks you to misrepresent the effectiveness of one of your company's products to a customer. You can immediately imagine how a story reporting the details of your conversation with the customer would appear in tomorrow's paper. Would you be comfortable having others read the details of that conversation? The ideal is to conduct business in such a way that your activities and conversations could be disclosed without your feeling embarrassed.

Another method might be to ask a question asked by the Seneca people (one of the original five nations of the great Iroquois Confederacy located in the northeastern United States and Southeastern Canada) in their guidelines for self-discipline: "how will I be remembered when I'm gone?"[11] Americans don't often think about this question, but it's a good one. Will you be remembered as an individual of integrity or not?

7. *Think Creatively about Potential Actions*

Before making a final decision, be sure that you haven't unnecessarily forced yourself into a corner. Are you assuming that you have only two choices, *either* "a" or "b"? According to Jack Edwards, Vice President of Cummins Engine Company, who spoke at the 1994 Conference Board meeting on ethics, it's important to look for creative alternatives. Perhaps if you've been focusing on "a" *or* "b", there's another answer "c." For example, he told the story of an American business person who received an extravagant gift from a foreign supplier. This situation could easily be conceptualized as an "a" or "b" situation. Should I accept the gift (which is against company policy) or should I refuse it (which will likely be interpreted as a slap in the face by this important supplier). The "c" solution was to accept the gift as a gift to the company that would be displayed in the headquarters entrance.

In another overseas location, the company was having difficulty with local children cutting through a wire fence and stealing valuable electronic components. The "a" or "b" solution was to arrest or not arrest these young children when they were caught. After involving the community, the managers involved were able to arrive at a "c" solution. They discovered that the children were stealing because there weren't enough classrooms at the local school, leaving the children with little to do but get into trouble. Cummins made classrooms available on their site. The mayor provided accreditation, books, and teachers. This "c" solution cost the company very little and accomplished a great deal. Three hundred and fifty students were accommodated, the stealing problem disappeared, and Cummins became a valued corporate citizen.

8. *Check Your Gut*

The emphasis in these steps has been on a highly rational fact gathering and evaluation process once you know that you're faced with an ethical dilemma. But, don't forget your gut. Intuition is gaining credibility as a source for good business decision making. In ethical choices, if your gut is bothering you, it probably means that something isn't right. In fact, it may be your only clue that you're facing an ethical dilemma to begin with and it can be a source of empathy for those affected by a decision or action. So, pay attention to your gut. But, don't let your gut make your decision for you. Once you know you're facing an ethical dilemma, use the rational decision-making tools developed here to guide your decision making.

PRACTICAL PREVENTIVE MEDICINE

Doing Your Homework

There's no doubt that you'll encounter ethical dilemmas—every employee probably encounters hundreds of them during a career—the only thing in doubt is when. Your mission is to be as prepared as possible before you run into a problem. The more informed you are, the more effective you'll be in protecting yourself and your employer. The best way to do that is to learn the rules of your organization and your profession, and to develop relationships that can help you if and when the need arises.

You can learn the rules in various ways. First, read your company's code of ethics (if it has one) and policy manual. Since most policy manuals are huge, you obviously can't memorize one. But if you skim the contents, some of the rules will sink in—you may not remember the exact policy, but you'll probably remember at least that one exists and where to find it.

Second, ask questions. Managers, executives, and peers will admire your initiative when you ask what they think is "important around here." Since many organizational standards are unwritten and they differ from company to company, the only way you'll find out about them is by asking. While you're asking questions, query your co-workers (including management) about what kinds of ethical situations are most common in your organization and how your organization generally handles those issues. Ask your manager how to raise ethical issues within your organization. Since he or she will certainly tell you to raise an issue with him or her first, be sure to find out how you raise an issue in his or her absence. This not only gives you a road map for raising issues, it also sends a signal to your manager that ethics are important to you.

Finally, develop relationships with people who are outside of your chain of command. Get to know people in human resources or personnel, legal, audit, and in other departments who might be able to provide information, help you raise an issue or determine if something even is an issue, or vouch for your credibility in a crisis. You might also want to join a professional group or association. Many professions have developed ethical standards—apart from those that may exist in your company—and it can be very helpful to know other people in your profession to confidentially consult with if a crisis arises in your company. Some may say that this is being political, but we think it's just plain smart to network with people outside of your immediate job and company. It's the difference between being a victim of circumstance and having the power, the knowledge, and the network to help manage circumstances.

Frankly, after you've done your homework and learned about your company's standards and values, you may find that your values and your employer's values are in conflict. If the conflict is substantial, you may have no choice but to look for work in another organization.

When You're Asked to Make a Snap Decision

Many business people place value on the ability to make decisions quickly, and as a result many of us can feel pressure to make up our minds in a hurry. This can be a particular issue when people are inexperienced for whatever reason—this may be their first job or a new one, or they may have changed companies or industries— and they may feel a need to prove their competence by making decisions quickly. Obviously, that can be dangerous. The ethical decision-making tools described earlier in the chapter assume that you'll have some time to devote to the decision. Therefore, consider the following guidelines when a quick decision seems called for:

1. Don't underestimate the importance of a hunch to alert you that you're facing an ethical dilemma. As we said earlier, your gut is your internal warning system. As one senior executive at a multinational computer company said, "The gut never lies." When your gut tells you something's wrong, consider it a warning siren.

2. Ask for time to think it over. Most snap decisions don't have to be that way. Say something like, "Let me think about it and I'll get right back to you." Bargaining for time is a smart way to give yourself a break—then you can really think about the decision and consult with others. It's better to take the time to make a good decision than it is to make a bad decision quickly and have lots of time to regret it. Would you rather be known as cautious or reckless?

3. Find out quickly if your organization has a policy that applies to your decision.

4. Ask your manager or your peers for advice. You should consider your manager the first line of defense when you encounter an ethical dilemma. Regardless of your level within the organization, you should never hesitate to ask for another opinion. This is where the network comes in handy. If you have friends in human resources or the legal department, you can float the issue with them on a casual basis to see if there even is an issue.

5. Use *The New York Times* test. As we said earlier, this is a quick check kind of test. If you'd be embarrassed to have your decision disclosed in the media or to your family, don't do it.

You're upgrading your department's data processing capabilities and have just placed an order for four personal computers and two laser printers with a computer company representative. When you mention that you wish you had a printer at home like the ones you just ordered, the representative tells you that because of your large order, she can give you a 50% discount on a printer for your home. However, all items must be ordered now. You feel that this is not quite right, but you're not sure why.

In this case, the employee could have real doubt about whether or not to accept a 50% discount on a printer for his home. Even though he feels funny about the offer, he might be thinking that he does a lot of work at home, so accepting a discount on a personal printer could be justified. And, since the computer representative made the offer after the order was placed, there's no conflict of interest—his decision to purchase obviously wasn't influenced by the offer of a discount.

But he should listen to his gut, which is feeling that this isn't quite right. He can first stall the computer representative by telling her he'll get back to her later in the day or tomorrow. He can find out what his company policy says about making purchases. (Many companies would equate the discount with a gift and forbid accepting it unless it's available to all employees.)

Suppose he finds nothing in the policy manual to prohibit the discount, and other workers have said "go for it." Then he can use *The New York Times* test. How would the public react to his decision? Some people would probably think that his order was influenced by the offer of a discount. He knows that's not true, but it might be difficult to convince other people of that. This is called an appearance of a conflict of interest, and as discussed in Chapter 3, an appearance can be as damaging as an actual conflict. If someone could think your judgment has been affected by a relationship or, in this case a discount, it could be viewed as the appearance of a conflict, and should be avoided. Appearances are extremely important in business, and may not be accounted for by the philosophical tools provided earlier in the chapter. Whether you *appear* to be fair may be as important as whether you're really fair.

The bottom line is: If you think that your decision could be misinterpreted or if someone could think the objectivity of your decision has been compromised, re-think the decision. The representative's offer can be refused politely by saying something like, "My company doesn't allow personal discounts," or "I just don't feel right about it."

If you ever feel that accepting a favor from a vendor will place you under an obligation to the vendor, be very careful. For example, a public relations manager, Mary, described an incident with a printing company (we'll call it Type Co.) sales representative who was trying to get her business. Type Co. already did business with a number of departments within her company, but Mary was satisfied with her current printer and saw no reason to switch. Just before the holidays, Type Co. sent a miniature television to Mary and to all of Type Co.'s other clients in her company. She immediately felt that the gift was inappropriate, but to check out her judgment, she called one of Type Co.'s other clients in her company. Mary's colleague assured her that there was nothing wrong with accepting the gift and that it was simply a token of good will. (If Mary had been friendly with one of her company's lawyers or human resources managers, she would probably have received very different advice.) However, Mary was still uneasy and sent the television back.

When asked why she returned the gift, Mary said, "I felt like I was being bribed to do business with Type Co." Mary listened to her internal warning system, despite what her colleague said. A reader of *The New York Times* would probably agree that Mary was being bribed to do business with Type Co.

CONCLUSION

This chapter has presented a *prescriptive approach* to individual ethical decision making. When you're confronted with an ethical choice, you should find it helpful to inform your choice by considering the ideas and steps offered in this chapter. The end-of-chapter questions and case should give you some practice in applying these ideas and steps to real ethical dilemmas.

However, the prescriptive approach needs to be complemented by the *descriptive approach* offered in Chapter 5. In the next chapter, you'll learn about psychological research that can help us understand how people actually make ethical decisions—the individual characteristics and cognitive processes that impact the decisions people make.

DISCUSSION QUESTIONS

1. If you had to choose one of the philosophical approaches discussed in this chapter to guide your decision making, which would you choose? Why?

2. Think about an ethical dilemma situation that you've faced. Apply the eight steps recommended in this chapter. Does it change your thinking about the situation? Would it change your action?

3. Some corporations and other organizations have designed ethical decision-making tests that incorporate some of the principles and systems described in this chapter. For example, Carl Skooglund, Vice President and Ethics Director at Texas Instruments, outlines the Ethics Quick Test recommended for use by Texas Instrument employees:[12]

   a. Is the action legal?
   b. Does it comply with your best understanding of our values and principles?
   c. If you do it, will you feel bad?
   d. How will it look in the newspaper?
   e. If you know it's wrong, don't do it, period!
   f. If you're not sure, ask.
   g. Keep asking until you get an answer.

   Think about this list in terms of the decision-making guides discussed in the chapter. Which ones are being used here? Which are not? What recommendations, if any, would you make to alter this list? If you had to make up a list for your company, what would be on it? Why?

   Do the same with the Rotary International Four-Way Test:

   a. Is it the truth?
   b. Is it fair to all concerned?

    c. Will it build good will and better relationships?

    d. Will it be beneficial to all concerned?

       Think about the rest of the Seneca people's guidelines for self-discipline.[12] Could they serve as guides for ethical decision making in business? Why or why not?

    a. Am I happy in what I'm doing?

    b. Is what I'm doing adding to the confusion?

    c. What am I doing to bring about peace and contentment?

    d. How will I be remembered when I am gone?

4. What limitations, if any, can you think of to the prescriptions provided in this chapter? Can you think of reasons why they might not work?

CASE

Pinto Fires

by Dennis A. Gioia

On August 10, 1978, three teen-age girls died horribly in an automobile accident. Driving a 1973 Ford Pinto to their church volleyball practice in Goshen, Indiana, they were struck from behind by a Chevrolet van. The Pinto's fuel tank ruptured and the car exploded in flames. Two passengers, Lynn Marie Ulrich, 16, and her cousin, Donna Ulrich, 18, were trapped inside the inferno and burned to death. After three attempts Lynn Marie's sister, 18-year-old Judy Ann, was dragged out alive from the driver's seat, but died in agony hours later in the hospital.

    They were merely the latest in a long list of people to burn to death in accidents involving the Pinto, which Ford had begun selling in 1970. By the time of the accident, the car had been the subject of a great deal of public outcry and debate about its safety, especially its susceptibility to fire in low-speed rear-end collisions. This particular accident, however, resulted in more media attention than any other auto accident in U.S. history. Why? Because it led to an unprecedented court case in which the prosecution brought charges of reckless homicide against the Ford Motor Co.—the first time that a corporation had been charged with criminal conduct, and the charge was not negligence, but murder. At stake was much more than the maximum penalty of $30,000 in fines. Of immediate concern, a guilty verdict could have affected 40 pending civil cases nationwide and resulted in hundreds of millions of dollars in punitive damage awards. Of perhaps greater concern, however, were larger issues involving corporate social responsibility, ethical decision making by individuals within corporations, and ultimately, the proper conduct of business in the modern era.

    How did Ford get into this situation? The chronology begins in early 1968 when the decision was made to battle the foreign competition in the small car market, specifically the Germans, but also the growing threat from the Japanese. This decision came after a hard-fought, two-year internal struggle between then-president Semon "Bunky" Knudsen and Lee Iacocca, who had risen quickly within the company because of his success with the Mustang. Iacocca strongly supported fighting the competition at their own game, while Knudsen argued instead for letting them have the small car market so Ford could concentrate on the more profitable medium and large models. The final decision ultimately was in the hands of then-CEO Henry Ford II, who not only agreed with Iacocca, but promoted him to president after Knudsen's subsequent forced resignation.

Iacocca wanted the Pinto in the showrooms by the 1971 model introductions, which would require the shortest production planning period in automotive history to that time. The typical time span from conception to production of a new car was more than 3 1/2 years; Iacocca, however, wanted to launch the Pinto in just over 2 years. Under normal conditions, chassis design, styling, product planning, advance engineering, component testing, etc. all either were completed or nearly completed prior to tooling of the production factories. Yet, because tooling had a fixed time frame of about 18 months, some of these other processes were done more-or-less concurrently. As a consequence, when it was discovered through crash testing that the Pinto's fuel tank often ruptured during rear-end impact, it was too late (in other words, too costly) to do much about it in terms of redesign.

A closer look at the crash-test reports reveals that Ford was aware of faulty fuel tank design. Eleven Pintos were subjected to rear-end collisions with a barrier at average speeds of 31 miles per hour to determine if any fuel would be lost after impact. All eight of the Pintos equipped with the standard fuel tank failed. The three remaining cars, however, survived the test because special measures had been taken to prevent tank rupture or fuel leakage. These measures included a plastic baffle placed between the axle housing and the gas tank, a steel plate between the tank and the rear bumper, and a rubber lining for the gas tank.

It should be noted that these tests were done under guidelines established by Federal Motor Vehicle Safety Standard 301, which was proposed in 1968 by the National Highway Traffic Safety Administration (NHTSA), but not officially adopted until the 1977 model year. Therefore, at the time of the tests, the Pinto met the required standards. Standard 301 had been strenuously opposed by the auto industry, and specifically Ford Motor Co. In fact, the lobbying efforts were so strong that negotiations continued until 1976, despite studies showing that hundreds of thousands of cars burned every year, taking 3000 lives annually; the adoption of the standard was projected to reduce the death rate by 40%. Upon approval of Standard 301 in 1977 all Pintos were provided with a rupture-proof fuel tank design.

Despite the crash test results, Ford decided to go with its gas tank design. Because the typical Pinto buyer was assumed to be extremely price conscious, Iacocca set an important goal known as "the limits of 2000"—the Pinto could not cost more than $2000 and could not weigh more than 2,000 pounds. Thus, to be competitive with foreign manufacturers Ford felt it could not spend any money on improving the gas tank. Besides, during the late 1960s and early 1970s American consumers demonstrated little concern for safety, so it was not considered good business sense to promote it. Iacocca echoed these sentiments when he said time and time again "Safety doesn't sell," a lesson he had learned after a failed attempt to add costly safety features to 1950s Fords.

Ford had experimented with placing the gas tank in different locations, but all alternative locations reduced usable trunk space. A design similar to that of the Ford Capri was successful in many crash tests at speeds over 50 miles per hour, but Ford felt that lost trunk space would hurt sales too much. One Ford engineer, when asked about the dangerous gas tank said, "Safety isn't the issue, trunk space is. You have no idea how stiff the competition is over trunk space. Do you realize that if we put a Capri-type tank in the Pinto you could only get one set of golf clubs in the trunk?"

The last of Ford's reasons for not making adjustments to the fuel tank design, however, was unquestionably the most controversial. After strong lobbying efforts, Ford and the auto industry in general convinced NHTSA regulators that cost-benefit analysis would be an appropriate basis for determining the feasibility of safety design standards. Such an analysis, however, required the assignment of a value for a human life. A prior study had concluded that every time someone died in an auto accident there was an estimated "cost to society" of $200,725 (detailed in the exhibit entitled, "What's Your Life Worth?")[13]

Having this value in hand, Ford calculated the cost of adding an $11 gas tank improvement versus the benefits of the projected 180 lives that would be saved (via an internal memo entitled "Fatalities Associated with Crash-Induced Fuel Leakage and Fires"). This is presented in the exhibit labeled, "The Cost of Dying in a Pinto."[14] As is demonstrated, the costs outweigh the benefits by almost three times. Thus, the cost-benefit analysis indicated that no improvements to the gas tanks were warranted.

Having decided to go ahead with normal production plans, the Pinto's problems soon surfaced. By early 1973, Ford's recall coordinator received field reports suggesting that Pintos were susceptible to "exploding" in rear-end collisions at very low speeds (under 25 miles per hour). Reports continued to indicate a similar trend in subsequent years, but no recall was initiated despite the mounting evidence. At every internal review, those responsible decided not to recall the Pinto.

Prior to the Indiana accident, the most publicized case concerning the Pinto's gas tank was that of Richard Grimshaw. In 1972, Richard, then 13, was riding with a neighbor on a road near San Bernardino, California, when they were hit from the rear. The Pinto's gas tank ruptured, causing the car to burst into flames. The neighbor was burned to death in a crash that was survivable—if there had been no fire. Richard suffered third-degree burns over 90% of his body and subsequently underwent more than 60 operations, with only limited success. A civil suit was settled in February 1978, when a jury awarded a judgment of over $125 million against Ford, most of which consisted of punitive damages (later reduced to $6 million by a judge who nonetheless accused Ford of "callous indifference to human life"). This judgment was based on convincing evidence that Ford chose not to spend the $11 per car to correct the faults in the Pinto gas tanks that its own crash testing had revealed.

The Pinto sold well until the media called special attention to the Pinto fuel tank story. As a consequence, in June 1978, in the face of pressure from the media, the government, pending court cases, and the potential loss of future sales, Ford ordered a complete recall of all 1.5 million Pintos built between 1970 and 1976. During the 1980 Indiana trial that resulted from the fatal accident of 1978, differing views continued to be expressed about the Pinto fires case. Ford representatives argued that companies must make cost-benefit decisions all the time. They claimed that it is an essential part of business, and even though everyone knows that some people will die in auto accidents, buyers want costs held down; therefore, people implicitly accept risks when buying cars.

However, in a scathing article accusing Ford of criminally mismanaging the Pinto problem, investigative reporter Mark Dowie framed the case in a different and rather more sensational way, with this often-quoted speculation: "One wonders how long the Ford Motor Company would continue to market lethal cars were Henry Ford II and Lee Iacocca serving twenty-year terms in Leavenworth for consumer homicide."[15]

What's Your Life Worth?

The chart below, from a 1971 study by the National Highway Traffic Safety Administration, is a breakdown of the estimated cost to society every time someone is killed in a car accident. The Ford Motor Company used the $200,725 total figure in its own cost-benefit analysis.

Component	1971 Costs
Future productivity losses	
Direct	$132,000
Indirect	41,300
Medical costs	
Hospital	700
Other	425
Property damage	1,500
Insurance administration	4,700
Legal and court	3,000
Employer losses	1,000
Victim's pain and suffering	10,000
Funeral	900
Assets (lost consumption)	5,000
Miscellaneous accident cost	200
TOTAL PER FATALITY:	$200,725

The Cost of Dying in a Pinto

Printed below are figures from a Ford Motor Co. internal memorandum on the benefits and costs of an $11 safety improvement (applicable to all vehicles with similar gas tank designs) which would have made the Pinto less likely to burn.

Benefits

Savings: 180 burn deaths, 180 serious burn injuries, 2100 burned vehicles.

Unit Cost: $200,000 per death, $67,000 per injury, $700 per vehicle.

Total Benefit: $180 \times (\$200,000) + 180 \times (\$67,000) + 2,100 \times (\$700) = \$49.5$ million.

Costs

Sales: 11 million cars, 1.5 million light trucks.

Unit Cost: $11 per car, $11 per truck.

Total Cost: $11,000,000 \times (\$11) + 1,500,000 \times (\$11) = \$137$ million.

CASE-BASED QUESTIONS

Put yourself in the role of the recall coordinator for Ford Motor Co. It's 1973 and field reports have been coming in about rear-end collisions, fires, and fatalities. The decision you must make is whether to act to recall the automobile or not.

1. Identify the relevant facts.

2. Identify the pertinent ethical issues/points of ethical conflict.

3. Identify the relevant affected parties.

4. Identify the possible consequences of alternative courses of action.

5. Identify relevant obligations.

6. Identify your relevant community standards that should guide you as a person of integrity.

7. Check your gut.

8. What will you decide?

NOTES

[1]Rachels, J. 1983. *The elements of moral philosophy.* New York: McGraw-Hill.

[2]Peach, L. 1994. An introduction to ethical theory. In *Research Ethics: Cases and Materials*, R. L. Penslar, ed. Bloomington: Indiana University Press.

[3]Fritsche, D. J. & Becke, H. 1984. Linking management behavior to ethical philosophy—An empirical investigation. *Academy of Management Journal*, 27: 166–175.

[4]Rachels, J. 1983. *The elements of moral philosophy*. New York: McGraw-Hill.

[5]Solomon, R. C. 1988. *Ethics and excellence*. New York: Oxford University Press.

[6]Bebeau, M. 1994. Developing a well-reasoned moral response to a moral problem in scientific research ethics. Paper distributed at the Teaching Research Ethics conference, Poynter Research Center for the Study of Ethics and American Institutions, Bloomington: Indiana University, May, 1994.

[7]Nash, L. 1989. Ethics without the sermon. In *Ethics in Practice*, K. R. Andres, ed. Boston: Harvard Business School Press.

[8]Larson, D. E. 1990. *Mayo clinic family health book*. New York: William Morrow.

[9]Nash, L. 1989. Ethics without the sermon. In *Ethics in Practice*, K. R. Andres, ed. Boston: Harvard Business School Press.

[10]Messick, D. M. & Bazerman, B. 1994. Ethics for the 21st century: A decision making perspective. Unpublished manuscript.

[11]Steiger, B. 1984. *Indian medicine power*. Atglen, PA: Whitford Press, 92.

[12]Skooglund, C. 1992. Ethics in the face of competitive pressures. Business Ethics Resource, Fall: 4.

[13]Dowie, M. 1977. How Ford put two million fire traps on wheels. *Business and Society Review*, 23: 51–55.

[14]Ibid.

[15]Ibid.

CHAPTER FIVE

Deciding What's Right: A Psychological Approach

INTRODUCTION

CHAPTER 4 INTRODUCED several *prescriptive* ethical theories. These theories, developed by philosophers, have been designed to help individuals decide what they *should* do in response to ethical dilemmas. But, people don't always make the best decisions, and even when they identify the best decision, they may not have the will to follow through. Research points to some reasons why. This chapter focuses on the psychology of individual ethical decision making. As opposed to discussing what individuals *should* do, it introduces the psychological factors—the individual differences and cognitive processes that describe how people think and what they actually do in response to ethical dilemmas. It also discusses some of the barriers that can keep well-intentioned people from good ethical decision making and suggests some ways to overcome these barriers.

INDIVIDUAL DIFFERENCES AND ETHICAL JUDGMENT

Much of the rest of this book focuses on the situational pushes and pulls that influence ethical conduct. For example, people follow leaders or their peers. They tend to do what's rewarded. Yet, despite these powerful pushes and pulls, people do bring something of themselves to situations. Heroes emerge when you least expect it. People blow the whistle despite severe negative consequences. Others embezzle funds or lie to customers despite all of management's efforts to support good conduct. How can we explain these ethical and unethical behaviors? Very simply, ethical conduct is influenced by both situational pushes and pulls AND characteristics of the individual that we'll call individual differences.

When people are hired, they come with personalities—individual predispositions to think and behave in certain ways. Research has uncovered a number of individual traits that influence the way people think and behave in ethical dilemma situations. Moral psychology research provides insight into how people think when confronted with ethical dilemmas. In addition, personality characteristics such as locus of control may contribute to how people think and behave.

Cognitive Moral Development

The best explanation for ethical behavior based on individual characteristics comes from the moral reasoning research of Lawrence Kohlberg.[1] When people behave morally, they must, among other things, decide what course of action is morally right (as we just discussed in the preceding chapter), and they must choose the morally right path over others.[2] In other words, if they decide that blowing the whistle is the morally right path, they must have follow through and do it.

Kohlberg's moral reasoning theory is a cognitive developmental theory that focuses primarily on the first activity—how people actually decide what course of action is morally right. His research began by following 58 American boys ranging in age from 10 to 16 years old. He interviewed them every 3 years over a 12-year period, asking for their open-ended responses to hypothetical moral dilemmas. Their responses were systematically analyzed and resulted in new understanding of how moral reasoning gradually transforms from middle childhood to adulthood. The resulting theory proposes that moral reasoning develops sequentially through three broad levels, each composed of two stages. As individuals move forward through the sequence of stages, they can comprehend all reasoning at stages below their own, but cannot comprehend reasoning more than one stage above their own. Development through the stages results from the cognitive disequilibrium that occurs when an individual perceives a contradiction between his or her own reasoning level and the next higher one. This can occur through formal training, but generally occurs through interaction with peers and life situations that challenge the individual's current way of thinking. According to Kohlberg, the actual decision isn't as important as the reasoning process used to arrive at it. However, he argued that the higher the reasoning stage, the more ethical the decision because the higher stages are more consistent with normative ethical principles of justice and rights.

The theory has been successfully applied to studies of adults in business settings.[3] For example, Weber interviewed business managers about their responses to the following hypothetical dilemma:[4]

Evelyn worked for an automotive steel casting company. She was part of a small group asked to investigate the cause of an operating problem that had developed in the wheel castings of a new luxury automobile and to make recommendations for its improvement. The problem did not directly create an unsafe condition, but it did lead to irritating sounds. The Vice-President of Engineering told the group that he was certain that the problem was due to tensile stress in the castings. Evelyn and a lab technician conducted tests and found conclusive evidence that the problem was not tensile stress. As Evelyn began work on other possible explanations of the problem, she was told that the problem had been solved. A report prepared by Evelyn's boss strongly supported the tensile stress hypothesis. All of the data points from Evelyn's experiments have been changed to fit the curves, and some of the points which were far from where the theory would predict have been omitted. The report "proved" that tensile stress was responsible for the problem.

Among a number of questions presented to the interviewees, they were asked whether Evelyn should contradict her boss's report and why. We will use this hypothetical dilemma to understand the theory and how responses to the above question (along with others) help to identify an individual's placement in Kohlberg's moral reasoning stage framework. Table 1 outlines the levels and stages involved.

Level I. At level I (labeled the preconventional level and including stages 1 and 2), a person views rules as imposed and external to the self. The decision about what's right is explained in terms of rewards and punishments and the exchange of favors. Stage 1 individuals are guided by obedience for its own sake. Avoiding punishment is the key consideration. It's easy to image a small child thinking, I should share my toy with my brother because if I don't Mom will yell at me. A stage 1 response to the Evelyn situation might argue that it would be wrong to contradict her boss because she must obey her superiors and she would certainly be punished if she disobeyed.

At stage 2, concern for personal reward, satisfaction and a sense of duty to oneself are important. Additionally, a kind of market reciprocity is considered. What is right may be judged in terms of a "you scratch my back, I'll scratch yours" reciprocity. A stage 2 child might think that if I share my toy with my brother, he might share his with me later. A stage 2 response in the Evelyn situation might argue that Evelyn should support her boss because he is responsible for her performance appraisals, and if she lets this one go, he might overlook some of her problems from the past. Also, if her boss has been kind or helpful to her in the past, she may express some obligation to repay the favor.

Level II. At level II (labeled the conventional level and including stages 3 and 4) the individual has internalized the shared moral norms of society or some segment like a family or work group. What's morally right is explained in terms of living up to roles and the expectations of relevant others, fulfilling duties and obligations, and following rules and laws. Kohlberg's research placed most American adults at this level and Weber's research found that most managers' responses to the Evelyn dilemma were at level II, stages 3 and 4.

At stage 3, what's morally right is thought to be that which pleases or helps others or is approved by those close to you. Interpersonal trust and social approval

TABLE 1 Levels of Cognitive Moral Development According to Kohlberg

Stage	What is considered to be right
LEVEL I—PRECONVENTIONAL	
Stage 1—*Obedience and Punishment Orientation*	
Sticking to rules to avoid physical punishment. Obedience for its own sake.	
Stage 2—*Instrumental Purpose and Exchange*	
Following rules only when it is in one's immediate interest. Right is an equal exchange, a fair deal.	
LEVEL II—CONVENTIONAL	
Stage 3—*Interpersonal Accord, Conformity, Mutual Expectations*	
Stereotypical "good" behavior. Living up to what is expected by peers and people close to you.	
Stage 4—*Social Accord and System Maintenance*	
Fulfilling duties and obligations of the social system. Upholding laws except in extreme cases where they conflict with fixed social duties. Contributing to the society or group.	
LEVEL III—POSTCONVENTIONAL OR PRINCIPLED	
Stage 5—*Social Contract and Individual Rights*	
Being aware that people hold a variety of values; that rules are relative to the group. Upholding rules because they are the social contract. Upholding nonrelative values and rights regardless of the majority opinion.	
Stage 6—*Universal Ethical Principles*	
Following self-chosen ethical principles of justice and rights. When laws violate principles, act in accord with principles.	

Adapted from Kohlberg, L. (1976) Moral stages and moralization: The cognitive-developmental approach. In T. Lickona (Ed.), *Moral development and behavior: Theory, research, and social issues*. New York: Holt, Rhinehart and Winston, pp. 34–35.

are important. For example, a stage 3 response to the Evelyn dilemma might say that Evelyn shouldn't contradict her boss because she would be perceived as disloyal by her boss and might lose the social approval and trust of her boss and peers. On the other hand, what if Evelyn shares her dilemma with close family members whose opinions are important to her, and they feel strongly that she must contradict her boss? In this case, she would likely reason that she should contradict her boss because the people she trusts believe it's the right thing to do.

At stage 4, the perspective broadens to consider society. The individual is concerned about fulfilling agreed upon duties and following rules or laws that are designed to promote the common good. Therefore, a stage 4 response might say that

Evelyn should contradict her boss because of her duty to society. What if the noises do represent a safety problem? She has a responsibility as a good member of society to report it. She would feel particularly strongly about this if she were aware of product safety laws that required her to report the problem.

Level III. Finally, we come to level III (postconventional, sometimes called principled reasoning—stages 5 and 6). The principled individual has gone beyond identification with others' expectations, rules, and laws to make decisions more autonomously and consistent with principles of justice and rights. It's important to remember that very few adults in our society actually reach stage 5, and that stage 6 is thought to be a theoretical stage only.

At stage 5, the emphasis is still on rules and laws because these represent the social contract, but stage 5 thinking considers the possibility of changing the law for socially useful purposes. And a stage 5 individual would take into account moral laws above society's laws, such as considering what decision would create the greatest societal good. A stage 5 Evelyn might reason that she should contradict her boss because doing so would be consistent with the ethical principle of the greatest societal good, particularly if she considered safety of the automobiles to be a potential problem. Her responsibility goes beyond that of a good law-abiding member of society. A stage 5 Evelyn is also responsible to principles of justice and rights. So, even if there is no law requiring her to report what she knows, a stage 5 Evelyn would consider the rights to safety of the potential automobile consumers as an important reason for her to tell.

People often mistakenly think that ANY principle qualifies as "principled" thinking in Kohlberg's theory. But, Kohlberg is quite precise about the kinds of principles that qualify as "principled" thinking and he details how a researcher would score an interview to determine an individual's stage. Without going into too much detail here, level three principles are principles of justice and rights generally consistent with the kind of principles introduced in Chapter 4 under deontological theories.

To understand Kohlberg's theory, you must remember that it is a *cognitive* theory. What counts is the reasoning processes involved in a decision, not the decision itself. So, a stage one individual and a stage 5 individual may make the same decision, but their reasons for making it are very different.

Are women and men different? In 1982, Carol Gilligan published *In a Different Voice*, a widely publicized book about women's cognitive moral development. Gilligan, who had been Kohlberg's student, claimed that Kohlberg's theory was flawed because he had studied only boys and then had simply applied the same theory to girls. Her own research with girls led Gilligan to question the exclusive focus on justice in Kohlberg's higher stages. She found that people raise both justice and *care* concerns when describing moral conflicts. She also found that while males focused almost exclusively on justice considerations, a care focus was almost exclusively a female phenomenon. Females were more likely to use a "morality of care" that emphasized relationships—raising issues related to caring for others, responsibility to others, and the continuity of interdependent relationships.[4]

Gilligan's claims have received a great deal of attention, particularly in the child and adolescent development fields. But, their applicablity to adults working in business organizations is limited. Gilligan's own research[5] comparing the moral reasoning of male and female medical students found no significant difference between the genders, suggesting that both men and women are strongly influenced by the powerful cultural norms of medical practice. Similarly, an interview study of business managers[6] based on Gilligan's theory, found no gender differences. All but one of the managers (male and female) who described a moral conflict at work based their moral reasoning on rights. Finally, cognitive moral development studies based on Kohlberg's theory and conducted by many other researchers over the years have found only trivial gender differences. When differences have been found, females generally have scored higher than men.[7]

We can now begin to address the second requirement for ethical behavior— doing what's right. Recall that to behave morally, people must first decide what course of action is morally right (probably depending to a large degree upon their stage of moral development), and then they must choose the morally right path over others.[8]

Looking up and looking around.   We've already learned that most adults are at the conventional level of cognitive moral development (level II), meaning that they're highly susceptible to external influences. Their decision about what's morally right, and therefore their likely action, is inextricably linked with what others think, say, and do. We call this *looking up and looking around*[9] for ethical guidance.

These individuals aren't autonomous decision makers who strictly follow an internal moral compass. They look up and around to what their superiors and their peers are doing and saying and they use these cues as a guide to action. Therefore, most people are highly likely to do what's expected of them as a result of the reward system, role expectations, authority figure demands, and group norms. That's why the remainder of this book focuses so heavily on these external influences and it's why it's so important that managers structure the work environment to support ethical conduct. The large majority of employees will be looking for guidance and they'll do what's right if guided and supported along those lines.

Autonomous principled thinking and action.   Higher stage thinking is more independent of these external influences. The postconventional principled thinker (level III, representing a minority of people) has developed his or her own justice and rights-based principles that guide ethical decision making. Research has demonstrated that these people are also more likely to behave consistently with their own principle-based decisions—they'll carry through and do what they think is right. More principled individuals also have been found to be less likely to cheat, more likely to resist pressure from authority figures, more likely to help someone in need, and more likely to blow the whistle on misconduct.[10] But it's important for managers to remember that level III individuals are rare. Autonomous decision making based on principles of justice and rights is the exception rather than the rule.

The bottom line for managers is this. Cognitive moral development theory and research tell us that most of the people you manage are going to be strongly influenced by what you do, say, and reward. They are *looking up and looking around* for guidance from **you** and their peers and they're likely to follow what they see around them. Therefore, it's your responsibility to structure the work environment in a way that supports ethical conduct. If you avoid this responsibility, these people will look elsewhere for guidance and the guidance they receive may not support ethical conduct at all.

Those few individuals who have reached principled levels of moral reasoning should be singled out to lead key decision-making groups. They can be identified with the use of instruments that have been developed by cognitive moral development researchers. Research on ethical decision making in groups suggests that when less principled individuals lead a group, the group's ethical decision making performance decreases. On the other hand, groups with leaders higher in moral reasoning either improve or stay the same.[11]

Moral reasoning can also be increased through training. Over the years, Kohlberg, his students, and colleagues have designed training approaches based upon cognitive moral development theory. In this type of training, facilitators give participants hypothetical ethical dilemmas for discussion. The facilitator promotes movement through moral reasoning stages by challenging participants' thinking and by exposing individuals to reasoning higher than their own. This creates cognitive conflict, leading the participant to question and eventually revise his or her own reasoning. Research has supported the effectiveness of this type of training with adults in dental, medical, and business schools.[12] So, managers may want to consider incorporating these ideas into their firms' ethics training.

Locus of Control

Another individual characteristic that has been found to influence ethical conduct is *locus of control*.[13] Locus of control refers to an individual's perception of how much control he or she exerts over the events in life. Locus of control can be thought of as a single continuum from a high internal locus of control to a high external locus of control. An individual with a high internal locus of control believes that outcomes are primarily the result of his or her own efforts, whereas an individual with a high external locus of control believes that life events are primarily determined by fate, luck, or powerful others. Locus of control is not something a person is born with. It develops over time through interaction with other people and the social environment. Therefore, although it is thought to be relatively stable, one's locus of control can shift. For example, if someone with a very high internal locus of control became a prisoner of war with little chance of escape, s/he would likely develop a more external focus over time.

External Locus of Control ◄————————► Internal Locus of Control

Relationship to ethical conduct. How is locus of control related to ethics? First, individuals with a high internal locus of control see the relationship between their behavior and its outcomes more clearly than do those with an external locus of control. They see themselves as *in control* of things that happen. Therefore, they're more likely to take responsibility for the consequences of their actions. It would be more difficult for such an individual to say, "well, it's not my responsibility. I just work here" or "I'm just following orders." Studies have found that internals are more likely to help another person, even if there's a penalty for doing so.[14]

Internals see themselves as in charge of their own fates. Therefore, they should also be less willing to be pressured by others to do things they believe to be wrong. One interesting study asked subjects to complete a story in which the main character was pressured to violate a social norm.[15] The more internal the subject's locus of control, the more likely the story completion had the hero resisting the pressure. In an obedience to authority experiment (explained in more detail in Chapter 7), externals were more likely to give apparently (but not really) harmful electric shocks to someone if told to do so by the experimenter.[16]

For managers, it may be helpful to know where your workers fit on the locus of control continuum. It can help you understand how they think and how they react to a variety of situations, including ethical situations. For example, workers who constantly blame bad luck and other external factors for performance failures or ethical lapses may be doing so because of an external locus of control—that's the way they view the world. You can work with such individuals to help them see the relationship between their actions and the outcomes by consistently holding them responsible and accountable for what they do. As a result, their locus of control may shift over time and they will take more responsibility for the consequences of their actions.

COGNITIVE BARRIERS TO GOOD ETHICAL JUDGMENT

Individual differences aside, all human beings share certain ways of thinking about the world. The steps offered in Chapter 4 assume a rational ethical decision making process, prescribing how an ethical decision *should* be made. However, studies of human decision making have found that actual decision making falls short of this rational ideal. Although people intend to be rational in their decision making, for a variety of reasons they're not. In recent years, psychologists have discovered a number of weaknesses and biases in how people make decisions.[17] Some of these have direct implications for ethical decision making in organizations[18] and for the advice given in Chapter 4. Think of this part of the chapter as a kind of "reality check." If you're going to manage your own and others' ethical behavior, you need to understand how people *really* think in addition to how they *should* think.

As a backdrop for your thinking, recognize that the cognitive weaknesses and biases we will be discussing operate primarily because people try to reduce uncertainty and simplify their world. Although uncertainty is a fact of organizational life, business people want very much to deny the uncertainty they face. Therefore, they tend to act as *if* the world is rational and they're in control. Being "in charge" and able to predict events is a highly valued characteristic, especially in business. But, this focus on being in charge is an illusion that can get managers into trouble. What if you really don't know all of the facts—what the risks are—who the potential affected parties are—what all the consequences of your decisions are? You'll see in this chapter that the best way to avoid decision-making weaknesses and biases is to become aware of them and to incorporate steps into your decision making that are explicitly aimed at reducing their impact.

Script Processing—The Pinto Fire Case

Dennis A. Gioia is a management scholar and an expert on social cognition in organizations, who has provided us with a rare opportunity to look inside the head of someone who was involved in a widely publicized ethical dilemma situation. He has analyzed his own thoughts and behavior as recall coordinator at Ford Motor Company shortly after the Ford Pinto was introduced in both a lengthy article in the *Journal of Business Ethics*[19] and personal reflections that you'll find at the end of this chapter.

In the summer of 1972, Gioia graduated with an MBA. His value system included opposition to the Vietnam War and deep concerns about the ethical conduct of business. "I cultivated my social awareness; I held my principles high; I espoused my intention to help a troubled world; and I wore my hair long. By any measure I was a prototypical 'Child of the '60's."[20] A car enthusiast, Gioia was hired by the Ford Motor Company to be a "Problem Analyst." One year later he became Ford's Field Recall Coordinator, in charge of coordinating all current recall campaigns and identifying developing problems.

In analyzing his participation in the decision NOT to recall the Pinto, Gioia suggests that his behavior was highly influenced by *script processing*. Scripts are cognitive frameworks that guide human thought and action. Information processing is made much more efficient because a cognitive script allows the individual to call on an established behavior pattern and act automatically without contemplating every case in great detail. Active thinking is not required because the situation fits the mental prototype, which triggers the script and the prescribed behaviors. According to Gioia, this is something like "cruising on automatic pilot." Many of us have discovered that we were cruising on automatic pilot when we arrive at a familiar destination but we can't recall how we got there. We were following an established behavior pattern. The route was so familiar that we didn't have to think about it anymore. Somehow we were magically there. Similar things happen at work. They become routine and we do them pretty much without thinking.

Given the huge information load expected of someone who was simultaneously managing hundreds of files on potential safety problems, scripts provided a great information processing advantage. Rather than treating every potential problem situation as unique, Gioia could save time and mental energy by making quick and efficient decisions about problems as they arose. As early reports about the Pinto began to trickle in, they didn't raise any flags because they fit the scripted criteria for a "normal" accident. Therefore, he filed the claims automatically and gave seemingly more important problems his active attention.

However, in addition to its contribution to information processing efficiency, script processing clearly has disadvantages. Gioia admittedly "looked right past" potential problems because he had seen similar information patterns hundreds of times before. The scripted definition of a crisis case was not met by the information he received, so the Pinto wasn't singled out for attention. Consistent with research on script processing, he selectively perceived information that was consistent with the script and ignored information that didn't fit the pattern.

Muffled emotions can also become part of a script. Many jobs require the control of emotions, particularly negative emotions. The recall coordinator's job fit this category. In order for him to function in his job every day, Gioia's emotions had to be squelched to some degree. Even when one event penetrated his script, it didn't lead to recall of the Pinto. He had received a photograph of a burned Pinto and subsequently saw the burned hulk of an actual automobile. These powerful visual images moved him to bring the case before members of the Field Recall office. However, at the meeting, it became clear that the characteristics of the Pinto problem didn't meet the group's shared scripted criteria for a recall. All members, including Gioia, voted not to recall.

Script processing can be particularly problematic for ethical decision making. First, ethical decision making requires active consideration of the moral dimensions of the situation and a "custom" decision, tailored to the complexities of that particular case. Yet, Gioia argues that in many situations organizational members are not even aware that they are dealing with an ethical dilemma. They handle situations by following scripts that are likely to exclude ethical considerations. In other words, ethical dilemmas do not lend themselves to "automatic pilot" decisions. Yet, the realities of our hectic work lives make this sort of default decision making very common.

Cost-Benefit Analysis

Frequently, in addition to the cognitive processing limitations of individual decision makers, institutionalized decision-making processes can powerfully influence the decisions that are made by individuals or groups. In the Pinto fire case, a controversial decision-making process was used to justify the decision not to change the gas tank design. The National Traffic Safety Association had approved the use of cost-benefit analysis to establish automotive safety design standards. This involved the assignment of a dollar value for a human life, deemed to be approximately $200,000 in 1970. As an internal memo revealed, Ford had tabulated the costs of altering the tank design (for all similarly designed vehicles) to be $137,000,000 or $11 per vehicle. The benefits were calculated to be $49,530,000. These included the savings to society that would be accrued by preventing 180 deaths at $200,000 each, plus 180 projected burn injuries at $67,000 per injury, and 2100 burned cars at $700 per car. Using the cost-benefit analysis made the decision look straightforward. The costs of redesign outweighed the benefits and would therefore not be undertaken. Moral considerations didn't figure into the equation.

Attempts to reduce complex decision making to quantitative terms aren't uncommon, especially in a highly competitive business environment. In this way, complex decisions can be simplified, an apparent advantage. But, the potential disadvantages should be clear. Such simplification removes moral criteria from the decision-making process.

The Pinto Fire example also points to the importance of *multiple selves* and *role behavior* that will be discussed more in Chapter 7. Gioia was an idealistic young student, but he admittedly dropped his idealism at the corporation door, picking it up on his way out each day. In performing his job of recall coordinator, the role expectations and guiding scripts were more influential. As he says:

> The recall coordinator's job was serious business. The scripts associated with it influenced me more than I influenced [them]. Before I went to Ford I would have argued strongly that Ford had an ethical obligation to recall. After I left Ford, I now argue and teach that Ford had an ethical obligation to recall. But, *while I was there*, I perceived no obligation to recall and I remember no strong *ethical* overtones to the case whatsoever. It was a very straightforward decision, driven by dominant scripts for the time, place, and context.

Clearly, these processes that individuals and organizations use to simplify complex decisions can have significant implications for the ethical decisions managers make. Although script processing and quantitative decision-making criteria clearly help us to do our jobs more efficiently, they can also strip ethical considerations from the decision making process.

One way to address this problem is to make ethical considerations part of the script. Gioia suggests that this may be possible, although he warns that "it will take substantial concentration on the ethical dimension of the corporate culture (see Chapter 9), as well as overt attempts to emphasize ethics in education, training, and decision making before typical organizational scripts are likely to be modified to include the crucial ethical component."[21] You can help your subordinates by working with them to make the scripts explicit and to analyze them for their ethical components.

You can also require decision-making groups to analyze the ethical aspects of their decisions and to include this analysis in their report(s). Just as environmental impact statements are now a routine part of many business decisions, an ethical analysis could require that managers focus on the influence of a particular decision on stakeholders' rights and consequences for the community or communities affected by the decision. You can also require groups to justify their decision-making *process* (e.g., decision-making criteria and weighting) in moral as well as quantitative terms.

Thinking about Fact Gathering

In Chapter 4 we advised you to "get the facts" as an important first step in good ethical decision making. But be aware that your thinking about the facts is likely to be biased. Research evidence suggests that you may look for the wrong ones or stop looking too soon because you think you already have all the facts you need.

We know that most people, including business students and business executives, are overconfident about their knowledge of the facts. For example, in research studies, people were asked factual questions. Then they were asked to judge the probable truth of their answers. In response to the question, "Is Rome or New York farther north, most people chose New York, and they believed that the probability was about 90% that they were right. Actually, they were wrong. Rome is slightly north of New York. Being overconfident can make you fail to search for additional facts or for support for the facts you have.[22]

Even if you gather additional facts or support, another cognitive bias termed the *confirmation trap*[23] may influence your choice of which facts to gather and where to look. All of us have the tendency to look for information that will confirm our preferred answer or choice and to neglect to search for evidence that might prove us wrong. If you're a pharmaceutical executive who wants to believe that a new product is safe, you're more likely to ask your managers something like, "Does it meet all FDA regulations?" In this case, the executive expects, and will probably get a confirming response and a quick decision to go ahead with the drug can be made. However, the meeting might take a very different turn if the executive asks, "What health and safety problems are still possible with this drug?"[24]

In an attempt to overcome these limitations and biases, it's important that you consciously try to think of ways you could be wrong. Incorporate questions in your individual and group decision-making processes such as, "How could I/we be wrong?" "What facts are still missing?" and "What facts exist that might prove me/us to be wrong?" You may still miss some important facts, but you'll miss less of them than if you didn't ask these questions at all.

Thinking about Consequences

In Chapter 4, we also introduced consequentialist theories and we advised you to think about all the potential consequences of your decision for a wide variety of stakeholders. Who can argue with such sage advice? But psychologists have found a number of problems with how people think about consequences.

Reduced number of consequences.   Psychologists have found that one way people simplify their decisions and make them more manageable is to reduce the number of consequences they consider. They're especially likely to ignore consequences that are thought to affect only a few people. But consequences that affect only a few people can be serious. For example, a highly beneficial drug may have beneficial consequences for many and adverse consequences for only a few people. But what if those few people could die from side effects of the drug?[25] Obviously, you wouldn't want to ignore such serious consequences no matter how few people are affected. In attempting to consciously deal with this, it helps to consult a broad range of people who have a stake in the decision you're making. Invite input from all interested parties, especially those who disagree with you and those with the most to lose. Ask them what consequences they're concerned about and why. Then, incorporate these consequences in your decision making.

Consequences as risk.   One way to think about consequences is to think in terms of decision making about risk. Research suggests that people tend to underestimate potential risks because of an *illusion of optimism*. They overestimate the likelihood of good future events and underestimate the bad. People also generally believe that they're less susceptible to risks than others. This belief is supported by the *illusion of control*, the general belief that we really are in charge of what happens. And if we think we can control events, we also think bad things are less likely to happen. This illusion of control has been demonstrated to exist in MBA students from top U.S. business schools, suggesting that managers are certainly vulnerable.[26] Managers whose judgment is influenced by these cognitive biases are likely to underestimate the risk facing the firm as a result of a particular decision. But if managers ignore risks, they're also ignoring important consequences. So, it's important to recognize this tendency to ignore risk, and design risk analysis into your decision making processes.

Even if we attend to risks, we still have difficulty thinking about them in a completely rational way. One tendency that can contribute to downplaying risk was already discussed—the tendency to attend to information that will help to confirm the decision we would prefer to make (confirmation bias). In the famous space shuttle *Challenger* disaster, everyone knew that there was risk. The question was how much, and was it too much? There were many economic and political factors pushing NASA to launch this shuttle with the teacher on board. Researchers now believe that the confirmation bias may have influenced decision makers to focus on the information that confirmed their preference, which was to launch, and to discount available information about risks that would have supported a delay.[27]

Consequences over time—escalation of commitment.   The prescription to think about consequences also fails to take into account the fact that decisions are not isolated choices but often become part of a series of choices within the context of a larger decision or project. Consider the following scenario:

You finally graduated from college and landed a great job and you invested most of your savings in the car of your dreams—a used BMW. But, in a short time, the car began having mechanical problems. Every time you brought it to the mechanic, he claimed that it was fixed for good, but the problems continued and your bank account was being drained. Should you quit trying to fix the car?

Because you've already made the decision to buy the car and you've already invested a lot of money in it, your tendency will be to continue to be committed to this previously selected course of action. This tendency has been called "escalation of commitment to a losing course of action" or "throwing good money after bad."[28] A perfectly rational decision maker would consider the time and expenses already invested as "sunk costs." They aren't recoverable and shouldn't be considered in a decision about what to do. Only future costs and benefits should be considered. But, this is difficult. Norms in our society and in our organizations support trying, persistence, and sticking with a course of action. Also, if others are involved, we're likely to feel the need to justify our original decision—whether it was to buy a car, a piece of equipment, or land.

One way to overcome escalation of commitment is, as with many biases, to recognize that it exists and try to adjust for it. Ask yourself explicit questions about whether you're committed to a decision just because failure would make your original decision look bad. Ask yourself, "If I took over the project today, with no personal investment, would I support the project?" Another approach is to bring in outsiders and ask for their opinions or turn the project over to them completely. That gets your own ego completely out of the decision-making process.

Thinking about Integrity

In Chapter 4, you were also advised to think about your own integrity—to ask yourself what a person of integrity would do in the particular situation facing you. But, cognitive biases can get in the way here too. If your thoughts about yourself are controlled by illusion rather than reality, how can you make a good decision about your integrity? The basic idea here is that individuals prefer to think positively about themselves. They're likely to unconsciously filter and distort information in order to maintain the positive self image they prefer.

Psychologists know that people have an *illusion of superiority*. Surveys have found that people tend to think of themselves as more ethical, fair and honest than most other people.[29] It's obviously an illusion when the large majority of individuals claim to be more honest than the average person, or more ethical than their peers. It's a little like Garrison Keillor's mythical Lake Wobegon where ALL the children are above average. There isn't a whole lot you can do here except to try to be honest with yourself.

Thinking about Your Gut

Finally, in Chapter 4, we advised you to listen to your gut. But, in this chapter, we've spent a great deal of time telling you that your gut may well be wrong—led by cognitive limitations and biased thinking.

We think that your gut can still be particularly useful in alerting you that something might be wrong—that you're facing an ethical dilemma—in the first place. But once that decision is made, you'll need to temper your gut with the knowledge gained in this chapter and the rest of the book. Hopefully, the combination of your gut and an informed brain will help you to make better decisions.

CONCLUSION

This chapter has introduced you to individual differences that can influence ethical decision making. The chapter has also outlined the cognitive limitations and biases that can interfere with good ethical decision making. Hopefully, knowing about these and how they can be overcome will help you to be a better individual decision maker. Much of the remainder of the book will move beyond this focus on the individual decision maker to a focus on the group and organizational influences that can have a profound influence on your decisions and actions.

Personal Reflections on the Pinto Fires Case

by Dennis A. Gioia
The last chapter ended with a provocative case highlighting some of the sordid events in the history of the Pinto fires problem. As the authors have indicated in this chapter, I was involved with this infamous case in the early 1970s. They have asked me to reflect on lessons learned from my experience.

I take this case very personally, even though my name seldom comes up in its many recountings. I was one of those "faceless bureaucrats" who is often portrayed as making decisions without accountability and then walking away from them— even decisions with life-and-death implications. That characterization is, of course, far too stark and superficial. I certainly don't consider myself faceless, and I have always chafed at the label of bureaucrat as applied to me, even though I have found myself unfairly applying it to others. Furthermore, I have been unable to walk away from my decisions in this case. They have a tendency to haunt—especially when they have such public airings as those involved in the Pinto fires debacle have had.

But why revisit 20-year-old decisions, and why take them so personally? Here's why: because I was in a position to do something about a serious problem . . . and didn't. That simple observation gives me pause for personal reflection and also makes me think about the many difficulties people face in trying to be ethical decision makers in organizations. It also helps me to keep in mind the features of modern business and organizational life that would influence someone like me (me!, of all people, who purposefully set out to be an ethical decision maker) to overlook basic moral issues in arriving at decisions that, when viewed retrospectively, look absurdly easy to make. But they are not easy to make, and that is perhaps the most important lesson of all.

The Personal Aspect

I would like to reflect on my own experience mainly to emphasize the personal dimensions involved in ethical decision making. Although I recognize that there are strong organizational influences at work as well, I would like to keep the critical lens focused for a moment on me (and you) as individuals. I believe that there are insights and lessons from my experience that can help you think about your own likely involvement in issues with ethical overtones.

First, however, a little personal background. In the late 1960s and early 1970s, I was an engineering/MBA student; I also was an "activist", engaged in protests of social injustice and the social irresponsibility of business, among other things. I held some pretty strong values that I thought would stand up to virtually any challenge and enable me to "do the right thing" when I took a career job. I suspect that most of you feel that you also have developed a strongly held value system that will enable you to resist organizational inducements to do something unethical. Perhaps. Unfortunately, the challenges do not often come in overt forms that shout the need for resistance or ethical righteousness. They are much more subtle than that, and thus doubly difficult to deal with because they do not make it easy to see that a situation you are confronting might actually involve an ethical dilemma.

After school, I got the job of my dreams with Ford and, predictably enough, ended up on the fast track to promotion. That fast track enabled me to progress quickly into positions of some notable responsibility. Within two years I became Ford's vehicle recall coordinator, with first-level responsibility for tracking field safety problems. It was the most intense, information-overloaded job you can imagine, frequently dealing with some of the most serious problems in the company. Disasters were a phone call away and action was the hallmark of the office where I worked. We all knew we were engaged in serious business and we all took the job seriously. There were no irresponsible bureaucratic ogres there, contrary to popular portrayal.

In this context I first encountered the neophyte Pinto fires problem—in the form of infrequent reports of cars erupting into horrendous fireballs in very low-speed crashes and the shuddering personal experience of inspecting a car that had burned, killing its trapped occupants. Over the space of a year I had two distinct opportunities to initiate recall activities concerning the fuel tank problems, but on both occasions voted not to recall, despite my activist history and advocacy of business social responsibility.[30]

The key question is how, in the space of two short years, could I have engaged in a decision process that appeared to violate my own strong values—a decision process whose subsequent manifestations continue to be cited by many observers as a supposedly definitive study of corporate unethical behavior? I tend to discount the obvious accusations: that my values weren't really strongly held; that I had turned my back on my values in the interest of loyalty to Ford; that I was somehow intimidated into making decisions in the best interests of the company; that despite my principled statements I had not actually achieved a high stage of moral development, etc. Instead, I believe a more plausible explanation for my own actions looks to the foibles of normal human information processing.

I would argue that the complexity and intensity of the recall coordinator's job required that I develop cognitive strategies for simplifying the overwhelming amount of information I had to deal with. The best way to do that is to structure the information into cognitive "schemas," or more specifically "script schemas," that guide understanding and action when facing common or repetitive situations. Scripts offer marvelous cognitive shortcuts because they allow you to act virtually unconsciously and automatically, and thus permit handling complicated situations without being paralyzed by needing to think consciously about every little thing. Such scripts enabled me to discern the characteristic hallmarks of problem cases likely to result in recall, and also enabled me to execute a complicated series of steps required to initiate a recall.

All of us structure information all of the time; we could hardly get through the work day without doing so. But, there is a penalty to be paid for this wonderful cognitive efficiency: we do not give sufficient attention to important information that requires special treatment because the general information pattern has surface appearances that indicate that automatic processing will suffice. That, I think, is what happened to me. The beginning stages of the Pinto case looked for all the world like a normal sort of problem. Lurking beneath the cognitive veneer, however, was a nasty set of circumstances waiting to conspire into a dangerous situation. Despite the awful nature of the accidents, the Pinto problem did not fit an existing script; the accidents were relatively rare by recall standards and the accidents were not initially traceable to a specific component failure. Even when a failure mode suggesting a design flaw was identified, the cars did not perform significantly worse in crash tests than competitor vehicles. One might easily argue that I should have been jolted out of my script by the unusual nature of the accidents (very low speed, otherwise unharmed passengers trapped in a horrific fire), but those facts did not penetrate a script cued for other features. (It also is difficult to convey to the layperson that bad accidents are not a particularly unusual feature of the recall coordinator's information field; accident severity is not necessarily a recall cue—frequently repeated patterns and identifiable causes are).

The Corporate Milieu

In addition to the personalized scripting of information processing, there is another important influence on the decisions that led to the Pinto fires mess: the fact that decisions are made by individuals working within a corporate context. It has escaped almost no one's notice that the decisions made by corporate employees tend to be in the best interest of the corporation, even by people who mean to do better. Why? Because socialization processes and the overriding influence of organizational culture provide a strong, if generally subtle context for defining appropriate ways of seeing and understanding. Because organizational culture can be viewed as a collection of scripts, scripted information processing relates even to organizational level considerations. Scripts are context bound; they are not free-floating general cognitive structures that apply universally. They are tailored to specific contexts. And there are few more potent contexts than organizational settings.

There is no question that my perspective changed after joining Ford. In retrospect, I would be very surprised if it hadn't. In my former incarnation as a social activist, I had internalized values for doing what was right as I understood rightness in grand terms; but, I had not internalized a script for applying my values in a pragmatic business context. Ford and the recall coordinator role provided a powerful context for developing scripts—scripts that were inevitably and undeniably oriented toward ways of making sense that were influenced by the corporate and industry culture.

I wanted to do a good job and I wanted to do what was right. Those are not mutually exclusive desires, but the corporate context affects their synthesis. I came to accept that it was not feasible to fix everything that someone might construe as a problem. I therefore shifted to a value of wanting to do the greatest good for the greatest number (an ethical value tempered by the practical constraints of an economic enterprise). Doing the greatest good for the greatest number meant working with intensity and responsibility on those problems that would spare the most people from injury. It also meant developing scripts that responded to typical problems, not odd patterns like those presented by the Pinto.

Another way of noting how the organizational context so strongly affects individuals is to recognize that one's personal identity becomes heavily influenced by corporate identity. As a student, my identity centered on being a "good person" (with a certain dose of moral righteousness associated with it). As recall coordinator, my identity shifted to a more corporate definition. This is an extraordinarily important point, especially for students who have not yet held a permanent job role, and I would like to emphasize it. Before assuming your career role, identity derives mainly from social relationships. Upon putting on the mantle of a profession or a responsible position, identity begins to align with your role. And information processing perspective follows from that identity.

I remember accepting the portrayal of the auto industry and Ford as "under attack" from many quarters (oil crises, burgeoning government regulation, inflation, litigious customers, etc). As we know, groups under assault develop into more cohesive communities who emphasize commonalities and shared identities. I was by then an insider in the industry and the company, sharing some of their beleaguered perceptions that there were significant forces arrayed against us and that the well-being of the company might be threatened.

What happened to the original perception that Ford was a socially irresponsible giant that needed a comeuppance? Well, it looks different from the inside. Over time, a reasonable value for action against corporate dominance became tempered by another reasonable value that corporations serve social needs and are not automatically the villains of society. I saw a need for balance among multiple values, and as a result my identity shifted in degrees toward a more corporate identity.

The Torch Passes to You

So, given my experiences, what would I recommend to you, as a budding organizational decision maker? I have some strong opinions. First, develop your ethical base now! Too many people do not give serious attention to assessing and articulating their own values. People simply do not know what they stand for because they haven't seriously thought about it. Even the ethical scenarios presented in classes or executive programs are treated as interesting little games without apparent implications for deciding how you intend to think or act. These exercises should be used to develop a principled, personal code that you will try to live by. Consciously decide your values. If you don't decide your values now, you are easy prey for others who will gladly decide them for you or influence you implicitly to accept theirs.

Second, recognize that everyone, including you, is an unwitting victim of his or her own cognitive structuring. Many people are surprised and fascinated to learn that they use schemas and scripts to understand and act in the organizational world. The idea that we automatically process so much information so much of the time intrigues us. Indeed, we would all turn into blithering idiots if we did not structure information and expectations, but that very structuring hides information that might be important—information that could require you to confront your values. We get lulled into thinking that automatic information processing is great stuff that obviates the necessity for trying to resolve so many frustrating decisional dilemmas.

Actually, I think too much ethical training focuses on supplying standards for contemplating dilemmas. The far greater problem, as I see it, is recognizing that there is a dilemma in the first place. The insidious problem of people not being aware that they are dealing with a situation that might have ethical overtones is another consequence of schema usage. I would venture that scripted routines seldom include ethical dimensions. Is a person behaving unethically if the situation is not even construed as having ethical implications? People are not necessarily stupid, ill-intentioned or Machiavellian, but they are often unaware. They do indeed spend much of their time cruising on automatic, but the true hallmark of human information processing is the ability to switch from automatic to controlled information processing. What we really need to do is to encourage people to recognize cues that build a "Now Think!" step into their scripts—waving red flags at yourself, so to speak—even though you are engaged in essentially automatic cognition and action.

Third, because scripts are context-bound and organizations are potent contexts, be aware of how strongly, yet how subtly, your job role and your organizational culture affect the ways you interpret and make sense of information (and thus affect the ways you develop the scripts that will guide you in unguarded moments). Organizational culture has a much greater effect on individual cognition than you would ever suspect (see Chapter 9).

Last, be prepared to face critical responsibility at a relatively young age, as I did. You need to know what your values are and you need to know how you think so that you can know how to make a good decision. Before you can do that, you need to articulate and affirm your values now, before you enter the fray. I wasn't really ready. Are you?

DISCUSSION QUESTIONS

1. What does it mean to say that everyone is victim of his or her cognitive structures?

2. Do you believe that scripts can override your value system?

3. Answer the question posed in the reflections: Is a person behaving unethically if the situation is not even construed in ethical terms?

4. What does it mean to say that organizational culture is a collection of scripts?

5. Who should make the decision about taking risks with others' lives in designing products?

6. Should someone be permitted to place a value on a human life? Should a company? Should the government?

7. How do you feel about the use of cost-benefit analysis where human life is part of the cost calculation?

8. Can you articulate your most important ethical values and prioritize them?

NOTES

[1]Kohlberg, L. 1969. Stage and sequence: The cognitive-developmental approach to socialization. In *Handbook of socialization theory and research*. D.A. Goslin, ed. Rand McNally, 347–380.

[2]Rest, M. 1986. *Moral development; Advances in research and theory*. New York: Praeger.

[3]Treviño, L. K. & Youngblood, S. A. 1990. Bad apples in bad barrels: A causal analysis of ethical decision-making behavior. *Journal of Applied Psychology*, 75 (4): 378–385.

Weber, J. 1988. The relationship between managerial value orientations and stages of moral development: Theory development and empirical investigation with behavioral implications. Unpublished dissertation, The University of Pittsburgh.

[4]Gilligan, C. 1982. *In a different voice*. Cambridge, MA: Harvard University Press.

[5]Gilligan, C. & Attanuci, J. 1988. Two moral orientations. In *Mapping the moral domain.*, C. Gilligan, J. V. Ward, & J. M. Taylor, eds. Cambridge, MA: Harvard University Press, 73–86.

[6]Derry, R. 1987. Moral reasoning in work-related conflicts. *Research in Corporate Social Performance and Policy*, 9: 25–50.

[7]Rest, M. 1986. *Moral development; Advances in research and theory*. New York: Praeger.

[8]Ibid.

[9]This phrase was used with different meaning by R. Jackall in *Moral Mazes*, by Oxford University Press.

[10]Treviño, L.K. 1992. Moral reasoning and business ethics. *Journal of Business Ethics*, 11: 445–459.

[11]Dukerich, J., Nichols, M.L., Elm, D.R. & Vollrath, D.A. 1990. Moral reasoning in groups: Leaders make a difference. *Human Relations*, 43: 473–493.

[12]Treviño, L.K. 1992. Moral reasoning and business ethics. *Journal of Business Ethics*, 11: 445–459.

[13]Rotter, J.B. 1966. Generalized expectancies for internal versus external control of reinforcement. *Psychological Monographs: General and Applied, 80:1–28.*

[14]Midlarski, E. 1971. Aiding under stress: the effects of competence, dependency, visibility, and fatalism. *Journal of Personality*, 39: 132–149.

Midlarski, E. & Midlarski, M. 1973. Some determinants of aiding under experimentally induced stress. *Journal of Personality*, 41: 305–327.

Ubbink, E.M. & Sadava, S.W. 1974. Rotter's generalized expectancies as predictors of helping behavior. *Psychological Reports*, 35: 865–866.

[15]Johnson, R.C., Ackerman, J.M., Frank, H. & Fionda, A.J. 1968. Resistance to temptation and guilt following yielding and psychotherapy. *Journal of Consulting and Clinical Psychology*, 32: 169–175.

[16]Propst, L.R. 1979. Efforts of personality and loss of anonymity on aggression: A re-evaluation of deindividuation. *Journal of Personality*, 47: 531–545.

[17]Bazerman, M.H. 1994. *Judgment in managerial decision making.* New York: John Wiley & Sons.

[18]Messick, D.M. & Bazerman, M. 1994. Ethics for the 21st century; a decision-making perspective. Unpublished manuscript. The International Consortium for Executive Development Research.

[19]Gioia, D. 1992. Pinto fires and personal ethics: A script analysis of missed opportunities. *Journal of Business Ethics*, 11(5,6): 379–389.

[20]Ibid.

[21]Ibid.

[22]Messick, D.M. & Bazerman, M. 1994. Ethics for the 21st century; A decision-making perspective. Unpublished manuscript. The International Consortium for Executive Development Research.

[23]Bazerman, M.H. 1994. *Judgment in managerial decision making.* New York: John Wiley & Sons.

[24]Messick, D.M. & Bazerman, M. 1994. Ethics for the 21st century; A decision-making perspective. Unpublished manuscript. The International Consortium for Executive Development Research.

[25]Ibid.

[26]Ibid.

[27]Ibid.

[28]Staw, B.M. & Ross, I. 1987. Understanding escalation situations. In *Research in Organizational Behavior*, Vol. 9. B.M. Staw & L.L. Cummings, eds. Greenwich, CT: JAI Press.

[29]Messick, D.M. & Bazerman, M. 1994. Ethics for the 21st Century; A decision-making perspective. Unpublished manuscript. The International Consortium for Executive Development Research.

[30]See Gioia, 1992, for a more thorough description and analysis of my experience.

SECTION III

Ethics and the Manager

CHAPTER SIX

Ethical Problems
of Managers

INTRODUCTION

ETHICAL ISSUES for individual employees and managers are very differ-ent, since managers are responsible for the entire range of human resources activities such as hiring, firing, disciplining, and performance evaluation. Also, since managers are responsible for employee supervision, they are increasingly being held accountable by the courts for the activities and behavior of the people who report to them. Finally, because managers are role models for the workers in their depart-ment, it's critical that managers be able to discuss the ethical implications of deci-sion making and provide advice to employees who find themselves in an ethical quandary. These facts of corporate life have many managers nonplussed. "How can I possibly manage the ethics or morality of the people I manage? Is it even possible to manage ethics? Where are the special pitfalls for me as a manager?"

In this chapter, we're going to examine what responsibilities managers have, and how you as a manager can influence your direct reports to make ethical decisions.

TODAY'S MANAGERS NEED
NEW SKILLS

Here's what the experts tell us about dramatic changes in the role of the modern manager:

111

Trend #1: experts predict that the work force is becoming less educated and less skilled. There'll be increased competition to hire and retain the best workers. The result: managers need to be proficient at hiring the best people, evaluating their performance, and if necessary, disciplining them, and even terminating them.

Trend #2: experts also predict that the work force is becoming more diverse and that persuading all of these diverse groups to sing together as a well-tuned chorus is key to future success. Companies that best address the needs of a diverse population will probably be in a better position to succeed than companies that ignore this new reality. The result: managers need to be able to deal with individuals of both sexes, and all ages, races, religions, and ethnic groups. And managers not only need to have this ability themselves, but also they need to be able to encourage this ability in team members. Managers must become "conductors" who orchestrate team performance—sometimes teaching, sometimes coaching, always communicating with employees and empowering them to learn and make decisions.

Trend #3: even though employees may be empowered, the buck (according to the federal government) continues to stop at the manager's desk. If your employees break the law, they're not the only ones who will suffer the consequences; you may, also. The result: managers need to recognize their responsibility to supervise, and to help create an environment where ethical decisions are valued. Each of these trends has implications for the ethical issues modern managers face.

Trend #1—Managing the Basics

It's imperative that managers hire the best-trained workers and accurately appraise their performance. It's also essential that managers know how to discipline, and perhaps even terminate a worker who is an unsatisfactory performer.

Hiring and Work Assignments

After two years of complex negotiations and hand-holding, your bank has finally signed Big Holding Co. as a client. Big Holding has three main divisions: a chemicals business in Louisiana, a heavy equipment division outside of Cleveland, and an agricultural business in Iowa. Since the business is so enormous, you assign three junior employees to the company—one employee per division. Joe Patterson, a talented chemical engineer will head effort for the chemicals business.

When you and your three employees meet with the senior management team from Big Holding to plot long-term strategy, the Chief Financial Officer pulls you aside to chat. "You shouldn't send Joe to Louisiana," he says. "There have been numerous violent incidents there involving people of his race, and I would be afraid for his safety. Why don't you assign him to one of the other divisions, and send someone else down South?"

. . .

You're planning to hire a new marketing manager and one of the leading candidates is very short. He's so short that he could be classified as a dwarf and would have difficulty doing things like reaching light switches. If you hired him, his office would have to be modified, although that really isn't much of a problem. The real problem is your concern about how your customers would react. The specific job he's applying for requires extensive customer contact and his appearance is frankly disconcerting. On the other hand, his credentials are excellent and he's certainly qualified for the job.

A manager hires, or brings new people into the organization, and determines employee work assignments once employees are on the job. The new people may be permanent employees, or they may be part-time employees, temporary workers, or consultants.

Federal law prohibits discrimination based on race, religion, sex, color, ethnic background, and age, and it protects those who are pregnant or handicapped. In the first example above, which involves an African-American male, the correct answer is not as clear-cut as it may appear. The worker is certainly qualified for the job—and he should be given the opportunity to be assigned to the part of the business he seems most qualified to manage. Although federal legislation supposedly protects him from discrimination, the element of danger in this case caused at least one company to reassign an employee in a very similar case. A better solution might have been to give the employee the choice of whether to go or accept another assignment. A thoughtful manager might have said, "Here are the facts as I know them—it's your decision and I'll support whatever you decide."

In the second example, which involves a very short candidate, many people might think that the solution is even more ambiguous. He is "certainly qualified" for the job and his size may very well include him in protectionist handicapped legislation. But the larger issue is: what qualities should determine whether or not an individual should be hired?

All protectionist legislation—at all levels—points to the answer, as does the concept of fairness. Hiring, promotions, and terminations should be based on ability, period. However, it's one thing to ignore someone because of your own prejudice, and quite another to hesitate to put someone in a situation where they might suffer discrimination from an external audience that's out of your control such as your customers. It's difficult to say whether you're doing someone a favor by setting him or her up for possible failure in an environment that's hostile. Perhaps the best course of action in both circumstances is to frankly describe the situation and let the candidate make the choice about whether or not to accept the job.

Prejudice is difficult to overcome. Everyone has biases: some people don't like very tall people, or very short people, or fat ones, or skinny ones, or old ones, or young ones. Others have biases against brown eyes, or blue eyes, or eyes with wrinkles, or big noses, or aquiline noses, or balding heads, or heads that are too hairy. Some people like individuals from certain schools or from particular parts of the country. What if someone interviews for a job and he is just plain unattractive, or she's deaf, or he had cancer three years ago, or she speaks English with an accent? Do those qualities have anything to do with an ability to do the job, or with talent?

Some employers have a "corporate profile" in mind when they hire, especially when they're trying to fill positions with "extensive public contact." They look for healthy, young people with regular features, moderate height, a medium build, and who have no discernible accents. Do employers with a conscious, or subconscious "corporate profile" think that the public or their customers are somehow homogeneous? If history had used a "corporate profile" as a yardstick, Abraham Lincoln, Benjamin Franklin, Marian Anderson, Albert Einstein, Sammy Davis, Jr., and Franklin Roosevelt may have been relegated to positions with "no public contact."

Talent and ability come in a variety of packages. When managers use anything other than those two factors to evaluate qualifications for hiring, promotions, or work assignments, they not only shortchange the individual, they shortchange their employer. And they may help to perpetuate stereotypes in the work place.

Performance Evaluation

You were recently promoted to manager of a department with five professionals and two clerical staff. One of the professionals, Joe, is a nice guy, but he simply hasn't been able to match the performance of the others in the department. When he tells you he's been interviewing for another job in a different part of your company, you pull his personnel file and see that the person who previously managed the department had rated Joe's performance as "good to excellent." You frankly disagree. Joe has asked you for a recommendation. Based on the written appraisals, you could give him a good one—but your personal observation is at odds with the written evaluations. Joe's prospective manager—your peer in another department—asks for your opinion. What do you say?

When we talk about performance evaluation, we're really talking about two things. First, there's a written assessment of an employee's performance. Most large companies have a formal performance appraisal system, with forms to standardize the process, and a mandate to complete a written evaluation on every employee usually once each year. These written appraisals usually have some influence on any salary adjustments and they usually become part of the employee's permanent personnel file. Second, there's the informal process of performance evaluation that ideally is an ongoing process throughout the year. When a manager gives continuous feedback—when objectives are stated and then performance against those objectives is measured—employees generally aren't surprised by the annual written performance appraisal.

Why is continuous evaluation important? A training manager in New York City tells a story about the importance of accurately and continuously appraising performance. "Imagine you're bowling," he says. "A sheet is stretched across the lane and you can't see what you're doing. Your manager is the only person who can tell you how you're doing. What would happen if your manager told you how you were doing only occasionally, or once a year? How would your performance be affected if he or she told you about your performance only when you got a gutter ball? What would happen if he or she only commented just when you did well?" It's only when your manager gives you consistent feedback—reflecting the complete range of your behavior—that you can improve your performance.

The problem with performance evaluation is that most managers hate to do it. It's certainly easier to recognize an employee's achievements than his or her shortcomings, but many managers are so busy that they forget to recognize either. Pointing out an employee's deficient performance is extremely difficult for most managers. It's such a thorny issue, that in a survey of 4000 Fortune 500 executives, five out of seven executives said that they would rather lie to employees about performance than confront them.[1]

In the example above, the manager thinks Joe has been inaccurately (and perhaps even dishonestly) evaluated in the past. Since most employers require a rating of "good" or "satisfactory" before an employee can transfer to another job, the manager will probably feel pressure to supply such a recommendation so Joe can qualify for the transfer. This is a common problem. Many organizations have employees like Joe, who are less than stellar performers, but who are never confronted with their poor performance. In Joe's company, no manager has been brave enough to bite the bullet and either try to get Joe to improve his performance or initiate the termination process. It's easier to pass Joe along to someone else—to turn him into a ping-pong ball, bouncing from department to department, never really improving his performance because no one will confront him with the truth. And because his written appraisals have been less than honest, prospective managers get buffaloed into thinking Joe's performance is adequate. It's a vicious cycle and a real disservice to the employee, his or her co-workers, and the organization.

One good way to ensure continuous performance evaluation is to establish a formal system with the employees who report to you, whether or not your company requires it. Meet with each employee every six months or every year, and jointly agree to job objectives and to what measurement would constitute success for each objective. Then meet monthly with each employee and discuss how the employee is meeting his or her objectives. When objectives and measurement standards are established in advance and progress is tracked, it's much easier for employees to perform. They know what the target looks like, how to get there, and how they'll know when they've met it. An ongoing process eliminates the need to blast a non-performer once a year, and can greatly reduce misunderstanding, resentment, and charges of discrimination or bias.

As Joe's manager, you have at least two choices that would meet the objectives of fairness and honesty. First, you can present Joe with your honest rating of his performance and refuse to approve a transfer until you and he have set objectives, he understands how he'll be measured, and you have enough time to evaluate his performance based on those objectives. Second, you could approve the transfer, but be frank with Joe and his prospective manager in your evaluation of Joe's performance.

Discipline

Steven is a salesman who reports to you, the regional director of sales for an office supply company. He has a great track record and has consistently surpassed his sales targets, but he has a terrible flaw. He's not on time for anything. He's late for meetings with you, lunches with clients, and the problem extends to his paperwork. His expense reports, sales reports—everything is handed in a day or sometimes even a week late. As his manager, you've counseled him about his tardiness and he has improved. Now instead of being 15 minutes late for a meeting, he's only 5 minutes late. And instead of submitting his expenses a week late, they're only two days late. His lateness seems minor in view of his achievements, but it's driving you and his co-workers crazy.

Most managers view disciplining employees as something to be postponed for as long as possible. Many people in a work environment try to ignore a worker's shortcomings in the hope that the situation will improve. Discipline, however, is important for a number of reasons: not only to ensure worker productivity, but also to set the standard that certain behaviors are expected from all employees, and to meet the requirements of the U.S. Sentencing Guidelines. The Sentencing Guidelines specify that all employees in an organization must receive consistent discipline for similar infractions. For example, in the case of employee theft, a secretary and a senior vice president must be treated in the same way. The Guidelines are violated if one receives a slap on the wrist and the other is suspended or fired.

In the case of Steven, the late salesman, you as a manager could be tempted to view disciplining his lateness as nitpicking. He's a star after all, right? However, to expect promptness from all of your other employees and not from Steven is unrealistic and unfair.

Research has given us clues about the most effective ways to discipline employees. First, the discipline must be constructive and done in a professional manner. For example, although you might be tempted to scream at Steven and call him a jerk, that's not going to change his behavior. It's much more effective to meet with him, explain the consequences of his lateness, and focus the discussion on his behavior, not on him personally.

Second, the discipline should be done privately. Employees should never be criticized in front of other employees. It's just as embarrassing as being criticized in public by your parent or your spouse, and it encourages nothing but hard feelings. Those discussions should always be held behind closed doors.

Third, employees should have input into the process and be encouraged to explain their side of the story. The entire idea of "team" management revolves around individuals being encouraged to share their view of a situation. The real problem may not be with the particular employee you want to discipline. Steven, for example, may be late with reports because people are late in submitting data to him. To solve problems at the simplest point, it's wise to ask for an employee's explanation.

Finally, discipline should be appropriately harsh and consistent with what other employees have received for similar offenses. This aspect of discipline is perhaps the most important in terms of ensuring good performance in the future.[2]

For example, a highly respected financial professional (let's call her Beth) was fired from her position at a large commercial bank for providing an inaccurate calculation in a report to senior management. The head of human resources for the bank gave Beth a herculean task: to calculate all pension obligations on current employees. The assignment was given at 6:00 p.m. on a Tuesday, and the report needed to be written, typed, and copied for a senior management meeting the next morning at 9:00 a.m. Beth and her secretary stayed at the office all night long, doing calculations, writing the report, and finally preparing it for the meeting the next morning. When one of the senior managers discovered an error in one of the complex calculations, Beth was summarily fired by the head of human resources. It sent a huge message, not only to Beth, but to the entire human resources department. Other mistakes had been made—even by the head of human resources—and those errors had been punished with a reprimand, certainly not a firing. And, of course, the impossible deadline constituted an extenuating circumstance in everyone's opinion except the head of human resources. The effects of unreasonable discipline are far reaching, and that's why discipline needs to be appropriate to the offense and consistent with what others have received.

In the case of Steven, the late salesman, unless you're willing to be consistent and accept tardiness in all other employees, Steven's behavior needs to be addressed.

Terminations

You're a manager in a large commercial bank. You discover that Patricia, a loan officer who reports to you, has forged an approval signature on a customer loan, which requires signatures from two loan officers. When you confront Pat with the forgery, she apologizes profusely and says that her husband has been very ill. The day she forged the signature, he was going into surgery and she just didn't have time to find another loan officer to sign the authorization for the loan. Pat has been with your bank for 15 years and has a spotless record.

Terminations come in many varieties and none of them are pleasant. There are terminations for cause, that means that an individual has committed an offense which can result in instant firing. "Cause" can represent different things to different companies, but generally theft, assault, cheating on expense reports, forgery, fraud, and gross insubordination (including lying about a business matter) are considered to be "cause" in most organizations. Many companies define "cause" in their employee handbooks.

In the case above, Patricia will most likely be fired for cause. In banking, there are few things as sacred as a signature, and a professional with 15 years of banking experience would certainly be expected to know this. Forgery of any kind cannot be tolerated in a financial institution. It's a sad case, and any manager would surely feel compassion for Patricia. However, there are some offenses that are unpardonable in a financial institution, and this is probably one of them.

There are also terminations for poor performance. This type of firing is most often based on written documentation such as performance appraisals and attendance records. Many employers have a formal system of warnings that would occur before someone is actually terminated for poor performance. A verbal warning is usually the first step in the process, followed by a written warning, and then termination. The process can differ from company to company.

Then there's downsizing and "right sizing," which are just fancy words that mean layoffs. Layoffs can result from many kinds of reorganizations such as mergers, acquisitions, relocations, or as the result of economic reasons, or changes in business strategy. A layoff can result from a decision to trim staff in one department, or from a decision to reduce head count companywide. Whatever the reason, layoffs are painful, not only for the person losing his or her job, but also for the co-workers who'll be left behind. Co-workers tend to display several reactions: they exhibit low morale; they become less productive; they distrust management; and they become extremely cautious.[3] These are just a few reasons why layoffs have to be handled well.

Whatever the reason for a termination, there are steps you can take as a manager to make it easier for the employee being terminated and for yourself. Again, the main goals are to be fair, and to allow the employee to maintain personal dignity. First, get all the facts ready before you meet with the employee. Prepare a brief explanation of why this particular termination is necessary. Also, prepare a personal statement of what financial and benefit arrangements are being made for the employee. If outplacement services are being offered, have that information ready. Also, try to assess what the employee's reaction might be. If you're about to fire a violent person for cause (like assaulting a co-worker), you might want to have security nearby when you deliver the news. If you're laying off numerous employees, you might want to have outplacement counselors or human resources professionals on hand to meet with people after they've heard about the layoffs.

Second, most outplacement counselors advise managers to give the bad news to terminated employees early in the day and early in the week, if possible. This gives the employee time to meet with a counselor if necessary. (Obviously, this advice probably doesn't apply to employees who are fired for cause.) Third, when you deliver the news, be objective, don't get abusive, be compassionate, and do it quickly, if possible. Fourth, keep all information about the termination private. Never discuss the reasons for a firing with anyone who doesn't have a need to know. The exception to this advice is when numerous layoffs occur. Survivors—co-workers who are left behind—will require some explanation of why layoffs were needed. In this case, you might want to speak about general, never specific or personal, reasons for the layoff.

Terminations for cause don't go unnoticed and the employee grapevine will certainly carry the news of a termination around your organization. And that's a good thing because it's important for employees to understand that bad acts get punished. However, it's generally improper to publicly explain why an individual has been punished; the primary objective is to protect the dignity and privacy of the person who has been punished.

Why are these ethical problems? Hiring, performance evaluation, discipline, and terminations can be ethical issues because they all involve fairness and the dignity of the individual. Rice & Dreilinger[4] say that the desire for justice is a "fundamental human characteristic. People want to believe that the world operates on the principles of fairness; they react strongly when that belief is violated." In fact, the majority of calls to corporate ethics hotlines (discussed more in Chapter 10) relate to just these types of issues.

Costs Much federal legislation exists to protect the rights of individuals in situations which involve hiring, performance evaluation, discipline, and terminations. (See Discrimination—Costs in Chapter 3 for more details.)

There are few accusations as disturbing as one of discrimination, not only to the individuals directly involved, but also to others in the department or on the team. If, as a manager, you're accused of discriminating against an employee, the least you'll endure is an investigation. If your management decides that there's justification for the employee's charge, you may be penalized or even fired. However, many of these cases are not decided by a company's management. Frequently, the first you'll hear of a discrimination charge in hiring, promotion, or termination is from an external lawyer or from a government agency after a lawsuit has been filed against you and your company. If you manage someone who has been accused of discrimination, expect a lot of questions concerning why you were unaware of it or tolerated it. If you were aware of it and didn't do anything about it, be prepared for disciplinary action, particularly if a lawsuit results.

Discrimination lawsuits can be extremely costly for employers—especially if a pattern of discrimination can be established. Depending on the nature of the discrimination, over what period of time it occurred, and how many people are involved, fines and damages can total in the millions. The damage to a company's reputation can be even more costly.

Trend #2—The Diverse Work Force

The second skill set required of the new manager involves positively influencing the relationships among other team members and creating an ethical work environment that enhances individual productivity. Everyone we work with has a range of issues that could affect the ability to perform well. Many people are responsible for children, parents, or other relatives. Many workers have chronic illnesses or conditions or allergies; and those workers who are lucky not to have a chronic condition can suddenly become ill or injured. Other employees have chemical dependencies, such as an addiction to drugs or alcohol. Managers need to be able to accomplish tasks and the mission of a department or team, in spite of the often painful events and conditions that can distract team members.

And since a bias-free person hasn't been born yet, managers also have to be able to counsel team members in their relationships with one another. Since every team will include a wide range of personalities, a manager frequently needs to be a referee—mediating and resolving disputes, assigning tasks to the workers who can best accomplish them, and ensuring that fairness is built into the working relationships of team members.

The examples that follow, while similar to those in Chapter 3, differ because they are written from the manager's, not the individual's, perspective. And, as we said earlier in this chapter, managers have a different level of responsibility.

Diversity

One of your best customers is a very conservative organization—a real "white-shirt" company. Reporting to you is David, a very talented African-American who could benefit greatly from working with this customer account—and the customer account would benefit greatly from David's expertise and creativity. The issue is that David dresses in vibrant colors and wears an African skull cap. Your company long ago recognized David's brilliance, and his dress within the company isn't an issue. But you know your customer would react with raised eyebrows at David's attire.

What is it?   A diverse work force is comprised of individuals of both sexes, and of myriad races, ethnic groups, and religions. The role of a manager is to create an environment where the contribution of each individual can be maximized. Since the population of the United States is remarkably diverse, it makes perfect sense to believe that products and services offered to this population should be developed, produced, and marketed by a diverse work force.

The danger of ignoring this diversity was illustrated during an interview with a chemical company executive. One of the company's products is wallpaper. Even though the wallpaper was of a very high quality and priced competitively, sales were down. This was even more of a mystery since home repairs and renovations—especially by do-it-yourself decorators—were at record numbers.

Baffled by the problem, several senior marketing managers conducted customer surveys and found that the patterns of the company's wallpaper were the problem. The patterns and styles were viewed by consumers as being outdated and old fashioned. The managers then investigated the process by which patterns and styles were selected. What kind of market research was performed before patterns were selected for the next season?

They discovered that, even though more than 90% of wallpaper purchases were made by female consumers, there were no women on the team of chemical company employees who selected patterns for production. All style decisions were made by male employees. The marketing managers and other executives insisted that women and other diverse voices be included on the selection committee. The results were immediate. As soon as the new styles of wallpaper appeared in stores, sales increased substantially.

In the example at the beginning of this section, David's attire could be viewed as problematic by some managers. In this case, and others like it, honesty is probably the best policy. You may want to frankly tell David that you want him to work on this account because his ability would benefit the customer. Perhaps say that the customer is conservative and might be distracted from his ability by his attire. Let David decide how he wants to dress when meeting with the customer. This approach honestly lets David know how his clothing might be interpreted by the client, but it doesn't force him into some narrow corporate box. The point is to balance your interpretation of what a customer might appreciate with David's individuality and diverse voice.

Dress codes tend to raise some people's hackles. The intention of most dress codes is not to restrict individuality, but to ensure a professional appearance in the work place. Ethnic garb shouldn't really be an issue, as long as it's modest. The aim of most dress codes is to eliminate clothing that could be viewed as immodest or too casual to a customer.

Harassment

Your profession has been traditionally a male-dominated one and Marcia is the only woman in your department. Whenever Sam—your senior engineer—holds staff meetings, he and the other males in the department compliment Marcia profusely. They say things like, "It's hard for us to concentrate with a gorgeous woman like you in the room," or "you've got to stop batting your eyelashes at us or the temperature in this room will trigger the air conditioning." They compliment her apparel, her figure, her legs, and the way she speaks. Although flattering, their remarks make her feel uncomfortable. She has mentioned her discomfort to you on several occasions, and you've told Sam and the others to cut it out. They just laughed and told you that Marcia was too sensitive. You think that while Marcia was being sensitive, she did have justification for being upset about her co-workers' remarks.

(For a review of the legal definitions of sexual harassment, please consult Chapter 3.)

Do compliments constitute harassment? They do when they embarrass someone and serve to undermine an individual's professional standing in front of co-workers. In a 1987 survey of 8500 federal government employees, 35% of the women polled said that sexual harassment took the form of offensive remarks.[5] So, Marcia's reaction isn't unusual.

If Marcia is disturbed by the remarks of her co-workers, it's your responsibility as her manager to do something about it. In cases like these, it's sometimes helpful to reverse the situation. Imagine that your department was predominately female, and that the women continually said to the lone male, "You're just a hunk." "We all get aroused when you bat your eyelashes at us." "That's a great suit you're wearing; those slacks really show off your gorgeous thighs." How ridiculous does that banter sound?

One drawback in reversing the situation is that men and women frequently have widely varying perceptions on just what qualifies as sexual harassment. In an 1981 survey of 1200 people in Los Angeles by sociologist Barbara Gutek, 67% of the men said they would be flattered if a female colleague propositioned them; 63% of the women said they would be offended by a proposition from a male colleague. In addition, companies or professions that have a preponderance of male employees have more to worry about. Companies with the lowest percentage of female workers report the highest sexual harassment complaint rate.[6]

In this case, Marcia's discomfort is the issue, and it's irrelevant whether or not you or others think she's being a "little too sensitive." She has already taken the appropriate steps, first by telling her co-workers to stop, and then approaching you when they didn't. You should meet immediately with the members of your department, individually or as a group. You could reverse the situation as in the previous paragraph and show the men how ridiculous their comments would sound if the sex of the players was reversed. Explain to them that inappropriate compliments are not acceptable and anyone who behaves inappropriately in the future will be disciplined. Make it clear that every member of the team has the right to feel comfortable on the team, and be treated with respect. In addition, if you don't act swiftly and firmly, and then back up future offenses with disciplinary action, you may be inviting a lawsuit.

Here's another kind of harassment:

> One of your direct reports, Robert, belongs to a fundamentalist church. While you have no problems with anyone's religious beliefs, Robert is so vocal about his religion that it's becoming a problem with other employees in your department. He not only preaches to his fellow employees, but also he has criticized the attire of some of his female co-workers, and continually quotes the bible in staff meetings. You've received complaints about his behavior from several employees. A few weeks ago, you suggested to Robert that he tone down his preaching, and he reacted as if you were a heathen about to persecute him for his beliefs. His behavior has since escalated.

The job of a manager is to try to maintain a balance between the rights of the individual and the rights of the group—in this case, the attempt by one individual to impose his or her opinions or behavior on other team members. The objectives are fairness and respect for each individual.

In the case of Robert, it appears that he has crossed the line from expressing diverse views to harassment. Although it's important to recognize the value of diverse backgrounds, it's just as important to have an environment where one individual can't constantly attempt to impose his beliefs on other team members. Robert has ignored your requests and those of his co-workers, and has continued his preaching. This kind of behavior will no doubt disrupt the performance of the team and the relationships among team members. In this case, it's probably reasonable to begin documenting Robert's performance since you've already verbally warned him. His hostility and his refusal to respect the opinions of his co-workers and his manager can be viewed as insubordination. In organizations that have a due process approach to discipline, the next step might be a written warning to curb his attempts to influence the religion of his co-workers, or termination will result. Then, if Robert's harassment of his co-workers doesn't stop, he could be fired.

Family and Personal Issues

One of your direct reports is Ellen, who just returned from maternity leave. She now has two children—her infant is four months old and her older child is three years old. Ellen is not only a talented worker, but she's also a wonderful person. Before the birth of her second child, she had no problem handling the workload and the demands on her time—she had a live-in nanny who could care for her child regardless of when she returned home. Recently, however, her live-in left and Ellen is now sending her children to a day care facility with strict opening and closing times. While Ellen is very productive when she's in the office, her schedule no longer has any flexibility—she must leave the office no later than 5:00 p.m. This has caused a hardship to all of her peers who must complete team assignments whether or not she's present. Although you don't want to cause problems for her, the situation doesn't seem fair to her co-workers.

Family and personal issues are those situations and conditions that, while not directly related to work, can affect someone's ability to perform. People simply can't leave their personal and family problems at home. The difficulty in situations like these is achieving a balance between maintaining a worker's job commitment, performance, and attendance with his or her right to privacy and with fairness to co-workers. The yardstick is: if someone is performing well, and his or her attendance is satisfactory, there's probably no cause for action on the part of the manager, beyond offering assistance if the worker wants it.

In Ellen's case, she has a temporary inability to match her co-workers' schedules. Sooner or later, every worker must deal with situations that place limitations on the ability to maintain certain working hours. Similar situations could result from a variety of other causes including illness, family responsibilities, home construction, and commuting schedules. The issue here is fairness in attendance, not performance or productivity. And the ideal solution may be to build more flexibility into the working hours, not just for Ellen, but for the entire team. The ideal solution would involve confronting the problem head-on by asking the people in your area to collaborate and find a solution. For example, you could make an attempt to hold all team meetings in the middle of the day, when everyone can attend. Individual activities could be relegated to the afternoon, so it's not essential that Ellen—or anyone else—stay late to work as a group. If your organization has flexible work hours, you could talk to your manager about the possibility of your area incorporating flexible work schedules, where people could arrive and leave at varying times, but where the office and department would always be covered. The objective is to make life easier for the person and fair for the entire group, and as a result enhance the team's overall productivity.

Personal illnesses and chemical dependencies of employees present a different set of issues. Not only can these situations affect work schedules, but also they can affect an individual's ability to perform. Most corporations have explicit policies for managing employee illness. Generally, employees are guaranteed a specific number of sick days and then go on some sort of disability program. If an employee, however, hasn't received a formal diagnosis and is simply taking sick days, acting erratically, or there's a change in his or her performance, you might suspect a physical or mental illness. Encourage the employee to see a doctor, and consult with the company medical department (if you have one) if you continue to be concerned about an employee's health. It's important to remember that illnesses of any kind—depression, cancer, AIDS—are private and should be kept confidential. These conditions do not cause any danger to co-workers, and many people who suffer from them can resume normal or modified work schedules. Managers can help these employees by protecting the employee's privacy and by being fair and compassionate.

Drug or alcohol abuse is a different matter. Most corporations have policies that prohibit any kind of drug or alcohol use on company premises, and many companies have severe penalties for employees who are caught working under the influence of alcohol or drugs. Both alcoholism and drug addiction are costly in terms of the abuser's health and they can both cause extreme danger in the work place. A corporate bond trader who's high on cocaine can wreak havoc on himself, his employer, and his customers. A pilot who's drunk poses obvious risks to an airline and its passengers. Would you like to ride with a railroad engineer who just smoked a few joints, or have the sale of your home negotiated by a real estate broker who's inebriated, or have your child's broken leg set by a doctor who's on amphetamines?

If you suspect that one of your employees is abusing drugs on or off the job, keep track of any changes in behavior and performance, in writing. (Even if an employee uses drugs or alcohol only off company premises, the residual effects of the substance may affect job performance.) This is an important step because some medications smell like alcohol on the breath, so it's important to be sure that you're dealing with abuse and not a medical condition. Once you're fairly certain that you're dealing with abuse, contact your human resources department. Substance abuse is considered an illness (and generally not a fireable offense—at least in many large corporations) and the employee usually will be counseled by human resources. If abuse is present, most large employers offer substance abuse programs for employees, and will probably insist that your employee participate in such a program. In most large companies, employees are given one or two chances to get clean. If the problem recurs, substance abusers can be terminated. The important issue here is to get fast help for the employee—for the sake of the employee, the company, and your customers.

Why are these ethical problems?   These are all ethical issues because they concern fairness and respect for the individual. A large percentage of the ethical issues that arise in business are human resources related and they can usually be addressed by local managers, who act quickly, fairly, and with compassion.

Costs   The personal, professional, and corporate costs of discrimination and sexual harassment are described earlier in this chapter and in Chapter 3. The costs for mishandling most issues connected to diversity are not clear cut and they're often difficult to quantify. One 1988 study estimated that sexual harassment alone costs the "typical Fortune 500 company $6.7 million a year in absenteeism, employee turnover, low morale, and low productivity."[7] If we could combine all of the fairness issues—performance evaluation systems, harassment, subtle and not-so-subtle discrimination, and how managers handle family, substance, and illness issues—and figure out how much it costs businesses when employees are treated unfairly, the result would probably be astronomical, and not just in financial terms. How many people leave a job because of unresolved problems with a co-worker? How many people choose not to go the extra mile because the organization doesn't treat its employees fairly? How many of the best performers choose to work for a company that allows them flexible hours to care for a child or an aging parent? How many people are depressed and frustrated because they're picking up the slack for a co-worker who's a chronic alcoholic? The toll in human suffering, morale, loyalty, productivity, and lost opportunity is inestimable.

Trend #3—The Buck Stops with You

If we could listen in on managers' prayers, or take a peek at their wish lists, they might very well contain the following desires: "I hope our work is terrific and that we get paid for it; I hope we meet our deadlines; and I hope there's nothing going on that I don't know about that could hit the fan."

As a manager, you'll discover sooner or later that your employees can do a lot. They can bring you glory, they can be alternately fun and frustrating, and they can get you into big trouble. Most managers would dearly love an insurance policy that would protect them from careless, dishonest, obnoxious, or belligerent employees. Unfortunately, we don't know of any insurance company selling that policy just yet.

One investment you can make to try to ensure that nothing will "hit the fan" takes time, effort, and only you can do it. But that is good news: you can do it. Because the buck stops with the manager, you need to actively manage ethics: you need to actively foster good communications, set standards and consistently enforce them, and understand that you are a role model and employees will follow your example.

Boris Yavitz, former dean of Columbia University's Graduate School of Business and a member of several corporate boards, has sage advice for managers. First, communicate your expectations both publicly and privately. Employees are much less likely to disregard a personal challenge—"are we doing it right?"—than they are if they have only seen that expectation expressed in an impersonal policy manual. Second, a manager should prove his or her commitment through personal example. They need to "walk the talk" or no one will take their spoken "expectations" seriously. Finally, since employees are naturally inclined to "protect" managers from bad news, managers should explicitly tell employees that they don't want to be protected. "Tell me everything." The best protection is to communicate loudly and clearly that you don't want "protection."

Communications

Mark was just promoted to head the Power Tool Division of Toolbox Manufacturing Co. Although he has previously worked in other divisions of Toolbox, this promotion is his first exposure to Power Tool. Shortly after he arrives, he discovers that his eight direct reports are scattered all over the division's headquarters location. This means that he can't just walk into their offices without traveling through the whole complex. And if he wants to see one of them, he has to wait for them to arrive from their far-flung offices. So, he makes an executive decision: he decides to create a private, restricted-access, executive building with offices for him, his direct reports, and their staff people. The building will even have a dining room. Then they can all get to know one another and work more efficiently as a team.

Good communication is the very heart of the new, team manager's ethics skill set. Without good communication, it's virtually impossible to encourage ethical behavior. And regardless of where you are in the management hierarchy, if you haven't made effective communication your top priority, you'd better get ready for some big surprises. The Big Truth is: if you don't communicate with your employees, they won't communicate with you. You won't know what's going on; you'll be out of the loop; you'll be ignorant; you'll be inviting an ethical transgression. And in business, ignorance definitely is not bliss.

Communicating with one group of employees isn't enough because you'll know only what's going on with them, and other employee information will be seen thorough the filter of that one group. This is why management "by-walking-around" and "open-door policies" receive so much praise in books about effective, innovative management. Only by listening to many different people, at many different levels, can a manager be knowledgeable about what's going on.

So, in the earlier example, does Mark have a problem? Well, it's admirable that he wants to be close to his senior managers and create an effective senior team. However, he has erected a giant roadblock to effective corporate communications. Essentially he has isolated himself—and the entire senior management team—from the rest of the company, and from the day-to-day decisions that could get the organization into trouble. His isolation has also pretty much ensured that employees are not going to know, much less understand, his expectations concerning their behavior. The isolation factor will also make it extremely difficult for an employee to report wrongdoing. This isn't as serious an issue for the other senior managers as it is for Mark. They have established networks within Power Tool and will presumably continue to visit their employees and friends throughout headquarters. Mark, however, is new to Power Tool, has no network, and has pretty much guaranteed that he's not going to have one aside from the senior managers. In addition, by creating separate quarters and dining facilities for senior managers, Mark has created an elitist environment with haves and have-nots. (For those of you you think no senior executive would be so shortsighted as to behave as Mark did: since 1985, the

CEOs of at least two Fortune 100 companies did exactly what Mark did. Both companies suffered enormous crises in management ranks as a result.)

Although it's usually easier for a senior manager to become isolated than it is for a middle manager (who is getting information from at least two directions), isolation can happen at any level. As Jack Welch,[8] General Electric's CEO, said, "Communication often breaks down in areas of the organization where the impact of change is felt most. I've seen it happen, literally, at the top of some businesses. No level of management has a monopoly on cement, and to make middle management synonymous with a cement layer is a bad rap—and inaccurate."

The importance of face-to-face communication has been documented in a study conducted by General Electric and Hewlett Packard.[9] Employee surveys at both companies have shown that "the better the manager communicates with his or her people on a face-to-face basis, the more satisfied employees are with their work life." General Electric researchers found that employee satisfaction was directly connected to how well managers communicated job performance feedback, complaints, appraisals, compensation, and career objectives. Hewlett Packard's survey produced very similar results and 93% of Hewlett Packard employees rated their manager as the preferred source for company information.

In addition to communicating a company and department mission, how employees' jobs fit into the big picture, benefits, policies, individual performance, objectives, etc., to employees, it's critical that managers communicate—in words and actions—that they're approachable. If a manager is seen as being unapproachable for whatever reason, employees will hesitate to ask questions, or seek clarification about an ethical issue, or alert the manager to an ethical problem. An unapproachable manager has laid the groundwork for being blindsided. The first time he or she may hear about a problem is from human resources, the company lawyer, a senior executive, a government agency, a district attorney, or a newspaper reporter. And since it's a natural inclination for employees to try to "protect" a manager from bad news, managers should flat out tell all employees, "Don't protect me from bad news. I want to know everything." Then, it's important that they *not* shoot the messenger or the first bad news alert they hear may be the last one.

In addition to giving positive reinforcement to employees, it's also important to avoid negative reinforcers. By that, we mean any phrasing that could be interpreted by employees to be license or even approval to misbehave. These phrases include: "I don't care how you do it, just do it," or, "the bottom line is what matters," or, "we have to meet our numbers (or deadline, etc.) at any cost." Phrases like these clearly communicate that a manager doesn't care how activities are accomplished, as long as they're accomplished: the ends justify any means. And they should be stricken out of any manager's vocabulary.

Setting Standards

Mary Ellen is the human resources manager for Little Manufacturing. She's not sure how the main time clock has been repeatedly damaged—by a frustrated employee or by intentional sabotage—but she knows it's expensive to fix. Every time it's repaired, the bill averages $1000. She decides to handle the problem by issuing an ultimatum. She distributes a memo that clearly states that any employee found tampering with the time clock will be fired. Two weeks after the memo goes out, the chief steward of the company's union slams his fist into the clock after he tries several times to get it to punch his card. Five employees and a manager witness his actions.

All organizations have standards. All departments and teams have standards, and managers establish standards. Some standards are written and appear in glossy manuals. Others are not written anywhere, but those may be the standards that are best understood by employees. "You must tell the truth here or you'll be fired," might be a standard, or "Don't rock the boat," or, "Don't tell me how you do it, just do it."

In this case, Mary Ellen—and by virtue of her position, human resources and senior management—are about to have their credibility tested. She has drawn a line in the sand; do not cross it or else. If she doesn't follow through on the "or else," she wasn't serious about the line, right?

Firing the union's chief steward would be messy. There would be protests from the union leadership, hourly employees will probably complain (and maybe hit the time clock), and there might even be a lawsuit. Mary Ellen might lose her job, too. It would be easier to ignore the incident, or make excuses for it, and repair the clock. But messy or not, Mary Ellen may have no choice. If the union's chief steward isn't terminated, a very loud and clear message will go out on the wire: "We may make threats, but we really don't mean them. At least not for people who are important or who might be troublesome."

Mary Ellen's problem began when she issued the ultimatum. If she didn't mean it, she shouldn't have said it. So, is it fair to fire the chief steward for Mary Ellen's mistake? Unfortunately, he knew the consequences of his actions, and he and Mary Ellen have left management little choice. Pick your poison: that steward stays and management loses it's credibility, or the steward goes and management faces the music and a mess with the union. Perhaps the most honorable course in this case is for the company to admit its mistake and convene meetings with the union to resolve the time clock problem and the resulting disciplinary issue. (This is the course the company took where this incident actually occurred. However, management credibility has sunk to a desperate level as a result of this and other incidents, and workers simply do not believe management. Productivity and employee commitment are at rock bottom, and the company is in real danger of going out of business.)

How about the manager of a food processing plant who consistently talks about the importance of customer service: "The consumer should always come first," he says. Then one day, a shipment of food is delivered for processing. The factory equipment is ready to go, the employees are waiting for this delivery, and the food is just this side of spoiled. "It's good enough," he says, "the processing will kill any contaminants and the consumer will never know the difference. We'll lose a lot of money if we don't process something now." What message has he sent to his employees? Suppose a month later, an employee finds a few rodent droppings in a food processing unit. It'll cost a lot of money and time to stop the machinery and clean it. And the food in the hopper right now would have to be destroyed. What do you think the employee will do? Does the customer come first? Or can a corner be cut to save money?

It's important to understand that no matter what you do, you are setting ethical standards. Failing to set standards is in itself a standard since employees will interpret it as meaning there are no standards. In this era of teams and empowered employees, managers certainly need to spell out "how things are going to be done around here." And those ethical standards have to be consistently upheld or employees won't believe them. It's called "walking the talk."

Managers Are Role Models

You manage a department that supports a sales and trading unit in an investment bank. A newly hired employee on your team, Jack, discovers what he thinks is a problem. Jack says he thinks that a salesperson, Will, has designed a very clever way to inflate sales points. Since bonuses can be influenced by sales points, Jack feels that this behavior is cheating. He describes an encounter he had with Will in a local bar; Jack told Will that he was surprised by his little scheme. Will replied, "What I'm doing is perfectly acceptable, and you obviously don't understand how our department works. Anyway, it's none of your business, is it?" When Jack objected, Will waved him off. When you review Will's numbers, you frankly don't see a problem; it looks as if Jack has misinterpreted some of them. But Jack feels strongly that this is an issue and wants to pursue it with the audit department. Will is one of your firm's biggest moneymakers.

Professional basketball player Charles Barkley made sports headlines when he proclaimed, "I'm not paid to be a role model."[10] A colleague on the courts, Karl Malone, responded in an issue of *Sports Illustrated*, "Charles, you can deny being a role model all you want, but I don't think it's your decision to make. We don't *choose* to be role models, we're *chosen*. Our only choice is whether to be a good role model or a bad one." Barkley may not have wanted to be a role model, and some managers may not want to be either. But Barkley and managers *are* role models, by virtue of their position and not their inclinations. Being a role model involves more than simply doing the right thing. It also involves helping your employees do the right thing. A role model inspires employees, helps them define gray areas, and respects their concerns.

In this example, Jack is behaving exactly the way he should if indeed he suspects wrongdoing. He is paying attention to his "gut" feelings about Will's activities, and he feels so strongly about this issue that he's willing to risk his manager's disapproval by pursuing it with the audit department. In this example, Jack's manager has reviewed the situation and has determined the Will's activities are not unethical in any way. Should this be the end of it? Should Jack's manager encourage him to get another opinion?

Managers can provide guidance to employees who encounter ethical dilemmas by encouraging them to assemble all the facts, and then evaluate the situation using any of the tests described in Chapter 4. How would this situation reflect on the company if it was described in a newspaper? Is this situation fair? Does it harm anyone, or violate someone's reasonable expectations? Have all the stakeholders been identified and considered? What does your gut tell you?

In this case, Jack has collected the facts, approached Will for an explanation, and brought the situation to his manager's attention. Even after his manager has found no cause for action, Jack still feels uncomfortable. Probably the most responsible action Jack's manager can take is to offer to go to audit with Jack and try to resolve the issue. By agreeing to accompany Jack in his visit to audit, his manager has sent clear messages to Jack: "First, it's good that you bring issues like this to my attention. Second, I take you seriously, even if I don't particularly agree with you. Third, I trust your instincts and so should you. Fourth, ethics are important to me; they're so important that even if I don't agree with you, I'm willing to pursue the issue with you in order to make you feel more comfortable and to find resolution in case I'm wrong about this." (Since 1990, in at least three Fortune 100 companies, major problems were discovered in just such a manner as this case describes. In all three cases, the problems were discovered by new employees, who were at first rebuffed by their managers, and who uncovered the problem after many people had reviewed the situation for many years.)

Why are these ethical problems?   Actually, effective communications, setting standards, and being a strong role model are not ethical problems. They are techniques managers can use to avoid ethical problems. If done well and consistently, they help to create an environment where workers understand the rules and management's expectations, and are comfortable in raising issues to management, ideally before the issues mushroom into problems.

Costs   Since the skills described in "The Buck Stops with You" are difficult to quantify, they're covered only indirectly by law. However, there are clear legal penalties for managers in the financial industry, who "fail to supervise."

When an ethical or legal problem is found to exist in a team, the manager of that team will be held responsible, regardless of whether the manager knew anything in advance. When a lawsuit against an organization results, many individual managers can be dragged into the suit. In some cases, managers can be sued individually, and in others, managers can be charged for the activities of their employees. Even if no legal action results, a manager's career can be ruined if he or she mishandles a legal or ethical issue.

MANAGING UP AND ACROSS

Gone are the days when a person can advance in an organization by impressing only the next level of management. The new team structures mandate that workers treat everyone well. An example of how some corporations are institutionalizing this approach is an increasingly popular method of performance appraisal which some companies call "360 degree" feedback. This means that not only does a manager appraise a worker, but also co-workers and his or her manager. Feedback of this sort, which comes from all directions, is probably a much more effective barometer of performance than old methods which measure only how well people manage up. Of course, it also means that workers need to carefully consider *all* of their work relationships: up, down, and across. And it's also an indicator of what astute workers have always known: since you never know who you might end up reporting to, or who is going to be crucial to your success in the future, it's critical to effectively manage all of your work relationships.

In team situations, managers can still have a profound impact on your future. They sign off on or approve performance appraisals, pay raises, transfers, and generally are a primary influence on your career mobility and trajectory. It can be difficult to overcome a poor relationship with a manager unless you have solid relationships with individuals on or above your manager's level. That's why it's important for you to cultivate your manager's respect.

Although it may appear that your peers don't have as direct an impact on your career as your manager does, they nevertheless can have a profound effect on your future success. Since you generally "get as good as you give," if you don't cooperate with your peers, they'll probably refuse to cooperate with you, and that lack of cooperation could cripple you. In addition, peers can be promoted to management positions, which can prove to be truly unfortunate if you haven't developed good relationships with them.

Honesty Is Rule One

Michael is a lawyer who reports to Paula, the corporate counsel for a chemical company. During one particularly busy period, Paula asks Michael to prepare a summary of all pending lawsuits and other legal activity for the company's senior management. Since Michael has several court appearances and depositions cluttering his schedule, he assigns the report to one of his paralegals, who completes the report in several days. Since he's so busy, Michael simply submits the report to Paula without reviewing it. When Paula asks him what he thinks of the report, he assures her that he's fine with it. The next day, Paula asks Michael into her office and says that she has found a major omission in the report. Michael has no choice but to admit that he didn't have time to review the report.

There's probably nothing that trips up more people than the temptation to lie or stretch the truth. And there's also probably nothing that will trip up your career faster than a lie or an exaggeration. In business, your reputation is everything, and lying or exaggerating can quickly undermine it.

Michael has basically lied to his manager. Even if he can weasel his way out of the hot seat by saying he didn't have time to thoroughly review the report, he has created an indelible impression with Paula. She may question, not only his future reports, but also his activities in general. Michael could have told Paula up front that he didn't have time to prepare a report. He could have suggested that one of the paralegals prepare it. He could have asked for a time extension so that he could carefully review it. Paula may not have been thrilled with his analysis of the situation, but she probably would have understood and helped him look for another solution. However, by implying that he had completed and reviewed the report, when in fact he hadn't looked at it, Michael has severely damaged his reputation with his manager. A worker's responsibility includes identifying a problem, and then proposing a solution. If you provide a solution when you report a concern, you stand a good chance of having your idea implemented. If you just report an issue with no solution, you'll probably have one imposed on you.

Managers and peers rely on the information they receive from the people who report to them and who work with them. Obviously, that information must be truthful and accurate or someone else's work will be skewed. Once someone has reason to doubt your veracity, it may be impossible for you to recover. As one executive said, "Lying will end someone's relationship with me, period." The caveat is: be completely honest about all aspects of your work, including your ability, the information you provide, and your ability to meet deadlines. Keep your promises.

Standards Go Both Ways

It began when Bruce asked Andy to lie to his wife about his whereabouts. "If Marcia calls, tell her I'm in Phoenix on a business trip," he told Andy. Of course, he had also confided to Andy that in case of an office emergency, he could be reached at a local golf tournament or at a nearby hotel where he was staying with his mistress. Since Bruce was senior to Andy and was a powerful contributor in the department, Andy went along with his request. When Marcia called, Andy told the lie about Bruce being in Phoenix. Bruce asked several more "favors" of Andy, and Andy complied. Then Bruce asked for a big favor: he instructed Andy to inflate monthly sales figures for a report going to senior management. When Andy objected, Bruce said, "Oh, come on Andy, we all know how high your standards are."

Earlier in this chapter, we discussed the responsibility of managers to set ethical standards. It's equally important that workers set ethical standards with their managers and peers. The best way to ensure that you're not going to be asked to compromise your values is to clearly communicate what people can expect from you.

In Andy's case, he made his first mistake by going along with Bruce's lie to his wife. Although it's tempting to help out a colleague—especially one who's powerful and senior to you—you're sliding down a slippery slope when it involves a lie. And the chances are excellent that Bruce would not have asked Andy to lie about the monthly sales figures if he hadn't already known that he could manipulate Andy. If Andy had refused to lie for Bruce on that first occasion, Bruce would probably have vastly different expectations of him. When Bruce asked Andy to lie to his wife, Andy could have replied (with a smile), "Hey, Bruce, don't drag me into that one! I'll tell her you're not in the office, but I'm not going to outright lie to her." Andy could have said it in a nonthreatening way and Bruce probably would have understood. Bruce might even have been embarrassed. But once Andy got caught up in Bruce's conspiracy, Bruce felt he would probably go along with other untruths. The caveat: Say it nicely; say it with a smile; but say it firmly and unequivocally. If a co-worker or manager asks you to betray your standards—even in the tiniest of ways—refuse to compromise your standards or you'll end up being confronted with increasingly thorny dilemmas.

When It's Impossible

John and Maria were peers in a large corporation's marketing department until John accepted a transfer to another area within the company. They had an unusually close working relationship and parted as good friends and colleagues. After John was in his new position, they continued to meet for lunch, and they called one another frequently. Since they had worked so creatively together, it took a while for Maria to adjust to John's absence. In a few months, however, Maria had created a new team in the department and was producing highly acclaimed projects with her new partner. When Maria's manager, Carol, retired, she recommended Maria as her successor. However, the senior manager in charge of the area ignored Carol's recommendation and brought John back as department manager. Now that Maria reports to John, their relationship has changed dramatically. John tries to aggressively manage her in an effort to exert his authority, and the more aggressively he behaves, the more Maria resists, since she feels cheated out of a promotion and resents the dramatic change in his attitude.

It's not unusual in business, to end up reporting to someone you dislike, don't respect, or find it extremely difficult to work with. And perhaps the touchiest situation is one like the case above, where an individual suddenly finds herself or himself reporting to a former peer. This situation is so tricky to manage, that it should be avoided unless the position represents a unique career opportunity.

In Maria's case, her real problem is not only with John, but also with the next level of management, which ignored her ability and contributions, and installed someone else (anyone else) to manage the department. It's a clear signal to Maria that she should either transfer to another area of the company, or look for another job. If she can't or won't look for another position, she's going to have to manage her relationship with John.

Her first step is to stop reacting to John, and ask him for a truce. They both need to negotiate rules for their new working relationship. In the real case on which this example is based, John and Maria didn't negotiate a truce. They talked about one another to co-workers, and in innumerable ways betrayed the relationship they had previously had with one another. The resulting cat fight took a tremendous toll on both of their careers. Their behavior was frowned on by their management chain (even though they had created the problem), and they both looked out of control. They finally left the company, but the period of fighting was an emotionally draining time for both of them.

The lesson to be learned from John and Maria is that it's foolhardy to take things personally. Treat everyone as if you might someday report to them, because someday you might. Those people who can find a way to work with everyone are the people who are most valued by organizations. Negative emotions like jealously, dishonesty, and betrayal will serve no purpose except making the participants look ridiculous to observers. Work is work—you don't have to make love to someone you work with, or live with them, or get so emotionally charged over a situation that you lose control. As soon as you see a relationship start to get out of control, call a truce, discuss the situation, and establish rules for future dealings. If that doesn't work, get out of the situation.

Why are these ethical problems? Honesty is obviously an ethical issue because it involves the truth. Setting standards and knowing how to deal with "impossible" relationships are not ethical problems. They are preventive measures to help you avoid getting caught up in situations which could damage your career.

Costs Honesty, setting standards, and knowing how to handle relationships are critical skills for the establishment of your reputation. As one executive says: "A good reputation is a prerequisite for success. The way to cultivate a good reputation is to be cooperative, do a good job, treat people with respect, keep your promises, meet deadlines, and be accurate and fair in your appraisal of events and activities." Effectiveness at work is all about influence, and reputation is one important key to influence.

WHEN ALL ELSE FAILS—BLOWING THE WHISTLE

A section on managing up and across wouldn't be complete without a discussion of what happens when you suspect a co-worker or your manager has done something very wrong. If their activities are keeping you awake at night, you may have to report it—blow the whistle—and you need to proceed with great caution.

How *not* to blow the whistle might be best illustrated in a case that involves a high-level investment banker who discovered that some of his colleagues were engaged in unethical dealings with several customers. The investment banker brought the situation to the attention of his manager, who told him to forget it. Determined to raise the issue, the banker wrote an irate memo outlining the situation and naming names to his company's CEO. The banker copied the memo to several other top managers. Even though there were only three levels of management between the banker and the CEO, and even though the banker was right about his colleagues and they were eventually fired, the banker was also fired.

In another large, multinational company, a young trainee in an Asian country felt he was being treated unfairly by his local management. In a pique of anger, he wrote a long message outlining his grievances on his company's electronic mail system. Although he addressed his message to the company CEO, president, and head of human resources (all three senior managers were based in New York), he copied everyone else on the system—approximately 30,000 employees worldwide. The trainee was fired, not because of the message, but because of how he communicated it. The head of human resources commented, "He was being groomed for management, and we couldn't have someone with such poor judgment in that role. If he had complained only to senior management, he would have been heard, he would have been protected, and we would have corrected the situation. After copying the world with his complaint, we felt he was a loose cannon and we had no choice but to get him out."

Unless you want to be branded as someone with poor judgment, you have to be very careful about how you raise issues. Usually, the CEO is one of your last resorts, and should be approached only after you've exhausted every other internal resource and are ready to go outside the company to resolve the issue. An exception to this would be in a company like PPG Industries, where the former CEO, Vince Sarni, asked and encouraged employees to contact him directly with issues. A hot line for that purpose sat on his desk, and he personally answered that phone.

So how do you blow the whistle? First, let's talk about when.

When Do You Blow This Whistle?

Let's assume first that your concern involves a serious issue. Reporting the dumping of toxic materials, for example, is a serious issue. One of your colleagues padding an expense report probably isn't. Once you've informed your manager about a fudged expense report, your responsibility is probably fulfilled. However, one colleague fudging an expense report is a far cry from a group of employees systematically altering all of their expense reports with their manager's knowledge. If you suspect something of that magnitude, of course you should report it to someone outside of your chain of command such as your internal auditor.

Many might disagree with this approach, but few people in business have the time to be "on patrol"—once a manager is alerted, it's his or her responsibility to deal with issues like expense reports, except in extraordinary circumstances. This could be termed "picking your battles"—and responding appropriately to your gut feelings. A new approach can help you determine the seriousness of an issue by evaluating its "moral intensity." Thomas Jones,[11] at the University of Washington, theorizes that every ethical issue has six moral components that contribute to moral intensity: magnitude of consequences, social consensus, probability of effect, temporal immediacy, proximity, and concentration of effect. And the more morally intense the situation, the more likely you are to recognize it as a moral issue

Magnitude of consequences   The sum of the harms (or benefits) done to victims (or beneficiaries). For example, a product that causes an allergic reaction in 10,000

people has greater consequences than if the product causes a similar reaction in 10 people.

Social consensus   The degree of social agreement that an action is good or evil. For example, there is probably more social agreement that discriminating against handicapped workers is wrong than there is agreement about affirmatively hiring minority candidates.

Probability of effect   The probability that the action will actually take place *and* will cause harm. For example, a pharmaceutical product that causes extreme dizziness every time someone takes it has a higher probability of effect than a drug that causes dizziness in a few allergic individuals only when it's taken in combination with another drug.

Temporal immediacy   The length of time between now and the onset of consequences. For example, firing 300 employees next Friday has more temporal immediacy than telling 300 employees that they'll be let go in six months.

Proximity   The feeling of nearness (social, psychological, or physical) of the victims. For example, a toxic dump located one mile from your home has greater moral proximity than one located in the next state.

Concentration of effect   This is "an inverse function of the number of people affected by an act of given magnitude." For example, stealing $1000 from one person has a more concentrated effect than stealing $10 from 100 people.

In addition to the moral intensity of a situation, there are other triggers to help you determine if an issue is serious—serious enough to be raised beyond your immediate manager. Some of these triggers include an issue that involves truth, employee or customer (or other stakeholder) rights, trust, harm, your personal reputation, or the reputation of your organization, and whether the law is being broken or compromised. In the toxic dump case, for example, harm could certainly result, customer (and other stakeholder) rights are involved, your organization's reputation is at risk, a public trust may be violated, and law may very well be compromised or broken if you keep quiet about the dumping of toxic wastes. A situation like that has all the earmarks of a serious ethical dilemma.

Suppose your manager asks you to supply inaccurate numbers in a financial report to another level of management. That situation not only involves a breach of truth, but it also involves potential harm and could damage your reputation. It's a serious issue that you'll probably want to report.

How to Blow the Whistle

Let's assume that you're dealing with a serious issue, you've assembled the facts, they're accurate to the best of your knowledge, you've asked you peers or your manager for advice, and there's a law or company policy about to be violated or the moral intensity test indicates a serious problem. Now what?

1. As we've said throughout this book, approach your immediate manager first. If your manager tells you to ignore a situation or belittles your concern approach him or her again. The second time you approach your manager, you may want to write a memo and spell out your concerns in black and white so it's more difficult for your manager to ignore or dismiss them. Frequently, writing a memo will be enough to convince your manager that this is serious and you'll get a more favorable response. You should also do some soul searching to make sure your decision to pursue this issue is an objective one, and not based in any feeling of revenge you might have for your manager, co-workers, or company. Also, you should find out exactly how your company wants issues raised and if there is a special process for doing it. If there is, follow the process to the letter.[12]

Now is the time to discuss the issue with your family. Since any whistleblowing activity can affect not only you, but also your family, it's imperative that your family know what's going on. It's also the time to document your activities. Obtain copies of correspondence that relate to the issue and any memos you've written in an attempt to alert management. It's also a good idea to keep a diary to track activities related to the issue and describe any conversations you've had concerning the issue.[13]

2. If you receive no satisfaction from your manager, it's time to go to the next level of management. The most diplomatic way of going around your manager is to say to your manager something like, "I feel so strongly about this that I'd like a meeting with you and your manager to discuss it." The positive aspect of asking your manager to go with you to the next level is that he or she won't feel betrayed and you'll appear to be a team player. The negative aspect is that your manager may forbid you to approach his or her manager. If that happens, or if you're still not satisfied after meeting with the next level of management, you'll need to consider going outside of your chain of command.

3. If your company has an ethics officer, department, or ombudsman, now is the time to contact that person. It's also a good idea to do some research to find out if your state has any special legislation regarding whistleblowing. Your state may have legislative protection for whistleblowers, but it may require you to follow certain procedures.[14]

4. If your company has no formal ethics department, you'll need to think about areas outside of your chain of command which would be the most receptive to your concerns. If your issue is human resources related—if it involves relationships or activities within your company like discrimination or sexual harassment—approach your human resources officer or department. If the issue is business related—if it involves external relationships such as those with customers, vendors, regulators, etc.—you can still approach human resources, but a better choice would probably be the legal department or your company's internal auditors. Obviously, if the issue involves the law or an actual or potential illegality, you should contact the legal department. And if the issue concerns a financial matter, it's probably better to approach your organization's auditors. Most auditors have a system of internal checks

they can trigger which will confirm or refute your suspicions and even protect you. Also, some auditors in some industries have an underground network of sorts—there are relationships that exist among auditors from various organizations. They can investigate situations very quietly and keep the situation from blowing out of proportion if that's indicated and appropriate.

Since the role of human resources, legal, and audit departments is to protect the corporation, they should be receptive to any concerns which could put the company at risk. If, however, the activity you're concerned about has been approved or condoned by the highest levels of management, these internal departments may go along with "business as usual." And since their role is to protect the company, you are likely to find that their first allegiance is to the company, and not to you.

It's usually safe to approach these departments, but it's not completely without risk. You can reduce the risk if you can persuade one or more of your colleagues to join you in the process. Having an ally can encourage lawyers and auditors to take you more seriously. It may also be wise to consult your personal lawyer at this point in the process. According to Hoffman and Moore[15] he or she can "help you determine if the wrongdoing violates the law, aid you in documenting information about it, inform you of any laws you might be breaking in documenting it, assist you in deciding to whom to report it, make sure reports are filed on time, and help you protect yourself against retaliation."

5. Once you've approached your management, the ethics office (if your company has one), and human resources, legal, and audit, you should have received some satisfaction. The vast majority of whistleblowing cases are resolved at one of those levels.

However, if you're still concerned, the risks to you personally escalate significantly from this point on. Your last resort within your company would be your organization's senior management, including the CEO, President, or Board of Directors. Obviously, you should contact whomever has a reputation for being most approachable. Understand that your immediate management will most likely be irate if you approach senior management. However, if you're right about your concerns, you may end up a big hero if the issue you're raising is a localized problem and senior management is unaware of what's going on.

Before contacting your senior management, be sure to have your facts straight and documented. (This is where a diary and copies of correspondence will be useful.) If you're wrong, few people are going to understand or forgive you. You may be harassed, reprimanded, or penalized, or there may be some pretext found to fire you.

6. If you've raised the concern all the way to the top of your company, still have a job, and are still unsatisfied, your only choice now is to go outside. If your company is part of a regulated industry, like defense contractors and commercial banks, you can contact the regulators who are charged with overseeing your industry. Or you can contact the press.

However, if you've already contacted numerous individuals in your company, it won't take a genius for people to figure out who is talking outside of the company.

Even if you contact the press or the regulators anonymously, your co-workers probably will be able to figure out who's blabbing.

7. There are situations that might be so disturbing to you that you may have no alternative but to quit your job. The toxic dump situation described earlier might just be one of those situations. And frankly, the stress involved in blowing the whistle is so intense that you might consider quitting your job after step 3 or 4. Whistleblowing is so stressful that in one study by Soeken and Soeken (1987), one-third of the whistleblowers surveyed would advise other people not to blow the whistle at all.[16] Many people, however, would find it extremely difficult, and perhaps impossible, to live with certain situations on their conscience. The knowledge of a toxic dump about to poison private wells would probably be almost impossible to live with for most people. When knowledge becomes unbearable, blowing the whistle and ultimately quitting your job may be the only solution.

CONCLUSION

Employees are strongly influenced by the conduct of management. That's why it's so critical that individual managers understand how employees view them, the impact managers can have on how decisions will be made in their area, and that they have the power to create an environment that permits employees to behave ethically. It's equally important that workers appreciate the importance of managing their relationships with the manager and their peers, and how to alert the company's senior executives to wrongdoing in the safest way possible.

DISCUSSION CASES

Employment Basics

You've recently been promoted to a supervisory position and are now responsible for coordinating the work of four other employees. Two of these workers are more than 20 years older than you are, and both have been with the company much longer than you. Although you've tried to be supportive of them and have gone out of your way to praise their work, whenever there is some kind of disagreement, they go to your boss with the problem. You've asked them repeatedly to come to you with whatever issues they have; they just ignore you and complain to other workers about reporting to someone your age. Design a strategy for dealing with these workers and your manager.

Diversity

After two years of sales calls and persuasion, a large, multinational petroleum company—Big Oil Ltd.—decides to sign with your employer, Secure Bank. Since

Big Oil is headquartered in Saudi Arabia and most of the meetings with the client have been in the Middle East, Secure Bank's senior executive in charge of oil and oil products companies—Julie—has not attended. Although the Secure Bank employees who have met with the company have told the Big Oil executives that the lead on their account will be a woman, the news must not have registered, perhaps because of language difficulties. Today, the Big Oil reps are in Chicago to sign on the dotted line and meet with Secure Bank's senior managers, and of course, they've met with Julie. A member of the original Secure Bank sales team calls you to say that Big Oil's senior team member has told him that Julie will not work on their account, period. Because of cultural issues, Big Oil execs are uncomfortable dealing with women from any country. As Julie's manager, what do you do?

Effective Supervision

You return from vacation and find that while you were away, your assistant forged your name to a cash advance to cover the cost of office supplies. Although the purpose of the advance is appropriate, you're frankly shocked that your assistant would forge your signature. How do you handle this employee?

Blowing the Whistle

A young man you manage tells you that one of your female peers has made a sexual advance toward him. Your peer is married, has children, and is a popular and respected department head. The young man is very flirtatious and has mentioned unwanted sexual attention from other women in the company on at least two other occasions. However, this is the first time he has named names and has made what appears to be a "formal" complaint. How do you handle this?

DISCUSSION QUESTIONS

1. How can performance be measured as an ongoing process, and not just as a once-a-year event?

2. Should high performers be allowed to work by rules that are different from those that apply to other workers?

3. Imagine that you're the manager of a facility where 200 layoffs are scheduled. Design an action plan for how the layoffs would occur.

4. Are there ways in which managers can avoid harassment issues among employees who report to them? What would your strategy be?

5. Imagine that someone who reports to you is on a prescription medication that makes this employee's breath smell like alcohol. How would you handle this situation?

6. Design a list of ethical standards you'd implement if you were managing a department of 20 employees.

7. List ways you can establish and communicate your standards to your employees and to your peers.

NOTES

[1]Halper, J. 1988. *Quiet desperation, the truth about successful men*, New York: Warner Books.

[2]Ball, G., Treviño, L. & Sims, H.P. Jr. 1994. Just and unjust punishment incidents: Influence on subordinate performance and citizenship. *Academy of Management Journal*, 37: 299–332.

[3]Rice, D. & Dreilinger, C. 1991. After downsizing. *Training and Development Journal*, May: 41–44.

[4]Ibid.

[5]Deutschman, A. 1991. Dealing with sexual harassment. *Fortune*, November 4: 145–148.

[6]Sandroff, R. 1988. Sexual harassment in the Fortune 500. *Working Woman*, December: 69.

[7]Ibid.

[8]Welch, J. 1989. *Monogram* (G.E.'s employee publication), Fall: 4.

[9]Smith, A. 1991. *Innovative employee communication: New approaches to improving trust, teamwork, and performance.* Englewood Cliffs, NJ: Prentice Hall. 3, 107–108.

[10]Gelman, D. 1993. I'm not a role model. *Newsweek*, June 28: 56.

[11]Jones, T.M. 1991. Ethical decision making by individuals in organizations: *An issue-contingent model*. Academy of Management Review, 16(2): 366–395.

[12]Webber, R. 1989. Whistleblowing. *Executive Excellence*, July: 9–10.

[13]Ibid.

[14]Dunkin, A. 1991. Blowing the whistle without paying the piper. *Business Week*, June 3: 138–139.

[15]Hoffman, W.M., and Moore, J.M. 1984. *Business ethics: Reading and cases in corporate morality*. New York: McGraw-Hill. 257

[16]Miceli, M. & Near, J. 1992. *Blowing the whistle*. New York: Lexington Books. 303.

CHAPTER SEVEN

Managing for Ethical Conduct

INTRODUCTION

MANAGERS NEED simple and practical tools for managing ethical conduct. Therefore, this chapter introduces some basic management concepts that provide a foundation for understanding how to manage for ethical conduct in an organizational setting. Consistent with the focus of the book, each section concludes with practical implications for managers. Underlying our recommendations to managers are several key assumptions:

1) that managers want to be ethical

2) that managers can and should work to develop their own ethical decision-making skills (see Chapters 4 and 5)

3) that, based on their experience, managers will have insight into the unique ethical requirements of the job

4) that managers will want their subordinates to be ethical as well

IN BUSINESS, ETHICS IS ABOUT "BEHAVIOR"

In business, when people talk about ethics, they're talking about "behavior." In this context, ethics isn't mysterious or unusual, nor does it depend on the individual's innate goodness, religious conviction, or understanding (or lack thereof) of esoteric philosophy. People find themselves in work situations every day where they're faced with questions of right and wrong where values are in conflict. Should I hire, fire, promote, or demote this individual? Should I offer or accept a gift in this or that situation? How should I respond when my supervisor asks me to act against my own beliefs?[1]

The study of ethical behavior in business has to do with understanding the factors that influence how people behave in these situations. Although we've seen that internal factors such as individual moral development are important, ethical conduct depends, to a large extent, on such external factors as the rules of the context they're in, the reward system, what their peers are doing, what authority figures expect of them, the roles they're asked to play, and more. We're going to focus on these external factors because they're the ones that managers can influence the most. Once managers understand how management principles apply to ethical conduct, they can manage ethical behavior more proactively and effectively. On the other hand, if managers fool themselves into thinking that ethical conduct is determined exclusively by some mysterious character trait, they'll throw up their hands and walk away from situations that they could proactively manage. Or they'll think that by simply getting rid of a "bad apple," unethical conduct won't recur. This kind of thinking is a copout. Unethical behavior is rarely as simple as a "bad apple." It's often something about the work environment that allows the bad apple to behave badly. And the work environment is something that managers can influence.

Practical Advice for Managers

What are the practical implications for managers? First, think of ethics in concrete behavioral terms. Specifically, what kind of behavior are you looking for in your subordinates and how can you create a context that will support ethical conduct? Specifying concrete goals for ethical behavior means going beyond abstract statements like, "integrity is important around here" to more concrete statements such as, "I expect sales representatives to be absolutely honest with our customers about such things as the characteristics of our products and our ability to deliver by a certain date." Finally, it's the manager's responsiblity to create a work environment that supports ethical behavior and discourages unethical behavior just as much as it's the manager's responsibility to manage for productivity. Don't just set ethical behavior goals. Follow up to make sure that they're being met and model ethical conduct yourself. Your people will pay more attention to what you do than to what you say. Take advantage of opportunities to demonstrate the ethical conduct you expect.

OUR MULTIPLE ETHICAL SELVES

To understand ethics at work, we must understand that people are socialized to accept different behavior depending upon the context. Cultural anthropologists have known for years that we have multiple selves and that we behave differently depending upon the situation we confront.[2] Children in our society are taught very early that it's allright to be loud and boisterous on the playground, but they must be reverent at the church, synagogue, temple, or mosque. Table manners are important when visiting, but eating with one's fingers may be acceptable at home. As adults, we play highly differentiated roles, and we assume that each social context presents different behavioral expectations. Football players are expected to tackle each other deliberately and aggressively on the playing field, a behavior that they would be arrested for on the street. Businesspeople are expected to be aggressive against competitors, but gentle with their spouses and children. Game jargon is often applied to business dealings—like the term "playing field"—which makes the business dealings less subject to moral scrutiny. One "bluffs" and conceals information in business negotiations the same way one "bluffs" in a poker game. "Bluffing" sounds a lot better than lying, and the game analogy helps to distinguish business behavior from morality in other situations. So, although we might prefer to take a single ethical self from situation to situation, reality suggests that most people are willing to accept different rules for different contexts. All of this means that we can have multiple ethical selves.

The Dennis Levine example.   Dennis Levine's personal account of his insider trading activities suggests multiple ethical selves. He described himself as a good son, husband, and father, and a man who had been encouraged by his parents to "play straight." "I come from a strong, old-fashioned family . . . [my father] taught me to work hard, believe in myself, and persevere . . . as a kid I always worked."[3] Levine's wife, Laurie, had no idea that he had been secretly and illegally trading in stocks for years. In fact, the family lived in a cramped, one-bedroom apartment for nearly three years after his son was born despite his huge insider trading profits. So, the fact that someone is "from a good family" or is "a family man or woman" is no guarantee of ethical behavior in the office. At the office, the manager is dealing with the "office self" who may be very different from the "family self" or the "religious self" where the expectations and norms are different.

Levine was a good son, husband, and father. But he separated his family self from his insider trading self. Why was his insider trading self allowed to exist? We can only speculate that this office self fit into an environment where peers were engaging in insider trading and no one was getting caught. Most important, his continuing huge profits led him into a downward spiral of unethical behavior that he found difficult to stop despite his recognition that it was illegal.

Practical Advice for Managers

So what should managers do? The ideal is to make the organizational environment one that supports ethical conduct and "integrity." Integrity is defined as that quality or state of being complete, whole, or undivided. So the ultimate goal is to bring these multiple ethical selves together—to support the idea that a business person can be equally ethical at the office and at home. But managers should pursue that goal with the practical understanding that many people find it quite possible to divide themselves into multiple ethical selves.

Begin by analyzing yourself. Get to know your own office ethical self. Is it consistent with your personal ethical self? If not, what will be required to bring the two together? Again, you're an important role model for your subordinates. If you're clearly a "whole" person of integrity, they're more likely to aspire to "wholeness" themselves.

Then, be realistic. When thinking about your subordinates, make no assumptions about ethics at work based upon a person's background, religious affiliation, family life, or good deeds in the community. Instead, find out what norms and expectations guide their office selves and make sure that they support ethical behavior. You can learn a great deal simply by keeping your eyes and ears wide open. But the best way to find out how your people think about these issues is to ask them, either in person or in survey form. You may be surprised what they'll tell you. And you're sending an important symbolic message about what concerns you just by asking. Do they feel, as many surveys have suggested, that they must compromise their personal ethics to get ahead in your organization? If so, what do they think can be done about it?

Find out what influences their thoughts and behavior in ethical dilemma situations. Find out what inhibits them from being the best they can be—from doing the right thing. You can base your questions on real or hypothetical situations. Most supervisors have never bothered to ask the question. Is it any wonder then that most subordinates end up believing that their managers don't really care about ethics? Once you've had this type of discussion, it's essential that the organization follow up in ways that support ethical conduct. A number of practical ideas for how to do that follow.

REWARD SYSTEMS

People Do What's Rewarded and Avoid Doing What's Punished

Reward systems are probably the single most important formal influence on people's behavior at work. Ask any manager about reward systems and he or she can probably recite a few basics recalled from a college psychology or management class. For example, most of us remember something about **reinforcement theory**—*people are more likely to behave in ways that are rewarded and they're less likely to do what's punished.* That seems simple enough. But we often fail to recognize the power of these simple concepts. People in work organizations are constantly on the lookout for information about rewards and punishments—especially if this information isn't explicit. In fact, the more ambiguous the situation, the more people search for clues. They know that to be successful at work they'll have to determine what's rewarded and do those things while avoiding behaviors that are punished.

How Reward Systems
Can Encourage Unethical Behavior

The electronics appliance sales example. How does this simple idea apply to the management of ethical and unethical behavior? Imagine an employee in an electronic appliance store who works on a modest salary plus commission basis. In other words, the sales people are paid a percentage on the items they sell. The company frequently advertises specials on certain television models in the local newspaper and, of course, people come into the store asking about those models. But because of the lower profit margin on these sale items, the company also lowers the commission that sales personnel receive on these models. The higher rewards (higher commissions) come with sales of models that aren't on special. The company prefers to sell the higher-priced models, but advertises the lower-priced ones to get customers into the store. In fact, the company has set sales goals for each salesperson, with higher goals for the higher-priced models. The company offers little sales training. New salespeople spend a day or so working with the store manager and then they're pretty much on their own. The manager doesn't seem to care how sales are made— just that they are made. The manager's commissions are based on store sales.

If the sales people value money (and their jobs), and the assumption is that they do, they'll be motivated to sell the higher-priced models. They can do this in a variety of ways. For example, they might simply point out that some of the models not on special have features that the sale models don't have. Some customers will probably listen to the advice and buy the more expensive models. As buyers listen and go along, the connection between selling higher-priced items and positive outcomes (commissions, praise) strengthens and the motivation to sell more of these items grows.

But there are still probably lots of folks who insist on buying the sale models. To sell more of the higher-priced models, the salesperson might be tempted to discuss the importance of features (only available on the higher-priced models) that the customer doesn't really need. The salesperson may try this and find that a good number of people go along. There are more rewards—more money, praise from the manager—and no obvious negative outcomes. This behavior can even be justified or at least rationalized. These customers are getting features they wouldn't otherwise get, right?

Things are going so well that the salesperson might now be tempted to go a bit farther—perhaps playing with the controls to make it look as if the picture on the sale TV is a bit fuzzier than the picture on the more expensive models. That makes it even easier to sell the more expensive models.

Explained this way, the connection between rewards and unethical behavior seems pretty clear. Although no one was explicitly telling sales people to be unethical, the opportunity was there, management set higher sales goals for higher-priced models, and rewarded the sale of these models with higher commissions. The store manager didn't seem to care how the sales got made and didn't object to the salesperson playing with the controls to deceive customers.

The goal was to sell higher-priced models. But the exclusive focus on goals frequently obscures the means to the goal—how you get there. If managers are concerned about ethical conduct, it's essential that they also focus on how the goal is being achieved. They must let their subordinates know that they're interested in means as well as ends. If individuals are rewarded for meeting goals no matter what methods are used, they're much more likely to try methods that cross over the ethical/unethical line.

Many people have told us of their experience with managers who make a statement something like the following, *"I don't care how you do it, just do it."* Or, *"I don't want to know how you meet the goal, just meet it."* These statements are clearly giving permission to use any means necessary (ethical or unethical) to meet the goal. Managers who have uttered these words shouldn't be surprised to find that unethical behavior is often the result.

Practical Advice for Managers about Rewards

Here's the key for managers. People do what's rewarded. And these rewards don't have to be explicit. The company in our example would probably never have dreamed of saying that they were rewarding sales persons for being unethical. In fact, they weren't doing this explicitly. But, if the designers of the motivational plan had thought carefully about the plan's *potential* effects, they might very well have identified its fatal flaw—it focused on ends only and left it to the salespeople to figure out the means (how to accomplish the goals). Managers are more likely to identify these flaws in advance if they put themselves in their employees' shoes. Think about what an individual would be likely to do given the reward system that's in place or the one that's being recommended. What kinds of attitudes and behaviors are being rewarded explicitly or implicitly? How can you find out? Ask your staff. If you have good open communication with them, they'll tell you.

Finally, think about the goals you have set. Have you set goals for ethical conduct (e.g., honesty) as well as for bottom-line performance (e.g., number of TVs sold)? We believe in the *ethical pygmalion effect*. In tests of the more general pygmalion effect, researchers have found that people in school and work settings generally live up to the expectations that are set for them, whether high or low. Students and workers perform better in response to a teacher's or supervisor's high expectation. With the *ethical pygmalion effect*, expectations for ethical behavior are set high and people are expected to fulfill them. This ethical pygmalion effect appeals to people's desire to do what's right. It is also likely to get people to think about how they achieve their goals, not just whether they've achieved them.

Recognize the Power of Indirect Rewards and Punishments

It's equally important to recognize that workers don't have to be individually rewarded for the message to have an impact. An extension of reinforcement theory is **social learning theory**.[4] According to social learning theory, people also learn from observing the rewards and punishments of others. Recall that we said that workers are constantly on the lookout for information about rewards and punishments. But they don't have to experience the reward or punishment themselves in order for these to have their reinforcing effects. If they see that others get away with lying, cheating, or stealing, they're more likely to try these behaviors themselves, especially if the behaviors are personally rewarding.

The Tailhook example.   As an example of how people learn about rewards and punishments from observing others, think about the 1992 Tailhook scandal in the U.S. Navy. According to many insiders, the type of sexual harassment (of some 90 women) that occurred in the Las Vegas Hilton had been implicitly rewarded (or at least not punished) in the Navy for some time. These harassment rituals were regular events that the male participants experienced as fun (rewarding). And the Navy brass was known to turn a blind eye to reports, responding with a "boys will be boys" attitude. Investigations were torturously slow and resulted in little, if any punishment. The reward system became well known in the Navy and therefore the men continued to engage in "rewarding" behaviors that weren't punished.

Many (especially women) looked to the Navy's reaction to the Tailhook scandal as an opportunity to change the messages being sent about acceptable and unacceptable conduct in the Navy. Some early signs were encouraging, but the longer term results were disappointing. The Secretary of the Navy resigned his post at the outset of the scandal. The Navy's top admiral was asked to resign, but his job was saved by the Secretary of Defense. Investigations of potential criminal misconduct were also launched. However, the Navy's discussions with 1500 men resulted in only two suspects. When the Pentagon took over, 140 fliers were accused of indecent exposure, assault, or lying under oath. However, only 80 of these individuals were ever fined or even moderately disciplined. Perhaps most significant, in early 1994, the young woman who filed the first complaint, Lt. Paula Coughlin, resigned from the Navy, explaining that Tailhook "and the covert attacks on me that followed have stripped me of my ability to serve."[5] The Navy's top admiral, Frank B. Kelso, retired two months early "with a flowery note from the Defense Secretary praising him 'as a man of the highest honor and integrity.'" Lt. Coughlin left amid "rumormongering by officers trying to impugn her credibility" and with a "stack of hate mail."[6]

The message to Navy men (and women) remains mixed. Yes, the event has caused a lot of turmoil, perhaps enough to suggest to Navy men that assaulting their female colleagues isn't as "rewarding" as it used to be. And, sexual-harassment sensitivity training is now required in the U.S. Navy. But, the fact remains that 90 women were assaulted and none of those responsible were court-martialed or seriously disciplined. As a result, observers are likely to wonder whether anything worse would happen to them if such an activity were to reoccur. Finally, women in the Navy have learned that if you report sexual assault, you may be the one to resign, not your attacker.

Managers, take note of the messages you're implicitly sending to all of your workers by what you reward and punish (or fail to punish). Employees are constantly on the lookout for these cues. They want to know what's OK and not OK in your work environment. If they observe that people advance by stepping on others, by lying to customers, and by falsifying reports, they'll be more inclined to do so themselves. On the other hand, if unethical individuals are dismissed, and persons of integrity advance, the ethical lesson is also clear. Integrity is valued around here and unethical behavior won't be tolerated.

Can You Really Reward Ethical Behavior?

Reward systems assume the use of rewards **and** punishments. However, for years, management writers have preached that managers should use rewards whenever possible—that punishment is inherently a bad management practice. This idea, good as it sounds, may be impractical when the goal is to encourage ethical behavior and discourage unethical behavior. Relying on rewards means rewarding ethical behavior. So, let's think about how a manager might reward ethical behavior. Perhaps s/he could give awards or bonuses to those whose expense reports were honest and accurate or to those managers who didn't harass their secretaries. Ridiculous? Of course. Workers don't expect to be rewarded for behaviors that are expected of everyone—for simply doing the right thing. So in the short term it's quite difficult to reward ethical behavior.

In the long term, yes.   On the other hand, if we switch to longer term thinking, there may be rewards for doing the right thing. For example, in most organizations people are aware of how one gets ahead. Do people get promoted despite ethical lapses? If so, the message is clear. If you want to get ahead around here, you have to do whatever it takes. People who make it are likely the ones who've decided to go along to get along or, worse yet, the ones who stepped on others to get ahead. Or, are those who have advanced to the highest levels known for their integrity? If so, a general message about the importance of integrity is being sent. So, rewards are a limited tool for influencing specific behaviors today or tomorrow, but they can certainly set the tone for what's expected and rewarded in the long term.

What About Punishment?

As for punishment, we all know that managers sometimes have to discipline their subordinates, just as responsible parents are expected to discipline their children. It's part of the manager's job to guide an employee who is headed down the wrong path. We also know that punishment works. If people expect their misconduct to be detected and punished, they're less likely to engage in it. So, if it works, why not use it? Well, it turns out that punishment works best when it's carried out in a particular way—when workers perceive it as fair.

If we examine the idea that punishment should be avoided, we find that it's based on old psychological research that was conducted on rats and small children. It has little to do with adults in work settings who can distinguish punishment that's *fair* (i.e., punishment that is deserved and fairly administered) from punishment that's unfair. Have you ever heard an adult say, "I had it coming, I deserved it"? As Dennis Levine said of his arrest and imprisonment for insider trading, "I've gained an abiding respect for the fairness of our system of justice . . . When I broke the law, I was punished. The system works."[7] He also said, "my former life was destroyed because I figured the odds were 1000 to 1 against my getting caught."[8] If he had thought he would be caught and punished, the odds would have been reversed and he may never have cut an insider trading deal. Once caught and punished, he acknowledged that the punishment was just.

Punishment should be administered fairly. Research evidence[9] suggests that punishment results in more positive outcomes (e.g., the behavior improves and the employee becomes a better corporate citizen) if the receipient perceives it to be fair. These positive outcomes are linked primarily to the appropriate severity of the punishment and employee input. The punishment should "fit the crime" and it should be consistent with what others have received for similar infractions. It's also important that you give the employee an opportunity for input—to explain his or her side of the story. Also, the disciplined worker is more likely to respond positively to the punishment if you approach it in a constructive fashion, carefully explain the reasons why and if you punish in private. Punishment can be a humiliating experience and public punishment adds insult to injury. Therefore, to make punishment a more productive process that's perceived to be fair, be constructive, provide a good explanation that ties the punishment to the misconduct, conduct the punishment in private, and most importantly, give the employee input, and take care to ensure that the severity of the punishment "fits the crime."

Recognize punishment's indirect effects. However, the punished employee should not be the manager's only concern. Social learning theory suggests that other workers will be powerfully affected as well. Remember, we learn a great deal from observing the rewards and punishments of others. But, if the punishment occurs in private, how will others know about it? Anyone who has worked in a real organization knows about the "grapevine," the communication network that flashes organizational news throughout a department or organization. Good managers are aware of the power of the grapevine and rely on it to transmit important information. And, research has discovered that when people are aware that unethical behavior has taken place, they want the violators to be punished.[10] The idea here is that people want to believe that the workplace is "just"—that good guys are rewarded and bad guys are punished. They also want to feel that they aren't suckers who, in a sense, are being punished for following the rules when others get away with breaking them. This is an important reason why managers must discipline unethical behavior when it occurs. By doing so, they not only send an unequivocal message to the violator and all observers that this behavior won't be tolerated, but they support the notion that this is a just place to work where the rules are enforced fairly.

The Thomas J. Watson, Jr.—IBM example. In *Father Son & Co.; My Life at IBM and Beyond*, Thomas Watson, Jr. discussed the importance of swift, severe punishment for breaches of integrity and the indirect effects of punishing or not punishing. Watson said, "If a manager does something unethical, he should be fired just as surely as a factory worker. This is the wholesome use of the boss's power." But, as he explains in the following excerpt from his book, his managers didn't always follow his advice.

> On one occasion some managers in one of our plants started a chain letter involving U.S. savings bonds. The idea was that one manager would write to five other managers, and each of those would write to five more, who would each send some bonds back to the first guy and write to five more, and so on. Pretty soon they ran out of managers and got down to employees. It ended up that the employees felt pressure to join the chain letter and pay off the managers. I got a complaint about this and brought it to the attention of the head of the division. I expected him to say, at a minimum, "We've got to fire a couple of guys, I'll handle it." Instead, he simply said, "Well, it was a mistake." I couldn't convince him to fire anybody. Now, you could admire him for defending the team, but I think there is a time when integrity should take the rudder from team loyalty. All the same, I didn't pursue the matter any further, and my failure to act came back to haunt me.
>
> A couple of years later in that same division, a manager fired a low-level employee who had been stealing engineering diagrams and selling them to a competitor. Firing him would have been fine, except that the manager handled it in a brutal way. The employee in question had one thing in his life that he was proud of—his commission in the U.S. Army Reserve, where he held the rank of major. Instead of simply going to the man's house and telling him, "You swiped the drawings and we're going to fire you," the manager picked a week when the fellow was in military camp to lower the boom. Somehow the military authorities got involved as well and the man was stripped of his commission. The humiliation caused him to become insanely angry, and for the next few years he devoted himself to making me uncomfortable. He sent pictures of Tom Watson Jr. behind bars to his senators and his congressman and to every justice of the Supreme Court. And he kept harking back to that chain letter, because he knew we had tolerated the men responsible for it. Eventually he simmered down, but the incident really taught me a lesson. After that I simply fired managers when they broke rules of integrity. I did it in perhaps a dozen cases, including a couple involving senior executives. I had to overrule a lot of people each time, who would argue that we should merely demote the man, or transfer him, or that the business would fall apart without him. But the company was invariably better off for the decision and the example.[11]

Practical Advice for Managers about Punishment

Tom Watson learned the hard way what can happen when breaches of integrity aren't disciplined swiftly and severely. Workers have long memories about incidents such as the chain letter and how management handled them. They tuck that sort of information away for later use. When the employee who stole the engineering drawings was fired in a particularly humiliating way, he was outraged. His severe and public punishment seemed particularly unfair when compared with the way others had been treated. And he reacted in ways that managers are told to expect from punished employees. He was angry at the punisher and the organization.

The important point about punishment is that adults differentiate between fair and unfair punishment. If you use punishment consistently to enforce the rules, employees will expect to be punished when they break them. However, they expect punishment that fits the crime and that's consistent with how others have been treated. In most cases, if you impose discipline fairly, the problem behavior improves and the subordinate goes on to be a productive organizational citizen.

Finally, remember that you should be concerned about observers who pay a great deal of attention to how rule violations are handled. When the chain letter offenders weren't severely punished, an implicit message was sent to all who were aware of the scheme and expectations were set up for how management would respond to future breaches of integrity. A "just" organization is one that punishes rule violations fairly and consistently. Workers expect managers to do this and they're frequently morally outraged when management doesn't do its job.

"EVERYONE'S DOING IT"

People Follow Group Norms

"Everyone's doing it" is the refrain so frequently used to encourage (and rationalize or justify) unethical behavior. We've all heard it. From fraternity brothers who are expected to advise their peers about the content of exams, to college football players who accept booster money, to waiters and waitresses who don't claim all of their tip income for tax purposes, to auditors who sign off on financial statements that haven't been thoroughly checked, to insider traders who share secrets about upcoming financial deals, individuals are much more likely to engage in unethical behavior if they're convinced that others are doing it. It lets them off the hook by providing an acceptable justification and rationale for the behavior.

Rationalizing Unethical Behavior

There are at least two dynamics that may be operating here. For some behaviors, the refrain "everyone is doing it" is used primarily as a rationalization. The employee who inflates his or her expense reports feels that it's justified first because everyone else is doing it (and getting away with it, too). This group may develop other reasons to bolster the rationalization process. For example, inflating expenses may be explained in the group as a way of compensating for the extra hours spent away from home, to pay for the drink at the bar or a movie, and other expenses that aren't deductible under the organization's travel cost reimbursement policy. These rationalizations are often explicitly or implicitly supported by the boss who suggests the behavior or who engages in it himself or herself. Either way, the manager sends a powerful message that it's okay to bend the rules, a message that can easily be generalized to other rules in the organization.

A better way to manage the process is to state the rules clearly and then enforce them. In other words, if it seems reasonable to reimburse a traveling employee for a drink at the bar, a movie, or a telephone call home, then change the rules so that these expenses can be legally reimbursed under the organization's travel policy. Then abuses of the system can be disciplined.

Pressure to Go Along

For other behaviors, the "everyone is doing it" refrain represents not just a rationalization but actual pressure to go along with the crowd. The argument is used to encourage those who are reluctant. "Aw, c'mon everybody does it!" Not going along puts the individual in the uncomfortable spot of being perceived as some sort of "goody goody" who is highly ethical but also highly unlikable, and certainly not someone who can be trusted. The result can be ostracism from the group and most of us would rather go along than be ostracized.[12] Many individuals will go along with unethical behaviors because of the strong need they have to be accepted. If left to their own devices, they might very well follow the rules. But, in the group situation, they feel that they have no choice but to comply or at least remain silent about what others are doing.

Practical Advice for Managers

So what does this mean for the manager? Above all, you must be acutely aware of the power of group norms that may be consistent or inconsistent with the formal, written rules. They represent what's really happening in the group and you must be in touch with this reality. Any new employee brought into a group will be quickly schooled in "the way we do things in this group" and will be expected to go along. Loyalty to the group may be the most powerful norm and one that's extremely difficult to counteract. If the group norms support ethical behavior, you have no problem, but if they don't, you face a particularly tough situation. If the group is strong and cohesive, one approach you can use is to identify the informal group leader and attempt to influence that individual, hoping s/he will influence the others. It's also important to consider the reward system. Norms often arise to support behaviors that are implicitly rewarded. If people are doing something, it's usually because they find it rewarding and the system somehow encourages it. Changes in the reward system can lead to changes in group norms.

The Slade Company case example.   A classic Harvard Business School case explains how a highly productive manufacturing work group with a strong informal leader has created a problematic group norm for punching in and out. After the foreman leaves, all but one of the group members go home. The one person remaining behind punches out all of the other group members. The result is that group members are paid for more hours than they actually work. On occasion, when a group member is delayed in the morning, the group punches him in. But this is carefully controlled and the group has developed norms so that it's not abused. Although the punch-out practice seems to be clearly wrong, the case is complicated by the fact that management admits that although pay is low, productivity in the group is high. Furthermore, the group is highly cohesive and very willing to work hard when necessary to fulfill last-minute orders or to solve unusual production problems. The workers also value the ability to have some control over the work day. Finally, management has known about the practice for some time and has ignored it.

The solution to the case isn't clear cut. The case writers have suggested that management might be better off leaving well enough alone. "If it ain't broke, don't fix it." However, we believe that this is impossible if the ethical dimensions of the case are brought into focus. Leaving it alone implies tacit acceptance and approval of rule breaking and sends that message not only to this work group but to all of the others. Other groups that, for some reason, can't manage to do the same (perhaps because of less cohesion or because their supervisor stays later) will no doubt resent the injustice. Management must also accept some responsibility for tacitly approving this over a long period of time.

Remembering that people do what's rewarded, we believe that the norm is most likely to change via changes in the reward system. For example, moving to a five-day salary (somewhat higher than their current average take home pay) rather than hourly pay would reward people for getting the job done rather than staying a certain number of hours on weekdays. Group members could still be paid extra for weekend overtime work when it's available. If the late-arrival norm isn't being abused, it could be institutionalized. If someone must be late, a new rule could state that they must inform someone in the work group by a certain time. Like absences, a certain number of late arrivals would be allowed within a specified time period. The informal group leader should be involved in devising the solution with an appeal to his or her concern for fairness to other workers in the organization.

PEOPLE FULFILL <u>ASSIGNED ROLES</u>

Roles are strong forces for guiding behavior and workers are assigned roles that can powerfully influence their behavior in ethical dilemma situations. Roles can reduce a person's sense of his or her individuality by focusing attention on the role and the expectations that accompany it. It doesn't really matter who fills the role. It's the role requirements that are important. This focus on the role reduces the individual's awareness of the self as an independent individual who is personally responsible for an outcome. This psychological process is called *deindividuation*[13].

So, the individual acts "in role" and does whatever is expected. This is fine when behaving "in role" means doing the right thing. But, what happens when "in role" behavior involves behaving illegally or unethically? For example, some might argue that the police officers in the Rodney King beatings in Los Angeles were behaving "in role." Aggression has become a necessary part of the police officer's role in this country. Another important part of the police officer role is loyalty to other police officers and protection of one's peers. Police officers often travel in pairs and must rely on each other in difficult, life-threatening situations. Therefore, loyalty, protection, and trust within the ranks serve an important, positive purpose. But, loyalty can also end up supporting unethical behavior when, for example, a fellow police officer is unnecessarily aggressive and isn't reported.

The Cagney and Lacey Example

In an old "Cagney and Lacey" television segment, Cagney and Lacey (two female police detectives) were part of a stakeout to catch one of their fellow police officers stealing heroin. They realized that they faced a complex moral dilemma when he told them that he was stealing the heroin for his mother who was dying of cancer and in severe pain. He had clearly broken the law and the rules clearly said that they must turn him in. But, loyalty and protection were important parts of their role. Their colleague clearly had good intentions—to help his dying mother. After much discussion and individual soul searching, they decided to protect their colleague and keep silent about what they knew . Although we may disagree about whether they made the right decision, the point here is that the peer protection and loyalty aspects of the police officer role were clearly an important part of that decision.

The Zimbardo Prison Experiment

A powerful and widely cited social psychological study illustrates the power of roles to influence behavior. The researchers[14] created a prison environment in the basement of the psychology building at Stanford University. Twenty-four psychologically healthy subjects (people like us) were recruited and randomly assigned to play the roles of prisoners or guards. General rules were provided regarding how to fulfill the role, but subjects were left free to interact within those general guidelines. With the cooperation of the local police, the guards were actually sent out to arrest the prisoners, book them, and transport them to their simulated cells. The prisoners were given uniforms and were referred to by identification numbers. The guards were given comfortable quarters and a recreation area. The guards wore uniforms and silvered sunglasses, and worked standard eight-hour shifts where they were given a great deal of control over the prisoners, short of physical abuse. With rare exceptions, the guards enjoyed the social power and status of the guard role. Some "guards" were exhilarated by the experience, reinforcing their guard role with aggression, threats and insults. The "prisoners" quickly began to show dramatic signs of emotional change, including acute anxiety, helplessness, and passivity verging on complete servility. Some became severely distressed and physically ill.

Although the experiment was originally scheduled to last two weeks, it was halted after only six days. "At the end of only six days . . . it was no longer apparent to most of the subjects (or to us) where reality ended and their roles began. The majority had indeed become prisoners or guards, no longer able to clearly differentiate between role playing and the real self. There were dramatic changes in virtually every aspect of their behavior, thinking and feeling."[15]

After the experiment was concluded, guards expressed a combination of excitement and dismay at the darker side of themselves that had emerged. The simulated situation had become real very quickly and both sides readily assumed the roles expected of them as members of their respective groups (prisoner or guard). This occurred despite the other roles these individuals may have played in their "normal" lives just days before. Finally, when individuals attempted to deviate from the role behavior, the deviation was quickly suppressed by pressure to conform expressed by other group members. The experimental results were used to support the "situational" explanation for prison behavior. In other words, perfectly normal people behaved cruelly and aggressively when placed in a role where these behaviors were either expected or allowed.

Roles at Work

But prisons aren't your average work setting. How do the results of this experiment apply to work organizations? People enter work organizations in a state of "role-readiness."[16] In this state, they're likely to engage in behaviors that are consistent with their organizationally prescribed role, even if those behaviors violate other values they hold (another example of multiple ethical selves). A particularly interesting example is provided by corporate professionals such as lawyers and physicians. Professionals are thought to adhere most closely to their professional roles. In fact, this is part of the definition of a professional. Although there's little research evidence, much anecdotal evidence suggests that many corporate physicians or lawyers identify more closely with their organizational role. For example, Johns-Manville medical personnel conformed to corporate policy and remained silent, despite the known medical dangers of asbestos exposure.[17] In their dual roles of physician and organizational member, the latter took precedence.

Conflicting Roles Can Lead to Unethical Behavior

In their jobs, people play different roles that may make competing demands on them, causing internal conflict and stress that may be resolved via unethical behavior such as lying. For example, professional nurses are taught that patient education and patient advocacy are important aspects of the nursing role. Yet these nursing role expectations may conflict with physicians' orders or they may be difficult to implement because of time pressures and paper work that take nurses away from patients. In a research study,[18] nurses responded to scenarios, some of which placed them in role conflict situations. Those nurses who were in role conflict situations said that they would be more likely to lie by misreporting their behavior on the patient's chart.

Managers must be aware that conflicting role demands can pressure their subordinates to be dishonest. The best way to avoid this type of dishonesty is to minimize conflicting role demands. Ask your staff to analyze their jobs and to identify sources of conflict that could cause them to feel that they have to lie to you or someone else in order to successfully accomplish some aspect of their job. Then, see if the job can be redesigned to minimize these conflicts.

Roles Can Support Ethical Behavior

Roles can also work to support ethical behavior. For example, whistleblowing (reporting the misconduct of others) is sometimes prescribed for individuals in certain jobs. This makes a difficult behavior easier to carry out. A survey of internal auditors found that whistleblowing was more likely when the auditors saw auditing as a prescribed job requirement.[19] Therefore, managers should consider the extent to which organizational roles encourage either ethical or unethical behavior. Obviously, those that support and encourage unethical behavior should be changed. Those that encourage ethical behavior (e.g., whistleblowing) should be bolstered. For example, research has found that, although reporting a peer's misconduct is a distasteful and difficult act, people are more likely to report a peer if reporting is explicitly made a part of their role via an honor code or code of conduct.[20] In other words, if their role requires them to report misconduct when they see it, they're more likely to do so. The requirement makes it easier because the behavior becomes a duty, a role responsibility rather than a voluntary ethical act.

Practical Advice for Managers

The key for managers is that roles influence behavior. Think about the roles people play in your department or organization. What are the implications of their role expectations for ethical and unethical behavior? Do some individuals experience conflicts between their roles? For example, are professionals torn between their organizational and professional roles? Or do employees experience conflicts within a role, like nurses who are supposed to play the often conflicting roles of patient advocate and subordinate to the physician? Again, the individuals who hold the jobs are probably the best source of information about their role expectations and potential conflicts. Once you've analyzed roles and role conflicts, determine whether jobs need to be altered to reduce conflict. If change isn't possible, at least you can anticipate the problems that are likely to arise for people in these jobs.

PEOPLE DO WHAT THEY'RE TOLD

In a "60 Minutes" segment (October 4, 1992), Americans working for a Japanese company in the United States reported that their supervisor told them to unpack machine tools manufactured in and shipped from Japan, remove the "Manufactured in Japan" label, change a few things, replace the label with a "Manufactured in the

U.S." label and recrate the machine tools for shipping. These products were then shipped as if they had been manufactured in the United States to, of all places, the American military (where U.S. manufacture of machine tools was a requirement). An American accountant at the firm finally blew the whistle, but when the workers who had been doing the unpacking and recrating were asked why they did it, they replied that they were doing what their supervisor had told them to do. One of the men who had attempted to protest was told that he could find another job if he didn't like it. So he continued doing what he was told to do.

This is just one of many examples we could cite of workers at all levels doing what they're told by managers. Participants in the Watergate break-in in 1972 referred to their unquestioning obedience to superior orders in testimony before the Senate investigating committee, as did Nazi SS officers in war crimes trials and participants in the Iran-Contra affair.[21] Organizations (corporate, political, or military) are authority structures whose members accept that, to be members in good standing, they must give up a certain amount of independence and autonomy. They expect that managers will tell them what to do. That's the managerial role. And, they assume that they should do what's expected of them. That's the subordinate role. These assumptions and expectations allow organizations to avoid chaos and function in an orderly fashion. Also, individuals often feel that they owe the organization and their manager their loyalty, further reinforcing the pressure to comply.

The Milgram Experiments

Classic social psychological studies conducted by Stanley Milgram[22] provide uncomfortable insights into how normal adults behave in authority situations. Most adults will carry out the authority figure's orders even if these orders are contrary to their personal beliefs about what's right.

In a number of laboratory experiments, Milgram paid subjects recruited from the New Haven, Connecticut, area to participate in a one-hour study on the effects of punishment on learning. The subject was asked to play the role of teacher in a learning experiment, while a second individual (a part of the research team who unbeknownst to the teacher/subject was in on the experiment) was asked to play the role of learner. The learner was strapped into a chair with an electrode attached to his or her wrist. The teacher/subject was seated at a shock generator and posed questions to the learner. Each time the learner provided an incorrect response to a question, the teacher/subject turned a dial to administer an increasingly severe shock. As the shocks intensified, the learner verbally expressed increasing discomfort, finally screaming and then going silent. During the experiments, many teacher/subjects would question the experimenter and express the desire to stop. The experimenter, dressed in a white lab coat, would say, "Although the shocks may be painful, there is no permanent tissue damage, so please go on." If the teacher/subject continued to resist, the experimenter would respond with three successive prods: "the experiment requires that you continue"; "it is absolutely essential that you continue"; "you have no choice, you must go on." If the teacher continued to resist, the experiment was finally terminated.

To the surprise of Milgram and other observers, most of the teacher/subjects in these experiments continued to the end, obeying the authority figure's instructions despite the conflict they felt and expressed. It's not that they felt OK about what they were doing. In fact, their emotional appeals to the experimenter suggested that they very much wanted to stop. But most of them didn't. They may have felt that refusing to continue would challenge the experimenter's authority, the legitimacy of the experiment, and that they would risk embarrassing themselves.[23] They acted as if they were constrained to do as they were told by the authority figure, rather than as independent adults who could end the experiment at any time.

Obedience to Authority At Work

This behavior is similar to behavior observed over and over again in work organizations. The notion of legitimate authority is an accepted tenet of organizational life. In 1968, American military men massacred hundreds of innocent civilians at Mylai, Vietnam. They didn't ask questions. They did what they were told to do. Twenty years later, Colonel Oliver North who was tried for arranging the illegal sale of arms to the Nicaraguan contra forces, claimed that he was only following the order of his superiors. Individuals who testified to the U.S. Congress about price-fixing practices in the electrical industry were asked why they didn't report these practices to higher authorities. They responded that they felt they couldn't because they reported to a prescribed superior only.[24] And, Roger Boisjoly, who questioned the safety of the O-rings and who attempted to convince managers to cancel the launch of the Challenger, never went outside the chain of command to protest.[25]

Practical Advice for Managers

The bottom line is that managers must realize the power they hold as legitimate authority figures in work organizations. Old concepts die hard. And even today in team-oriented organizations, most people will do as they're told. Therefore, authority figures must exhibit ethical behavior and they must send powerful signals that high ethical standards are expected of everyone. This message should begin at the top of the organization and work its way down through every level. Second, when unethical behavior is uncovered, the investigation must consider the explicit or implicit messages being sent by authority figures. Don't assume that the individual acted alone and without influence. Our tendency is to try to isolate the problem, find the one "culprit" (bad apple) and get on with our lives. But, the culprit may have been explicitly or implicitly encouraged by a superior and this possibility should be taken into account.

RESPONSIBILITY IS DIFFUSED IN ORGANIZATIONS

In order for a relationship to exist between what people think is right and what they do, they must feel responsible for the consequences of their actions.[26] Therefore, the feeling of personal responsibility is a prerequisite for moral action. If you feel that a decision YOU made to market a particular product might hurt small children or the environment, you are much more likely to seriously consider the moral implications of the decision. But, in organizations the individual often becomes disconnected from the consequences of his or her actions and doesn't feel personally responsible for them. Responsibility becomes *diffused*. No individual feels the need to take responsibility, so in the end no one does, and unethical behavior is more likely.

There are at least four reasons why individuals may not feel personally responsible for their organizational actions. Responsibility is diffused because it is taken away, shared with others in decision making groups, obscured by the organizational hierarchy or by psychological distance to potential victims.

"Don't Worry—We're Taking Care of Everything"

First, at work, individuals are often encouraged to turn responsibility over to those at higher levels. This is related to our earlier discussion of obedience to authority. But in this case, the individual is simply told not to worry—that the problem or decision is someone else's responsibility. For example, an individual who expresses concern about a safety or environmental problem may be told, "we appreciate your concern, but you don't need to worry about it. We're taking care of everything." This type of response absolves the subordinate of feelings of responsibility for the consequences of the organization's action. Someone, particularly someone at a higher level, has taken the responsibility.

However, even if the superiors are highly responsible and highly ethical, the act of absolving subordinates of responsibility may have significant implications for their subsequent ethical behavior. Because of the feeling that they must do as they're told by authority figures, most people feel that they have no choice but to follow superiors' orders. In this case, the orders are to hand over responsibility for decision making and the individual feels that s/he has no choice but to give it up. If this sort of response becomes routine, individuals will come to believe that it isn't their responsibility to be on the lookout for ethical violations and they may stop bringing potential problems to the attention of superiors.

Diffusing Responsibility in Groups

Second, important organizational decisions are often made in groups. Therefore, responsibility for the decision becomes diffused among all group members. No single individual feels responsible. Diffusion of responsibility in groups is used to explain the results of classic research on the likelihood that bystanders will help a seizure victim.[27] This research suggests that when others are present, responsibility is diffused among all of the bystanders and individuals are less likely to help.

Diffusion of responsibility also operates in group decision making through processes such as "groupthink."[28] Groupthink occurs in cohesive groups where group members have a commitment to the group and a strong desire to remain a group member. A major characteristic of groupthink is the conformity of individual group members to the decision they think the majority of group members prefer. Individual group members find it very difficult to express disagreement and tend to censor themselves even if they disagree with the group decision.

One important symptom of groupthink is the group's "illusion of morality," the sense that the group simply wouldn't do anything wrong. In a classic film on groupthink, a group of managers makes a decision to market a new drug despite disturbing evidence that it may produce dangerous side effects. The illusion of morality is expressed by a group member who states that the company has a well-earned good reputation and would never do anything to hurt the customer.

Clearly, decisions with ethical overtones that are made in a group setting require special attention. The manager must make sure that the ethical implications are identified and carefully analyzed. The group leader should be careful not to state his or her preference up front because group members will tend to censor their own beliefs to conform with those of the leader. Other techniques can be used to make sure that alternative points of view are aired. For example, an individual can be appointed to the role of devil's advocate or multiple individuals can be appointed to voice multiple alternative perspectives. It's easier for these individuals to take an alternative stance when it's their *role* to do so.

Diffusing Responsibility by Dividing Responsibility

Third, responsibility in organizations is often so divided that individuals see themselves as only a small cog in a large machine. Division of responsibility is essential for the kind of specialization required in modern jobs. But this means that organizational members essentially do their jobs with blinders on - they see only what's directly ahead of them and no one sees (or takes responsibility for) the whole picture.

Scott Peck is a psychiatrist and author who was part of a group dispatched to study the My Lai massacre after it occurred. His interviews with military people revealed a bureaucratic organizational structure that allowed individuals to see only their own narrow part of the problem, thereby allowing them to avoid feelings of responsibility. When he wandered the halls of the Pentagon, questioning those involved in directing the manufacture of napalm and its transportation to Vietnam as bombs, the replies he received were something like the following: "We appreciate your problem and your concerns, but we are not the department you want. We are in ordnance. We supply the weapons, but we don't determine how they're used." Down the hall, another group suggested that the broad issues were also beyond their purview. "We simply determine how the war will be conducted—not whether it will be conducted."[29] Peck termed this process "the fragmentation of conscience." "Any group will remain inevitably potentially conscienceless and evil until such time as each and every individual holds himself or herself directly responsible for the behavior of the whole group—the organism—of which he or she is a part. We have not yet begun to arrive at that point."[30]

Research has documented the diffusion of responsibility process. In a variation on the Milgram obedience to authority experiments discussed earlier, the diffusion of responsibility was simulated by dividing the teacher's role between two people, a "transmitter" and an "executant." The transmitter would inform the executant when a shock had to be administered and at what level. The experiment found that transmitters were significantly more likely to obey than executants.[31] One can imagine that it was easier for the transmitter to rationalize his or her actions. "I didn't actually do the harm—someone else did." This rationalization should become easier and easier, the greater the distance between the individual decision maker and the actual outcome.

Diffusing Responsibility by Creating Psychological Distance

Finally, responsibility can be diffused because of the psychological distance between the decision maker and potential victims.[32] When potential victims are psychologically distant or out of sight, it's more difficult to see oneself as responsible for any negative outcomes. This was exemplified in further variations on the obedience to authority studies in which Milgram[33] varied the closeness of the learner victim to the teacher. For example, when the learner was placed in the same room with the teacher, the level of obedience dropped more than 20% (to 40%). In another variation, when the teacher was asked to physically force the learner's hand onto the shock plate, the obedience level dropped another 10%. In these situations, as psychological distance decreased, the teacher felt personal responsibility more strongly and was less likely to comply with the authority figure's demands to harm the learner.

This research suggests that personal responsibility for the outcomes of our organizational decisions will be less clear in situations where the potential harm is far removed. For example, when the plant is not in our community, but in Mexico or somewhere in Asia, potential negative consequences are more distant, we may feel less personal responsibility, and may be more willing to make decisions that would harm people.

Practical Advice for Managers

People are much more likely to act ethically if they perceive themselves as responsible for the outcomes of their decisions and actions. As a manager, you can increase this perception of responsibility by making responsibility a highly relevant issue. When a subordinate brings up an ethical concern, don't take it completely off his or her hands. Or, if it becomes necessary to do so, be sure to keep the individual informed of the progress and outcome of the decision. Second, make it clear that every group member will be held personally responsible for the outcome of group decisions. Ask groups to present minority reports or recommendations so that a communication mechanism exists for those who don't agree with the group. Appoint a devil's advocate or multiple advocates to question the assumptions of the group and the group's decision.

The current movement to decrease levels in the organizational hierarchy may have a positive side benefit. With fewer levels, it should become more difficult for organizational members to rationalize their actions in such a way. Also, accountability can be enhanced by spelling out the expectations associated with specific positions in the organization and by holding individuals to those expectations. Finally, personal visits to geographically distant work sites should decrease psychological distance and increase the manager's felt responsibility for the outcomes of any decisions or actions that impact people in these locations.

CONCLUSION

You now have some important management concepts that can be applied to the maangement of ethical and unethical conduct. The remaining challenge is to analyze yourself (or your manager) in relation to these ideas. A common phrase used by today's managers is "walking the talk." If your intention is to be an ethical manager, here are some questions to ask yourself to see if you're "walking your ethical talk."

AM I "WALKING MY TALK?"

1. Do I talk about the ethical implications of decisions with the people who report to me and with candidates I'm interested in hiring? With my peers? With my manager?

2. Have I made it clear to the people who report to me that I don't want to be protected from bad news? Do they understand that they can tell my anything without fear of retribution? Do my reports come to me with ethical concerns?

3. Do I provide guidance on ethical decision-making and have I participated in the ethics training of those who report to me?

4. When evaluating the performance of my staff, do I consider ethical goals as well as performance and quality goals? Do I focus on the means as well as the ends in decision-making and performance appraisals?

5. Do I reward ethical conduct and discipline unethical conduct?

6. Do I require my people to take responsibility for their decisions?

7. What are the informal norms in my department? If my employees were asked to list the "rules" of working for me, what would they say? Are any of these "problematic" if ethical conduct is the goal?

8. If I were to die tomorrow, would the people who report to me say that I had integrity? How would my peers describe me? And what would my manager say?

The answers to these questions should form a sound beginning for understanding and managing ethical behavior in your work group. We'll discuss the important broader issue of organizational culture in Chapter 9.

DISCUSSION QUESTIONS

1. Have you ever been in a situation, especially a work situation, where the norms supported unethical/ethical behavior—where you felt pressured to go along? Explain.

2. Have you ever been in a situation where the rewards explicitly or implicitly supported unethical conduct (ethical conduct)? Explain.

3. Can you think of situations in which unethical behavior was dealt with appropriately (punished justly) or inappropriately? What were the reactions of others in the organization?

4. What do you think would be appropriate punishment for those found guilty of assault or indecent exposure in the Tailhook situation? Why?

5. Have you ever felt obligated to do something you felt was wrong because a person in a position of authority told you to do it?

6. Think about how you might design work to maximize workers' taking responsibility for the consequences of their actions.

7. Evaluate yourself or a manager you know using the "do you walk your talk" questions above.

CASE

Sears, Roebuck, and Co.: The Auto Center Scandal

Sears, Roebuck, and Co. began in the late 1800s as a mail-order company that sold farm supplies and other consumer items. Its first retail store opened in the mid-

1920s. Responding to changes in American society, such as the move from farms to factories and the presence of the automobile in many homes, hundreds of retail stores opened over the years. The company expanded rapidly and eventually it diversified to include other businesses: insurance (Allstate Insurance), real estate (Coldwell Banker), securities (Dean Witter Reynolds), and credit cards (Discover). Each of these other businesses became its own division, in addition to the merchandising group which included retail stores, appliances, and auto service centers. By the early 1990s, the company was reporting earnings and revenues in the billions of dollars.[34]

Despite its long history of high earnings and its penetration into the U.S. market, Sears' retail business began to experience serious financial difficulties in the 1980s. Discount retailers such as Wal-Mart and K-Mart were pulling ahead in market share, leaving Sears lagging. Sears responded by adding non-Sears name brands and an "everyday low price" policy. But, despite these efforts, in 1990 Sears reported a 40% decline in earnings, with the merchandising group dropping a whopping 60%! Cost-cutting measures were planned, including the elimination of jobs and a focus on profits at every level.[35]

In 1991, Sears unveiled a productivity incentive plan to increase profits in its auto centers nationwide. Auto mechanics had traditionally been paid an hourly wage and were expected to meet production quotas. In 1991, the compensation plan was changed to include a commission component. Mechanics were paid a base salary plus a fixed dollar amount for meeting hourly production quotas. Auto service advisors (the counter people who take orders, consult with mechanics, and advise customers) had traditionally been paid a salary. In order to increase sales, however, commissions and product-specific sales quotas were introduced for them as well. For example, a service advisor might be given the goal of selling a certain number of front-end alignments or brake repairs during each shift.[36]

In June 1992, the California Department of Consumer Affairs accused Sears, Roebuck and Co. of violating the state's Auto Repair Act and sought to revoke the licenses of all Sears auto centers in California. The allegation resulted from an increasing number of consumer complaints and an undercover investigation of brake repairs. Other states quickly followed suit. Essentially, the charges alleged that Sears Auto Centers had been systematically misleading customers and charging them for unnecessary repairs. The California investigation attributed the problems to Sears Auto Centers' compensation system.[37]

In response to the charges, Sears CEO and Chairman Edward A. Brennan called a news conference where he denied that any fraud had occurred and he defended Sears' focus on preventive maintenance for older cars. He admitted to isolated errors, accepted personal responsibility for creating an environment where "mistakes" had occurred, and outlined the actions the company planned to take to resolve the issue. These included:

- elimination of the incentive compensation program for service advisors
- substitution of commissions based upon customer satisfaction

- elimination of sales quotas for specific parts and repairs
- substitution of sales volume quotas

According to Brennan, "we have to have some way to measure performance."[38]

Sears also introduced "shopping audits" of its auto centers in which employees would pose as customers and Brennan published a letter to the company's customers in *The Wall Street Journal* and *USA Today* on June 25, 1992.

Note that the compensation system for mechanics, based on number of tasks performed and parts replaced, was maintained. During the summer of 1992, Chuck Fabbri, a Sears mechanic from California, sent a letter about Sears' wage policy for mechanics to U.S. Senator Richard Bryan. He said:

> . . . It is my understanding that Sears is attempting to convince your committee that all inspections in their auto centers are now performed by employees who are paid hourly and not on commission. This is not the case. The truth is that the majority of employees performing inspections are still on commission . . .
>
> The Service Advisors . . . sell the repair work to the customer . . . The repairs that they sell are not only based on their inspections, but to a larger degree based on the recommendations of mechanics who are on commission . . .
>
> On January 1, 1991 the mechanics, installers and tire changers had their hourly wages cut to what Sears termed a fixed dollar amount, or FDA per hour which varied depending on the classification. At present the mechanic's FDA amount is $3.25 which, based on current Sears minimum production quotas, is 17% of my earnings. What this means is that for every hour of work, as defined by Sears, that I complete, I receive $3.25 plus my hourly base pay. If I do two hours worth of work in one hour I receive an additional $3.25 therefore increasing my earnings.
>
> Sears calls this type of compensation incentive pay or piece work, however a rose by any other name is still a rose. This is commission plain and simple. The faster I get the work done the more money I make, and as intended, Sears' profits increase. It is therefore obvious to increase his earnings, a mechanic might cut corners on, or eliminate altogether, procedures required to complete the repair correction. In addition to this, since the mechanic often ispects or performs the diagnosis, he has the ideal opportunity to oversell or recommend more repair work than is needed. This would be especially tempting if it has been a slow day or week. In part greed may create this less than ethical situation, but high pressure to meet quotas by Sears' management also presents a significant contribution. I have recently been threatened with termination if my production didn't at least equal Sears' minimum quotas. I might add that prior to this new wage policy, management had only positive response to my production, and my record proves this . . .
>
> There is no doubt in my mind that before their auto center employees were put on commission Sears enjoyed the trust of its customers. Today presents a different story. The solution is obvious not only for Sears, but for the industry.[39]

Sears agreed to a multimillion-dollar settlement with the state of California and the 41 other states that had filed similar charges. The company was placed on three-year probation in California. It also settled a number of consumer class-action suits. In July 1992, the U.S. Congress held hearings on fraud in the auto repair industry.

The long-term impact of the scandal is unclear. Sears has now sold off its securities firm, the Discover card, most of its real estate and mortgage business, and 20% of Allstate Insurance. At the end of 1992, auto center sales lagged behind prior levels.[40] Also, in 1992, *Business Week* reported that employees in other areas of Sears' business such as insurance and appliance sales, were feeling the same kinds of pressures from sales quotas.[41]

Case-Based Questions

1. Identify the ethical issues involved in the case (refer to Chapter 4).

2. Identify the management issues involved in the case. For example, think about the case in terms of multiple ethical selves, norms, roles, reward systems, diffusion of responsibility, obedience to authority. What factors contributed the most to the alleged unethical conduct on the part of service advisors, mechanics?

3. How would you evaluate Sears' response to the allegations and the changes they made? Has Sears resolved its problem? Why or why not? If you think not, can you propose a better plan?

5. What do you think is the potential long-term impact of the scandal on Sears' longstanding reputation for quality and service?

6. Respond to Brennan's comment that, "we have to have some way to measure performance." What can management do to prevent "overselling?"

7. Should anyone be disciplined? If so, who, and when?

NOTES

[1]Toffler, B. 1986. *Tough choices.* New York: John Wiley & Sons.

[2]Barrett, R.A. 1984. *Culture and conduct: An excursion in anthropology.* Belmont, CA: Wadsworth.

[3]Levine, D. B. 1990. The inside story of an inside trader. *Fortune,* May 21: 80–89.

[4]Bandura, A. 1986. *Social foundations of thought and action: A social–cognitive theory.* Englewood Cliffs, NJ: Prentice-Hall.

[5]Goodman, E. 1994. Nobody deemed accountable for Tailhook. *Centre Daily Times,* February 15: 6A.

[6]Waller, D. C. 1994. Tailhook's lightning rod. *Newsweek,* February 28: 31.

[7]Levine, D. B. 1990. The inside story of an inside trader. *Fortune,* May 21: 80–89.

[8]Ibid.

[9]Ball, G., Trevino, L.K. & Sims, H.P., Jr. 1994. Just and unjust punishment incidents. *Academy of Management Journal,* 37: 299–322.

[10]Trevino, L.K. & Ball, G.A. 1992. The social implications of punishing unethical behavior: Observers' cognitive and affective reactions. *Journal of Management,* 18: 751–768.

[11]Watson, Thomas J. Jr. 1990. *Father son & co.: My life at IBM and beyond.* New York: Bantam.

[12]Treviño, L.K. & Victor, B. 1992. Peer reporting of unethical behavior: A social context perspective. *Academy of Management Journal*, 353: 38–64.

[13]Zimbardo, P. G. 1970. The human choice: Individuation, reason, and order versus deindividuation, impulse, and chaos. In *Nebraska Symposium on Motivation, 1969*. W.J. Arnold & D. Levine, eds. Lincoln: University of Nebraska Press, 237–307.

[14]Haney, C.C., Banks & Zimbardo, P. 1973. Interpersonal dynamics in a simulated prison. *International Journal of Criminology and Penology*, 1: 69–97.

[15]Zimbardo, P. 1982. Pathology of imprisonment. In *Readings in social psychology: Comtemporary perspectives, 2nd ed.* D. Krebs, ed. New York: Harper & Row.

[16]Katz, D. & Kahn, R. 1978. *The social psychology of organizations, 2nd ed.* New York: John Wiley & Sons.

[17]Brady, F.N. & Logdson, J.M. 1988. Zimbardo's "Stanford prison experiment" and the relevance of social psychology for teaching business ethics. *Journal of Business Ethics*, 7: 703–710.

Brodeur, P. 1985. *Outrageous misconduct: The asbestos industry on trial.* New York: Pantheon.

[18]Grover, S. 1992. Why professionals lie: The impact of professional role conflict on reporting accuracy. *Organizational Behavior and Human Decision Processes*.

[19]Miceli, M.P. & Near, J.P. 1984. The relationships among beliefs, organizational position, and whistle-blowing status: A discriminant analysis. *Academy of Management Journal*, 27: 687–705.

[20]Treviño, L.K. & Victor, B. 1992. Peer reporting of unethical behavior: A social context perspective. *Academy of Management Journal*, 353: 38–64.

[21]Kelman, H.C. & Hamilton, V.L. 1989. *Crimes of obedience.* New Haven: Yale University Press.

[22]Milgram, S. 1974. *Obedience to authority; An experimental view.* New York: Harper & Row.

[23]Kelman, H.C. & Hamilton, V.L. 1989. *Crimes of obedience.* New Haven: Yale University Press.

[24]Waters, J.A. 1978. Catch 20.5: corporate morality as an organizational phenomenon. *Organizational Dynamics*, Spring: 3–19.

[25]Kelman, H.C. & Hamilton, V.L. 1989. *Crimes of obedience.* New Haven: Yale University Press.

[26]Schwartz, S.H. 1968a. Words, deeds, and the perception of consequences and responsibility in action situations. *Journal of Personality and Social Psychology*, 10: 232–242.

Schwartz, S.H. 1968b. Awareness of consequences and the influence of moral norms on interpersonal behavior. *Sociometry*, 31: 355–369.

[27]Darley, J.M. & Latane, B. 1968. Bystanders' intervention in emergencies: Diffusion of responsibility. *Journal of Personality and Social Psychology*, 8: 373–383.

[28]Janis, I. 1982. *Group Think, 2nd ed.* Boston:Houghton Mifflin.

[29]Peck, M., Scott, M.D. 1983. *People of the lie; The hope for healing human evil.* New York: Simon & Schuster.

[30]Ibid.

[31]Kilham, W., & Mann, L. 1974. Level of destructive obedience as a function of transmitter and executant roles in the Milgram obedience paradigm. *Journal of Personality and Social Psychology*, 29: 696–702.

[32]Kelman, H.C. & Hamilton, V.L. 1989. *Crimes of obedience*. New Haven: Yale University Press.

[33]Milgram, S. 1974. *Obedience to authority; An experimental view*. New York: Harper & Row.

[34]Santoro, M.A. 1993. *Sears auto centers*. Boston: Harvard Business School.

[35]Santoro, M.A. 1993. *Sears auto centers*. Boston: Harvard Business School.
Kelly, K. 1992. How did Sears blow this gasket? *Business Week*, June 29: 38.

[36]Santoro, M.A. 1993. *Sears auto centers*. Boston: Harvard Business School.

[37]Kelly, K. 1992. How did Sears blow this gasket? *Business Week*, June 29: 38.

[38]Gellene, D. 1992. New state probe of Sears could lead to suit. *Los Angeles Times*, June 12, part D: 1.

[39]Hearing Before Subcommittee on Consumer of the Senate Committee on Commerce, Science, and Transportation, 102nd Congress, 2nd Sess., July 21, 1992 (S. Hrg. 102–972), p. 83.

[40]Santoro, M.A. 1993. *Sears auto centers*. Boston: Harvard Business School.

[41]Flynn, J. 1992. Did Seras take other customers for a ride? *Business Week*, August 3: 24–25.

SECTION IV

Ethics and the Organization

CHAPTER EIGHT

Ethical Problems
of Organizations

INTRODUCTION

THERE'S BEEN INCREASED concern in recent years over the state of business ethics. The media is responding to the public's concern over ethics by providing more coverage of ethical lapses by organizations. It's easy to wonder if any organization is doing the right thing.

Wonder no more. There are thousands of organizations who struggle every day to uphold an ethical standard. If you try to imagine the hundreds of thousands of transactions that occur every day, and then think about how many you hear about as being illegal or unethical, the proportion of wrongdoers is probably quite small. However, there are those few who do cross the line.

In this chapter, we're going to examine some of the classic cases in business ethics. Some are examples of catastrophes that can strike a corporation without warning. They aren't the result of corporate wrongdoing; rather, they are bolts from the blue, acts of nature, and they're sometimes the result of unfounded rumors or external sabotage. Although some are basically "accidents" and the company or organization is initially a victim, they can become ethical debacles depending on how a company reacts. A company's behavior in a crisis says a lot about what the company stands for. Because a crisis strikes suddenly and unexpectedly, a company tends to show its "true colors" by how it handles disaster. The corporate reaction frequently becomes more widely know than the event that prompted it.

Other examples are ethical lapses that result from a purposeful activity. The company, in other words, has been an active participant in its own mess. It has made its own bed, so to speak, and it's in trouble because of a conscious action or decision it has taken. The ethical dilemma may result from ignorance, negligence, arrogance, and sometimes because of plain old greed. In some of these famous cases, severe cost controls caused the problem, and in others, companies didn't know how to handle bad decisions made by their predecessors. Frequently, when a company is suspected of having made an unethical decision, it takes a long time for the company to admit the mistake. In some of these cases, not only did the company behave unethically, but also they obfuscated and stalled when the mistake was discovered.

In other examples, a company may have made an unconscious mistake. It has instituted a process, or introduced a product, or is somehow involved in another kind of activity that has had a profoundly different outcome than the company expected. The company may have begun with the best of intentions, but they ended with a vastly different outcome. Nevertheless, the companies involved in those cases probably should have known they were in dangerous waters and acted upon that information.

The cases you'll read about here are thumbnail sketches of famous incidents. All of the cases here have been extensively documented in the press, and you can find lengthy descriptions of them in business and scholarly publications. We've divided the cases into four categories that represent the four major stakeholders in every business decision: consumers, employees, shareholders, and the environment (or the community as a whole). The famous cases are followed by a hypothetical case for you to ponder on your own.

ETHICS AND CONSUMERS

It might surprise many people to learn that there were few laws protecting consumers before the 1960s. In fact, at the turn of the last century, consumers didn't even have the right to sue a manufacturer for defective equipment. The first real consumer law took effect early in the 20th century when, in *McPherson* v. *General Motors*, a consumer was given the right to sue the auto manufacturer for a defective vehicle. Until then, the only recourse for the owner of an auto was to go after the dealer who sold him or her the vehicle. Another landmark law was the Pure Food and Drug Act, which was passed in 1906 to prohibit adulteration in food and drugs.[1]

Although more consumer laws were passed in the first half of this century, consumers had to wait until the early 1960s for any real protectionist legislation. The framework of consumer protection as we know it today was constructed during the Kennedy administration. In his speech to Congress on consumers in 1962, President John F. Kennedy outlined four consumer "rights."[2] The four rights he outlined included the right to safety, the right to be heard, the right to choose, and the right to be informed. This message and the legislation that resulted laid the groundwork for today's consumer movement.

Exactly what do companies and organizations owe their customers? According to some, products and services should be produced and delivered according to the "due care" theory.[3] This theory stipulates that due care involves:

1. Design—products and services should meet all government regulations and specifications and be safe under all foreseeable conditions, including misuse by the consumer.

2. Materials—materials should meet government regulations and be durable enough to withstand reasonable use.

3. Production—products should be made without defects.

4. Quality control—products should be inspected regularly for quality.

5. Packaging, labeling, and warnings—products should be safely packaged, should include clear, easily understood directions for use, and should include a clear description of any hazards.

6. Notification—manufacturers should have a system in place to recall products that prove to be dangerous at some time after manufacture and distribution.

Although we've certainly alluded to some organizational responsibilities in earlier chapters, we're going to concentrate on three duties in this chapter: to respect the customer and not engage in activities that conflict with the interests of an established customer base, to produce a safe product that is free from any known defects, and to honestly advertise a product or service.

Conflicts of Interest

Although we usually think of conflicts of interest as situations involving individuals, they can also involve organizations. For example, what happens to Small Bank, a client of a larger financial institution—Big Bank—when Big Bank purchases a small company that supplies other financial institutions with computerized information? Small Bank isn't just a customer of Big Bank, it's also a competitor. Big Bank could, in theory, delay information over the wires until it has had an opportunity to act. Even if Big Bank never takes advantage of the situation, it could appear as if it could delay or manipulate information because it owns the company that supplies it to itself and to other corporations. In an industry like finance, where information is the fuel that drives the engine, it's difficult to imagine how one institution could justify owning an information company to its customers, who also are competitors. In the financial institution where this happened, the information company became a black hole, where the financial institution poured money and resources until it finally sold the information company. Customers (competitors) could not accept the relationship between the financial institution and its subsidiary.

Take a look at this hypothetical case and see what ethical issues it presents:

Big Insurance Co. is a large supplier of health care services that is under fire from the government to lower costs and increase efficiency. Big Insurance has an excellent reputation and is widely acknowledged as one of the best-managed companies in the country. In spite of its reputation, however, Wall Street has reacted negatively to government efforts to reform the industry as a whole, and Big Insurance's stock price has lost 30% of its value in the last year. To counter the effect of possible government intervention, Big Insurance has just purchased Little Co., a discount health care supplier and traditionally one of Big Insurance's feistiest competitors. Wall Street has greeted the acquisition with enthusiasm and Big Insurance's stock price has rebounded by more than 10% since news of the acquisition was made public.

While this acquisition could provide Big Insurance with a foothold in tomorrow's health care industry, a real problem lies in the mission of Little Co. Little has made its reputation by providing objective health care advice to its customers. Now that it's owned by Big Insurance, customers have expressed doubts about how objective Little can be in recommending health care services if it's owned by a health care provider.

As the senior executive charged with bringing Little Co. into the corporate fold, how do you proceed? What are your obligations to Big Insurance, Little, and the customers of both? What do you owe to shareholders and the financial community? What provisions would you include in an ethics code for Little Co.?

In Chapter 3, we defined a conflict of interest as occurring when someone could think that your judgment might be clouded because of a relationship you have. The definition is the same for organizations: if an organization's customers or other stakeholder group could think that an organization's judgment is biased because of a relationship it has with another company or firm, a conflict exists. Corporate or organizational conflicts are just as dicey as those that exist between individuals and should be avoided at all costs.

Product Safety

Obviously, a major ethical obligation of any organization is to produce a quality product or service. And just as obviously, nothing will put a company out of business faster than offering a product that is dangerous, poorly produced, or of inferior quality. The competition in the marketplace generally helps to assure that goods and services will be of a quality that is acceptable to consumers. However, sometimes a company will become the victim of external sabotage (like Johnson & Johnson), and sometimes a company will make a foolhardy decision (like A.H. Robins or Beech-Nut), and the result is a product that is not safe. Let's look at a few of the classic cases:

Company: **Johnson & Johnson**
Industry: Pharmaceuticals
Situation: In September 1982, seven people in the Chicago area were killed when they ingested Tylenol, a pain killer produced by McNeil Labs,

a division of Johnson & Johnson. The Tylenol in question was found to have been laced with cyanide, and it was not known for several weeks whether the contamination was the result of internal or external sabotage. A thorough investigation later proved that the poisonings were the result of external sabotage.

How the Company Handled the Crisis: First, the company pulled all Tylenol from shelves in the Chicago area. That was quickly followed by a nationwide recall of all Tylenol—31 million bottles with a retail value of over $100 million. Johnson & Johnson sent Mailgram messages explaining the situation and the recall to over 500000 doctors, hospitals, and distributors of Tylenol. It also established a crisis phone line where consumers could call an 800 number to ask questions about the product. In addition, its CEO, James Burke, and other executives were accessible to the press and were interviewed by a variety of media.

Since Tylenol had captured over a third of the painkiller market before the poisoning, Johnson & Johnson decided to try to rebuild the brand and its franchise. That wasn't going to be easy since consumer fear ran high immediately after the poisoning. In one survey conducted a month after the incident, 87 percent of the respondents understood that Johnson & Johnson was not to blame for the Tylenol deaths, yet 61 percent declared they would be unlikely to buy Tylenol in the future. So even though most consumers knew the poisonings were not the fault of Johnson & Johnson, a majority wouldn't buy the product again. Johnson & Johnson tackled this problem head-on by offering coupons to entice consumers back to Tylenol, and ultimately, by redesigning Tylenol's packaging to be tamper resistant.

The Result: Johnson & Johnson's reaction to the Tylenol poisoning has been hailed as the benchmark for how organizations should react to a crisis. As we've mentioned in other chapters, Johnson & Johnson's reaction to the Tylenol crisis proved that its famous credo wasn't hollow. Its commitment to its consumers is not only the first tenet of the credo, it was also that concern for the customer that drove its response to the crisis. And by being accessible to the press, its executives displayed concern for the consumer by refusing to dodge responsibility or blame any other party for their difficulties.

The results of the crisis have been far reaching. The tamper-resistant packaging pioneered by Johnson & Johnson has become commonplace in a wide variety of products—from food to pharmaceuticals. Johnson & Johnson's reputation as a quality producer of pharmaceuticals and as a company that cares about its customers is still strong, more than a decade after the crisis. Its former Chairman, James Burke, is renowned for his concern about ethical issues and is a sought-after speaker on a wide variety of topics related to ethics. Also, by the mid-1980s, Tylenol had regained almost all of its market share.

Comments: The background of former Johnson & Johnson CEO James Burke was critical to the company's behavior during the Tylenol crisis.

Burke was a marketing man, who knew and understood the value of timely, accurate communications. Not many executives are comfortable with open communications, and their natural reticence can be enormously harmful to their organizations when a crisis strikes.[4]

Company: **Beech-Nut**
Industry: Food Processing
   The Situation: In the mid-1980s, Beech-Nut, a wholly owned subsidiary of Nestle, was burdened with debt and trying to cut costs wherever it could. The facility in question produced apple juice for babies and was located in Canajoharie, NY, a small hamlet on the Erie Canal. In an effort to contain costs, Beech-Nut began ordering apple juice concentrate from a new supplier, which offered the concentrate at a significantly lower cost than the previous supplier.
   By 1981, Beech-Nut's director of research and development, Jerome LiCari, was suspicious of the difference in price, and worried that the concentrate was adulterated. After lengthy testing, LiCari determined that it was indeed adulterated and alerted Beech-Nut's top management. All attempts by LiCari to blow the whistle on the fraud were ignored by Beech-Nut's executives and LiCari resigned in January, 1982. An investigator later described the apple juice as being "a 100 percent fraudulent chemical cocktail," because there was no apple juice in the apple juice.
   How the Company Handled the Crisis: Both the Food and Drug Administration (FDA) and an industry trade association began investigations of the apple juice supplier in 1982. In fact, the trade association asked Beech-Nut to join other manufacturers in a lawsuit against the supplier. Beech-Nut refused and, since it had several million dollars worth of concentrate in inventory, it continued to manufacture apple juice from the concentrate for almost a year, although it stopped purchasing any additional concentrate from the supplier. Because Beech-Nut was afraid that the State of New York would seize the product, it shipped truck loads of the apple juice to another state and to overseas markets in the dead of night, and continued to sell the apple juice until May 1983.
   The Result: As in many other examples, the original offense didn't get Beech-Nut in as much trouble as the cover-up did. The company eventually pleaded guilty to 215 criminal counts and paid over $25 million in fines. Two of its top executives were indicted on criminal charges, found guilty of conspiracy, fraud, and other counts, and received fines and jail sentences. (Its president, Neils Hoyvald, pleaded guilty to 351 felonies; its vice president of operations, John Lavery, pleaded guilty to 448 felonies.) In addition, its market share dropped by approximately 20% after the debacle, leading to more record losses. Beech-Nut later closed its baby apple juice business.
   Comments: A resulting tragedy, which is seldom mentioned, is how the "company town" of Canajoharie was affected. Since over 1000 townspeople

were employed at the Beech-Nut plant, the eventual closing of the plant there because of the apple juice scandal, has had a profound effect on an already depressed area.[5]

Company: **A.H. Robins**
Industry: Pharmaceuticals

Situation: In 1970, A.H. Robins, a small, family-owned pharmaceutical company best-known as the manufacturers of Chap Stick and Robitussin cough syrup, purchased ownership of the Dalkon Shield, a new intrauterine device (IUD). Interest in birth control measures had dramatically increased in the 1960s, and big profits were being made from contraceptives. This was a new market for Robins; in fact, it had no obstetrician or gynecologist on its staff. The problems with the Dalkon Shield were present from the very beginning, although A.H. Robins was initially ignorant of the time bomb they just bought. Because it was a medical device, the Dalkon Shield wasn't required to undergo the rigorous testing the government required of new drugs. And the Dalkon Shield had had precious little testing before Robins purchased the rights to it. Robins aggressively marketed it anyway. By 1975, there were more than four million Dalkon Shields in use by women all over the world, and more than half of those were in use in the United States.

The major problem with the Dalkon Shield was the "tail" that allowed for its removal. Other IUDs had monofilament tails—the tails were one, solid piece of plastic. The Dalkon Shield by contrast had a multifilament tail—it was made up of hundreds of pieces of plastic that proved to be an efficient breeding ground for bacteria. This tail could introduce bacteria into a woman's body and the result could be severe sepsis that could cause massive infection, sterility, miscarriage, or death.

How the Company Handled the Crisis: A.H. Robins stonewalled at every opportunity. Their executives falsified medical data, lost or destroyed key company files and records related to the IUD, and completely denied knowledge of the danger under oath. It finally alerted 120000 doctors to the danger in 1975. However, it didn't recall the IUD until 1984, when it conducted a massive press campaign to encourage women to have the device removed at Robins' expense.

The Result: The results of their inaction were tragic. Fifteen women died as a result of severe pelvic inflammatory disease, and over 60000 women suffered miscarriages. Hundreds more women gave birth to children with severe handicaps such as blindness, cerebral palsy, and mental retardation. In 1984, Robins established a fund of $615 million to deal with claims from the Dalkon Shield. Shortly thereafter, it became apparent that with hundreds of thousands of claims against the company, the fund would prove inadequate, and the company declared Chapter 11 bankruptcy in late 1985. In 1988, the company was acquired by American Home Products.[6]

Company: **Dow Corning**

Industry: Silicone and related products

Situation: Dow Corning (a joint venture of Dow Chemical and Corning Glass Works) began marketing silicone breast implants in the early 1960s. By the mid-1970s, women began to complain that their implants were rupturing or leaking. There are primarily two kinds of breast implants, saline and silicone, although both are encased in a thin layer of silicone. The problem is that over time, the silicone case can break down in the woman's body and either rupture or leak small amounts of silicone into the chest cavity and ultimately into the bloodstream.

The problem was not well known until a California lawsuit propelled the issue into the public eye. At that trial, a former Dow Corning employee who had been involved in the development of silicone implants, testified that, "The manufacturers and surgeons have been performing experimental surgery on humans."[7] Company documents showed numerous complaints about the implants, including ruptures, leakage, infections, immune system problems, and tumors.

How the Company Handled the Crisis: As with the Dalkon Shield, silicone breast implants were considered to be a medical device, and were not subject to lengthy government approvals before implantation. In an effort to protect its image, the company delayed delivering key documents and research to the authorities. And it delayed informing physicians and patients about the mounting complaints regarding implants. They reasoned that the number of women suffering ill effects from the implants were overshadowed by the number of women who were pleased with the operation.

The Result: In many ways, this story is still unfolding. By 1992, more than 3500 women had registered complaints about their implants to the Food and Drug Administration, and more than 1000 women had filed lawsuits against Dow Corning. The company has established a fund in the hundreds of millions of dollars to compensate women for their injuries, although the figure may change before the issue is settled. In early 1992, Dow Corning got out of the implant business and it announced that it would provide subsidies of up to $1200 to women who wanted their implants removed. In addition, the FDA announced that it would begin re-evaluating more than 100 common medical devices in use before 1976, when regulations covering their use were implemented.

Comments: Dow Corning, if indeed a villain in this episode, has company. Some plastic surgeons became aware of the controversy before it was made public and continued to implant silicone devices into women. It's a very lucrative business—and generated up to $450 million in medical fees per year before the controversy.[8]

Now let's take a look at a hypothetical product safety case:

As a brand manager at a large food manufacturer, you're positioning a new product for entry into the highly competitive snack food market. This product is low fat, low calorie, and should prove to be unusually successful, especially against the rapidly-growing pretzel market. You know that one of your leading competitors is preparing to launch a similar product at about the same time. Since market research suggests that the two products will be perceived as identical, the first product to be released should gain significant market share.

A research report from a small, independent lab—Green Lab—indicates that your product causes dizziness in a small group of individuals. Green has an impressive reputation and their research has always been reliable in the past. However, the research reports from two other independent labs don't support Green's conclusion. Your director of research assures you that any claims of adverse effects are unfounded and the indication of dizziness is either extremely rare or the result of faulty research by Green Lab. Since your division has been losing revenue because of its emphasis on potato chips and other high-fat snack food, it desperately needs a low-fat money maker. Since you were brought into the division to turn it around, your career at the company could depend on the success of this product.

What are your alternatives? What is your obligation to consumers? What is your obligation to your employer and to other employees at your company? What should your course of action be?

As we saw in Chapter 4, one of the most common faults in ethical decision making is to ignore the long-term consequences of a decision. Although most organizations try hard to produce a product or service of high quality (to stay in business, if for no other reason), many don't take the time to identify all stakeholders and think long term about the consequences of its decisions. In issues that involve product safety and possible harm to consumers, thinking long term is critical. Is this product going to harm someone? Even if it might harm only one person, is there a way that can be avoided? Is there a way we can warn against possible harm? What can we do to ensure this product's safety? If the product is sabotaged by angry insiders or outsiders, or if we discover problems with this product or service at a later date, how can we protect the public, consumers, and ourselves? How closely did the companies involved in the classic cases adhere to the due care theory described earlier? How can you apply the due care theory to the hypothetical case?

Advertising

The subject of ethics in advertising is a murky one, simply because there are varying opinions of exactly what truth is, and furthermore, what responsible is. Does a certain moisturizer really make skin look younger, or is it the 20-year-old model who has a young, dewy complexion? How would that moisturizer work for a 50-year-old? Do automakers and beer makers really need young women in skimpy bathing suits to sell their products? Do companies have a responsibility to respect all consumers? Are certain segments of the population fair game when it comes to the art of selling? Should we attempt to protect children from sugary cereal ads or teen-agers from ads for expensive athletic shoes? How truthful, or responsible does advertising have to be to qualify as ethical? Let's take a look at a classic case:

Company: **G. Heileman Brewing Co.**
Industry: Beer makers (brewers)
   Situation: Although beer sales in general were off by several percent in 1991, one segment of the market—the malt liquor segment—was experiencing tremendous growth. Depending on the brand, malt liquors can have almost twice the alcoholic content of regular beer. Heileman's brew, PowerMaster, had an alcohol content of 5.9% compared to 3.5% for ordinary beer.
   The company got into trouble when they focused on inner city youth as a target market. The company developed commercials featuring rap musicians who glorified in song (rap) the virtues of being a PowerMaster, and drinking a beer that was the "power." African-American activists like the Reverend Calvin Butts in New York City and others, denounced the company's efforts to sell what could be a dangerous product to a group that already had serious problems with drugs and alcohol and gang-related violence.
   How the Company Handled the Crisis: Pressure from African-American leaders (particularly the clergy) mounted, and their outrage was documented in a wide range of media. However, all calls to discontinue the production of PowerMaster were unheeded until the federal government got involved. The Bureau of Alcohol, Tobacco, and Firearms finally ordered Heileman to stop marketing PowerMaster. Heileman was allowed to sell its remaining inventory—about a month's supply, and the brand died shortly after that.
   The Result: This advertising campaign began a wave of controversy, not only about PowerMaster, but about malt liquors in general, and the appropriateness of some advertising messages. It also prompted a hard look at how companies target certain groups of consumers. Heileman no longer makes PowerMaster. It does continue to produce Colt 45, another high-alcohol malt liquor.[9]

Here's a hypothetical case that involves slightly different advertising issues:

   As a bottler of natural spring water, your advertising department has recently launched a campaign that emphasizes the purity of your product. The industry is highly competitive, and your organization has been badly hurt by a lengthy strike of unionized employees. The strike seriously disrupted production and distribution, and it caused your company to lose significant revenues and market share. Now that the strike is over, your company will have to struggle to recoup lost customers, and pay for the increased wages and benefits called for in the new union contract. The company's financial situation is precarious to say the least.

You and the entire senior management team have high hopes for the new ad campaign, and initial consumer response has been positive. You are shocked then, when your head of operations reports to you that an angry worker has sabotaged one of your bottling plants. The worker introduced a chemical into one of the machines, which in turn contaminated 120000 bottles of the spring water. Fortunately, the chemical is present in extremely minute amounts—no consumer could possibly suffer harm unless they drank in excess of 10 gallons of the water per day over a long period of time. Since the machine has already been sterilized, any risk of long-term exposure has been virtually eliminated. But, of course, the claims made by your new ad campaign could not be more false.

List all of the stakeholders involved in this situation. Do any stakeholder groups have more to gain or lose than others? Develop a strategy for dealing with the contamination. How much does a company's financial situation determine how ethical dilemmas are handled?

In advertising, there's a thin line between enthusiasm for a product and high-pressure sales tactics, between optimism and truth, and between focusing on a target market and perhaps tempting that market into unfortunate activities. Can you think of any products where outrageous claims have been made? Is it fair to appeal to the emotions of a particular market segment? Why not? Can you think of particular advertising devices or symbols that are used to appeal to a specific group of consumers? How far is "too far" in advertising?

ETHICS AND EMPLOYEES

Organizations have myriad ethical obligations to their employees. Some of these could include: the right to privacy, the right not to be fired without just cause, the right to a safe work place, the right to due process and fair treatment, the right to freedom of speech (whistleblowing), and the right to work in an environment that is free of bias.[10] We've addressed a number of these rights in other chapters. In this chapter, we're going to focus on two specific rights: a safe work place and the right to keep a job unless just cause can be found for a firing.

Employee Safety

Certainly the most basic of employee rights is to work without being maimed or even killed on the job. In 1970, the Occupational Safety and Heath Administration (OSHA) was created in an attempt to protect workers from hazards in the work place. OSHA's mission is not only to protect workers against possible harm, but also to ensure that employees are informed of the hazards of their particular industry and job.

Let's look at a classic employee safety case:

Company: **Johns Manville**

Industry: Asbestos

Situation: For decades, asbestos was the favorite insulator in myriad construction products—some estimate that over 3000 products contained some kind of asbestos component. Millions of homes, schools, and other buildings contained asbestos insulation; thousands of ship workers in World War II installed asbestos in battle ships and other water craft; and thousands of auto mechanics had fixed innumerable automobile brakes lined with asbestos. The danger of inhaling even minute amounts of asbestos was not publicly known until the 1970s, mainly because the incubation period for many of the asbestos-related lung diseases and cancers is anywhere from 10 to 40 years. However, by the mid-1970s tens of thousands of people who worked with asbestos were beginning to suffer from the fatal diseases we now know are characteristic of asbestos exposure.

How the Company Handled the Crisis: According to company documents, Johns Manville became aware of the adverse health effects of asbestos exposure as early as the mid-1930s. (In fact, Prudential Insurance stopped insuring asbestos workers' lives in 1928.) Although some executives were disturbed by the connection between their product and workers' illnesses, the sentiments of the stonewallers prevailed. Warning labels were not placed on asbestos packaging until 1964. In addition, company doctors lied to asbestos workers at Manville facilities and told them they had no health problems. Johns Manville executives hid scientific data; lied to the public, the government, and their employees; and kept quiet about the danger to which tens of thousands of workers were being exposed.

The Result: By 1982, more than 17000 lawsuits had been filed against Johns Manville. That was the tip of the iceberg. Many more thousands are expected to be filed as more workers developed fatal diseases that were the result of World War II exposure. Many of these deaths are lingering ones, where the quality of life is greatly diminished over many years. As a result of the massive litigation, Johns Manville established a fund containing hundreds of millions of dollars to settle claims. The company filed for Chapter 11 bankruptcy protection in 1982, has been reorganized, and renamed the Manville Corporation. The new corporation has a strong commitment to funding the costs of the claims filed against its former self, and Manville executives have voiced what appears to be a real commitment to ethics within the corporation in an effort to prevent what happened from happening again.[11]

Comments: One of the real mysteries with this case is: how could so many senior executives over so many years manage to live with themselves while keeping the awful secret of asbestos-related illness? It's one thing to hide something for a few years. But to keep something this devastating secret for more than 40 years, throughout many changes in management, is a staggering notion to contemplate.

Would Manville's liability have been lessened if they had informed employees of the risks in working with asbestos? Can you think of examples in other industries where safety and health are major issues? Are there health and safety issues in service (nonmanufacturing) industries? Are employers responsible for conditions such as carpal tunnel syndrome, which is a condition where the wrist is injured as a result of repeated movements like entering data into a computer? What recourse do employers have in situations where the performance of a job, in itself, can cause injury? If a company discovers that its employees are at risk for injury, is it under any obligation to inform the public?

Employee Downsizings

Employee downsizings or layoffs can result from many business conditions including economic depressions, the desire to consolidate operations and decrease labor costs, increased competition and unmet corporate objectives, to list just a few causes.[12] However justifiable the reason may be, the result always involves human misery. Organizations may not have an ethical obligation to keep labor forces at a specific number. They do, however, have an obligation to hire and fire responsibly. One major Fortune 500 company, with recent memories of a painful layoff, sent a directive to all of its managers when conditions began to improve in 1992. The directive stated that no unnecessary hirings were to take place. In other words, "This upturn may be temporary. Don't hire people today who we may have to lay off next year."

Let's look at a hypothetical case about a company's ethical obligations to its employees:

Giant Co. is a large company that has experienced significant decreases in sales and profits. It has become apparent to key stakeholders—employees, customers, and the financial community—that Giant has focused on the wrong product lines. Consequently, numerous small competitors have eroded Giant's place in its industry, and Giant's sales and profits have plummeted. Over the last year, Giant's board of directors has reduced the company's dividend, replaced Giant's CEO with someone from outside of the industry, and has demanded strict cost controls, including reduced employee benefits and headcount reductions. The experts suggest that 30% of Giant's employees will be terminated.

The new CEO, who has a reputation as a turnaround artist, is known for his propensity to make deep cuts in personnel, and to radically alter organizational structures. The employees are reeling from the layoffs, insecurity, and critical press accounts that suggest that Giant is having an identity crisis that could put it out of business if change doesn't happen fast. As a result, Giant's CEO asks you, the head of human resources, to design a plan to cut the oldest—and most highly paid and experienced—employees from the company. He supplies you with a target number that he says will accomplish his goal and yet keep government regulators at bay.

As we mentioned in Chapter 6, employees have the right to be treated fairly, without bias, and on the basis of their ability to perform a specific job. And, if a layoff or downsizing is necessary—if it involves one person or many—the layoff should be done with respect, dignity, and compassion. In the hypothetical case we just described, what is your obligation to Giant's employees and to the new CEO? Does the CEO's mandate conflict with your profession's notion of responsibility? If there is a conflict, how could you resolve it? What factors would you consider in structuring a plan that would be as fair as possible to all involved?

ETHICS AND SHAREHOLDERS

Organizations also have a clear ethical obligation to shareholders and other "owners." This ethical obligation includes serving the interests of owners and trying to perform well, not only in the short term, but also over the long term. It also means not engaging in activities that could put the organization out of business, and making good short-term decisions that might jeopardize the company's health in the future. As Kotter and Heskett[13] say in their book, *Corporate Culture and Performance*, ". . . only when managers care about the legitimate interests of stockholders do they strive to perform well economically over time, and in a competitive industry that is only possible when they take care of their customers, and in a competitive labor market, that is only possible when they take care of those who serve customers—employees." Thus taking care of shareholders also means ultimately taking care of other key stakeholder groups. Let's examine how a recent case involving the investment banking giant, Salomon Brothers, impacted shareholders:

Company: **Salomon Brothers**
Industry: Investment Banking
   Situation: In December 1990, the head of Salomon's government bond trading desk, Paul Mozer, decided to test the regulatory resolve of the U.S. Treasury. Annoyed by the federal limits on the percentage of Treasury bonds any one firm could bid for in Treasury auctions—the ceiling was 35%—Mozer devised a plan to evade the regulation. He submitted a bid for Salomon Brothers, and he submitted an unauthorized bid in the name of one of his customers. The two bids combined represented 46 percent of the auction—a clear violation of the rules. Mozer got his bonds, and repeated this maneuver in February, April, and May 1991.
   How the Company Handled the Crisis: In April, Mozer described the tactic to these Salomon executives: Chairman John Gutfreund, President

Thomas W. Strauss, Vice Chairman John W. Meriwether, and General Counsel Donald M. Feuerstein. These executives told Mozer to stop his scheme but did not report Mozer's activities to the SEC at that time. (In May, Mozer rigged the bidding again.) In June, the Securities and Exchange Commission (SEC) subpoenaed Salomon for its auction records. In August, Salomon finally alerted the SEC to Mozer's activities. Immediately following the disclosure to the SEC, Mozer was suspended from his job and shortly afterward, the four Salomon executives mentioned above, as well as Salomon's outside law firm, were asked to resign from the firm by the Board of Directors. The Board named one of its own members, Warren Buffett, as interim chairman.

The Result: The publicity generated by the Salomon scandal was devastating to the firm. Its market value dropped by over one-third—$1.5 billion—in the week following the disclosure. Their debt was downgraded by various rating agencies and major banks reevaluated Salomon's loan terms. Because of the firm's decreased liquidity, its ability to trade was dramatically reduced. In addition to the immediate financial debacle, teams of Salomon Brothers personnel left the firm. For a year after the crisis, the financial press was awash in reports of high-level Salomon employees joining other firms. The defections will no doubt damage the firm for many years. Also, at a time when the profits of other investment banks were soaring by as much as 50% over previous years, Salomon's underwriting revenues were down 26%—a huge and humbling disparity. Their profits were off substantially, customers left, and they were barred from some kinds of transactions or were rendered ineffective because of their weakened financial position. It will take years for the firm to recover.[14]

Comments: In the investment banking industry, reputation is everything. It's the yardstick by which customers evaluate quality and a firm's ability to do business. There is nothing more devastating for a financial services firm than the loss of reputation. Salomon is lucky it survived. It very well could have gone the way of E.F. Hutton and Drexel Burnham Lambert. E.F. Hutton was acquired by another financial firm after it could not survive pleading guilty to 2000 felony counts of fraud in a check-kiting case. Drexel closed its doors after charges of wrongdoing in the high-yield market effectively crippled its ability to do business.

Let's look at a hypothetical case that could affect shareholders:

You work for an investment bank that provides advice to corporate clients. The deal team you work on also includes Pat, a marketing manager, and Joe, who serves as the credit manager for the team, as well as several other professionals. Just before your team is scheduled to present details of a new deal to senior management, Pat suggests to Joe that the deal would have a better chance of being approved if he withheld certain financials. "If you can't leave out this information," Pat says, "at least put a positive spin on it so they don't trash the whole deal."

The other team members agree that the deal has tremendous potential, not only for the two clients, but also for your company. The financial information Pat objects to—while disturbing at first glance—would most likely not seriously jeopardize the interest of any party involved. Joe objects and says that full disclosure is the right way to proceed, but that if all team members agree to the "positive spin," he'll go along with the decision. Team members vote and all agree to go along with Pat's suggestion—you have the last vote. What do you do?

In this hypothetical case, what is your obligation to the shareholders of your organization, and to the shareholders of the two organizations which are considering a deal? Are shareholders a consideration in this case? Are customers? Are employees? Could the survival of any of the three companies be at stake in this case? In a situation like this one, how could you best protect the interests of key stakeholder groups?

ETHICS AND THE ENVIRONMENT

The public's concern with the effect of business on the environment really began in earnest in 1962 with the publication of Rachel Carson's, *Silent Spring*.[15] In her book, Carson outlined the hazards of pesticides, and DDT in particular, to the environment. The public was alarmed by Carson's predictions and that public outcry resulted in the Environmental Protection Act in 1969, and with the creation of the Environmental Protection Agency in 1970. The goal of both the act and the agency is to protect the environment—air, water, earth—from the activities of businesses and individuals. Of course, the ethical obligations implicit for all of us is to think long term about the health of the planet and its environs for ourselves, our children, and other generations to follow. Let's look at some classic environmental cases:

Company: **Union Carbide**
Industry: Chemicals
   Situation: Late in 1984, Union Carbide's plant in Bhopal, India, experienced a catastrophe unparalleled in corporate history. Forty tons of methyl isocyanate (MIC), a lethal chemical used in pesticide production, leaked from a storage tank, formed a toxic cloud, and began heading for the unsuspecting people who lived near the plant. Experts estimate that 2500 people died, and more than 300000 suffered injuries as a result of being exposed to the chemical cloud. In addition to the human casualties, there was significant damage done to the surrounding countryside and to the animals living nearby. A complicating factor in the disaster is that, although Union Carbide was the majority stockholder in the Bhopal plant, the Indian government owned 49.1% of the operation, and all of the workers and

managers in Bhopal were Indian nationals. The links between the Indian plant and Union Carbide's U.S. headquarters were tenuous. To complicate the situation, only two international telephone lines existed between Bhopal and the rest of the world at the time of the disaster.

How the Company Handled the Crisis: Because of a dearth of accurate information about the disaster, Union Carbide had difficulty ascertaining the exact details of the accident. Even with sketchy information, however, the company's reaction was swift and compassionate. It immediately shut down its other MIC-producing plant in West Virginia. It quickly sent medical supplies and a doctor who was an expert in dealing with the effects of the chemical to India. In addition, and even more impressive, Union Carbide's CEO, Warren Anderson, flew to India the day after the disaster to inspect the damage and lend support to the local Union Carbide management team. Anderson was arrested by Indian officials when he arrived, although he was later released. The company also sent a team of experts to Bhopal to investigate the accident.

Meanwhile, Union Carbide's communications team in Danbury, CT, was gearing up an enormous effort to communicate the company's position to all its stakeholders. In the year following the accident, "press requests increased from an average of 250 per year to more than 5000; employee bulletins increased from annual levels of 40–50 to more than 200; and employee videotapes increased from 3–5 a year to 45."[16]

The Result: Wall Street investors reacted immediately to the Bhopal disaster, and Union Carbide lost almost $900 million in market value. In addition, the company image took a beating, with 47% of the public being able to identify Union Carbide as the company involved in the Bhopal tragedy. The disaster turned into a five-year nightmare for Union Carbide: besides the negative publicity and a plummeting stock price, the company endured a two-year investigation, an attempted hostile takeover by GAF Corporation, a gas leak at its West Virginia facility, as well as reorganizations, recapitalizations, and major divestitures. In February, 1989, Union Carbide paid a total damages of $470 million, and $58 million in litigation costs. After the debacle, Union Carbide is still whole and profitable, albeit, much wiser.[17]

Comments: A long-term result of the accident is hopefully an increased awareness on the part of multinationals to keep closer tabs on their foreign operations, especially those located in less-developed countries. Although Union Carbide handled the accident with incredible speed and compassion, its original mistake was to allow a foreign facility to operate with lax controls and poor links to the mother corporation.

Company: **Exxon**
Industry: Petroleum
   Situation: In 1989, the *Exxon Valdez*, an oil tanker bound for Long Beach, CA, from the Port of Valdez in Alaska, ran aground in Prince Wil-

liam Sound. The *Valdez* contained 52 million gallons of crude oil, 10 million gallons of which began to quickly leak into the pristine Alaskan waters. The captain of the tanker, Joseph Hazelwood, was later tested for alcohol consumption and showed an increased blood alcohol level. Although it was never proven that Hazelwood was drunk at the time of the accident, he did violate company regulations by not being on the bridge of the tanker when navigating in those waters

In addition, Aleyeska, the consortium of seven oil companies that originally established Alaska as an oil capital with the construction of the Trans Alaska pipeline, was charged with safeguarding Alaska from just such an accident and with providing immediate help should such a catastrophe occur.

How the Company Handled the Crisis: Although Exxon attempted to immediately begin cleanup efforts, critical equipment was either damaged and in the process of being repaired, or not on the scene. And although CEO Lawrence Rawls did place full-page apology ads in various newspapers one week after the accident, he did not visit Alaska and was roundly criticized for that seeming insensitivity. In addition, Exxon appeared to blame everyone but itself for its problem. And Aleyeska was not much help—like Exxon, it was unprepared for a crisis of the magnitude of the *Exxon Valdez* spill.

The Result: Although over 800 miles of Alaskan beaches were initially covered with oil, by 1990, 85% of them had been cleaned. Wildlife in the area was not so lucky—more than 30000 birds died, as well as at least 2000 sea otters. In addition, the fish population was contaminated and may take years to recover. Exxon spent more than $2 billion on the clean-up and paid additional hundreds of millions to the city of Valdez and Alaskan fishermen. Captain Joseph Hazelwood was fired for not following the regulation about being on the bridge of the tanker.[18]

However, Exxon's image is what really took a beating. Environmentalists publicly hammered the company and approximately 40000 consumers destroyed their Exxon credit cards in protest. (At the time this book was sent to press—five years after the Valdez disaster—Exxon was still embroiled in lawsuits and may be for years.)

Comments: The difference between the personality of Exxon CEO Lawrence Rawls and Johnson & Johnson CEO James Burke could be why Exxon received such poor marks on its handling of the Valdez crisis. Rawls was an engineer and uncomfortable with the media. His reaction appeared slow and seemingly dispassionate, and the lemon he was handed remained a lemon. Burke knew how to make lemonade.

Now, imagine that you are the chief executive of a small chemical company. Think about how you would handle the following hypothetical case:

You have just been named CEO of a small chemical refinery in the Northeast. Shortly after you assume your new position, you discover that your three predecessors have kept a horrifying secret. Your headquarters location sits atop thirty 5000-gallon tanks that have held a variety of chemicals—from simple oil to highly-toxic chemicals. Although the tanks were drained over 20 years ago, there's ample evidence that the tanks themselves have begun to rust and leech sludge from the various chemicals into the ground. Because your company is located in an area that supplies water to a large city over 100 miles away, the leeching sludge could already be causing major problems. The costs involved in a cleanup are estimated to be astronomical. Because the tanks are under the four-story headquarters building, the structure will have to be demolished before cleanup can begin. Then, all 30 tanks will have to be dug up and disposed of, and all of the soil around the area cleaned.

You're frankly appalled that the last three CEOs didn't try to correct this situation when they were in charge. If the problem had been corrected 15 years ago before the building had been erected, the costs would be substantially less than they will be now. However, as frustrated as you are, you're also committed to rectifying the situation. After lengthy discussions with your technical and financial people, you decide that a cleanup can begin in two years. Obviously, the longer you wait to begin a cleanup, the riskier it becomes to the water supply. Before you begin the cleanup, it's imperative that you raise capital, and a stock offering seems to be the best way to do it. However, if you disclose news of the dump problem now, the offering would likely be jeopardized. But the prospect of holding a news conference and explaining your role in keeping the dump a secret keeps you up at night.

Who are the stakeholders in this situation? What strategy would you develop for dealing with the dump and its disclosure? Are you morally obligated to disclose the dump right away? How will Wall Street react to this news? Does your desire to correct the situation justify keeping it a secret for another two years?

Think about the due care theory presented earlier in this chapter. Can we draw parallels between due care for the consumer and due care for the environment? What if the oil tank dump mentioned in the hypothetical case was located in a foreign subsidiary of a U.S. company and the country in which it was located had no laws against such a dump? Would the CEO be under any obligation to clean it up? Should American companies uphold U.S. laws concerning the environment in non-U.S. locations? How much protection is enough?

Why Are These Ethical Issues?

These are all ethical issues because they involve obligations to key stakeholder groups. Consumers, shareholders, employees, and the environment are the major constituencies of any organization that is not operating in a vacuum. What groups are more important to a company than the people who pay to have goods made, the people who make them, the people who buy them, and the place where the goods are made? These ethical obligations all involve fairness and honesty to the four main stakeholders of any organization.

Costs

As we've seen in the classic cases we've described in this chapter, the costs for bungling an ethical obligation to any of the four major stakeholder groups can not only be crippling, but it also can be fatal. Just as individuals who cross the line can short circuit their careers or end up fired or prosecuted, organizations pay the same kind of price: their ability to function can be severely limited and they can even be forced out of business. At the very least, if a company's misdeeds are discovered, they will most certainly be excoriated in the press and by the pubic. Their reputation can suffer long-term damage that may be impossible to repair.

It's impossible to list here all of the regulatory bodies that watch over the rights of the four stakeholder groups. Certainly as you enter a particular industry or company, you will need to know what laws apply to that sector and what regulatory bodies govern compliance. In general, federal, state, and local governments have agencies charged with protecting the rights of stakeholder groups. Regulatory bodies like the Securities and Exchange Commission, the Comptroller of the Currency, and the Federal Reserve Board guard rights of shareholders. The Food and Drug Administration, the Federal Trade Commission, and the Federal Communications Commission are federal watchdog agencies for consumer rights. Employee rights are protected by a wide range of agencies including the Equal Employment and Opportunity Commission, the Labor Board, the Occupational Safety and Health Administration, and others. Finally, the Environmental Protection Agency is the primary protector of the environment.

CONCLUSION

The cases we've described in this chapter represent a few of the more memorable business ethics cases. No industry, and really no company, has been immune from ethical problems and unethical employees. Even Johnson & Johnson has taken its licks in recent years because of so-called inflated prices for some medications prescribed for chronic medical conditions. The point of examining these cases is that truly smart managers should learn from the mistakes of others.

DISCUSSION QUESTIONS

1. What factors might have contributed to Johns Manville's long silence on the dangers of asbestos?

2. What role do you think the personality of a CEO plays in the handling of an ethical problem?

3. Imagine that you're the CEO of a large firm like any of the ones described in this chapter. What concrete steps would you take to restore your company's reputation?

4. How much testing is enough testing when launching a new product?

5. Is Dow Corning's attitude acceptable regarding the number of women injured not outweighing the number of women helped?

6. Does it make sense for "company towns" like Canajoharie, NY to try to impose ethical standards on the "company?"

NOTES

[1]Ferrell, O.C. & Fraedrich, J. 1994. *Business ethics: ethical decision making and cases.* New York: Houghton Mifflin Co., 76.

[2]Hay, R. D., Gary, E. R. & Smith, P. H. 1989. *Business & society: Perspectives on ethics & social responsibility.* Cincinnati: South-Western Publishing Co., 288.

[3]Boatright, J. R. 1993. *Ethics and the conduct of business.* Englewood Cliffs, NJ: Prentice Hall, 332–335.

[4]Donaldson, T., & Werhane, P. H. 1988. *Ethical issues in business: A philosophical approach.* Englewood Cliffs, NJ: Prentice Hall, 89–100, 414–424.

Hartley, R. F. 1993. *Business ethics: Violations of the public trust.* New York: John Wiley & Sons, 112–125, 145–167, 220–252, 295–305.

[5]Hartley, R.F. 1993. *Business ethics: Violations of the public trust.* New York: John Wiley & Sons, 112–125, 145–167, 220–252, 295–305.

[6]Donaldson, T., and Werhane, P. H. 1988. *Ethical issues in business: A philosophical approach.* Englewood Cliffs, NJ: Prentice Hall, 89–100, 414–424.

Hartley, R. F. 1993. *Business ethics: Violations of the public trust.* New York: John Wiley & Sons, 112–125, 145–167, 220–252, 295–305.

[7]Hartley, R. F. 1993. *Business ethics: Violations of the public trust.* Englwood Cliffs, NJ: John Wiley & Sons, 112–125, 145–167, 220–252, 295–305.

[8]Ibid.

[9]Ibid.

[10]Carroll, A. B. 1989. *Business and society: Ethics and stakeholder management.* Cincinnati: Southwestern Publishing, 23–441.

[11]Donaldson, T., and Werhane, P. H. 1988. *Ethical issues in business: A philosophical approach.* Englewood Cliffs, NJ: Prentice Hall, 89–100, 414–424.

[12]Carroll, A. B. 1989. *Business and society: ethics and stakeholder management.* Cincinnati: Southwestern Publishing, 23–441.

[13]Kotter, J. P. and Heskett, J. L. 1992. *Corporate culture and performance.* New York: The Free Press, 46.

[14]Smith, C. W. 1993. *Ethics and markets. Restructuring Japan's financial markets.* Homewood, IL: Business One Irwin, 335–345.

[15]Wood, D. J. 1994. *Business and society.* New York: Harper Collins, 664.

[16]Smith, A. L. 1991. *Innovative employee communications.* Englewood Cliffs, NJ: Prentice-Hall, 41–44.

[17]Hartley, R. F. 1993. *Business ethics: Violations of the public trust.* New York: John Wiley & Sons, 112–125, 145–167, 220–252, 295–305.

[18]Hartley, R. F. 1993. *Business ethics: Violations of the public trust.* New York: John Wiley & Sons, 112–125, 145–167, 220–252, 295–305.

CHAPTER NINE

Ethics as Organizational Culture

(This chapter has been adapted with permission from Treviño, L.K. 1990. Developing and changing organizational ethics: A cultural approach. *Research in Organizational Change and Development*, Vol. 4, 195–230.)

INTRODUCTION

O VER THE LAST 10 years, "culture" has become a common way of thinking about and describing an organization's internal world—a way of differentiating one organization's "personality" from another. In this chapter, we apply this culture concept to organizational ethics. We will propose that organizations can proactively develop an *ethical organizational culture*, and that organizations with "ethics problems" should take a culture change approach to solving them.

A "COOKIE CUTTER" APPROACH WON'T WORK

The theme of this chapter is that a "cookie cutter" or "one size fits all" approach to developing an ethical organization simply will not work. Ethics is an integral part of the organization's overall culture. Therefore, designing an ethical organization means systematically analyzing all aspects of the organization's culture and aligning them so that they support ethical behavior and discourage unethical behavior. This kind of analysis and alignment requires a substantial and sustained effort over a long period of time.

Organizations Don't Have Cookie Cutter Ethical Problems

Standard cookie cutter ethics programs are likely to be ineffective because organizations don't have cookie cutter ethical problems. Although common ethical problems exist across virtually all organizations, organizations may vary in terms of the ethical problems that are most common or important for them. For example, a growing regional bank, a downsizing manufacturer of automobile parts, and an inner-city university probably have different ethics program needs. Forgery or embezzlement may be key ethical issues at the bank. Layoffs may be the hot ethical issue for the manufacturer, and research misconduct issues may be the major ethical concern at the university. Thus, each organization must identify and address the unique ethical problems that it faces.

Cookie Cutter Programs Are Superficial

Second, no matter how well-intentioned they are, cookie-cutter efforts are likely to be short lived or ineffective because they tend to be superficial, leaving deeper systems unanalyzed and untouched. For example, a one-day training program that emphasizes "doing the right thing" doesn't have any impact on an incentive system that rewards unethical behavior. The reward system is still there, awaiting employees when they return to the job.

"Ethics for a Day" Breeds Cynicism

As interest in ethics grew in the 1980s, more and more consultants offered packaged lectures and seminars. "The rule in ethics was spray and pray," said Mark Pastin, director of the Lincoln Center for Ethics in Arizona. "Consultants sprayed some ethics over [big companies] and prayed that something happened."[1]

However, these spray and pray programs can breed cynicism because they raise employees' awareness of ethics problems, while simultaneously suggesting, in many cases, how little the organization is actually doing about them. "We had our ethics-for-a-day training program. Now we're back to doing things the way we've always done them."

Proactively Develop an Ethical Organizational Culture

Align multiple systems to support ethical behavior. Rather than the cookie-cutter approach, organizations that are serious about ethics must proactively develop an ethical culture. Cultures are complex combinations of formal and informal systems. To create an ethical culture, these systems must be aligned to support ethical behavior. For example, if the formal ethics code tells people that honesty is highly valued in the organization, and high-level managers routinely tell customers the truth about the company's ability to meet their needs, employees receive a consistent message about the organization's commitment to honesty. The systems are aligned. On the other hand, if the same organization regularly deceives customers in order to land a sale, the organization is out of alignment. Its code says one thing while its actions say quite another. Deceit is what the organization is really about, despite the ethics code.

Dow Corning—An organization out of alignment?   An organization out of alignment may be lulled into thinking that its ethical house is soundly constructed (because it has an ethics code or program, for example), only to find that the roof has been leaking and it's about to cave in. This may be what happened to Dow Corning.

Dow Corning had been recognized as a corporate ethics pioneer. It was among the first to establish an elaborate ethics program in 1976. Then-chairman John S. Ludington set up a Business Conduct Committee, comprised of six company executives who each devoted up to six weeks a year to the committee's work and reported directly to the Board of Directors. Two of these members were given responsibility for auditing every business operation every three years. In addition, three-hour reviews were held with up to 35 employees who were encouraged to raise ethical issues. The results of these audits were reported to the Audit and Social Responsibility Committee of the Board of Directors. John Swanson, manager of Corporate Internal and Management Communication, headed this effort and was quoted as saying that the audit approach, "makes it virtually impossible for employees to consciously make an unethical decision."[2]

This impressive program failed to help the organization avoid its problem with breast implant safety, however, despite documented warnings from a company engineer in 1976 that suggested that the implants could rupture and cause severe medical problems. It isn't entirely clear why this well-intentioned ethics program failed. It's likely that, although it was designed to cultivate an overall environment of ethical conduct, aspects of the ethical culture were out of alignment—giving employees different messages.[3] "Layering in a bureaucracy is no substitute for a true corporate culture. Workers have a genius for discovering the real reason for a system and learn quickly how to satisfy its minimum requirements."[4] The system relied on managers to identify the key ethical issues covered by the auditors. Were these managers likely to alert the auditors to their most severe ethical problems? What would the consequences be? The system also relied upon periodic planned audits. Did commitment to ethics peak during the planned audit sessions, only to disappear into the woodwork after the auditors left.[5]

Audit of the ethical culture.   The only way to determine if the culture is aligned to support ethical behavior is to conduct a comprehensive audit of all relevant aspects of the ethical culture. This chapter provides guidelines for how to conduct such an audit. If the ethics audit determines that aspects of the current culture do not support ethical behavior, and the goal is to produce an ethical organization, then the culture must change.

ORGANIZATIONAL ETHICS AS A CULTURAL PHENOMENON

What Is Culture?

Anthropologists define culture as a body of learned beliefs, traditions, and guides for behavior shared among members of a society or a group.[6] This idea of culture has been found to be particularly useful for understanding work organizations and the behavior of people in them.[7] The organizational culture expresses shared assumptions, values and beliefs and is the social glue that holds the organization together.[8] Organizational culture is manifested in many ways, including norms, physical settings, modes of dress, special language, myths, rituals, heroes, and stories.[9]

Organizational cultures can vary widely, even within the same industry or organization type. For example, IBM has been long known for its formal culture, exemplified in part by a dress code that mandates dark suits, white shirts, and polished shoes. Apple Computer, on the other hand, has been known for its informality. Particularly in its early days, tee shirts, jeans, and tennis shoes were the expected Apple "costume."

Strong versus Weak Cultures

Organizational cultures can be strong or weak.[10] In a strong culture, standards and guidelines are known and shared by all, providing common direction for day-to-day behavior. Citicorp's culture was so strong that when Katherine Nelson traveled to Citicorp offices in the Far East to deliver ethics training, she felt right at home (despite huge differences in national culture). "You could tell that you were in a Citicorp facility," she said, "whether you were in London, Tokyo, or New York."

Kate facilitated an ethics training session for Japanese managers. She presented them with a common ethical dilemma—what do you do if you have raised an important ethical issue with your manager and nothing is done. In fact, the manager discourages you from pursuing the issue. The potential answers included do nothing, go around the manager to the next level, raise the issue in writing to the manager, or take the issue to a staff department such as Human Resources. The Japanese managers unanimously gave the "correct" answer according to Citicorp's culture and policies. They said that they would go around their manager and take the issue to the next level. Kate was shocked at their response, thinking that it conflicted with the wider Japanese culture's attention to authority, seniority, and honor. So, she asked these managers, "doesn't this conflict with Japanese culture?" To which, they responded, "You forget—we are much more Citicorp than we are Japanese." Citicorp's culture proved to be so strong that standards and guidelines spanned continents and superseded national culture.

In a weak organizational culture, subgroup norms or even individual norms are more influential than cultural norms. As a result, subcultures are more likely to guide behavior. Many colleges and universities can be thought of as having weak cultures. Departmental subcultures are often stronger than the overall university culture, with the romance languages department operating very differently from the accounting department, for example. Among students at a large state university, the fraternity/sorority subculture coexists with many other subcultures, and behavior is quite different within each subculture. It's important to note that weak doesn't necessarily mean "bad." In some situations, strong subcultures are desirable. They allow for diversity of thought and action. It's important to recognize, however, that in a weak culture, behavioral consistency is difficult, if not impossible to achieve.

Norms—"The Way We Do Things Around Here"

Norms are rules or standards of behavior that are accepted as appropriate by members of a group. They exert a powerful influence on individual behavior in organizations, and they can serve to support ethical or unethical conduct. For example, imagine an individual entering a sales job who is told immediately that customers should always be dealt with honestly because long-term customer relations are important. Here, the norm supports ethical conduct—honesty. On the other hand, consider the individual who begins a new job and is told by his or her boss that making the sale is all that counts. This norm supports unethical conduct. Either kind of norm (ethical or unethical) can become "the way we do things around here."

Socialization versus Internalization

Employees are brought into and are taught the organization's culture through a process called enculturation or *socialization*.[11] Through socialization, employees learn the prevailing norms—they learn "the ropes." Socialization can occur through formal training and/or mentoring, or through more informal transmission of norms by peers and superiors. When effectively socialized, employees behave in ways that are consistent with cultural norms. They know how to dress, what to say and what to do.

With *socialization*, people behave in ways that are consistent with the culture because they feel that they are expected to do so. Their behavior may have nothing to do with their personal beliefs, but, they behave as they are expected to behave in order to fit into the context and to be approved by people they care about.[12] An IBM employee whose personal preference is to work in jeans and a sweat shirt will nevertheless dress appropriately according to the more formal IBM dress code because of socialization. Similarly, individuals who don't personally believe in giving kickbacks—but are taught that it's the organizational norm—feel that if they don't go along they'll risk disapproval or they won't fit in. Those who conform to expectations are retained and promoted. Those who don't fit into the culture are likely to voluntarily leave. Obviously, socialization can support either ethical or unethical behavior.

Individuals may behave according to the culture for another reason—because they have internalized the norms. With *internalization*, individuals behave according to the norms because they have adopted the external cultural standards as their own. Their behavior, although consistent with the culture, also accords with their own beliefs about what's right. For example, an individual who prefers formal dress fits in with IBM's cultural expectations about attire. The standards have been internalized and are easily followed.

Organizational culture is created and maintained through a complex interplay of formal and informal organizational systems. Formally, leadership, structure, selection systems, orientation and training programs, rules, policies, reward systems, and decision making processes all contribute to culture creation and maintenance. Informally the culture's norms, heroes, rituals, stories, and language keep the culture alive and indicate to both insiders and outsiders whether the formal systems represent fact or facade. The next section will describe and provide examples of each of these important ethics culture components.

FORMAL CULTURAL SYSTEMS

Leadership

Leaders create culture. Leadership is a critical component of the organization's culture because leaders can create, maintain, or change culture.[13] The founder of a new organization is thought to play a particularly important culture-creating role.[14] Often, the founder has a vision for what the new organization should be. He or she may personify the culture's values, providing a role model for others to observe and follow, and guiding decision making at all organizational levels. For example, Thomas Jefferson founded the University of Virginia. Although he's long gone, it's said today that when the governing board of the university is faced with a difficult decision, they're still guided by "what Mr. Jefferson would do."

The same has been said of Walt Disney. The question, "what would Walt do," has been asked for many years after Disney's death. Walt Disney's moral influence is clear in the introduction to the company's code of ethics. "Walt Disney believed that the right kind of entertainment would appeal to all people . . . Walt believed that our audience would accept, above anything else, quality and good taste in entertainment. Time and time again throughout his career, he virtually bet his entire organization on this belief . . . often in the face of skepticism and predicted failure by others. His philosophy rejected gimmicks and the fast buck, embracing instead a different and vastly more difficult philosophy . . . to produce a quality family entertainment product. This philosophy has brought to the name "Disney" a hard-earned public trust unparalleled anywhere else in the entertainment business."[15]

Leaders maintain or change culture. Current leaders can also influence culture in a number of ways.[16] They can help to maintain the current culture or they can change it by articulating a vision, by paying attention to, measuring, and controlling certain things, by making critical policy decisions, and by recruiting and hiring personnel who fit their vision of the organization.

Jack Welch, CEO of GE since 1981, is held up as an example of a leader who has changed the staid bureaucratic culture of GE into a lean and highly competitive organization. Welch began the culture change effort by clearly articulating his vision that the new GE would be number one or number two in the world in each of its businesses. Businesses that could not measure up would be sold.

Traditional GE employees had been attracted to the job security of the old GE. But, Welch wanted to encourage competitiveness, risk taking, creativity, self-confidence, and dynamism. He recruited managers who were interested in doing a great job and then moving on, if GE no longer needed them. Many of the old-line GE employees found themselves out of sync and out of a job.

Welch also focused on identifying and eliminating unproductive work in the organization. He told managers to eliminate reports, reviews and forecasts, to speed decision cycles and move information more quickly through the organization by eliminating unnecessary bureaucratic layers. All of this has contributed to the "leaner and meaner" GE culture he created.

Leadership and ethical culture. Leadership is crucial to the organization's **ethical** culture, as integrity (or the lack of it) flows from the top, down. According to a report from the Business Roundtable, a group of senior executives from major American corporations, leadership is crucial to organizational ethics. "To achieve results, the Chief Executive Officer and those around the CEO need to be openly and strongly committed to ethical conduct, and give constant leadership in tending and renewing the values of the organization."[17] In surveys of practicing managers, honesty and competence emerge as the most important qualities identified as essential to good leadership.[18]

This view was echoed by Vin Sarni, former CEO of PPG Industries, a large multinational firm, in a 1992 speech to Penn State business school students. Sarni said that the title CEO stands for *Chief Ethics Officer*, a statement that recognizes how important it is for the organization's leader to set the firm's ethical standards. As CEO, Sarni eschewed the use of special staff departments to investigate ethical complaints. Rather, he personally headed the firm's ethics committee which is comprised of line officers, the organization's leaders. The symbolic message was clear. Ethical problems are important enough to be handled by leaders at the highest organizational levels.

Robert D. Haas is the 52-year old Chairman and Chief Executive of Levi Strauss, the maker of Levi's jeans, Dockers, and other apparel. He is also the great-great grand nephew of the company's founder, Levi Strauss. Since its founding in

1850, the company has been known for its extraordinary commercial success as well as its commitment to high ethical standards and social responsibility. Haas is following in a long company tradition with what he dubs "responsible commercial success"—combining profit making with making the world a better place. When he took over as CEO in 1984 (after stints as a Peace Corps volunteer, a White House Fellow, and a McKinsey consultant), however, the company had become bureaucratic and bloated. Haas took the company private through a $2 billion leveraged buyout of nonfamily stockholders. When announcing the buyout, Haas discussed not only its financial benefits but claimed that the buyout would allow management to "focus attention on long-term interests [and] would be the most appropriate way to ensure that the company continues to respect and implement its important values and traditions."[19] This chairman "guru" is known within and outside the company for his efforts to promote diversity, openness, empowerment, and ethical management practices. "He won't tolerate harassment of any kind. He won't do business with suppliers who violate Levi's strict standards regarding work environment and ethics. A set of corporate 'aspirations,' written by top management, is to guide all major decisions."[20] Some have asked if the company would behave differently if it were publicly traded. Haas replies, "It would take a lot more fortitude on the part of Levi's executives," but he insists that "it's a matter of leadership."[21]

On the other hand, if the organization's leaders seem to care only about the short-term bottom line, employees quickly get that message too. John G. Rangos, Sr., the founder of Chambers Development Co., a waste management firm, demanded bottom-line results. When executives reported to him in 1990 that profits would fall short of projections, he is quoted to have said, "go find the rest of it." And so they did, until an outside audit in 1992 found that the company had falsely reported strong profits in every year since 1985, when it was actually losing money all the time. Former employees say that, in the pursuit of growth, manipulated numbers were tolerated, or perhaps even encouraged. One former employee who found discrepancies in 1988 was told, "this is how the game is played." The future of the firm is now in question.[22]

The treatment of ethics in college sports organizations points to the expectation that leaders should set and enforce ethical conduct standards. Joe Paterno, the legendary Penn State football coach, and Dean Smith, of University of North Carolina basketball fame, are coaches who are held up as examples of positive ethical leadership in the college sports arena. They set expectations, create rules and policies, and enforce them.

Coaches are also held responsible when ethical violations are discovered among players, assistants, and boosters. A number of coaches have lost their jobs or have resigned because of these violations.[23]

When wrongdoing occurs in any type of organization, top managers are frequently held accountable even if they weren't personally involved. For example, the Chairman of Dow Corning was quickly replaced as a result of the controversy over breast implant safety in 1992.

Organizational Structure

In Chapter 7 we learned that individuals should take responsibility for their own behavior and question orders to behave unethically. However, the organizational structure frequently reinforces, and sometimes creates problems of authority and responsibility.

Most modern organizations are bureaucratic structures,[24] meaning that they have a hierarchy of authority, a division of labor or specialization, standardization of activities, and a stress on competence and efficiency. Bureaucracy provides many advantages, and large organizations require a certain amount of bureaucracy in order to survive. However, certain characteristics of bureaucracy such as specialization, division of labor, and hierarchy of authority can present problems for the organization's ethical culture.

Authority, responsibility, and ethical culture. With bureaucracy comes the idea of legitimate **authority**. Look at any organizational chart. It will tell you who supervises whom—who has authority over whom. These authority figures serve important bureaucratic roles. They direct work, delegate responsibility, conduct performance appraisals, and make decisions about promotions and raises.[25]

But, the idea of legitimate authority can present problems for the ethical culture. First, recall from Chapter 7 that people tend to obey authority figures no matter what they are ordered to do.[26] This natural tendency toward unquestioning obedience can be a real threat to the organization's attempt to build individual responsibility into its ethical culture.

Second, managers tend to expend a great deal of energy avoiding blame.[27] Their greatest fear is that when it comes time to blame someone, the finger will point their way, and their job will be at risk. By delegating responsibility to those at lower levels in the organization, the authority figure can often avoid blame for mistakes or ethical blunders. When it comes time to blame someone, the finger of blame frequently points down. Underlings, in particular, fear becoming the scapegoat for mistakes made at higher levels. CYA ("cover your ass") memos proliferate as managers look to blame someone in a relatively powerless position who is considered to be expendable.

The structure of an organization can also fragment jobs and roles.[28] It isn't necessarily that individuals don't want to take responsibility. But, jobs and roles get so divided up that they simply can't see the big picture.[29] We saw in Chapter 7 how military bureaucrats passed the buck for responsibility during an investigation of the My Lai massacre. They saw themselves only as cogs in a machine. No one felt responsible for the larger outcomes of their actions.

The ethical culture must incorporate a structure that emphasizes and supports individual responsibility and accountability at every level. Each person must be encouraged to take responsibility for his or her actions and must be held accountable for negative consequences when they occur. However, tracking responsibility is difficult and time consuming and is rarely done well. Many organizations don't do this kind of record keeping at all, perhaps preferring to keep responsibility ambiguous and scapegoating a viable possibility. Special Prosecutor Lawrence Walsh's attempt to track responsibility in the Iran-Contra affair provides a case in point. It's arguable that Colonel Oliver North served as a relatively low-level scapegoat. He received most of the blame, while others in the Reagan administration were able to claim (rightly or wrongly) that they were "out of the loop" (e.g., Ronald Reagan, George Bush, etc.).

New organizational structures. Organizations today are developing structures designed to remove bureaucratic layers, push responsibility down, and empower individuals to make decisions at every organizational level. Take the example of Herman Miller Inc. (HMI), the manufacturer of office and health care facility furniture that is committed to the values of "open communication, "the dignity of each individual," and "quality relationships based on mutual trust and integrity." Kevin Knowles, a crew leader for six years said, "What always surprises me is that everyone in the company . . . is free to talk with anyone in management about whatever they'd like to talk about." Managers at HMI cite workers' ability to go over their managers' heads as a major reason for the company's success. "There's no fear of retribution if you call someone three levels above." HMI touts a process its chairman calls "roving leadership" that allows anyone to be a leader on a particular issue.

Recently, roving leadership was tested successfully. An employee with AIDS decided that he should let others know about his illness. A co-worker took the roving leader responsibility and informed the human resources manager. Quickly, the entire plant was informed, and a physician from headquarters flew in with a training videotape and a question and answer session. According to the "roving leader," what's important is that HMI's value system "allows us to act on our instincts and know the company will support us. Because the value of each individual is important to us, we were able to stop the manufacture of furniture for one day to take care of Peter."[30]

These recent structural changes have powerful implications for taking responsibility and for ethical decision making, and they increase the importance of having a strong ethical culture. When individuals are independently making decisions, with less direct supervision, they need a strong ethical culture to guide them. An important part of this strong ethical culture is a structure that supports taking individual responsibility for ethical action.

Policies and Codes

Many organizations guide employees' behavior through formal organizational value statements, mission statements, credos, policies, and formal codes of ethical conduct. Generally, value and mission statements, and credos are abstract and general statements of guiding beliefs. Formal ethics codes are longer and more detailed, providing guidance about behavior in specific situations. Policy manuals are even lengthier and include more detailed lists of rules covering a multitude of job situations. An extended discussion of policies and codes follows in Chapter 10.

Formal ethics codes are most common. In a study of the largest American corporations by the Bentley College Center for Business Ethics, 93% of the 279 companies responding had ethics codes.[31] Little data exists on how well ethics codes actually work. Codes vary so much in content and implementation that it's difficult to generalize about their impact. We do know, however, that the existence of an ethics code alone will not solve an organization's ethics problems and can actually cause problems if it is implemented without attention to the rest of the ethical culture. A code can prescribe behavior. If that behavior isn't followed, we end up with an organization out of alignment (an organization that says one thing and does another). We also have cynical workers who can cite one more instance of organizational hypocrisy.

In many cases, codes are not widely distributed or enforced (an example of cultural misalignment). In one study, researchers found that only one-half of the codes were distributed beyond the level of officers and "key employees."[32] The Bentley College survey[33] found that only 18% of the respondents had an ethics committee to enforce the code and less than one percent had any type of judicial board to deal with code violations. Failure to enforce the code is a prime example of misalignment with the reward system. The code quickly loses legitimacy if ethical breaches aren't punished.

However, some firms distribute the code widely, even beyond their own employees. For example, in 1993, Wakefern Food Corp. (Shop-Rite supermarkets) distributed its code to its suppliers along with a letter, signed by the president, that said:

Dear Business Associate:

As the holidays draw near, we are mindful of the mutually satisfying and mutually profitable relationship which exists between Wakefern and our suppliers. We look forward to many more years of successful growth together through our joint efforts to provide our customers with quality products, excellent service and low price.

In recent years, we have found many of our staff members embarrassed by well-intentioned gifts from those with whom we do business. Our Board of Directors approved the enclosed Code of Ethics for Wakefern which clearly states our policy prohibiting Wakefern Associates from accepting gifts from our suppliers and customers. We feel that this policy should apply during the holidays as well as throughout the year.

With so much attention being given to practices which bring the business community's ethics into question, we urge your support of our efforts to maintain the respect and confidence of the industry for the objectivity of our dealings with suppliers.

Since failure to comply with our policy will result in disqualification from further business dealings with us, we request that you distribute this letter to those in your company who have business dealings with Wakefern Food Corporation and its subsidiaries.

The most significant means of expressing your appreciation to Wakefern staff continues to be your efforts to help us grow together by anticipating and meeting the changing consumers' needs and wants.

If you have any questions regarding this policy, please contact . . .

With our best wishes for happy holidays and a healthy and prosperous 1994.

Research on honor codes in colleges and universities suggests that students do cheat less in institutions with codes.[33] A recent study found, however, that students' perceptions of their peers' cheating had a more profound influence on their own cheating behavior than the existence of a code. In addition, the certainty of being reported and the severity of penalties were found to be important, supporting the idea that the code alone is not the most important influence.[34] It must act in concert with other aspects of the ethical culture. The code must not only be distributed, it must also be enforced and it must be consistent with other cultural systems. Otherwise, codes of conduct are more likely to serve as mere "window dressing" while being disregarded as guides for actual behavior.

Managers, especially middle managers, *want* to have a stated organizational policy or code when it comes to serious ethical matters. Remember that most people are looking outside themselves for guidance, and stated organizational policy can be an important source of that guidance. To determine where policy is needed, the organization can survey managers about areas of ethical concern and their perception of the need for policy in each area. In one study, managers made it clear that policy was needed in such areas as filing expense claims, gifts and bribes, and treatment of competitor information.[35]

Reward Systems

The importance of reward systems was discussed in Chapter 7. Here, we will focus on the reward system as a key component of the ethical culture and, in particular, the essential role it plays in alignment or misalignment of cultural systems.

Rewarding and punishing behavior.   To understand the ethical conduct of individuals in the organization, we need to look more specifically at the behaviors that are rewarded and punished, and how this system aligns with (or doesn't align with) the rest of the ethical culture. When managers are asked about ethics in their organization, reward systems are frequently cited as a significant problem. They report that concern about the bottom line often conflicts with and overwhelms any concern about ethics. They're rewarded for reaching a particular goal or for selling a certain amount of product, with little attention to how the goal is achieved. Because people tend to do those things that are rewarded, management must ensure that performance goals are realistic and can be achieved without resorting to unethical behavior. A classic case occurred at a GM plant several years ago. The plant manager had installed a device that periodically speeded up the assembly line beyond the rate agreed to in the union contract. When confronted, he pointed out that the firm's production specifications assumed that the line would run at maximum allowable speed 100% of the time. He installed the device to make up for inevitable down time.[36]

Misalignment of the reward system with other aspects of the ethical culture is quite common. We frequently hear this from managers who work in an organization with a code of ethical conduct that isn't enforced. Think about what happens when these cultural systems conflict. For example, imagine an organization where everyone knows that the top sales representative's sales frequently rest on unethical ground. Not only does the unethical conduct go undisciplined, but the sales representative receives large bonuses, expensive vacations, and is celebrated at annual sales meetings. Members of the sales force recognize that the reward system carries the "real" message and the code becomes meaningless, or worse yet, an example of top management's hypocrisy.

The reward system and whistleblowers. The organization's treatment of whistleblowers is a very relevant reward system concern[37] and a frequent source of misalignment. In today's organizations, fewer employees are directly supervised. Therefore, organizations must rely more on their employees to report misconduct. However, as we all know, powerful norms exist against blowing the whistle. The words we use to describe this behavior, "tattling," "squealing," "snitching," "informing," and "ratting," all have negative connotations. In fact, there isn't a nice or even a neutral word to describe it.

Whistleblowers frequently suffer retaliation, particularly when whistleblowers report managerial or organizational misconduct.[38] They're punished rather than rewarded for doing what they think is right. If an organization claims that it's attempting to develop an ethical culture, retaliation against a whistleblower is a powerful example of misalignment. Again, the workers view this "punishment" of the whistleblower as an example of the organization's "real" ethical beliefs.

Roger Boisjoly, a Morton Thiokol engineer blew the whistle on his employer regarding O-ring safety and management problems leading to the space shuttle Challenger disaster. He lost his job as a result of his "ethical" behavior, sending the clear message to other employees that blowing the whistle gets punished. According to Boisjoly, "if you believe in practicing what you preach, it can mean career suicide."[39]

However, the ethical organization must view the whistleblower as an important cog in its control system, and must find ways to make whistleblowing a safe, if not rewarded, activity. Most people don't want a reward for doing the right thing. They just don't want to be punished for it. In an attempt to protect whistleblowers, many organizations have installed hotlines and ombudspersons. Whistleblowers can call these hotlines and speak confidentially and without fear of retaliation. Examples of how these work are included in Chapter 10.

Thus reward systems are important in themselves because they provide guidance about expected behavior, but they're particularly important in the sense that people look to them to reflect the "real" message about what is valued in the organization. Is there consistency between what the organization says (e.g., codes) and what it does (rewards and punishments)? Reward systems frequently represent the source of "cultural misalignment" that can lead to cynicism about organizational ethics.

Orientation and Training Programs

Socialization is often begun through formal orientation programs and reinforced through ongoing training. The organization's values and guiding principles can be communicated in orientation programs. More specific guidance in ethical decision making can be provided in subsequent training programs. Recently, an increasing number of firms have added ethics training to their list of management development programs. Surveys estimate that 44% of companies provide some ethics training.[40]

A former Chairman and CEO of Allied Corporation said, "through our ethics seminars, we encourage people to gain a broader perspective of their responsibilities at Allied. Our managers must be capable of recognizing the ethical dimensions of their business decisions."[41] By providing ethics training, the organization not only offers specific skills to managers, but indirectly communicates that ethical behavior is valued and that ethical dimensions should be considered in decision making. More specific examples of ethics programs are included in Chapter 10.

The ethics training must be consistent with the ethical culture because a training program that is out of alignment is thought of, at best, as a pleasant day away from the office. At its worst, the ethics training will be taken as a joke, when managers attempt to reconcile what they're hearing with their experience in the organization.

Decision-Making processes

Ethical decisions are influenced by the organization's formal decision-making processes. For example, managers may ignore the ethical dimension of decisions unless leaders state that ethical concerns must be a formal part of organizational decisions. This emphasis on ethics can also be reinforced by regularly addressing ethical concerns in meetings and by making them an expected part of managers' reports regarding new products or business ventures. Some organizations are creating special high-level "ethics" committees charged with reviewing major organizational level decisions from an ethical perspective.[42] Others have advocated the implementation of *moral quality circles*, groups set up to assess the morality of business decisions.[43]

Overreliance on quantitative analysis. Decision-making processes can also contribute to unethical behavior. For example, in Chapter 5, we discussed the decision-making process that kept the Ford Pinto from being recalled. In that situation, exclusive reliance on a quantitative cost/benefit analysis to the exclusion of moral considerations had disastrous consequences. In another example, Johns Manville, the former corporate giant and producer of asbestos, was brought down by decision-making processes that focused on the bottom line to the exclusion of worker health. More than 40 years ago, top management began to receive information implicating asbestos inhalation as a cause of severe lung disease in workers. Managers and medical staff suppressed the research and concealed the information from employees. During testimony, a lawyer reported on a confrontation with the corporate counsel about the failure to share X-ray results with employees. The lawyer reported asking, "you mean to tell me you would let them work until they dropped dead?: The lawyer replied, "Yes, we save a lot of money that way." It was apparently cheaper to pay workers' compensation claims than to develop safer working conditions. A New Jersey court found that the company had made a "conscious, cold-blooded business decision to take no protective or remedial action . . ." [44] Obviously, organizational decision makers must rely on quantitative analysis in making business decisions. However, their reliance on numbers, to the exclusion of moral considerations, is clearly problematic. Discussions about whether the decision is the "right" thing to do must accompany discussions about the effect of a particular decision on the bottom line.

Burden of proof.   In 1986, Beech-Nut Nutrition Corporation, the second-largest U.S. baby food manufacturer, pleaded guilty to 215 felony counts, and admitted to selling apple products that were actually a blend of synthetic ingredients. How did this happen? There were many causes, among them the company's financial difficulties, the belief that other companies were selling fake juice (industry norms), and the belief that the juice was perfectly safe.

A chief cause may also have been decision-making processes that were used. When Jerome LiCari, Director of Research and Development, recommended changing suppliers in 1981 (because he suspected adulteration), Operations Head John Lavery turned the traditional burden of proof around. Generally, baby food manufacturers would switch suppliers if the supplier couldn't demonstrate that the product was genuine. In this case, Lavery said that if LiCari wanted to go with a more expensive supplier, he would have to prove that the concentrate they were buying was adulterated (rather than genuine). Given the technology available at the time, this was difficult, and the supplier was retained. [45]

A similar decision-making criterion was used in the decision to launch the space shuttle Challenger despite engineers' concerns about O-ring failure in cold weather. In previous launches, engineers had been required to show evidence that the launch was safe (which would have been difficult, if not impossible). In the case of the Challenger, the burden of proof was changed. Engineers who balked at the impending launch decision were asked to prove that it was *unsafe*.

These examples suggest that it's relatively easy to alter decision-making processes to support whatever decision managers have already made. That's why it's extremely important that organizations design decision-making processes in good financial times and before a crisis occurs. Then, when trouble strikes, they can rely on these effective decision-making processes to guide them. The space shuttle Challenger might never have been launched if engineers had been required to prove that the launch would be safe, rather than unsafe. Managers must be particularly alert to changes in traditional decision-making criteria, particularly in times of crisis.

INFORMAL CULTURAL SYSTEMS

In addition to the formal systems described above, organizational culture is kept alive informally and symbolically through informal norms, heroes, rituals, myths, and stories. Information about these is carried through informal communication systems such as the grapevine. In this way, people come to know what behaviors are "really" rewarded, how decisions are "really" made, and what organizational leaders "really" expect. If the formal and informal systems are out of alignment, people are more likely to believe the messages carried by the informal system. Therefore, management of these informal systems is extremely important.

Informal Norms

As discussed above, organizational norms are a powerful factor influencing organizational behavior. At a fast food restaurant, new employees may be told about a rule against eating food without paying for it. However, once on the job, they may see co-workers eating while the supervisor looks the other way. These co-workers may rationalize their behavior because of their low pay, poor working conditions, or because the supervisor doesn't seem to care. Encouraged to join them, the new employee is likely to do so, having learned the informal or "real" norms. Thus, despite rules, regulations, codes, and credos, informal norms are frequently the most influential behavior guides.

Heroes and Role Models

Heroes personify the organization's values.[46] They're symbolic figures who set standards of performance by modeling certain behaviors. These heroes need not even be present in the organization. Tom Watson, former president and son of the founder of IBM, is still very much alive in the organization. Stories about his values and exploits continue to influence daily organizational behavior. Thus, a hero who champions integrity and stands up for what is right may influence the behavior of many in the organization.

When asked to identify the organization's heroes, Penn State students in a management class on organizational culture inevitably name football coach, Joe Paterno. Coach Paterno is clearly not only the formal leader of the football team, but a cultural hero as well. His values, including education first for college athletes, and winning by sticking to the rules,[47] are considered by many to expand far beyond the football program to permeate Penn State's culture. (For quotes from an interview with Coach Paterno about managing an ethical organization, see Chapter 12).

Much organizational socialization is informally conducted by role models and mentors who may be superiors or more experienced co-workers. Individuals who are passing through organizational "boundaries," such as new hires, or individuals who are transferring from one part of the organization to another, are most vulnerable to these socialization influences.[43] The mentor or role model may emphasize the importance of integrity and resistance to pressure to behave unethically, or the role model may indoctrinate the individual into accepted unethical practices, making it difficult for the individual to redefine the job to exclude them.[49] The new accounting graduate who was told by his superior in a public accounting firm, "you're too honest to be an auditor," received a powerful message about ethics (or the lack thereof) in that organization.

Rituals

Rituals tell people symbolically what the organization wants them to do and how it expects them to do it.[50] Rituals are a way of affirming and communicating culture in a very tangible way.[51] For example, General Motors of Canada introduced their new vision and values by asking each manufacturing unit to create a small float representing one of the key values. These floats were part of a parade that kicked off a full day of culture building ritual surrounding the theme, "customers for life" and the motto, "I am GM." During the day, the CEO unveiled a large painting of the group vision and told a story about their future. To reinforce the "I am GM" motto, employees were asked to see themselves as being responsible, at any moment, for the company, its products, and services. The day ended with the "GM Acceleration Song" performed by the 100-person Up With People singing and dancing group. The song had been revised to incorporate the new values created by the leadership team.[52]

Myths and Stories

Another extremely important way organizational culture is communicated and kept alive is through the informal communication network. People invent stories to give meaning to their world and life.[53] Organizational myths and stories explain and give meaning to the organizational culture. They're anecdotes about a sequence of events drawn from the organization's history. The story's characters are employees, perhaps company heroes, and the moral of the story expresses the organization's values.[54]

At IBM, a story that has been told and retold describes how a low-level employee denied Tom Watson, the former IBM president, entry into a restricted area of the company because Watson was not wearing his IBM identification badge. Watson praised the employee, suggesting the importance of upholding company rules and applying them to everyone.

Language

Cultures develop and use language to communicate values to employees. The old joke that business ethics is an oxymoron suggests that the language of ethics is considered by many to be out of place in the business context. A number of the ethics officers we interviewed suggested that the word "ethics" was still not well received in their organizations (see Chapter 12). When possible, they use other words to describe what they're trying to do. For example, managers seem to be more comfortable talking about their values than their ethics, and Martin Marietta calls its ethics hotline "Guide Line," not "Ethics Hotline."

Managers are reluctant to describe their actions in moral terms even when they are acting for moral reasons, a phenomenon referred to as *moral muteness*. This reluctance can be attributed to managers' avoidance of the interpersonal confrontation that may take place if they question an organizational practice or decision, to the value placed on "efficient" decision making such that moral talk can be thought of as a distraction, and to the desire to appear powerful and effective. Moral talk can appear idealistic and utopian and inconsistent with the expectation that managers can solve their own problems.[55]

Getting people to talk about ethics has also been likened to sex education. Although parents agree that sex education is a good thing, they find it difficult to broach the subject with their children. Similarly, managers may find it difficult to begin a conversation about ethics with other managers or with their subordinates. If these topics are typically not discussed, the manager who brings it up may feel like a "goody goody" or a spoil sport.[56]

Top managers can make ethics an acceptable topic of conversation by sending a message that it's not only OK, but expected, to talk about one's ethical concerns. They can do this by leading discussions in ethics training programs, discussing the ethics code and its application in a videotape that is shown to employees, and otherwise openly discussing ethical problems with managers and employees[57] Senior managers can also build "moral talk" into the fabric of the organization by requiring routine discussion of moral issues and inclusion of ethical issues in business proposals.[58]

Empire Southwest, a company in Phoenix, Arizona, supports "moral talk" in its code of conduct: "It is not enough that you are honest, but vital that you speak out for honesty and honor. The courage to confront a violator, even though embarrassing, is necessary if we are to remain trusted. One act of dishonesty can hurt the entire group, and it is the responsibility of each to act in safeguarding all."[59]

It's difficult to imagine discussing questions of organizational ethics without an acceptable vocabulary to support the discussion. Both educators and employers have a role to play in providing students and workers with the language that can be used to discuss and analyze organizational problems from an ethical perspective. It could be as simple as using words such as "right," "wrong," "honesty," "integrity," "values," and "character." How often does your organization ask whether the decision is the right one, in a moral rather than a business sense? Is this the "right" thing to do for customers, suppliers, the community? How often is a job applicant evaluated for integrity, values, and character, in addition to performance?

The use of ethical language may be related to decision-making behavior. In one study[60] individuals who discussed their decision-making process using the language of ethics were more likely to be the ones who made an ethical decision. These people talked about ethics, morals, honesty, integrity, values, and good character. Those who had made the unethical decision were more likely to recount the decision in the more traditional business language of costs and benefits. This research suggests a link between language and ethical behavior. The language subjects used varied systematically according to the type of decision they made. The implication for organizations is that their employees may need to be taught the language of ethics and its appropriateness for business decision making.

Special organizational language can also be used to avoid the moral implications of actions. For example, in Nazi Germany, the code names for killing and genocide were "final solution," "evacuation," and "special treatment." This use of euphemisms allowed people to avoid confronting the true meaning of their behavior.[61] Today's business organizations have created euphemisms to avoid some of the pain of downsizing decisions. "Rightsizing" and "targeted outplacement" are just a couple of the terms we've encountered. It may be easier to impose a "targeted outplacement" than a layoff, but are the moral considerations as obvious with "targeted outplacement" as they are with layoffs?

DEVELOPING AND CHANGING THE ETHICAL CULTURE

We can conclude from this cultural analysis that ethics at work is greatly influenced by the organization's culture. Both formal and informal organizational systems and processes channel and reinforce certain kinds of behavior. Each of the systems on its own can support either ethical or unethical conduct. In addition, these multiple systems can work together or at cross purposes to support ethical or unethical conduct in the organization. Imagine an organization with an ethics code that forbids giving kickbacks, but then promotes the salesperson who is widely known for giving them. This "we say one thing, but do another" approach leads to widespread cynicism. The code loses all credibility as workers pay more attention to what's done than to what's said. On the other hand, the organization that fires the kickback giver has reinforced the code, supporting its ethical stance with its workers.

Developing and/or changing organizational ethics, then, involves simultaneously developing or changing multiple aspects of the organization's ethical culture. If the effort is to be successful, this ethical culture development or change should involve the alignment of all relevant formal and informal organizational systems. Managers must recognize the complexity of the ethical culture and the importance of the alignment of formal and informal systems in support of ethical behavior.

Changing organizational culture is more difficult than developing it. In a new organization, workers are quite open to learning and accepting the culture of their new organizational home. However, anthropologists and organizational scientists agree that changing culture is an extremely difficult process.[62] This view is consistent with an idea basic to organizational change and development efforts—that changing individual and group behavior is both difficult and time consuming. The human tendency to want to conserve the existing culture is referred to as "cultural persistence" or inertia. Culture has an addictive quality, perhaps because culture members are aware that culture components can not be altered without affecting other, cherished values and institutions.[63] Also, an unethical culture tends to feed on itself. Why would successful (but unethical) managers want to change? They wouldn't. They would tend to hire people like themselves and perpetuate the culture that exists.

In general, the catalyst and pressure for culture change comes from the organization's environment. For example, companies in deregulated industries (banking, telecommunications, airlines) were forced to change their cultures to become more innovative and more marketing oriented.

The pressure to change organizational ethics can come from stockholders, the government, and other outside stakeholders. The public's general mistrust of business executives[64] and the threat of increased government regulation may encourage leaders to look more closely at their ethical cultures. In addition, organizations whose members have been "caught" engaging in unethical behavior, or those faced with costly lawsuits, are prime candidates for such ethical culture change attempts. Finally, the government's new sentencing guidelines for corporate crime have turned the attention of many organizations to an evaluation of their ethical cultures.

However, the influence of bad publicity and costly lawsuits extends beyond the targeted organization. Organizations scan the environment for information that is relevant to their concerns. When one organization in an industry is called on the carpet for a legal or ethical violation, other organizations in the industry may take notice and act. Exxon's mishandling of the *Valdez* oil spill in 1989 sullied the reputation of the entire oil industry. And insider trading scandals put the entire financial industry on alert. Thus, any organization that senses increased vulnerability to external pressure is also more likely to consider the need for attention to the management of its ethical culture.

A CULTURAL APPROACH TO CHANGING ORGANIZATIONAL ETHICS

Any attempt to develop or change organizational ethics can benefit from an organizational change approach that includes a systemwide, long-term view. In addition, it should be based on the assumption that human beings are essentially good and capable of development and change.

A Cultural Systems View

The cultural approach relies on the idea that to be successful any attempt to develop and/or change the organization's ethics must take the entire cultural system into account.[65] The change effort must target multiple formal and informal organizational subsystems. All of these must work together to create clear, consistent messages about what is and is not appropriate behavior in the organization. If subsystems conflict, confusion and mixed messages will result. Thus, the entire range of formal and informal subsystems must be analyzed and targeted for development and change.

This complex, multisystem approach to managing organizational ethics argues against any short-term, quick-fix solutions that target only one system. The idea that an organization could solve its ethics problem simply by establishing a code of ethics becomes ludicrous when the complexity of the ethics culture is understood. The management of ethical conduct must be complex because it's influenced by multiple systems, each of them complex in itself. Thus the complexity of the solution must match the complexity of the problem. A solution that isn't sufficiently complex will miss important information, make incomplete diagnoses, and produce overly simple and short-sighted solutions. The organization that creates a code of ethics in response to external pressure and files it away without making changes in other systems such as the reward system and decision-making processes is more likely making a negative statement about organizational ethics rather than a positive one. The informal message is that management is hypocritical and that the code of ethics serves no useful purpose beyond the creation of a false facade.

A Long-Term View

The development of organizational culture takes place over a number of years. Effective culture change may take even longer, as much as 6 to 15 years.[66] It requires alterations in both formal and informal organizational systems that take time to implement and take hold. Resistances must be overcome. New rules and values must be reinforced via training programs, rites and rituals, and reward systems. Although not all organizational change efforts take this long, deep interventions in the organizational culture should be considered long-term projects.

Assumptions about People

Mainstream economics rests on the assumption that human beings are driven by self-interest and opportunism and are likely to shirk responsibility.[67] Acceptance of this assumption logically leads to change efforts focused almost exclusively on behavioral control.

However, we believe that human beings are essentially good and open to growth and change. Most employees prefer being associated with a just organization that supports ethical behavior and disciplines unethical behavior. Given this type of environment, most individuals can be expected to choose ethical behavior. Individuals who engage in unethical behavior should not simply be labeled "bad" people. They are often responding to external pressures or are behaving according to organizationally sanctioned definitions of what's appropriate. Although unethical behaviors must be disciplined, the organization should also treat unethical behavior as a signal to investigate itself and the cultural context in which the behavior occurred. Through culture, the organization can change definitions of what is appropriate and inappropriate, and relieve pressures to behave unethically.

Diagnosis—The Ethical Culture Audit

Formal attempts to develop or change organizational ethics should begin with diagnosis. Diagnosing culture calls for time-consuming techniques such as auditing the content of decision making, coding the content of organizational stories and anecdotes, and holding open-ended interviews with employees at all levels.[68] It also requires systematic analysis of formal organizational systems such as the structure and criteria for rewards and promotion.

The framework presented in this chapter can provide guidance for an audit of the organization's ethical culture.[69] The audit should include probes into the formal and informal organizational systems that are maintaining the ethics culture in its current state. First, formal organizational systems can be analyzed in a number of ways. Through surveys, interviews, observation at meetings, orientation and training sessions, and analysis of organizational documents, perceptions of how formal organizational systems either encourage or discourage ethical behavior can be identified. A sample of the kinds of questions that can be asked are listed in Table 1.

TABLE 1.   Selected Questions For Auditing the Formal System

1. How are organizational leaders perceived in terms of their integrity?

2. How are ethics-related behaviors modeled by organizational leaders?

3. Are workers at all levels encouraged to take responsibility for the consequences of their behavior? To question authority when they are asked to do something that they consider to be wrong? How?

4. Does a formal code of ethics and/or values exist? Is it distributed? How widely? Is it used? Is it reinforced in other formal systems such as reward and decision making systems?

5. Are whistleblowers encouraged and are formal channels available for them to make their concerns known confidentially?

6. Is misconduct disciplined swiftly and justly in the organization?

7. Are people of integrity promoted? Are means as well as ends important?

8. Is integrity emphasized to recruits and new employees?

9. Are managers oriented to the values of the organization in orientation programs? Are they trained in ethical decision making?

10. Are ethical considerations a routine part of planning and policy meetings, new venture reports? Is the language of ethics taught and used? Does a formal committee exist high in the organization for considering ethical issues?

TABLE 2. Selected Questions For Auditing the Informal System

1. Identify the organization's heroes. What values do they represent? Given an ambiguous ethical dilemma, what decision would they make and why?

2. What are some important organizational rituals? How do they encourage or discourage ethical behavior? Who gets the awards, people of integrity who are successful or individuals who use unethical methods to attain success?

3. What are the ethical messages sent to new entrants into the organization—must they obey authority at all costs, or is questioning authority acceptable or even desirable?

4. Does analysis of organizational stories and myths reveal individuals who stand up for what's right despite pressure, or is conformity the valued characteristic? Do people get fired or promoted in these stories?

5. Does acceptable language exist for discussing ethical concerns? Is this language routinely incorporated and encouraged in business decision making?

6. What informal socialization processes exist and what norms for ethical/unethical behavior do they promote? Are these different for different organizational subgroups?

Audit of informal systems is equally important. The culture can be analyzed to identify the organization's heroes, as well as the behaviors that are reinforced through stories, rituals, and language. This can be accomplished through open-ended interviews, observation of organizational rituals, and analysis of the organization's stories. Some questions that might be asked in an audit of the informal system are offered in Table 2. The questions in Tables 1 and 2 are designed to suggest the general direction of an ethical culture audit. Specific questions that arise out of the particular system being analyzed must be developed to tap that system's unique problems and needs. Canned approaches to discovering culture that assume they can identify the relevant dimensions in advance are bound to fail.[70] In addition, the multisystem nature of organizational culture suggests that responses must be compared within and across systems to answer the key question of whether formal and informal systems are aligned within themselves and with each other.

As you may have determined by now, a full-fledged ethical culture audit is a complex process that the average manager isn't prepared to conduct. Although large organizations may have staff with the required expertise, many organizations will find that they will need to hire consultants to assist with these diagnoses and intervention efforts. In fact, when dealing with a sensitive topic such as ethics, outsiders may be preferable for other reasons as well. Employees may be more willing to discuss these sensitive issues with a trusted, external consultant. On the other hand, understanding the cultural issues addressed in this chapter can help any manager become more sensitive to the complex nature of organizational ethics, and the importance of cultural alignment.

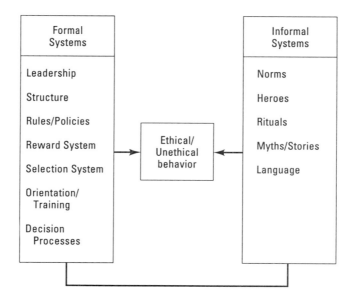

FIGURE 1 Developing and changing organizational ethics—
a multisystem cultural framework

Ethical Culture Change Intervention

Once the audit is complete, the data should be discussed with employees who can then be enlisted in the development of a culture change intervention plan. The plan will be guided by the diagnosis and the cultural, multi-system framework shown in Figure 1. Complementary changes in both the formal and informal organizational systems should be a part of any recommended change effort (see Figure 1).

Although difficult, changing formal systems is a more straightforward process than changing informal systems. Gaps and problems identified in the diagnosis can be addressed in a number of ways. Structure can be altered to encourage individuals to take responsibility for their behavior and to discourage unquestioning deference to authority. Codes of ethics can be designed participatively, distributed, and enforced. Reward systems can be designed to clearly punish unethical behavior. Whistleblowers can be encouraged and provided formal communication channels and confidentiality.[71] Orientation programs can be designed to incorporate the organization's values and training programs can be set up for the individuals most likely to be faced with ethical dilemmas in their work. Integrity can be emphasized in selection and promotion decisions. Decision-making processes can incorporate attention to ethical issues by devoting time at meetings and space in reports.

It's more difficult to change the informal systems, particularly those that have been found to maintain unethical behavior in the organization. However, these changes must be undertaken if the total change effort is to be effective. These changes require attention to the "art" rather than the science of management and are consistent with ideas about the importance of "symbolic management." With symbolic management, organizational leaders and managers are encouraged to be heroic, and to create rituals, symbols, and sagas that will influence those they manage.[72]

The organization may have to be "remythologized"[73] by reviving myths and stories of its founding and resurrecting related tales that can guide organizational behavior in the desired direction. For example, Alexander Bell's comment, "Come here, Watson, I need your help," set up Bell's concept of service that was so important to the telephone company's success. However, myths must also be frequently evaluated for their continuing usefulness. New ones may have to be found or developed in order to fit the current needs and goals of the organization. Remythologizing should be done carefully and infrequently. Employees generally know what's "really going on" in the organization. If the revived myth doesn't fit with organizational reality, it will only increase their cynicism. Also, myths can't be changed frequently. Their strength and value in the culture come from their stability across time.

Ethical Culture Change Evaluation

As with any organizational change and development effort, results should be evaluated over an extended period of time. Evaluation, like diagnosis and intervention, should be guided by the multi-system framework. Surveys and interviews can be repeated regularly to determine if norms have changed and to pinpoint potential problem areas. Documents can be analyzed to determine if ethical issues are being consistently considered. Other outcomes, such as number of lawsuits or reports of unethical behavior can also be tracked. However, interpretation may need to go beyond simply the numbers. Increased reporting to a hotline, for example, may only mean that ethical sensitivity has been raised, and should be viewed as a positive outcome rather than a negative one. This is probably the part of culture building that is most neglected. Most organizations are unwilling to make the investment in evaluation and therefore they really can't calculate the effectiveness of their efforts.

THE ETHICS OF MANAGING ORGANIZATIONAL ETHICS

An effort aimed at changing organizational ethics requires us to face a particularly knotty ethical dilemma. Whose values or ethics are to prevail? How do we know they're worth emulating? A change and development approach that involves employees is not manipulative or coercive and is most consistent with a concern for the ethics of the change effort itself. Employees should participate in the problem diagnosis and planning process. They should be aware of what's happening and should take part in identifying problems and recommending solutions.

CONCLUSION

This chapter has proposed a cultural framework for thinking about ethical and unethical behavior in the organizational context. Although individual character traits may predispose a person to ethical or unethical behavior, the cultural context also has a powerful influence on the behavior of most employees. An organization that wishes to develop or change its ethical culture must attend to the complex interplay of formal and informal systems that can support either ethical or unethical behavior. Thus, quick-fix solutions are not likely to succeed. A broad, multi-system approach to developing and changing organizational ethics was outlined to guide organizations in diagnosing, and if necessary, changing their ethical culture.

Although most managers are not prepared to conduct a broad culture change effort themselves, this chapter has provided managers with the understanding that organizational ethics is a complex cultural phenomenon. With this knowledge, the manager can certainly begin to assess the ethical culture of the organization, and will know what questions to ask the consultant who is brought in to help with a culture change effort.

DISCUSSION QUESTIONS

For the following questions, focus on an organization with which you are familiar. Or, if you are a student without significant organizational experience, discuss the questions with someone who is currently in a managerial role.

1. Does your organization address ethical issues in a formal, systematic way? If so, is it a cookie cutter, one size fits all approach, or has the organization customized an ethical culture to match its unique needs?

2. To the best of your ability, use the questions in Tables 1 and 2 to conduct an ethics audit of the formal and informal systems in your organization.

3. Having conducted the ethics audit, identify the formal and informal systems that are in need of attention. Design a change program to address weaknesses and to align formal and informal systems into a strong ethical culture.

CASE

VideoTek Corp.

Jeremy Campbell is the Chief Executive Officer and Chairman of a relatively young, publicly held, Boston high tech company we'll call VideoTek (for video technology). VideoTek was founded in 1980 by Earl Mantz who created a device that could convert black and white computer monitors into color monitors and would sell for $85.00.

The company started with two people and grew quickly to a core of 35 people who respected Earl as a visionary. Some in the founding group described him as a "deep thinking, spiritual type of person, with high ethical standards." The company culture evolved naturally out of his style. It was a hard work/high trust culture. Good people were hired and trusted to work hard and well for the company, and they did. It was common for people to work 60 to 80 hours a week for VideoTek. They believed in what they were doing and they believed in their product.

The company grew explosively from just two employees in 1980 to 1500 employees and over $200 million in sales in 1994. In 1989, when the company had achieved approximately $40 million in sales, it went public. A professional manager, Jeremy Campbell, was recruited from a large company to bring operational sanity to this small company that was growing out of control. He was named President and CEO. Earl, now a multimillionaire, happily became a member of the Board.

Jeremy brought in his own team—big company types—to manage the company. However, he recognized the value of Videotek's culture and he vowed to perpetuate it. Management today still prides itself on the company's flat organizational structure (e.g., few layers of management) and efficient, open communication via the company's electronic mail system originally set up by Earl. Just about everything that needs to be communicated within the company is communicated by electronic mail. Employees who are on the road keep in touch via their laptops. In support of communication openness, a unique feature of the system allows messages to be sent anonymously.

But, all is not rosy at VideoTek. Not long after Jeremy's arrival, long-time employees began to question top management's commitment to all aspects of the culture. They felt that he especially liked the "hard work" part, but what happened to "high trust?" Something was amiss. Jeremy seemed to be big on words, but short on follow through. He was doing some things that seemed highly questionable and supporting the questionable conduct of his friends. The key question seemed to be, "Could this top management team be trusted?"

Finally, the company has been experiencing a slowdown in growth. It needs new products to sustain its growth, but so far new products introduced under Jeremy's leadership have had disappointing results.

Following are two ethics-related electronic mail messages. The first is a message sent to all employees by Jeremy Campbell in response to an incident of unethical behavior that the grapevine was buzzing about. The second communication is an electronic mail message also sent to all employees a month later by an anonymous employee.

E-MAIL COMMUNICATION FROM THE CHAIRMAN AND CEO

From: Jeremy Cam@VTK 1-MAR-1993

To: All Staff

Subj: Ethical Conduct. Actions, Not Words.

The VideoTek Philosophy is a blueprint for action, a template for daily life at VideoTek. The second we forget that, we are vulnerable to internal challenges which threaten the very foundation of our continued success.

One precept of the VideoTek Philosophy must not be compromised under any circumstances: we live and work ethically. It is imperative to remind ourselves of certain key values which support this commitment:

> The goal of any business is to make a sound profit. Our dedication to quality will help us realize that goal. We do not compromise our integrity in the name of profits.

> VideoTek is changing the way people do business. Because we truly have an impact on people's lives, we must set a positive example of leadership and credibility in all things we do.

> We are honest and fair in all transactions with our customers, suppliers, shareholders and each other.

As specific challenges to these values have arisen, we have addressed them swiftly and decisively. In order to maintain focus on ethical behavior throughout the organization, I have formed a task force consisting of Joe Donaldson, Bill Sykes, Alan Golden, and Joyce Eldridge. This group will examine the following issues in depth and provide me with specific recommendations for corrective action:

* Relationships between VideoTek employees and customers and suppliers

* Outside business activities of VideoTek employees

* Protection of company assets and intellectual property rights

Beyond your own conduct, you have an obligation to report circumstances which you believe to be in conflict with VideoTek's ethical standards. Our ethics committee—composed of Joe Donaldson, Leslie Bolton, Alan Golden, and Joyce Eldridge—has been established to hear these reports and recommend the appropriate response.

VideoTek has been successful because of our ethics, not in spite of them. Only by remaining true to ourselves—resolute in our beliefs and consistent in our actions—will we continue to fulfill our mission. This requires both courage and wisdom, the very same qualities that have made us the company that we are today.
Jeremy.

E-MAIL COMMUNICATION FROM ANONYMOUS EMPLOYEE

From: SECRET@VTK 1-APR-1993

To: All Staff

Subj: Preliminary Report from VideoTek Ethics Committee

The VideoTek Ethics committee, consisting of Joe Donaldson, Leslie Bolton, Alan Golden, and Joyce Eldridge has been meeting to ensure that all VideoTek employees act in the most ethical possible manner. We must all remember the timeless words of our president Jeremy Campbell:

"One precept of the VideoTek Philosophy must not be compromised under any circumstances: we live and work ethically."

In light of this, we have prepared the 1992 Spearshaft of Ethics awards for cases of outstanding ethical behavior within VideoTek.

For instance, the Ethics Committee has received nominations from a few employees for one particular director of VideoTek who is also a major stockholder in one of VideoTek's customers, and whose son, a former employee of VideoTek, is also involved with this customer. Moreover, according to these employees, VideoTek has spent large sums of money and plans to spend even more to develop products for this customer, despite the fact that they have not lived up to the terms of their initial agreement with VideoTek. However, to avoid the slightest tiniest hint of a conflict of interest, the director in question stepped out of the meeting when the Board of Directors voted to approve the deal. Well, he didn't actually step out of the room, but he didn't vote on it, and that qualifies him for the Golden Spearshaft of Ethics. Even if VideoTek eventually loses money on the deal, we can still be proud to have lived by the highest of ethical standards.

From another employee who even read the annual report, we learned that the eight-person Board of Directors voted in 1992 to give all seven of the nonemployee directors stock options. We think that it was very important that the directors get these stock options. The directors do not have nearly enough money. In fact, some of them are practically living on the brink of poverty, or at any rate on the brink of being merely well off. For the eight of them to generously give the seven of themselves these options was the least they could do. After all, the options are only worth $850,000 between them. Because of this generous and self-sacrificing move we are awarding the entire Board of Directors the Silver Spearshaft of Ethics.

Don't believe the rumor that top management has been inconsistent in ethical word and deed. The malcontents who are spreading this rumor are woefully misinformed about a recent incident. As everyone knows, Amy Masterson has been one of our finest sales representatives for several years. However, her commitment to the firm recently came into question when she steadfastly refused to release customer confidential information, even when encouraged to do so by some highly placed VideoTek managers, and even when releasing the information would have clearly contributed to VideoTek's bottom line. Nor would Amy accept the $150,000 top management offered her to go quietly. The entire top management team has been awarded a Bronze Spearshaft of Ethics for their unending support of unquestioning loyalty to the firm. (By the way, donations to help Amy defray her legal expenses on her unjust discharge lawsuit may be sent directly to her home.)

Sadly, it has also come to our attention that some employees have said that our Human Resources Policies do not live up to VideoTek's ethical philosophy. Nothing could be further from the truth. The Human Resources Policies have been reviewed and considered as broadly as possible within the company. For instance, the company policy on nepotism was carefully evaluated by both Jim and Dana Swift. The company policy on termination of employees was scrutinized by a tremendous number of VideoTek employees within the BW and TC Divisions [two new product divisions that have been shut down, millions of dollars in losses, and hundreds of layoffs]. The ethics committee will also be inviting the employees who made the Spearshaft of Ethics nominations to personally review the termination policy, as soon as we can learn their names. Finally, VideoTek's policy on fair compensation was exhaustively studied by Jeremy himself, with the assistance of Business Week magazine, and he said he is fully satisfied that VideoTek is paying fair compensation.

In fact, the executive compensation committee has determined that the company's performance in 1992 was so outstanding that Jeremy has fully earned his compensation of $375,426 plus $50,000 bonus plus options, even thought the company's performance was so average that it would be totally unreasonable for any employees to receive bonuses for 1992. In light of this, we are jointly awarding the Tin Spearshaft of Ethics to the entire Human Resources Department and the executive compensation committee.

There are so many outstanding feats of ethical behavior within this company that we are sorry we can only honor an outstanding few. We hope that this will inspire everyone within the company to try harder in the coming year to live up to VideoTek's high ethical standards.

Lastly, we offer a few words from Jeremy himself:

"I am personally chagrined that anyone could have any perception that any VideoTek employee would do anything unethical. Whoever you are, you had better just change your perception, Buster!"

Joe Donaldson, Leslie Bolton, Alan Golden, and Joyce Eldridge—NOT!

April Fool's!

Case-Based Questions

1. Evaluate Jeremy Campbell's e-mail communication. Assume that this was the only "formal" communication employees had received from him regarding ethics (aside from a "Ten Commandments" type brochure handed to every new employee at orientation). Do you think electronic mail is an appropriate medium for this message? Why or why not? How would you evaluate the content of the communication itself?

2. Next, think about the anonymous e-mail communication. Assume that this communication represents the thinking of a large number of other employees, not just a lone dissenter. What does it say about the alignment or misalignment of VideoTek's ethical culture? For example, what does the communication say about the perception of ethical leadership, reward systems, honesty, and decision processes in the firm?

3. Shortly after this anonymous communication was sent, the ability to send anonymous communications was eliminated from the firm's electronic mail system. What kind of symbolic message do you think that action sent?

4. Earl Mantz, the founder, was a cultural hero while he ran the company during its early years. He had created and maintained the hard work/high trust culture and had the respect of the people who worked for him. Now, however, many see him as someone who sold out and a growing number of people from the original committed group are leaving to join other companies. In fact, less than 5 people remain from the original 35. They get together for a beer occasionally and reminisce about old times. Recently, one of them went on about how money and power can corrupt, "I wonder if the culture was ever real?" What has happened to the hard work/high trust culture? What happened to Earl's ability to provide decision-making guidance? Is there any hope for culture change in this organization? For remythologizing?

NOTES

[1]Byrne, J. 1992. The best laid ethics programs. *Business Week*, March 9: 67–69.

[2]Murphy, P. 1989. Creating ethical corporate structures. *Sloan Management Review*, 30 (2): 221–227.

[3]Ibid.

[4]Wesslund, P. 1992. Ethics are no substitute for the real thing. *Business Week*, April 7.

[5]Murphy, P. 1989. Creating ethical corporate structures. *Sloan Management Review*, 30 (2): 221–227.

[6]Barrett, R. A. 1984. *Culture and conduct; An excursion in anthropology.* Belmont, CA: Wadsworth, Inc.

[7]Deal, T. E. & Kennedy, A. A. 1982. *Corporate cultures.* Reading, MA: Addison–Wesley.

Louis, M. R. 1981. A cultural perspective on organizations: The need for and consequences of viewing organizations as culture-bearing milieux. *Human Systems Management*, 246–258.

Martin, J. & Siehl, C. 1983. Organizational culture and counterculture: An uneasy symbiosis. *Organizational Dynamics*, Autumn: 52–64.

Pettigrew, A. M. 1979. On studying organizational cultures. *Administrative Science Quarterly*, 24: 570–580.

Schein, E. H. 1985b. *Organizational culture and leadership*. San Francisco: Jossey–Bass.

Smircich, L. 1983. Concepts of culture and organizational analysis. *Administrative Science Quarterly*, 28: 339–358.

[8]Smircich, L. 1983. Concepts of culture and organizational analysis. *Administrative Science Quarterly*, 28: 339–358.

[9]Deal, T. E. & Kennedy, A. A. 1982. *Corporate cultures*. Reading, MA: Addison–Wesley.

[10]Ibid.

[11]Van Maanen, J. & Schein, E. H. 1979. Toward a theory of organizational socialization. In *Research in organizational behavior. vol. 1*. L. Cummings & B. Staw, eds. New York: JAI Press.

Fisher, C. D. 1986. Organizational socialization: an integrative review. In K. Rowland & G. Ferris (Eds.), *Research in Personnel and Human Resources Management, vol 4*. Greenwich, CT: JAI Press, 101–145.

[12]Barrett, R. A. 1984. *Culture and conduct; An excursion in anthropology*. Belmont, CA: Wadsworth, Inc.

[13]Schein, E. H. 1985b. *Organizational culture and leadership*. San Francisco: Jossey–Bass.

[14]Pettigrew, A. M. 1979. On studying organizational cultures. *Administrative Science Quarterly*, 22: 570–580.

Schein, E. H. 1985a. How culture forms, develops, and changes. In *Gaining control of the corporate culture*. R. H. Kilmann, M. J. Saxtion, & R. Serpa, eds., San Francisco: Jossey Bass, 17–43.

Selznick, P. 1957. *Leadership in administration*. New York: Harper & Row.

[15]Manley, W. W. II. 1991. *Executive's handbook of model business conduct codes*. Englewood Cliffs, NJ: Prentice–Hall.

[16]Schein, E. H. 1985b. *Organizational culture and leadership*. San Francisco: Jossey–Bass.
Selznick, P. 1957. *Leadership in administration*. New York: Harper & Row.

[17]Business Roundtable. 1988. *Corporate Ethics: A Prime Business Asset*. New York: Business Roundtable.

[18]Posner, B. Z. & Schmidt, W. H. 1992. Values and the American series. *Wall Street Journal*, October 31–November 3: 33.

[19]Lacter, M. 1985. Levi's buyout—It's official. *San Francisco Chronicle*, July 16: 51.

[20]Managing by values; Is Levi Strauss' approach visionary—or flaky? 1994. *Business Week*, August 1: 46–51.

[21]Ibid.

[22]Stern, G. 1992. Audit report shows how far Chambers would go for profits. *Wall Street Journal*, October 12: 1.

[23]Borden, R. C. 1989. Sherrill's termination released. *Bryan College Station Eagle*, March 3: 1.

Hamilton, A. 1989. Switzer resigns. *Centre Daily Times*, June 20: D1.

Status of sports investigations on college campuses. 1989. *The Chronicle of Higher Education*, June 7: A34.

[24]Weber, M. 1947. *The theory of social and economic organizations*. Translated by A. M. Henderson and T. Parsons. New York: Free Press.

[25]Sjoberg, G., Vaughan, T. R. & Williams, N. 1984. Bureaucracy as a moral issue. *The Journal of Applied Behavioral Science*, 20 (4): 441–453.

[26]Milgram, S. 1974. *Obedience to authority: An experimental view*. New York: Harper & Row.

[27]Jackall, R. 1988. *Moral mazes; The world of corporate managers*. New York: Oxford University Press.

[28]Kanter, R. M. 1983. *The changemasters*. New York: Simon and Schuster.

[29]Kelman, H. C. & Hamilton, V. L. 1989. *Crimes of obedience; Toward a social psychology of authority and responsibility*. New Haven, CT: Yale University.

[30]Nelson–Horchler, 1991. The magic of Herman Miller. *Industry Week*, February 18: 11–12, 14,17.

[31]Murray, T. J. 1987. Ethics programs: Just a pretty face? *Business Month*, 130 (3): 30–32.

[32]White, B. J. & Montgomery, R. B. 1980. Corporate codes of conduct. *California Management Review*, 23, 80–86(4): 690–697.

[33]Bowers, W. J. 1964. *Student dishonesty and its control in college*. New York: Bureau of Applied Social Research, Columbia University.

Campbell, W. G. 1935. *A comparative investigation of students under an honor system and a proctor system in the same university*. Los Angeles: University of Southern California Press.

Canning, R. 1956. Does an honor system reduce classroom cheating? An experimental answer. *Journal of Experimental Education*, 24: 291–296.

McCabe, D. L. & Trevino, L. K. 1993. Academic dishonesty: Honor codes and other situational influences. *Journal of Higher Education*, 64 (5): 522–528.

[34]McCabe, D. L. & Trevino, L. K. 1993. Academic dishonesty: Honor codes and other situational influences. *Journal of Higher Education*, 64 (5): 522–528.

[35]Nel, D., Pitt, L. & Watson, R. 1989. Business ethics: Defining the twilight zone. *Journal of Business Ethics*, 8: 781–791.

[36]Labich, K. 1992. The new crisis in business ethics. *Fortune*, April 20: 167–176.

[37]Graham, J. W. 1986. Principled organizational dissent: A theoretical essay. In *Research in organizational behavior, vol. 8*. L. Cummings & B. M. Staw, eds. Greenwich, CT: JAI Press, 1–52.

Near, J. P. & Miceli, M. P. 1987. Whistleblowers in organizations: dissidents or reformers? In *Research in organizational behavior*. L. Cummings & B. Staw, eds. Greenwich, CT: JAI Press, 321–368.

[38]Glazer, M. P. & Glazer, P. M. 1986. Whistleblowing. *Psychology Today*, August.

[39]Murray, T. J. 1987. Ethics programs: Just a pretty face? *Business Month*, 130 (3): 30–32.

[40]Harrington, S. J. 1991. What corporate America is teaching about ethics. *Academy of Management Executive*, 5 (1): 21–30.

[41]Allied Corporation. 1984. Ethics education for managers. *Ethics resource center report*, 2: 1.

[42]Schwartz, H. & Davis, S. M. 1981. Matching corporate culture and business strategy, *Organizational Dynamics*, Summer: 30–48.

[43]Tiger, L. 1988. Stone age provides model for instilling business ethics. *Wall Street Journal*, January 11: 18.

[44]Gellerman, S. 1986. Why "good" managers make bad ethical choices. *Harvard Business Review*, Winter: 15–19.

[45]Welles, C. 1988. What led Beech-Nut down the road to disgrace? *Business Week*, February 22.

[46]Deal, T. E. & Kennedy, A. A. 1982. *Corporate cultures*. Reading, MA: Addison–Wesley.

[47]Paterno, J. 1989. *Paterno by the book*. New York: Random House.

[48]Van Maanen, J. & Schein, E. H. 1979. Toward a theory of organizational socialization. In L. Cummings & B. Staw (Eds.), *Research in organizational behavior. vol. 1*. New York: JAI Press.

[49]Waters, J. A. 1978. Catch 20.5: Corporate morality as an organizational phenomenon. *Organizational Dynamics*, Spring: 3–19.

[50]Deal, T. E. & Kennedy, A. A. 1982. *Corporate cultures*. Reading, MA: Addison–Wesley.

[51]Beyer, J. M. & Trice, H. M. 1987. How an organization's rites reveal its culture. *Organizational Dynamics*, 15 (4): 5–24.

[52]Channon, J. 1992. Creating esprit de corps. In *New Traditions in Business; Spirit and Leadership in the 21st century*. San Francisco: Berrett Koehler Publishers, 53–66.

[53]Mitroff, I. & Kilmann, R. H. 1976. On organizational stories: An approach to the design and analysis of organization through myths and stories. In *The management of organization design; Strategies and implications*. R. Kilmann, Pondy, L. & Slevin, eds. New York: North–Holland.

[54]Martin, J. & Siehl, C. 1983. Organizational culture and counterculture: An uneasy symbiosis. *Organizational Dynamics*, Autumn: 52–64.

[55]Bird, F. B. & Waters, J. A. 1989. The moral muteness of managers. *California Management Review*, Fall: 73–88.

[56]Berney, K. 1987. Finding the ethical edge. *Nation's Business*, August: 18–24.

[57]Ibid.

[58]Bird, F. B. & Waters, J. A. 1989. The moral muteness of managers. *California Management Review*, Fall: 73–88.

[59]Berney, K. 1987. Finding the ethical edge. *Nation's Business*. August: 18–24.

[60]Trevino, L. K. 1987. *The influences of vicarious learning and individual differences on ethical decision making in the organization: An experiment*. Unpublished doctoral dissertation, Texas A & M University, College Station, Texas.

[61]Kelman, H. C. & Hamilton, V. L. 1989. *Crimes of obedience; Toward a social psychology of authority and responsibility*. New Haven, CT: Yale University.

[62]Barrett, R. A. 1984. *Culture and conduct; An excursion in anthropology*. Belmont, CA: Wadsworth, Inc.

Uttal, B. 1983. The corporate culture vultures. *Fortune*, October 17: 66–71.

[63]Barrett, R. A. 1984. *Culture and conduct; An excursion in anthropology*. Belmont, CA: Wadsworth, Inc.

[64]Ricklees, R. 1983. Ethics in America series. *Wall Street Journal*, Oct. 31–Nov. 3: 33.

[65]Tichy, N. 1983. *Managing strategic change*. New York: John Wiley & Sons.

[66]Uttal, B. 1983. The corporate culture vultures. *Fortune*, October 17: 66–71.

[67]Nord, W. R. 1989. OD's unfulfilled visions: Some lessons from economics. In *Research in organizational change and development*. R. W. Woodman & W. A. Pasmore, eds. Greenwich, CT: JAI Press, 39–60.

[68]Uttal, B. 1983. The corporate culture vultures. *Fortune*, October 17: 66–71.

[69]Wilkins, A. L. 1983. The culture audit: A tool for understanding organizations. *Organizational Dynamics*, Autumn: 24–38.

[70]Luthans, F. 1989. Conversation with Edgar H. Schein. *Organizational Dynamics*, 17 (4): 60–76.

[71]Near, J. P. & Miceli, M. P. 1987. Whistleblowers in organizations: dissidents or reformers? In *Research in organizational behavior*. L. Cummings & B. Staw, eds. Greenwich, CT: JAI Press, 321–368.

[72]Peters, T. 1978. Symbols, patterns, and settings; An optimistic case of getting things done. *Organizational Dynamics*, Autumn: 3–23.

[73]McWhinney, W. & Batista, J. 1988. How remythologizing can revitalize organizations. *Organizational Dynamics*, 17 (2): 46–79.

CHAPTER TEN

Creating an Ethical Organizational Culture: Model Ethics Programs

INTRODUCTION

CHAPTER 9 PRESENTED ethics as organizational culture. But, it may have raised as many questions as it answered, such as, "what are organizations *actually doing* to create and communicate an ethical organizational culture?" This chapter is more concrete and is designed to answer that question. It details specific principles, programs, and communication mechanisms that contribute to building and maintaining an ethical organizational culture. It begins by discussing ethics infrastructure, the structure within which ethics programs and communications take place. It then introduces basic communication principles that should guide all ethics communications. This is followed by a discussion of ethics-specific communication mechanisms such as mission statements, policy manuals, codes of conduct, ethics training programs, and leader communication strategies. Finally, we've incorporated a number of corporate examples from model ethics programs—corporations that manage and communicate ethics in ways that are consistent with their cultures. Much of the information and many of the quotes in this chapter come from interviews we conducted with top executives who manage ethics for their firms. As was suggested in Chapter 9, any ideas gleaned from this chapter should be adapted to the unique characteristics and culture of each organization.

Whatever your level in the organization, you should find this chapter helpful. If you're at a high organization level, it could help you make decisions about how to create an ethical culture in your firm. If you're at a lower or midmanagement level, it should help you to understand your own organization's approach and how it relates to what other organizations are currently doing. For example, you won't be surprised to find that the organization you join has an ethics office, a code of conduct and a hotline for reporting violations.

STRUCTURING ETHICS MANAGEMENT: THE ETHICS INFRASTRUCTURE

Whether it's a response to the 1980s "decade of greed," or concern about the 1990s "decade of retribution," many organizations are now allocating significant resources toward ethics programs. Where in the organization are these activities housed? Who manages them, and how do they go about it?

Until the mid-1980s, the title "ethics officer" didn't exist in American business. However, more and more firms are now hiring vice-president level ethics officers or are designating an existing executive as the key person charged with creating and maintaining a company's ethics or business conduct program (as recommended by the U.S. Sentencing Guidelines). There are enough of these high-level ethics executives today that they have formed a professional organization, the Ethics Officer Association (EOA). The organization's stated mission is "to promote ethical business practices, serving as a forum for the exchange of information and strategies." The organization began in 1991 when over 40 ethics/compliance officers met at the Center for Business Ethics at Bentley College in Waltham, Massachusetts. The organization was officially launched later that year and began holding annual meetings in 1993.

The establishment of an ethics office often accompanies the designation of an ethics officer. The corporate ethics office concept can be traced to 1985 and General Dynamics, then the second largest U.S. defense contractor. The Secretary of the Navy, out of concerns about the allowability of certain indirect expenses that had been billed to the government, directed General Dynamics to establish and enforce for all officers and employees a rigorous code of ethics with sanctions for violators. The company turned to a nonprofit consulting firm in Washington, DC, the Ethics Resource Center, for help in developing the code. As part of this process, an ethics office was set up and an ethics officer was hired.[1]

The 1991 U.S. Federal Sentencing Guidelines gave impetus to the move toward naming ethics officers and establishing formal ethics offices. The guidelines list seven requirements (see Chapter 2 for details) for due diligence and an effective compliance program. Recall that organizations that adhere to these requirements face lower penalties in court if someone in the organization is found to have broken the law. One of the requirements calls for the assignment of specific high-level individuals with responsibility to oversee compliance standards. This responsibility can be held by one individual or it can be divided among a number of individuals such as the legal counsel, internal auditors, and/or human resource professionals.

Some organizations delegate these responsibilities widely, finding that a strong statement of values and a strong ethical culture can bind the ethics management effort together. Others look to a corporate ethics committee to manage ethics programs and processes. However, more and more organizations, especially large ones, are deciding that ethics initiatives need to be coordinated from a single office with a single individual ensuring that all of the program's pieces fit together and that all of the Sentencing Guidelines requirements are being met.

The Corporate Ethics Committee

In many organizations, ethics is managed by a corporate committee staffed by senior-level managers from a variety of functional areas. This committee is set up to provide "ethical oversight and policy guidance for CEO and management decisions." It also represents an affirmation that top management really cares about ethics. At Honeywell, the corporate committee manages the overall ethics program whose "principal purposes are to formulate, endorse and promote compliance with Honeywell's business conduct policies and value statement and to ensure that employees, customers, and the public recognize that Honeywell places a high priority on ethical business conduct. The committee reviews issues, makes decisions, formulates policy, and directs program implementation through its program director.[2]"

PPG Industries also places responsibility for ethics management on a high-level ethics committee, chaired by the Chairman. According to former Chairman Vin Sarni:

> I don't think there can be any greater example of the importance of ethics in the company than the ethics committee structure. Anyone can bring a problem to the ethics committee, and it will be handled quickly and discreetly, with full protection and full confidentiality. Problems are investigated by the committee members who are line managers. On the committee we have an attorney who is a labor expert, the head of Human Resources, the Treasurer, and business managers. It's a very diverse group of six very high-level leadership people. The committee meets as required, maybe eight times last year [1992]. Inquiries are not handled in committee meetings, but ad hoc by assignment. I assign one of the committee members to be in charge of that particular situation and they carry it through to its conclusion unless they feel a need for the committee's input. The meetings are for discourse and for policy matters and changes that may be important in terms of communication. We communicate what we do through the worldwide ethics committee, by virtue of periodic articles in our company publications, and by virtue of proliferation of the ethics committee—for example, by establishing a subcommittee of the corporate committee in Europe.

Ethics Officers

More firms are hiring or naming an ethics officer. Approximately one-third of the respondents to a 1992 survey reported having an ethics officer function. Many firms designate their general counsel as the ethics officer. Others create a title like director of ethics compliance, director of internal audit, or just plain ethics officer. Most firms locate the ethics officer at the corporate level, and these high-level executives generally report to the CEO, the board of directors, a committee of the board or some combination.

Shirley Peterson shared the published outline of her responsibilities as Corporate Vice President, Ethics and Business Conduct at Northrop.

> Provides overall leadership and companywide strategies to effectively integrate the Northrop Ethics and Business Conduct Program and the Northrop values into all aspects of company operations. Works with corporate and division executive management and division ethics directors to define, implement and maintain effective strategies to ensure strong, consistent standards of business conduct, and adherence to company policies and values. Maintains an effective working relationship with customer and government organizations that have concerns in this area, including the Defense Plant Representative Office (DPRO), the Defense Contract Audit Agency (DCAA), the Defense Logistics Agency (DLA), the Department of Defense Inspector General (DOD IG) and other oversight agencies.

Insiders versus outsiders.   An ethics officer may be an insider or someone brought in from the outside. We talked to ethics officers who represent both categories. Shirley Peterson and Kent Druyvesteyn were both brought into their firms from the outside while Carl Skooglund had been with Texas Instruments since 1965 before being tapped for the Ethics Vice President position. The consensus seems to favor a respected and trusted insider. According to George Sammett, Jr. Vice President, Office of Corporate Ethics at Martin Marietta Corporation, insiders are more likely to know the company's culture and policy, know what buttons to push and whom to believe. Results of the 1992 ethics officer survey supports the insider preference. Eighty-two percent of the firms responding to the question hired their ethics officer from inside the firm. However, if the organization needs to make a drastic change, the CEO may feel it necessary to bring in an unbiased outsider who can help guide the organization through a culture change process.

Here's what the ethics officers said about choosing an ethics executive and the insider/outsider question:

> *Shirley Peterson—Northrop.* About a year after I had gone to Northrop, I asked the CEO, "I'm curious, why did you hire me?" And he thought for a minute and said that first, as an outsider, I would come with an unbiased look at what was there. Most companies take an old line manager who's been in the company forever and they make it clear to the person that this is your last stop before you go out to pasture. By doing that they get someone who's been around the horn, who knows where all the skeletons lie, where the problems are, and someone who will not be threatened. But, there are tradeoffs there. If the CEO wants a fresh look, he doesn't want somebody who's been around forever and speaks the old party line.

> *Kent Druyvesteyn—General Dynamics.* General Dynamics was in unusual circumstances. We had had tremendous negative publicity. And given the political envi-

ronment in which this decision had to be made, it was probably mandated that someone be brought in from the outside. But otherwise, if at all possible, you should find someone inside the organization. It should be someone who is well known in the organization, someone who has the reputation for being a good listener, for fair play, and someone who can be trusted to maintain confidentiality.

Carl Skooglund—Texas Instruments. An inside person who knows the organization is key. I think it ought to be somebody who has put in enough time with the company to have a realistic chance of knowing what's really going on. It would be a mistake to put someone in the ethics officer job who is 35 and has been with the company only 10 years. But I also think it ought to be somebody who has a chance to move into another slot.

Ethics Officer Background.   The job of ethics officer has been called "the newest profession in American business."[3] But, there are no special programs designed to train ethics officers, so they come from many backgrounds. With insiders, the job is often assigned to someone in a staff function (e.g., someone in the Corporate Secretary's Office, Office of the Legal Counsel, Audit, Human Resources or Public Affairs). According to the 1992 ethics officer survey, law was the most common background despite the fact that some believe that lawyers shouldn't be considered for the job. According to George Sammett, Jr. (ethics officer, Martin Marietta), corporate lawyers face a conflict of interest because they're hired to defend the corporation and therefore can't objectively handle an ethical issue that calls the corporation's behavior into question. Sammett asks, "Would you be willing to spill your guts if you knew the lawyer represented the other side?" The ethics officers we interviewed agreed that there is no single preferred background. What seems to be most important is that the individual is respected for being fair, trustworthy, credible, and discreet.

Carl Skooglund has spent most of his career at Texas Instruments. He worked his way up through engineering and manufacturing and held a variety of operational jobs. He was a product department manager, a division manager, and head of quality training and development and procurement, before being asked to set up the ethics office. When interviewed, Carl said,

A lot of people have asked me why I was selected for this job and I think it's probably because I had a lot of experience on the factory floor. People also tell me I come across as nonthreatening. I've always dealt with people well. I've had good communication relationships both up and down the organization. People at lower levels have generally felt that I'm approachable and I guess they trusted me. If you were to ask me what are the characteristics I would look for if I were selecting an ethics officer, it would be somebody who would be reasonably well known and trusted, somebody who has had experience on day-to-day workplace issues and the kinds of pressures that people are under, and clearly somebody who is perceived to be very discreet.

The Ethics Office, the Organizational Structure, and the CEO

Ethics offices can be centralized or decentralized. For example, NYNEX has business conduct offices in each major business unit and varies its offices based on each unit's unique work environment. Martin Marietta also has a decentralized system. Texas Instruments has a single ethics office that manages and coordinates all corporate ethics activities. The decision to centralize or decentralize may depend upon the overall structure of the firm, and whether different business units have different ethics management needs. If the firm is highly decentralized, it may be difficult to centralize the ethics function. Also, a local ethics office might better meet the needs of different units that are in different businesses. But, decentralized ethics offices must communicate with each other to ensure a certain amount of consistency through commitment to the organization's key values.

Ethics officers seem to agree that, whatever other reporting relationships exist, the ethics officer should have a direct reporting relationship to the CEO. They were particularly concerned about the ethics function being "stuck" under law, human resources, audit, or finance where it could "have its strings yanked," and where it would be just another part of the "silo mentality" that still exists in many organizations. Ethics would then be perceived as Audit's job or HR's job rather than as a part of the total culture. According to Shirley Peterson, the person who leads the ethics office is in a much better position to "press the envelope" if they report directly to the CEO.

Corporate ethics offices are generally small. For example, at Texas Instruments, Carl Skooglund has a staff of four that handles all ethics issues worldwide. At Martin Marietta, three staff members report to George Sammett, Jr. in the central ethics office. But, deputy directors are scattered throughout the organization to speed up issue response. Small ethics staffs make it essential that the ethics office staff work very closely with many others in line and staff positions throughout the company to assess the state of ethics in the organization, develop standards and programs, and implement and evaluate those programs.

COMMUNICATING ETHICS

Within the ethics infrastructure, good communication—downward, upward, and two way—is essential if an organization is to have a strong, aligned ethics culture. The organization must evaluate the current state of ethics communication and initiatives. It must communicate its values, standards, and policies in a variety of formal and informal ways that meet its employees' needs. These communication efforts should be synergistic, clear, consistent, and credible. They also need to be executed in a variety of media, because people learn things in different ways. In general, the old advice to speech writers still holds. "Tell 'em what you're going to tell 'em, then tell 'em, then tell 'em what you told 'em." In addition to downward communication from management, employees must also be provided opportunities to communicate their ethical concerns upward. Finally, an open communication environment must be created that says it's OK to ask questions and it's OK to talk about ethics. In the following section, we begin with some corporate communications basics—principles that should guide all ethics communication initiatives.

Basic Communications Principles

Corporate credibility—Align the formal and informal communication systems. When most people think of a corporate communications system, they think of the obvious—the company newspaper, the annual report, and other written materials. However, like culture, a corporate communications system consists of formal and informal components. Formal communications include all written communication like newspapers, magazines, memos, recruiting literature, policy manuals, annual reports, and advertising, as well as formalized oral communication like meetings, and speeches. But, perhaps the most powerful component in a corporation's communications system is the informal component—the grapevine.

The grapevine—a continual stream of information among employees about "what's really going on"—exists in every organization. It contains news, rumors, impressions, and perceptions. Surprisingly, research has shown that from 70–90% of the information that passes through the grapevine is accurate.[4] And, in survey after survey of employees in numerous and varied businesses, the grapevine is where they said they received most of their information about their employer. (In those same surveys, most people responded that they would rather receive information from their managers). The grapevine can be examined to shed light on a corporation's credibility since most employees are plugged into it, it provides information fast and continually, and it contains the "inside" scoop on corporate events.

One way to determine corporate credibility on various issues—specially ethics—is to compare the messages on the formal and informal communications systems. For example, suppose that XYZ Co. has a policy prohibiting employees from excessively entertaining customers. The policy is spelled out in a manual, and the President of XYZ has reinforced the policy in speeches to employees. Now imagine that XYZ's head of marketing repeatedly wines and dines clients. The costs of the lavish entertainment are detailed in expense reports that are approved by management and that are processed by clerical and financial control employees. In addition, other employees are invited along when the clients are entertained, and still more employees observe the head of marketing entertaining guests in expensive restaurants. Regardless of how strongly XYZ's formal communications system states the official policy, the informal communication system—the grapevine—will communicate what's really going on: XYZ is saying one thing and doing another. The company says it prohibits lavish entertainment, yet it condones that forbidden behavior in at least one high-level employee. As a result, XYZ's ethics culture is out of alignment and it has no corporate credibility on the subject of customer entertainment. Furthermore, its credibility on other ethical issues is probably suspect.

Now, imagine another situation. LMN Co. has a strongly worded policy regarding sexual harassment. And, LMN's senior executives have frequently stated that sexual harassment will not be tolerated. Suppose a manager, Pat Green, is accused of sexual harassment. The charge is investigated, found to be accurate, and Pat is fired. The exact details of the incident may not be on the grapevine, but in most cases, just the bare bones of that story will send a strong message. The messages on the grapevine will match what's said by LMN's formal communications system. Employees will get the word very quickly that LMN means business on the issue of sexual harassment, and the corporation will have increased its credibility by "walking the talk."

The importance of informal communications can't be overstated. Since truth and honesty are at the core of any ethics effort, if a company is saying one thing and doing another—if the messages on its formal communications system and its grapevine don't match—it has little or no credibility and probably shouldn't attempt a formal ethics communications effort until it has regained its credibility. How can you compare the formal and informal messages? Ask employees. Employee surveys and focus groups can provide feedback that will serve as the beginning of an effective comparison. How does an organization establish or regain credibility? Designing consistent policies and enforcing those polices are the only route an organization can take to gain credibility on ethics issues. If policies are enforced for only part of the employee population, or if there are different rules and treatment for different employees, there's little an organization can do to gain credibility until consistency is established.

Analyze the audience.   The first thing to do when designing a communications program is to analyze your audience's needs. Consider what employees already know, what they need to know, what biases and abilities they have, what the desired and required behaviors look like, when they should be asking questions, and where they can go to report their concerns and to ask for help?

When designing ethics communication for a typical employee population, organizations need to consider three kinds of people. We use military jargon to describe the three types because it's easy to visualize and remember.

Good soldiers.   Group I are "good soldiers"—these people understand and follow the rules and policies of the organization, and they have good ethical compasses—they have the judgment or experience required to discern between right and wrong and they have the moral grounding to do the right thing. Be careful to note that these aren't just soldiers who follow orders, right or wrong. They know that "good" soldiers are expected question an order they believed to be illegal or morally wrong—and they would.

Loose cannons.   Group II is called "loose cannons"—they're people with good ethical compasses, but they don't know their corporation's policies, and they may not even be familiar with general ethical standards in business. Loose cannons may be inexperienced; or transferring from another, unrelated industry with very different norms; or these people may never have read a policy manual. Whatever the reason, loose cannons may be well meaning, but they're naive.

Grenades. Group III are "grenades" and they're neither ignorant nor benign. These people may or may not know the rules, but they don't care. They have their own agenda and are lacking any company or professional loyalty. We call this group grenades because their activities can blow up suddenly and severely damage the organization.

While the communication needs of the three groups overlap, the emphasis for each specific group is clear. Good soldiers need support because good people often feel as if they need to compromise in order to "fit in." Good soldiers need to know that their instincts are right, and that their behavior is not the exception. It represents the organizational model. Loose cannons need to be educated; they need to know and understand basic norms of ethical conduct and specific company policy and standards. Grenades need to know unequivocally that ethical lapses will not be tolerated. They need to see good behavior rewarded and ethical lapses dealt with swiftly, consistently, and firmly.

There are probably few grenades in any organization. But, they surely exist everywhere and the system must be prepared to deal with them. Good soldiers may account for a substantial portion of employees, but probably not the majority. Since very few employees ever read a policy manual cover to cover—most people learn policy on a need-to-know basis—the majority of employees fit into the loose cannon category. The challenge in designing effective ethics communication programs is meeting the needs of all types of employees.

This focus on the ethics audience assumes that most employees don't come to the organization perfectly principled and perfectly prepared to make the right decision in every situation. Recall from chapter two that most employees are highly susceptible to influence from outside themselves, so the organization has to provide guidance, and, despite advances, the perfect integrity test hasn't been invented. Since polygraphs were outlawed for most types of employee screening in the United States, more organizations have turned to paper-and-pencil honesty or integrity tests to screen prospective employees. Most of these tests attempt to predict the prospective employee's propensity to steal from the organization, although others have a more general focus on workplace deviance. Integrity tests have recently been evaluated by the American Psychological Association and the government's Office of Technology Assessment. The two organizations' reports generally agree that research on integrity tests is improving and that evidence supporting the tests' ability to predict dishonest behavior has increased.[5] Nevertheless, many problems remain, and organizations will continue to have far from perfect employees who need guidance on ethical issues.

Evaluate the current state of ethics communications. Before beginning the actual design of an ethics communication program, it's essential to conduct an evaluation that asks the following questions:

What kinds of ethical dilemmas are employees likely to encounter? In addition to the typical ethical dilemmas outlined in Chapter 3, organizations need to identify additional dilemmas that might be unique to their particular industry. For example, a chemical company needs to consider environmental and safety dilemmas. A financial firm should pay extremely close attention to fiduciary and confidentiality issues. A manufacturing company may have to look at the ethical issues involved in worker safety, product liability, and labor relations. In addition to determining possible dilemmas specific to their industry, organizations also need to examine the various jobs within their organization to uncover what specific professional dilemmas their communication program will have to address. For example, an internal auditor will face one set of dilemmas, while a manufacturing supervisor will face an entirely different set. Once typical dilemmas are identified, it's possible for an organization to develop a program that's useful for employees—one that shows them how to deal with the most common dilemmas.

What don't employees know? Is the company hiring numerous midcareer hires, who may come from other industries with different standards of conduct? Does the company regularly hire large numbers of recent college or business school graduates who may have little knowledge of business standards, much less specific corporate policy or industry standards?

How are policies currently communicated? How is policy communicated now? Does the policy manual weigh in at 40 pounds? When a manager has a policy question, what does he or she do—look it up in the manual, ask human resources, or guess? What role does human resources play in disseminating policy? Is corporate policy ever discussed in orientation or training programs? No one is ever going to memorize a policy manual. Therefore, an ethics communications program needs to take a "snapshot" of key policies and concentrate on communicating those, plus the message that employees need to know when to ask questions, and that the organization encourages employees to inquire. Companies generally do a very good job of telling new hires how to succeed; what they usually don't do nearly as well is telling new hires how they're going to fail or get fired or worse. It's key that new employees understand what their employer's standards are. What does the company expect from them?

What communications channels exist? How do employees receive messages from management? How does management receive messages from employees? Is "management by walking around" a common practice, or is senior management isolated from most employees? Is there a suggestion program? Are employees generally comfortable approaching their managers with problems, concerns, and questions? Is there a grievance process or a whistleblowing procedure? Can most employees describe the three most important goals of the organization? Do most employees know where to go for help if their managers are unavailable, or if their manager is part of the problem? Are human resources, legal, and audit professionals accessible to most employees? Analyzing the answers to these questions will give an organization a good idea of where effective communications channels exist, where they don't, and where to build new ones.

Multiple Communications Channels for Communicating Ethics Messages

The company's ethics message can and should be communicated in a wide variety of ways. The most obvious ethics communication channels include a mission or values statement, a code of conduct, policy statements, a formal whistleblowing process, and communications from leaders. In addition to these, the ethics message needs to be reinforced in all printed materials including recruiting and orientation materials, newsletters and magazines. Specific ethics-related printed materials can also be developed.

The following list suggests just some of the types of communications materials that can contain an ethics message:

Recruiting brochures. These can include the mission or values statement, a discussion of corporate values, and a description of how people in the organization succeed and fail. Ethical conduct can be highlighted.

Orientation materials. These can include the mission or values statement, descriptions of common ethical dilemmas and advice for handling them, explanations of resources to help employees make ethical decisions, and how to raise an ethical issue or report an ethical concern.

Newsletters/magazines. These can include the mission statement, stories about corporate "heroes"—employees who illustrate the corporate values (including integrity), features that describe ethical dilemmas with comments from employees and managers about how they would deal with the problems.

Ideally, printed materials should continuously reinforce one another. If an organization is really serious about communicating an ethics message, it can also include mission statements and descriptions of corporate expectations in marketing materials and annual reports. That not only reinforces the ethics message with employees, but it also declares a company's intentions with other stakeholders—customers, investors, and the public.

Finally, including ethics messages across a wide variety of corporate communications means that the ethics message is continuously reinforced across an employee's entire career. For example, a candidate for employment would get an initial message in recruiting materials. New hires would get additional ethics information in orientation materials. This information would be reinforced through ongoing training programs, stories in newsletters, annual reports, and marketing materials. The big message is that ethics really is important around here.

A novel approach to ethics communication at Texas Instruments. Most of the communication channels we've addressed so far are relatively formal and one way (from management to employees). But, it's important that organizations also provide less formal opportunities for two-way communication about ethics.

To help employees learn from each other, Texas Instruments has introduced an internal corporate communication tool it calls "Instant Experience," aimed at helping organizational members deal with everyday kinds of ethical crises that they may not have experienced themselves. "Instant Experience" uses the corporate electronic mail system to transmit information about ethical issues weekly to all employees on T-News, the company's worldwide electronic newspaper, and to interact with employees about ethical issues. It frequently posts anonymous ethical questions and the ethics office's answers. This allows employees to raise timely issues quickly and without a lot of bureaucracy and it provides the ethics office with a constant line to the ethical pulse of the organization.

The idea was the brainchild of Glen Coleman, a retired Air Force helicopter pilot and an aerospace engineer who joined TI's ethics office about five years ago. Coleman admitted that, in Vietnam, he and his fellow helicopter pilots sometimes made potentially life-threatening mistakes. But, on their return, they would freely enter their "stupid mistakes" into a book they called "Instant Experience" so that their buddies wouldn't make the same mistakes and lives could be saved.

Coleman thought that something like this could work at TI. In a variation of the idea that not everyone should have to get burned to find out that the stove is hot, he reasoned that the ethics office could be a clearinghouse for ethical experiences that members of the organization were willing to share with others. As a result, these "instant experiences" are regularly transmitted to all employees on an electronic mail communication system, and are retained on the system so that new employees can get up to speed, and ongoing employees can check the system whenever they wish.

Here's an example of an anonymous question posed by a TIer that was posted on the communication system on May 20, 1991.

> Suppose I'm in a restaurant and I happen to overhear a conversation from behind me. It's two TI competitors discussing sensitive, competitive information that would be very valuable to TI. What do I do? Continue to listen? Put my fingers in my ears? Tell them to stop? And what should I do with the information that I've already heard? Forget it and pretend it never happened? Mark it TI STRICTLY PRIVATE and distribute it?
>
> I didn't go out looking for the information and I couldn't change my table location to get away from the conversation. It seems a little ridiculous to just throw away an opportunity to use valuable information that I've acquired but didn't solicit in any way. What's the right course of action?

And, here's how Carl Skooglund, TIs Ethics Director responded:

> . . . there is nothing illegal or unethical about accidentally being in the right place at the right time and overhearing a competitor's conversation. They must accept the responsibility for irresponsibly discussing sensitive information in a public place. If you have overheard the conversation, your best course of action is to document to your best ability what you heard and notify TI Legal, telling them how you acquired it. The TIer who raised this question is correct. It would be ridiculous to pretend that you never heard the information. Under these circumstances you can share the

information with TI. The competitor must accept responsibility for his carelessness. Our ethical principles do not exclude common sense.

Skooglund's response then took the issue a step further, asking TIers if the response should be different if the TIer had *intentionally* sat at a table adjacent to known competitors. Many TIers responded and over 95% of the responses agreed that intentional eavesdropping was clearly unethical. Here are some of their responses:

"We are not in the spy business. It's totally unethical."

"I was disappointed that you would even ask us this."

"Spying is spying."

"What happened to the golden rule?"

"My grandmother told me that if something makes you feel guilty, don't do it."

"If our customers knew about this, would their opinion of us suffer?"

"I would be ashamed."

"It's unmitigatedly unethical."

"Would I be proud to have my TI badge on?"

"Let's leave trickery to magicians."

"Stay far enough away from legal limits so that TIs character is never questioned."

Skooglund agreed with the large majority of responses and assured the respondents that their ethical compasses were pointing in the right direction. This instant experience system is useful because it allows employees to openly share their ethics-related questions and experiences and everyone in the organization can learn from the open exchange. In an organization without such a system, this individual may have struggled silently with the issue or may have asked a few peers or a manager for advice. But, with the system, the entire organization learns from one individual's experience.

"Instant Experience" is one of the most creative ethics communication tools we've discovered in talking with ethics managers. In addition to the weekly transmissions, and interactions, a collection of the weekly articles is retained on the Instant Experience system with a chronological and a subject index. As of May, 1993 the system had 187 separate articles on it—everything from ethical issues surrounding fax machine use to guidelines on the use of frequent traveler programs. The archive can be used by new employees or anyone with a question. A survey of TI employees found that 25–30% read it every week, and about two-thirds read it at least monthly. Supervisors are also encouraged to print the messages and post them on a bulletin board.

We think this system is particularly effective because it fits TI's culture and is based upon sound communication principles. First, TI is a high tech company where electronic mail is a part of the culture. So, e-mail ethics discussions are a natural extension of that culture. Second, electronic mail is appropriate for "ethics" discussions because it allows for interaction with reflection. Ethical issues generally require some introspection, perhaps even a trip to the file cabinet to check the code of conduct. The "instant experience" system allows employees to think about the issue and then participate in relatively informal discussions with other TIers. Finally, research on electronic communication suggests that people are less inhibited when communicating electronically. Therefore, they may be more willing to discuss sensitive ethical issues electronically than they would be face to face, contributing to the "it's OK to talk about ethics" atmosphere.

Mission or Values Statements

In recent years, many corporations have developed mission or values statements. A mission statement, values statement, or credo is a succinct description of "how we do business"—the corporate principles and values that guide how business is to be conducted in an organization. A mission statement is a codification of essential corporate behavior. It's a sort of "Ten Commandments" for an organization. If it's to be effective, it should be short, memorable, and in plain language so that everyone can be clear about its message. It's also essential that the organization's own employees develop it because a mission statement must accurately reflect the organizational culture. A mission statement scribed by outsiders just won't ring true.

An example of a corporate mission statement that reflects the culture of its organization is Citicorp's:

Citicorp's Principles of Ethical Behavior

- We'll behave toward others the way we wish them to behave toward us.

- Each of us will be personally responsible for our actions and won't seek refuge or anonymity behind Citicorp's reputation.

- We'll behave personally and professionally in accord with the letter, spirit, and intent of relevant laws and regulations.

- We believe in the free enterprise system and the appropriateness of earning a profit from providing fair and efficient service to our customers.

- While our headquarters are in the United States, we'll do business in other countries in a manner that recognizes our status as a guest.

- We'll be completely candid with our fellow employees in all business matters so that decisions can be based on all relevant facts.

- We won't directly or indirectly use Citicorp's reputation or resources to enhance our personal opportunities for material gain.

To understand why this statement is appropriate for Citicorp and may not be for another company, we need to analyze the company and the statement. Citicorp's statement specifically addresses the need to avoid conflicts of interest and the importance of honesty—both are essential in a financial institution. Citicorp's code is very specific about the kind of behavior that's acceptable and not acceptable, and it's especially interesting because it stipulates how it will operate outside the United States—as a guest. Of course, that's critical to Citicorp because it has a presence in over 90 countries. Citicorp's statement also concentrates on the behavior of the individual, where many corporate mission statements seem to concentrate more on the organization as a whole. Again, that's appropriate because Citicorp's culture is individualistic. So, although some elements of Citicorp's statement may be transferable to another company— the golden rule element, for example—the entire statement is not. It's a unique expression of a unique organization, and that's why it rings true for Citicorp employees.

Obviously, it's possible to have a meaningless mission and values statement when the words are posted on bulletin boards, but aren't really a part of the organizational culture. On the other hand, we know of many examples where corporate values actually guide corporate and individual decision-making on a regular basis. The role of the "customer first" value in Johnson & Johnson's decision making in the Tylenol crisis is the most famous example. However there are many others. At Alcoa, for example, worker safety has become a top priority value. According to a number of Alcoa's top executives, corporate decisions are not made without considering their implications for worker safety.

Policy Manuals

A policy manual is important because it's the one place where all relevant company rules are housed. Generally, policy manuals describe, not only laws and regulations pertaining to the company and its industry, but also all company policy, including human resources policy. While it's critical for a corporation to define its policies and communicate them—it's one of the stipulations of the U.S. Sentencing Guidelines—most employees don't read policy manuals cover-to-cover. Employees consider policy manuals to be reference manuals and, as a result, employees consult policy manuals in the way they use a dictionary—periodically and on a need-to-know basis. Many managers *never* consult a policy manual, however—it's much easier to ask someone than to look up the rules in a voluminous book—and, depending on whom they ask, they may or may not get the right answer.

The very nature of policy manuals—they're usually large and written in "legalese"—makes them a poor way to communicate the rules. Also, since all policy is detailed, all policy may be viewed as having the same importance. Obviously, some policies are much more important than others and should receive special emphasis.

When designing policy communications, analyze the audience. Who needs to know all the policy? Does some corporate policy only apply to a portion of the employees? What do employees really need to know, and what's nice for them to know? Here are some guidelines to follow:

- Communicate relevant rules to the people who need them. Although there's certainly policy that applies to everyone, there's surely some policy that applies only to specific employee groups. For example, if there's specific policy needed by accountants in the organization—either separate it from the main manual under a specific heading, or leave it out of the main manual and distribute accounting policy only to accountants. If some policy applies to all employees, it can be developed into a code of conduct.

- Prioritize policy. The material describing confidentiality is clearly more important than a description of how to code a time sheet for sick time. Policy should be presented in a way that lets employees see, at a glance, what the most important rules are.

- Make it understandable. First, eliminate the legalese—the only people who like legalese are lawyers. The rest of us like real language. Second, tell employees what the policy means. Most policy manuals prohibit conflicts of interest, yet few employees can define what a conflict is. Give examples of conflicts, and tell employees what a conflict looks like. If people can't tell you what a conflict is, it will be difficult for them to avoid one.

- Make policy come alive. Effective communication occurs, not when you send the message, but when people receive it and understand it. Policy needs to be communicated in short brochures that highlight important rules, and communicated in person in staff meetings, orientation programs, and training sessions.

Codes of Conduct

As stated in Chapter 9, a code of conduct is not a substitute for an ethics program; a code is only the start of an ethics effort. Codes come up frequently because most ethics programs, good or bad, seem to have them. Codes vary substantially in length, content, and readability, but they're generally perceived as the main road map, the ground rules for ethical conduct within the organization.

It's probably fair to say that the longer the code, the less employees are likely to read it. On the other hand, the shorter the code, the broader and more abstract the guidelines. The Marriott Corporation manages to get its code (including Spanish translation) onto four pages. The first page is a brief letter from the Chairman of the Board and President, J.W. Marriott, Jr.

Dear Marriott Associate:

Ethical conduct, acting fairly and honestly in all dealings with each other, our suppliers and our customers, is our Company's most important core value.

Unyielding commitment to these standards and principles is necessary to maintain the pride and confidence of our associates, and to provide quality products and services. Our Board of Directors recently affirmed our commitment to high ethical standards by adopting an Ethical Conduct Policy, CP-1. Please read it carefully, so that you will understand the conduct expected from all associates.

If you have any questions or concerns, please discuss them with your immediate supervisor, manager, Human Resources Representative or contact the Internal Audit Department at [telephone number].

The main headings for the three-page code include obey all relevant laws, treat all associates fairly, with dignity, and with respect, report financial condition and results of operations fairly and honestly, deal honestly and fairly with clients, customers, suppliers and financial partners, avoid conflict of interest, avoid the improper giving and receiving of gifts, safeguard the company's assets, separate personal political activities from the company's business; and report observed violations of standards. Each topic is then discussed in a paragraph. For example, under "obey all relevant laws," the code states,

> Obey All Laws
> including those that apply to alcoholic beverages, antitrust, campaign finance, civil rights, copyright protection, environmental protection, foreign corrupt practices, securities and taxes. While the Company does not expect its associates to be experts in legal matters, it holds each associate responsible for being familiar with the laws governing his or her areas of responsibility. Associates should seek advice from the Law Department whenever they have a question concerning the application of the law. From time to time, the Law Department will prepare a "Business Conduct Guide" and circulate it to the appropriate management.

Many organizations deal with a longer code by dividing the code into parts. The first part provides the broad guiding principles. These are followed by a more detailed section that includes more specific application to cases, answers to commonly asked questions, and reference to more detailed policy manuals. Some organizations create separate booklets for workers in particular functions such as purchasing or human resources management. These can provide details and answers to questions that are likely to arise in that particular type of job and the individuals in that job are more likely to read those details.

Code content may vary depending on the industry and the degree to which the firm has entered the global marketplace. Specific issues are addressed depending on the industry. Firms in the defense industry carefully outline the guidelines for charging one's time to particular government projects. If the firm is global, the code almost certainly deals with issues of doing business abroad.

If the code is to be taken seriously, it should be updated regularly and redistributed throughout the organization. For example, Texas Instrument's 32-page code of ethics has been revised four times since 1961. Many organizations ask employees to sign a statement acknowledging that they have read the code and abided by it during the previous year. Opinions differ as to whether this is a wise and/or necessary practice. Some see it as a necessary step that can convince workers that the company is serious about the code and expects it to be followed. Others see such statements only as efforts by the organization to cover itself in case of a lawsuit. If workers see it this way, they may end up with a cynical attitude toward the statement signing and the organization.

Here's what Carl Skooglund had to say about the card-signing issue:

> I have actually polled our managers and about 80 percent of them said "No", it comes across as a CYA for the company and that's not the kind of tone that we want. Now, I am not saying it's wrong. There are other companies that have taken the card-signing track and used it very effectively. If you are doing a corrective action type of program then it's a very useful tool. Fortunately, we were trying to reinforce a culture that was already there. We hadn't had an event that we were trying to work our way around.

NYNEX won the first Business Ethics Award from the Center for Business Ethics at Bentley College in 1993. The award focuses on the internal efforts companies have made to promote and support ethical behavior by its employees. According to NYNEX, their code provides the unifying guide to ethical behavior across the entire firm. NYNEX's "Code of Business Conduct" is booklike, covering a wide variety of topics in 58 pages, including special sections on business practices (privacy, sexual harassment, safety, alcohol, drugs, political contributions , competitive information, etc.), conflicts of interest, accountability for company property, and laws and regulations. It also includes a question and answer section. Here's an example:

> *Question:* A supplier has invited me to attend a one-day conference at a resort area. There will be a seminar in the morning. The remainder of the day may be used for recreational activities. May I attend?

> *Answer:* Generally, if this type of activity brings business benefit to NYNEX, you may consider attending. You should discuss the situation with your supervisor. You should be aware of the fact that some suppliers may attempt to influence you through an activity of this kind and that your action may be adversely perceived by another supplier. However, if the determination is made that you should attend, NYNEX should pay for all business expenses, such as travel and accommodations.

Finally, the end of the code book is devoted to a series of questionnaires to be completed by NYNEX employees. For example, a five-page conflict of interest questionnaire is completed once each year and is signed by every NYNEX management employee. Forms are also included for reporting gifts received and meals paid for by suppliers, competitors, or customers. NYNEX also keeps in touch with employees through a regular newsletter called the "Ethics Leadership Review." It includes articles on business ethics in general. However, much of the space is devoted to specific questions that relate to the NYNEX code and its interpretation.

Ethics Training Programs

Values statements, policy manuals, and conduct codes aren't enough. Organizations that are serious about ethics distribute these materials widely and then provide regular training in their meaning and application. Effective training programs are ongoing efforts to train everyone from new recruits to high-level managers. Most executives charged with responsibility for ethics don't claim to "teach ethics," however; as George Sammett, Jr. (ethics officer at Martin Marietta Corp.) said in a 1993 speech at the Conference Board conference on business ethics, "We don't teach ethics, we teach ethics awareness. I got half way through Aristotle and quit. We teach what the company expects of you and what kind of company we want to be, what kind of climate we want."

Training should be designed to suit the group of individuals being trained. A new employee needs different training from a manager who has been with the firm for 10 years. An assembly line worker might only require an hour of training, with regular refresher sessions, whereas a manager might require days of training that address a variety of issues.

New recruits. Many firms provide ethics training to new recruits through new employee orientation. For example, all new Honeywell employees are introduced to policies and procedures on their very first day. They view a videotape, listen to a presentation on Honeywell's values and their relation to business ethics from a key executive. They're also introduced to Honeywell's code and "info line" system and the Three R's. The Three R's state that "Under our ethical behavior model, every employee has the following responsibilities: 1) Recognize an issue or situation; 2) Raise the issue or situation to the appropriate levels; 3) see them through to Resolution.

Existing employees. Training is also provided to existing employees. Honeywell initially (in 1986) provided a basic two-hour training module designed to introduce the basic business ethics program to about 23,000 U.S. employees. The following year, it supplemented the initial training with another two-hour module delivered to about 35,000 employees. In 1988, it turned its attention to training 3,000 key management employees, using a three-hour training module. In 1989 and 1990, specialty training focused on employees who have contacts outside the organization.[6]

Supervisors. All new supervisors also receive a day of training on ethics that is a part of the organization's formal management development system. The one-day module focuses on recognizing and resolving ethical dilemmas, motivating employees, using the code of conduct and the three R's. Executives (Vice President level and above) attend a one-week course entitled "Ethics and Values: A Leadership Model."

Top management involvement. When an organization begins ethics training for the first time, it's useful to begin the training at the top of the organization. For example, at NYNEX, the CEO conducted the first ethics training workshop and then the training "cascaded" down through the organization. In the first phase, 1500 mid and senior-level managers attended a one-day workshop. As of 1992, nearly 50000 employees had attended workshops. "Cascading" is a term frequently used to describe ethics initiatives that begin at the top of the organization and work their way down, level by level. This technique is often used because of the import-ance of leadership to the credibility of ethics initiatives.

Although top executive involvement is generally considered to be important, few organizations have gone as far as Syntex, a 50-year old California pharmaceuti-cal company with 10000 employees in a dozen countries. The Vice Chairman and Chief Executive Officer, Hans Wolf, addressed the Conference Board meeting in 1992. He discussed the fact that he personally conducted ethics training on a regular basis and the symbolic meaning of the simple fact that the Vice Chairman would be willing to spend this much time dealing with real ethical issues faced by the firm's managers. Five hundred U.S. and international managers had participated in his ethics training program in groups of from 12 to 30. Here's how it works. Managers request a workshop with Mr. Wolf. He then solicits a brief description of situations these individuals have actually encountered on the job in which it was hard to decide what to do. The entries can be anonymous. He then creates cases that can be dis-cussed in the workshop setting. He has learned that the concern for good ethical behavior is not just an American concern. Requests come from their managers at multiple locations around the world.

Local management involvement. Many organizations recommend having local management conduct the ethics training and using common everyday ethical dilem-mas as the basis for discussion. TI subscribes to that model. According to Carl Skooglund, training sessions are more useful and effective if they address real ethical issues that people face every day. When he conducts the training himself, he uses examples of calls that have come in to the Ethics Office. He was inspired to do this in part by focus groups he held early in his tenure. He wanted to find out what people were thinking, what questions they had, what they thought about TI and ethics. He was shocked to learn that many employees felt that what they did on a day-to-day basis really didn't have any impact on TI's ethics.

> TIers make ethical decisions every day. Anybody who reports the time that they work or decides how to divide their time across different government contracts, or decides whether they are going to engage in some kind of an outside business activ-ity that might be in conflict with their TI job—these are all ethical decisions. Using common everyday issues in training gives employees a feeling of comfort that the issue they've faced has faced other TIers and that they're not some screwball who's worrying about something that doesn't matter.

Finally, ethics training must be refreshed regularly. This doesn't necessarily have to be done in formal classroom training sessions. But, regular updates are im-portant for a variety of reasons: 1) people forget; 2) ethical issues change with changes in law, technology, etc.; and 3) refreshers send the signal that the organiza-tion is constantly thinking about ethics—it isn't a one-shot deal.

A model—The ethics game. A powerful example of how to communicate a cor-porate ethics message is through an ethics game. As mentioned in Chapter 1, Katherine Nelson, coauthor of this book, created the first corporate ethics game, "The Work Ethic: An Exercise in Integrity." You've probably already experienced the game in this class. If not, you may want to review information about the game in Chapter 1.

Senior managers are frequently asked to address employee groups on the subject of integrity and ethics. Senior managers often feel intimidated by this mission, however. Ethics is a personal subject—it's like asking people to talk about their marriage, or their relationship with their mother, or whether they believe in God. It's also perceived to be such a soft subject that most people find it difficult to think of something meaningful to say. This is a major advantage of the game—most people find it easier to discuss ethics if they can focus on specific, practical issues. They can relate war stories along the way. "I remember when something like this happened to me and, boy, if I had ever done this, it would have been a disaster." It's this kind of interplay that employees find most interesting and informative. They can see how senior managers work through an ethical dilemma and what factors they consider important in making decisions.

The senior management appeals board is one of the most important aspects of the game. Groups can disagree with the scoring and appeal to a group of senior managers who have the power to change scores if they're convinced. This somehow "stamps" participating managers as approachable. Managers who participate in appeals boards frequently report there is a marked increase in the number of employees seeking them out and asking for advice. One manager described how he had been stopped in hallways, rest rooms, cafeterias, and even on the street to be asked advice by employees who had seen him as a judge on an ethics game appeals board. Most companies would do just about anything to have their employees seek advice from managers on ethical issues.

Senior managers can also learn a lot from participating in the game. It provides an opportunity for employees to raise issues directly to management. In one session, several male managers were made aware of how offensive young female trainees found any kind of sexual stereotyping. The young women were so determined to let management know how strongly they felt on this issue that the discussion continued at a reception after the game had officially ended.

The ethics game meets many communication goals, but it's especially effective in creating a dialogue and describing expected dilemmas and how employees might handle them. However, in order for an ethics program to be effective over the long term, training and communications should continue over time. A game is an excellent beginning and can be used repeatedly with different dilemmas. However, it can't exist in a vacuum or be all things to all people. It needs to be part of an integrated ethics program with other media and complementary messages.

Another model—The Northrop "When Things Went Wrong" video. Northrop Corporation surprised a lot of people when it created a case study called "When Things Went Wrong," about a devastating incident that took place in the late 1980s at a small 30-person Northrop site in Pomona, California. At the time, Northrop had about 46000 employees. In the company's own words, "the incident shook the company to its roots and damaged its reputation." Because of testing ir-regularities, the facility was closed, the manager and engineer connected to the in-cident were fired and imprisoned, the division to which the facility reported was suspended from government contracting for two years, the company paid a $17 mil-lion dollar fine, and incurred legal and business costs in the many millions.

The company decided, however, that this painful incident could be used in a positive way to raise the ethical awareness and sensitivity of all Northrop employees. They also decided that the use of the case study would make it difficult for Northrop employees to claim that "it can't happen here." So they created a videotape. In frank interviews, the CEO, Department of Defense representatives (the customer), and the managers of the parent division discuss the facts and the causes of the incident. These causes include an interplay of both individual and organizational factors. Then, the video identifies what employees and the organization can do to prevent a recurrence.

Thousands of employees have viewed and discussed the video with their man-ager and co-workers. The response has been overwhelmingly positive. "It helped heighten everyone's awareness of just what is needed from us as individuals when serious problems arise," one employee commented. Management hopes that Nor-throp employees who view the videotape will reflect on and acknowledge their indi-vidual role in ensuring that the incident never happens again.

Communicating Senior Management Commitment to Ethics

In *Corporate Culture and Performance*, Kotter and Heskett[7] pointed to one factor that could turn around a company that was heading in the wrong direction - a strong leader who could communicate the culture. They cited corporations like Xerox and General Electric and described how their top managers led.

> Visions and strategies were communicated with words—spoken simply, directly, and often—and with deeds . . . they encouraged people to engage in a dialogue with them, not allowing the communication to flow in one direction only. In almost all cases, the leaders became living embodiments of the cultures they desired. The val-ues and practices they wanted infused into their firms were on display in their daily behavior; in the questions they asked at meetings, in how they spent their time, in the decisions they made. These actions seem to have given credibility to their words. The behavior made it clear to others that their speeches were serious. And successes, which seemed to result from that behavior, made it clear that the practices were sensible.

Without the buy-in and active support of senior management, ethics initiatives are doomed. But senior managers don't have a great track record in communicating a vision, ethical or otherwise. In a survey of 400 professional and management em-ployees[8] respondents revealed a serious lack of trust in their senior executives. Most said that their company's leaders failed to communicate a "clear understanding of a corporate vision, mission, and goals." They also said that they trust their top management only about 55 percent of the time.[9]

Nevertheless, most employees want to hear from senior executives. Another study of 14250 employees in 17 companies in the U.S. and Canada found that "62 percent of employees list top executives as their preferred source of information, but only 15 percent say they actually get their company news from this source."[10]

What can senior managers do to establish better communications and more trust with employees? How can they begin to build an organization where ethics are valued? They can take a look at the advice that Peters and Waterman[11] offered over a decade ago in their classic book, *In Search of Excellence*. "An effective leader must be the master of two ends of the spectrum: ideas at the highest level of abstraction and actions at the most mundane level of detail. The value-shaping leader is concerned, on the one hand, with soaring, lofty visions that will generate excitement and enthusiasm. . . On the other hand, it seems the only way to instill enthusiasm is through scores of daily events." With this advice in mind, here are some concrete steps senior managers can take:

- Set high standards and communicate them loudly and repeatedly in public and in private.
- Act swiftly and firmly when someone violates the standards. Be consistent—don't have special rules for special people.
- Insist on complete candor from your direct reports. Tell them that you don't want to be protected, especially from bad news.
- Never, never shoot the messenger.
- Talk to a wide variety of employees on different levels and in different locations. Get out there and find out what's really going on. Don't be satisfied with others' interpretations.
- In a crisis, take responsibility, be accessible, and be honest. Take the high road. If you do, the company will probably pull through the crisis with a minimum of damage. This is why Union Carbide received generally high marks for the handling of the Bhopal crisis (CEO Warren Anderson quickly flew to India) and why Exxon received horrible marks for its handling of the Valdez oil spill (CEO Lawrence Rawls didn't visit Alaska until three weeks after the incident).
- Finally, put your money where your mouth is—fund ethics initiatives. Without supporting systems, most corporate value statements are collections of empty platitudes that only increase organizational cynicism.[12] To develop ethics initiatives, get help from your communications and training professionals. Don't leave your ethics strategy just to the lawyers.

We've talked now about senior executives. Leaders at every level are important role models for ethical (or unethical) conduct. How can an organization be sure that its leaders at every level are behaving according to its stated values and serving as ethical role models?

Northrop's leadership accountability program.   Northrop has instituted a leadership program designed to make the organization's leaders accountable for conducting themselves in a manner that's consistent with the organization's values. All Northrop managers have completed two generations of a "Northrop Leadership Conference" that emphasizes the importance of translating Northrop's values into action and setting the right example. The program began with top executives and cascaded down through the organization. Getting the top executives to buy into the program was extremely important in Shirley Peterson's view.

> It's important to be able to say, the CEO did this, the Senior Vice Presidents did this, your boss did this. That's very powerful. . . In this whole process of trying to change a culture and move the values down, if you don't get the managers on board first, how can you ever expect the employees to go along?

Here's how it works. Direct reports (and sometimes peers and customers) fill out a survey evaluating the individual leader on the extent to which he or she is "living" each of 80 behaviors that are associated with Northrop's values. Examples of behaviors include:

- consistently treating customer satisfaction as a top priority
- giving people the authority they need to do their jobs
- consistently doing what is "right" instead of what is "expedient"

The responses are evaluated and confidential numerical feedback about the results is provided to each leader in a 30-page detailed "leadership inventory." With each item, leaders learn where they marked themselves, where the company average is, where others graded them on average and their percentile.

In the feedback session, a consultant from outside the firm plays the role of counselor, providing feedback and then working with the manager. The leaders are encouraged to discuss the evaluation with their employees and to talk about the two or three things they are going to try to change. They role play how they might do this. For example, a leader might tell his or her direct reports, "I'm going to work on being a better listener—I'm going to start holding regular staff meetings, I'm going to get out on the floor more, and I'm going to ask you if I'm getting better during the year."

The survey is completed annually. After the initial one, the inventory contains an additional page that asks such questions as "Did you fill this out for this person last year—have you noticed any change? Did this person follow up? Did they tell you what two or three things they were working on? The ethics office also follows up with regular notes to the leaders (all 3200) to offer help. The consultants call the executives personally to ask how things are going.

Shirley Peterson believes that one reason the program works so well is that it is treated separately from the formal performance appraisal system that's used to make promotion and salary decisions. Although the company's performance appraisal now includes a section on values and ethics, this separate leadership accountability program relies on the belief that, when people are given constructive feedback that says their behavior is inconsistent with stated corporate values, they will want to change.

> This is personal feedback to the individual only—we label it "your personal improvement plan." Let's face it. There's no performance appraisal system or bonus system in the world that's going to change you and your style unless you want to yourself. We all want to be liked by others. So, if you get feedback that basically says people think I'm an SOB, that's traumatic. But back to what's the hook to get them to listen? It's their own ego, their own desire to be liked . . .

She also believes that the program works well because it is tied to the organizational culture and to the bottom line.

> We tie our program to the bottom line through the use of the personal feedback on the behaviors that are tied so strongly to the values. There is no quick fix. Ethics is about organizational culture and that takes time. We take all our managers through an involved process which allows them to be introspective about themselves in relation to a set of guiding principles. They become aware of how they are perceived, and how they have improved. It's been exciting. I've had people stop me in the hallways and say, you're the one who started this values thing, aren't you? I want to tell you how this has changed my life. Or, I want to tell you how this has changed my boss.

Northrop CEO, Kent Kresa, sent Northrop managers a memo in December 1993 congratulating them on the success of the Northrop Leadership Inventory process. Here's what he said:

> I want to congratulate you on an important achievement. Since 1990, almost all Northrop managers have participated in the Northrop Leadership Inventory process and have received feedback twice. I have just reviewed a company-wide summary of "first" and "second" generation scores.

> The comparision shows that we as a group *improved our scores on all 80 inventory items.* The average score per person/ per item improved 12.5% as rated by direct reports, while the average score as rated by customers/suppliers improved 10% Categories with greatest improvement include:

> *Building Customer Importance*—Treats customer satisfaction as "top priority"

> *Acknowledging Contribution*—Personally recognizes performance improvement in others

> *Achieving Excellence*—Defines quality as meeting customer needs including cost/schedule

Personal Leadership—Takes responsibility and ownership for decisions.

Follow-up works! The [data] show there is a clear positive correlation between the amount of follow-up and the amount of perceived change and effectiveness. I encourage each of you to continue to follow up on your action plan and seek feedback. Make that one of your 1994 PMP improvement goals . . .

By asking, listening, learning, following-up, and staying the course, we will each continue to grow as effective leaders. We plan to continue this process which has worked quite well as measured by our "customers." . . . Again, thank you for your work and accomplishments.

A Formal Whistleblowing System to Resolve Questions and Report Ethical Concerns

The Sentencing Guidelines require that organizations "take reasonable steps to achieve compliance with written standards through monitoring, auditing, and other systems designed to detect criminal conduct, including a reporting system free of retribution to employees who report criminal conduct." Although most organizations encourage employees to bring their concerns to their immediate supervisor first, employees sometimes want to ask a question anonymously or have a concern about their supervisor's behavior.

In order to ensure that employees have a safe and comfortable place to take their concerns, more and more organizations are setting up a telephone line for employees to confidentially call and ask for help in resolving an ethical dilemma or to report an ethical problem or behavior they've observed in the organization. A number of names have emerged for these—"Communication Lines"—"GuideLine" (NYNEX)—"Open Line (Northrop)"—"Helpline (GE)." These lines generally ring in the ethics office if there is one. Some large organizations provide separate reporting lines for each business unit. For example, GE lists 14 telephone numbers in a 1993 publication entitled "Integrity; The Spirit and the Letter of our Commitment." The numbers include a corporate phone line as well as one for each business unit. In some firms, such as PPG Industries, the line rings on the Chairman's desk. Other firms have hired an outside consulting firm to take the calls at an 800 number and then transfer the information to the company.

Here's how NYNEX explains its GuideLine process in a booklet called "Ethics at Work; NYNEX. Our GuideLine Process." A flow chart begins with the employee seeking guidance or reporting an allegation. The system is designed to provide guidance for questions about business conduct "when an employee needs guidance to make the right decision" or to deal with an allegation when an employee suspects wrongdoing. The employee can begin the process by going either to his or her supervisor or by calling or writing the GuideLine. For questions requiring guidance, the Business Conduct Office acts as "coach," providing guidance and or interpretation. The assumption is that the "right choice isn't always obvious." The "Business Conduct Office offers a confidential avenue to ask questions, voice concerns, clarify gray areas or report a suspected violation of the Code." Based on that information, the employee can then make an informed decision. For allegations, confidentiality of the process is emphasized. The employee is assigned a confidential ID number and agrees to call back at a particular date and time for case status. Even if the caller chooses to identify himself or herself, privacy is protected. Meanwhile, the Business Conduct Office opens the case by assigning a case number, and then "coaches, interprets, mediates, investigates, or refers," whatever is needed to conclude a case. About 40% of the calls relate to personnel matters, 50% are calls requesting information or clarification about the code of business conduct, and the rest relate to specific allegations of misconduct or security matters, such as suspected fraud and misuse of company funds.

One concern often raised about these reporting lines is that individuals will make nonvalid reports—"tattling" on people they don't like. That's one reason why confidentiality is so important within the entire reporting and investigative system. Both the identity of the reporter and the alleged violator must be protected throughout the process. The alleged violator must be protected because allegations can result from simple misunderstandings. The reporter must be protected from any retaliation from the accused.

Organizations that have experience with telephone reporting lines find that a large majority of the calls are for information clarification. The individual says, here's what I want to do. Is it okay? Does it follow procedure? Many calls also relate to relatively minor personnel issues. At Martin Marietta, about half of the calls are personnel-related. Only a small percentage (10% at NYNEX) are alleged violations. NYNEX received 2700 calls and letters in 1992.

Carl Skooglund (of TI) said:

> we were concerned about nonvalid reports. But, we've found that most people call about valid issues. Their motives may not always be noble, but the content is usually correct. Most of the people who use the communication line are using it because they sincerely have a question or concern about something or a question about something that they think is wrong. They may be misinformed. They may be blowing something out of proportion, but I think they use it for positive reasons. I would be willing to bet that only a very small percentage are untruthful allegations made to try to hurt somebody for a vindictive reason. It just hasn't been a problem.

Another relevant question concerns how to interpret the meaning of the number of calls and letters. Obviously, if an organization institutes and promotes an easy way to ask questions, express concerns, and report violations, the number of calls should increase dramatically. Does this mean that there are more ethical problems? Probably not. The executives who run these programs generally interpret such increases as evidence that their programs are working. However, Carl Skooglund suggests that in an ideal world, the ethics office should aim to put itself out of business. In other words, ethical conduct should become so institutionalized that there would be no reason for people to call. Like the Maytag repairman, the ethics officer would have a very boring job. On the other hand, a quiet telephone may also signal a number of other positive or negative conditions: 1) lack of concern or recognition of ethical problems (negative), 2) an intimidating environment where people fear retribution (negative), 3) good problem solving at the local level (positive), or 4) no one knowing the ethics office exists (negative). Ultimately, it is up to the ethics office to devise ways to determine what the numbers and the changes in the numbers mean.

Finally, confidentiality and protection of callers remains an important issue. Some firms have hired outsiders such as Pinkerton Services Group (PSG) to manage their reporting lines.[13] Other companies have hired outside individuals often called "ombudspersons" whose roles extend beyond just answering a reporting line. Sam Scott Miller discussed his ombudsperson role for Kidder Peabody and Charles Schwab and Co. in a speech to the Conference Board in 1991. He described his roles as information receiver, information provider, and investigator. Callers use him as a sounding board to help them determine whether something is wrong. He might help individuals determine whether activities they want to engage in represent a conflict of interest. People would rather hear a "no" answer from him than to be embarrassed in front of a supervisor. As an investigator, he pursues the problem until closure. The firm's own facilities and processes are used in the investigation. Finally, the ombudsperson may serve in an alternative dispute resolution role. He tries to resolve issues before they become lawsuits or arbitration proceedings. At Kidder Peabody, Miller reports to a compliance committee, comprised of the CEO and other top managers. His reports are somewhat abstract to maintain confidentiality, but the group wants to assure that problems are resolved and wants to know about any actions it needs to take (e.g., education) to prevent the problem from recurring.[14]

Whether a hotline, an ombudsman, or some other formal procedure is most appropriate for a particular corporate culture, the important thing is to have some way for employees to raise issues without fear of retribution. If there's no way for employees to raise issues without fear of retribution, the first time an executive hears about a problem may be from a district attorney, a regulator, or a newspaper reporter.

EVALUATING THE ETHICS PROGRAM

Many organizations have committed significant resources to their ethics efforts—hiring high level executives, developing values statements and codes, designing and implementing training programs, etc. Few organizations, however, have systematically evaluated these efforts. Evaluation is particularly important at this relatively early stage in the development of formal ethics programs so that the organizational community can learn what works both in general and under specific circumstances. By evaluation, we don't mean asking employees at an ethics training program whether they "liked" it. Many employees will respond affirmatively just because they "liked" the idea of a few hours or a day away from the office. Whether they "liked" it or not should be secondary. The most important question is, is the program accomplishing its goals?

Surveys

Most large organizations already conduct regular employee attitude surveys. Many have added ethics to the list of survey topics. Surveys can target knowledge, attitudes, skills, and behaviors. For example, if ethics training has been recently required of all employees, surveys can evaluate the extent to which employees understand the company's expectations and standards. Baseline data can be collected before ethics training is begun and then several months after it's completed to analyze whether positive change has occurred. Surveys can help to evaluate employees' skill at recognizing and resolving ethical issues, and measure the extent to which employees observe unethical conduct in the organization. Finally, attitudes toward ethics management programs and processes can be evaluated. For example, the Ethics Resource Center has recently been combining data from a number of organizations across industries so that individual organizations can be compared to this overall data. They reported some disturbing findings at the 1993 Conference Board meeting on business ethics. For example, 33% of respondents said that they occasionally observed violations of the company's ethical standards and nine percent said they often did. Only about half of the respondents who observed a violation actually reported it. 36% of respondents said that nothing was done in response to their report. 27% said they never heard about the outcome and 19% claimed to be the victim of retribution for reporting the violation.

All survey results must be evaluated carefully. For example, many of firms that call upon the Ethics Resource Center for help do so because they are in some kind of trouble. Thus these cross-company results may be skewed in a negative direction. Also, because ethics is such a sensitive topic, it may be difficult to get employees to share their honest thoughts and feelings. They may be telling you what they think you want to hear, although the above findings suggest that this isn't the case. Furthermore, the numbers generated by a survey are ultimately ambiguous. Employees who are angry about a recent downsizing may evaluate the "ethics" of the organization more harshly than they otherwise would. A final suggestion from Carl Skooglund regarding surveys is that questions shouldn't be asked if you don't really want to know and you're not willing to accept the answer. He also suggests leaving the legal department out of the survey process. "They'll make it as content free as they possibly can, because, according to the lawyers, the safest way to communicate is—don't."

Johnson & Johnson's former Chairman, James Burke, had been on the board of IBM Corporation in the 1980s and became impressed with IBM's employee survey program. He decided that one way to keep the Johnson & Johnson Credo alive would be to survey employees about how the company was doing relative to the credo. The survey went through a number of iterations after being tested on employees at a variety of locations. The first survey was conducted in the United

States in 1986–1987. The first international survey was conducted the following year. The first part of the survey includes 118 items and takes about 25 minutes to complete. It asks employees to rate things like the company's "customer orientation" on five-point scales. The second section is open ended for written comments. About 30000 employees take the survey in any given year. One of the findings has been the impact of top leadership and corporate culture on survey results. For example, former Chairman Burke had emphasized the customer above all. President David Clare emphasized safety first. In an analysis of the survey results, ratings on these two survey dimensions were highest. Most of all, the survey is viewed as a way to keep the Credo alive, a way of "closing the loop on this thing called the Credo."[15]

Peer Review

Texas Instruments and Martin Marietta have had ethics offices since the mid to late 1980s. These firms' ethics officers entered into an agreement to provide peer review of each others' formal ethics programs via two day "open book" visits to each other's sites. They focused on processes, not cases, and reviewed everything from the ethics office's missions and strategies to its budgets, training, and videotapes. The tone was trusting and supportive rather than investigative or adversarial. In addition to getting feedback about their own programs, and discussion of common problems, the peer review process provided insight into what the other firm was doing that might have application at home.

Carl Skooglund:

> One of the primary things that I learned was that Martin Marietta has a very effective system for recording, cataloging, following up on inquiries. I went back and researched it and did an analysis as to whether we wanted to head that direction. I also saw some good training materials.
>
> One of the things that George [George Sammett, Jr. of Martin Marietta] would probably say he learned from us related to readability of ethics office materials. They had some documents that were hardly user friendly at all. Another thing that George learned from us is that they have their people in the Human Resources organization conducting training rather than the management of the local organization taking responsibility.

Skooglund and Sammett discussed the common finding that so many queries to the ethics office relate to human resource/personnel issues. They asked each other why and speculated that it suggests 1) lack of trust in the HR function—that HR is viewed as a management tool, 2) fear of retribution—that the ethics office is safer to use, and 3) that personnel issues are bona fide ethics issues if the callers believe they are—that ethics has to do with fairness and anyone with such a concern is a customer of the ethics office and should not be turned away.

COMMITMENT VERSUS COMPLIANCE

Taken together, all of these ethics initiatives can be categorized as emphasizing either a commitment and/or compliance approach to managing ethics. The commitment approach is proactive and aspirational. It emphasizes *expected behavior* and an effort to achieve high standards represented by the spirit of the law and organizational values. It relies on such techniques as leader communication and role modeling to affirm the organization's commitment to its stated ethical values and goals. Employees learn that these are not empty words, but words that organizational leaders believe and live by. Ethics becomes a point of pride in the organization. "We're so good we don't have to cheat!" The response to a commitment-oriented program is generally good until violations occur. Then, employees expect that commitment to be backed up with sanctions against the violator(s).

With a compliance emphasis, the focus is more on *required behavior*—obeying the letter of the law rather than aspiring to lofty ethical principles. Disciplinary procedures for violators are also important to compliance efforts. Many organizations are taking a compliance approach in response to the U.S. Sentencing Guidelines mandate. Employees are told that compliance with the law is essential, and that employees who break the law will be punished. The danger with a compliance-only focus is the possibility that employees will believe anything goes as long as there isn't a rule against it.

An effective ethics program should have both commitment and compliance components. By themselves, abstract values statements can appear hypocritical to employees. "Management makes these lofty statements, but they don't tell us what we should do." Values must be translated into rules for behavior, and, to give the rules meaning, violators must be punished. Employees welcome information that reduces ambiguity about what they can and can't do. And, if enforcement is applied consistently across all organizational levels, they are likely to perceive the system as fair and just.

On the other hand, employees often view a heavily compliance-oriented program with cynicism. Without a strong value base, compliance programs seem to focus on catching employees doing something wrong, rather than aspiring to do things right. Employees translate this emphasis into mistrust and a "CYA" approach. Either "the organization doesn't trust its employees," or "the organization is just out to protect its own behind." The best programs aim to focus on commitment first and foremost, supported by just and fair enforcement of the rules.

CONCLUSION

This chapter has offered specifics about how ethics is actually managed in organizations—through an ethics infrastructure and a synergistic system of ethics communications that is closely tied to the organization's culture. Communications must be credible and appropriate to the organization's audience. In general, we recommend a combined commitment/compliance approach to ethics management with an emphasis on commitment. Employees will learn, through a variety of communication channels, that the organization really cares about ethics and is committed to its values. They will also learn that violations of the organization's rules will not be tolerated.

DISCUSSION QUESTIONS

1. Imagine that you had to develop three guiding principles for a corporate ethics committee. What would they be and why?

2. Imagine that it's your responsibility to select an ethics officer for your organization. What qualities, background, and experience would you look for? Would you ever be interested in such a position? Why or why not?

3. What are the advantages of having an ethics office or officer report to a company's chief executive officer, the legal department, human resources, or audit? What are the disadvantages?

4. Think about an organization where you've worked. What kinds of ethical dilemmas are unique to that organization? To that industry?

5. Which of the following exist in the organization? Are they consistent and credible? Mission or values statement, policy manual, code of conduct, ethics training (who conducts it), hotline?

6. Is senior management committed to ethics? How do you know?

7. Are leaders at all levels held accountable for their ethical conduct? If so, how? If not, why not? What would you recommend?

8. What recommendations would you make for handling frivolous calls to the hotline?

9. Does the organization evaluate its ethics initiatives? How? If not, why not?

10. Would you characterize the ethics efforts in this organization as taking a commitment, compliance, or combination approach? Is it effective? Recommend improvements.

11. How would you raise an ethical concern in this organization? List all of the resources available to you. Which ones would you be likely to use? Why or why not?

12. Imagine that you're the CEO of a small manufacturing company. An employee has dumped toxic waste in a nearby stream. Who would you call into your office and what would you want to know? Develop an action plan for dealing with the crisis. Who would you talk to and what would you say?

CASE

What's Wrong With This Picture?

You're a management consultant who has been asked by Green Co. to help design an ethics communication and training program for all Green Co. employees. Your meetings to date have been with the head of human resources, and your contract with the company has been negotiated with him. Once the papers have been signed, you begin your research and are quickly stymied by Green's corporate counsel. He says that you will not be allowed to ask employees about ethical dilemmas that have occurred at Green. He specifically asks that you get your information from other sources such as press accounts of problems in the industry, or from other organizations with which you've worked. In addition, the head of human resources has told you that you'll be unable to meet the three most senior executives because they're busy negotiating a large acquisition. You will have access to other high-level managers who can tell you what they think the seniors want. You're instructed to write a code of conduct for the company, a mission statement, and prepare presentations for the senior managers to give to employees sometime next month on corporate expectations and values.

Case-Based Questions

1. Based on what you know about developing ethical cultures and programs, identify the problems presented by this case.

2. Why do you think the corporate counsel has responded in this way? What will be your response to him, if any?

3. As a consultant, what are your ethical obligations, if any?

4. How will you proceed?

NOTES

[1]Austin, N. K. 1994. The new corporate watchdogs. *Working Woman*, January: 19–20.

Personal communication, Kent Druyvesteyn, 1994.

[2]Towne, P. L. 1991. Training employees and communicating ethical standards. In Corporate ethics: Developing new standards of accountability. *Conference Board Report No. 980*. New York: The Conference Board, 25–26.

[3] Austin, N. K. 1994. The new corporate watchdogs. *Working Woman*. January: 19–20.

[4]Simmons, D. G. 1985. The nature of the organizational grapevine. *Supervisory Management*, November: 39–42.

[5]DeAngelis, T. 1991. Honesty tests weigh in with improved ratings. *APA Monitor*, 7.

Ones, D. S., Ziswesvaran, C., & Schmidt, F. 1993. Comprehensive meta-analysis of integrity test validities: Findings and implications for personal selection and theories of job performance. *Journal of Applied Psychology*, 78: 679–703.

Sackett, P. R., Burris, L. R., & Callahan, C. 1989. Integrity testing for personal selection: An update. *Personal Psychology*, 42: 491–529.

[6]Towne, P. L. 1991. Training employees and communicating ethical standards. In Corporate ethics: Developing new standards of accountability. *Conference Board Report No. 980*. New York: The Conference Board, 25–26.

[7]Kotter, J. P. & Heskett, J. L. 1992. *Corporate Culture and Performance*. New York: Free Press.

[8]Smith, A.L. 1991. *Innovative Employee Communication: A New Approach to Improving Trust, Teamwork and Performance*. Englewood Cliffs, NJ: Prentice-Hall.

[9]Ibid.

[10]Ibid.

[11]Peters, T. J. & Waterman, R. H. Jr. 1982. *In search of excellence: Lessons from America's best-run companies*. New York: Harper & Row.

[12]Hammer, M. & Champy, J. 1993. *Reengineering the corporation: A Manifesto for corporate revolution*. New York: HarperCollins.

[13]Powell, J. M. 1994. Pinkerton responds to the Federal Sentencing Guidelines. *Corporate Conduct Quarterly*, 3(1): 10.

[14]Miller, S. S. 1991. The ombudsperson. In Corporate ethics: Developing new standards of accountability. *Conference Board Report No. 980*. New York: The Conference Board, 29–30.

[15]Johnson & Johnson's credo survey: Genesis and evolution . 1993. *Ethikos*. vol. 7, No. 2, September/October: 2.

SECTION V

Wrapping It Up

CHAPTER ELEVEN

Managing for Ethical Conduct in a Global Business Environment

INTRODUCTION

WITH THE INCREASING globalization of business, more managers are finding themselves in an international environment full of ethical challenges. If managing for ethical conduct is a challenge in one's own culture, imagine how the difficulties multiply when the culture and language are foreign, and the manager is under increased stress.

Particularly in developing nations, business people face cultures, customs, and norms that may conflict with their own ethical standards. Although large multinational corporations with years of experience in the international arena sometimes provide their managers with training and policies to guide their actions, many representatives of American business are left to fend for themselves with little or no guidance.

In this chapter, we will address the difficulties of foreign assignments in general terms. Then, we will focus on the specific challenges of dealing with ethical issues that arise in the context of international business. These issues concern individuals' specific decisions about the actual conduct of business in different cultures as well as broader organizational decisions about whether and how to conduct business in foreign nations.

Focus on the Individual Expatriate Manager

We begin by focusing on the individual expatriate manager, the difficulties inherent in foreign business assignments, and the importance of training for cultural understanding and sensitivity.

The Difficulties of Foreign Business Assignments

The globalization of business has contributed to a huge increase in interactions between people from different cultural backgrounds. These interactions may occur during brief business trips or more lengthy overseas assignments. Unfortunately, many overseas assignments end early and unsuccessfully because of the expatriate manager's (and his or her family's) inability to adjust to the foreign work environment. The costs of individual failure are high, estimated at between $50,000 and $150,000. The estimated cost of these failures to U.S. business as a whole has been estimated to be over $2 billion a year.[1]

The Need for Training and Guidance

Despite these failures and their costs, studies have found that most American businesses don't provide cross-cultural training to their managers who are assigned to work overseas. Top managers seem to believe that an effective manager in New York can be an effective manager in Beijing, Beirut, Buenos Aires, or Budapest with no cross-cultural training. This isn't surprising given that only a small number of top managers of American multinational corporations have substantial international experience.[2]

Studies have found that cross-cultural training can be highly effective. For example, training contributes to:

1) greater feelings of well-being and self-confidence for the American manager

2) improvement in relationships with host nationals

3) the development of correct perceptions of host culture members

4) better adjustment to the new culture

5) higher performance[3]

Several of these training outcomes are relevant to the ethics of international business relationships, perhaps most importantly to the development of correct perceptions of members of the host culture.

Improving General Cultural Understanding

Culture had been defined as "collective mental programming."[4] This definition of culture suggests that patterns of believing differ across cultures, and that all of us use these patterns to interpret the world and to guide action. If an individual operating in a foreign culture doesn't understand its particular patterns of believing and behaving, the individual will interpret experience purely in terms of his or her own culture, inevitably misinterpreting and misunderstanding. For example, a gift could be interpreted as a friendly gesture, a thank you, or a bribe depending upon the cultural context and the resulting interpretation. In a collectivist culture such as Japan, giving gifts is considered to be an important part of relationship building. Giving a gift can also be an important step toward acceptance and becoming a member of the group, if it is done correctly.[5] Therefore, interpretations are extremely important because actions are likely to vary greatly depending upon the interpretation.[6]

Foreign Language Proficiency

Language is an essential part of the cultural learning that can contribute to productive international business relationships. First, the expatriate manager's effort to learn the language is generally taken as a symbol of his or her interest and commitment to understanding. Those who are fluent in a foreign language know that much cultural learning occurs implicitly as one develops fluency. For example, some languages have words for things that other languages take a tortured phrase or sentence to convey, or can't convey at all. Yet Americans speak fewer foreign languages than their trading partners[7] and some have argued that Americans pay a high price for this "monolingual arrogance."[8]

One senior executive of a Fortune 500 company frequently talks with business school student groups about how to be successful in their future business careers. He recommends, above all, that students find some way to experience an international environment and that they learn to speak a foreign language fluently. After they have learned one language, he suggests that they start on a second.

Language fluency isn't a matter of just knowing the words, but knowing how they are used within the particular cultural context. For example, an old story goes that a Scottish visitor to Japan had worked hard to develop a good relationship with his Japanese host. After several weeks, the Japanese host said (in Japanese), "I would like to sleep with you." Luckily, the Scot was sophisticated in cross-cultural communication and didn't react negatively or dismiss the remark while his mind raced to attempt to understand the statement's meaning. Despite his confusion, he agreed to the apparently odd request. The Japanese host had a second mattress brought to the visitor's room and the two slept through the night, comfortably and without incident. He later discovered that his Japanese host had paid him the highest compliment. The Japanese believe that an individual can easily be killed in his sleep. Therefore, the request indicated a relationship of total trust.[9] A note of caution—you might not want to try this one today. Our students tell us that "I would like to sleep with you" now carries the same meaning in Japan as it does in the United States!

Recognizing the Power of Selective Perception

Human beings are constantly bombarded with information. Therefore, they must perceive selectively or they would be totally overwhelmed. This *selective perception* process is largely determined by culture. For example, in the United States people focus more on another individual's behavior than the person's status or other qualities. The reverse can be true in other cultures. When President Richard Nixon was forced to resign, it was because of his behavior. Americans understood this, but members of some other cultures didn't. They focused on the fact that he was *president*, after all,[10] an issue of status and position. Similarly, in Latin cultures, people pay more attention to social relationships than to behavior. Thus if a close relative commits a crime, it may not even be perceived as a crime because the relationship is more important than the action.

Therefore, it is essential to recognize that the visitor to another culture will notice things that are important at home, but may not be important in the target culture. The visitor is also likely to overlook important behaviors, roles, and values because of selective perception. These aren't important at home, so they aren't even noticed. Furthermore, members of the target culture are equally selective, perhaps not noticing things that seem crucial to the visitor.[11]

On the other hand, with effective cross-cultural training, managers can be trained to be on the lookout for things that would otherwise be ignored, and they will be more able to interpret and understand their international business experiences in light of the belief patterns of the particular culture. Managers can't be expected to make intelligent, informed decisions, and to communicate effectively in the absence of this basic understanding.

Assumption of Behavioral Consistency

However, understanding the culture is not enough. Much theory and research on international business conduct is grounded in an inaccurate key assumption—that if we understand cultural behavior (how people think and behave in their native environment), we'll understand how a particular group will behave in relation to cultural outsiders. In other words, if I understand the Japanese culture better, I can predict how my Japanese counterparts will behave toward me, what their expectations will be, and so on. And, if I understand all of that, I'll know how to behave with them.

People are amazingly adaptable, however, and, just when you think you have them figured out, they change their behavior. In fact, they may be trying to figure out how to behave with you as much as you're trying to figure out how to behave with them. A colleague recently related a story about a meeting between business and philosophy professors on his campus. Recognizing the cultural differences between the two departments, the philosophy professors decided to leave their khakis at home, and dress up for the occasion—sporting crisp shirts and ties. The business professors all showed up in jeans! The moral of this story is that people adapt their behaviors to what they believe others expect of them, making it very difficult to predict behavior.

Here's another example from the international business environment. By all accounts, American women should experience great difficulty succeeding in some foreign business environments, particularly in cultures (e.g., Asia, the Middle East) where women have not attained the rights that American women have come to expect. We expect foreign nationals to think about and treat American women as they treat women in their own cultures. Yet a major study of North American women working as expatriate managers in a number of countries around the world found that these women are successful beyond anyone's expectations.[12] "Women succeed because they are seen as foreigners who happen to be women, not as women who happen to be foreigners."[13] The foreign nationals adapt their behavior in relation to these women rather than expecting an American woman to behave like a Japanese or Saudi Arabian woman.

A study of cross-cultural business negotiations also challenges the behavioral consistency assumption. Adler and Graham[14] found that, when dealing with an individual from a different culture, negotiators adapted their negotiation behavior to that of the negotiation partner. However, an important study result was the finding that the American negotiators were the *least flexible*, making fewer adjustments in response to their negotiation partner's behavior than Canadian or Japanese negotiators.

What can we learn from these studies? Although learning about the culture is an essential first step, don't assume that simply learning about another culture is enough. The foreign nationals you deal with in business interactions may behave differently with you than they would with individuals from their own culture. Thus, understanding cultural norms and behaviors is *only a starting point*. The foreign individuals you deal with may adapt their behavior based on what they expect you to do. Therefore, you must be flexible and open to learning from the situation at hand, despite research findings suggesting that flexibility is not the American manager's strong suit. Perhaps one of the most important things to learn, in preparation for a cross-cultural experience, is that you can't be fully prepared—that there will be surprises and daily opportunities for further learning and understanding.[15] The successful international businessperson will be open, flexible, and tolerant of ambiguity.

Assumption of Cultural Homogeneity

We should also not assume homogeneity within a culture—that individuals within a culture are all the same. Imagine if someone assumed that all Americans were all like the characters in American films. Obviously, this kind of simplistic thinking and stereotyping leads to grossly inaccurate expectations. Individual personalities and experiences vary widely within any culture, leading to behavioral differences. For example, a Japanese business person with an American MBA may behave quite differently from a Japanese business person who has never left the country[16] Be open to learning as much as possible about the *individuals* you are dealing with, and try to leave stereotypes behind.

Specific Training and Guidance

In addition to general cultural and language training, international business assignments require training in areas more specifically related to ethics such as how to recognize the ethical issues that are likely to arise in a particular environment, how to negotiate in a particular culture, and how to handle requests for payoffs and bribes.

Preparation to recognize and deal with ethical issues. Beyond general training in the culture, training with respect to business ethics beliefs and practices is essential. First, the expatriate manager must be prepared to recognize the ethical issues likely to arise in a particular business setting. Just as ethical issues at home vary somewhat from industry to industry (e.g., manufacturing versus hospitality) and profession to profession (e.g., marketing versus accounting), the ethical issues that are likely to arise vary from culture to culture. The treatment of employees (e.g., child labor, worker safety) may be more of a problem in one culture, while the disposal of toxic wastes may be more likely to arise in another, and bribes may be more problematic in yet another culture.

Second, the expatriate manager needs help making ethical decisions in the more ambiguous international business context. At home, it's easier to rely on your intuition or to simple guidelines such as "*The New York Times* Test." Intuition often falls short when home culture norms conflict with those of the host country, however.[17] Individual expatriate managers shouldn't be left to fend for themselves in these unfamiliar circumstances. The organization owes it to them to help navigate these unknown ethical waters. More and more organizations are doing just that.

Negotiating across cultures. The frequency of business negotiations is increasing with growth in foreign trade, joint ventures, and other inter-organizational agreements. When working within one's own language and culture, being an effective negotiator requires the utmost in sensitivity, understanding, and communications skills. These requirements multiply when negotiating in an international business environment.

A number of studies detail differences in negotiation styles and tactics across cultures.[18] Most relevant, given our focus on ethics, is an understanding of the use of "dirty tricks" and "psychological warfare"—negotiation "tactics designed to pressure opponents into undesirable concessions and agreements."[19]

The use of dirty tricks is possible in any negotiation, but it becomes more complex in an international negotiation because of possible misinterpretation. For example, Brazilians expect deception among negotiators who are not well acquainted. Therefore, they're more likely to use deception during early negotiation stages than are Americans. Consequently, it may be wise for an American negotiator to expect phony facts to be a part of the initial negotiation stage with a Brazilian counterpart.

It's also important to recognize that what seems like deliberate deception may not be. Eastern Europeans have limited authority to finalize agreements and are expected to check with their superiors about any changes. However, Americans often have wide authority to make important decisions at the negotiation table. Without this cultural knowledge, an American might interpret the Eastern European's claims about limited authority to be an attempt at deception when it isn't.

Psychological warfare—"tactics designed to make the other person feel uncomfortable"[20] and want to conclude the negotiation quickly—also has different meaning in different cultures. For example, too much touching or too much eye contact may make Americans extremely uncomfortable. Again, it's important to be able to distinguish real attempts at psychological warfare from the expression of typical cultural behavior. For example, Latins tend to touch more than Americans or Canadians, who touch more than Scandinavians. Arabs maintain greater eye contact than Americans, who use eye contact more than the Japanese. An understanding of the culture one is dealing with can help to prepare the negotiator to correctly interpret these types of behaviors.[21]

Payoffs and Bribes

Probably the most frequent source of anxiety for American business persons operating abroad is the expectation of payoffs and bribes. A bribe is a payment to someone to secure a sale, or to obtain approval or assistance from an individual or organization (often a government bureaucrat). Although an accepted part of commercial transactions in many Asian, African, Latin American, and Middle Eastern cultures, it is often against the law in these very same countries.

On arrival in a foreign airport, many a businessperson has faced a government official's extended hand, and the suggestion that payment was needed to facilitate the delivery of product samples to the hotel—no payment, no product. Without previous preparation, the expatriate is at a loss to know what to do. What is the meaning of this request in the context of the culture? Is making the payoff against U.S. or local law? What exactly is local custom? How much is expected? What's likely to happen if I don't pay? Will payment really expedite matters? What are the options? How will my company respond if my work is delayed?

American business people generally prefer to conduct business in a way that's consistent with the U.S. and local law. They would prefer not to make illegal payments to anyone. Despite local laws, however, bribes and payoffs are the custom in many cultures, dating back centuries.[22] Therefore, American businesspeople frequently feel that they are at a competitive disadvantage if they are prohibited from making payments especially if competitors make them freely.

A recent survey[23] suggested that U.S. business professionals hold wide-ranging opinions on the acceptability of payments to foreign officials, despite the illegality of bribery. Survey participants were asked to respond to the following vignette:

A company paid a $350,000 "consulting" fee to an official of a foreign country. In return, the official promised assistance in obtaining a contract which should produce a $10 million profit for the contracting company.

Responses varied from almost half saying that the behavior was "never acceptable," to 32.5% who said that it was "sometimes acceptable" to 18.5% who said that it was "always acceptable." Those who believed that it was never acceptable relied on their personal beliefs that bribery is illegal and that payoffs are always wrong. Others suggested that if you pay once, you'll be stuck doing it forever. Even if others operate that way, you shouldn't give in to the temptation. However, those who believed that it was sometimes acceptable suggested that it was customary in other cultures, practiced by the competition, and was at times the only way to do business. Some went so far as to say that Americans shouldn't impose their cultural values on others, particularly in countries where bribery is not illegal.

The Foreign Corrupt Practices Act.   In the 1970s, the Securities and Exchange Commission found that the practice of bribing foreign officials was widespread among U.S. multinational corporations, and that the amounts paid were becoming "excessive." For example, in the mid-1960s, a major Korean political party asked Gulf Oil for a $10 million donation. The CEO personally negotiated it down to $4 million, still a huge sum. In a notorious incident, Lockheed made an estimated $25 million in payments in connection with sales of its Tristar L-1011 aircraft in Japan. In all, 450 companies including more than 100 Fortune 500 firms admitted to making questionable foreign payments in amounts totalling more than $300 million.[24]

The U.S. Congress passed the Foreign Corrupt Practices Act in 1977,[25] making it the only nation with a law prohibiting bribery abroad. The act prohibits representatives of U.S. corporations from offering or providing significant payments to foreign political parties, candidates or government officials for the purpose of inducing the recipients to misuse their powerful positions to assist the company to obtain, maintain, or retain business—"to make a decision or take an action that he/she otherwise might not take."[26]

The law does allow for small payments to lower-level figures, so-called "grease payments" or "facilitating payments" that might be needed to persuade officials to perform their normal clerical or ministerial duties faster or better. Americans might think of these facilitating payments as "tips," a little extra for the individual involved, to assure courteous or efficient service. In order to be classified as a facilitating payment, it must not significantly change the final decision or result. It's against the law and considered to be subversion of the free market system if the money is paid to sway high-level people to make decisions they would not otherwise make. Companies are required to keep records of all such transactions which are not tax deductible as they are in other countries such as Japan.[27] Extortion payments are also excluded from prohibition under the law. For example, if a company official is kidnapped overseas and held for ransom, a company can legally pay the ransom.[28] Although the act has been criticized by some who argue that U.S. firms cannot compete effectively when they are constrained by this law and other companies from other countries are not, the evidence does not support this claim.[29]

Development of Guidelines, Rules, Codes, and Reward Systems

Given the wide diversity of opinion among managers and the ambiguity of U.S. legal requirements, organizations doing business abroad should develop guidelines, rules, and policies to guide expatriate managers in bribery and other ethical dilemma situations. This kind of guidance is even more important in these highly ambiguous international business situations than it is at home where the manager has the benefit of cultural understanding.

We learned in Chapter 7 about our "multiple ethical selves," the fact that people are frequently willing to accept different rules for different contexts. When applied to the international business ethics environment, the concept becomes cultural relativism. "When in Rome, do as the Romans do" is the guiding slogan of cultural relativists who claim that "no culture has a better ethics than any other."[30] However, Donaldson argues convincingly that relativism must be rejected because, at the extreme, relativists would have to accept any practice that is accepted within a culture, even murder. He proposes developing a "moral threshold" for corporate behavior abroad based on the language of rights, including such core human rights as personal freedom, physical security and well-being, political participation, informed consent, the ownership of property, and the equal dignity of each human person. "Rights establish bare minimums of ethical behavior without the ring of absolutism."[31]

Business organizations must then help their overseas managers to apply these complex notions of rights and responsibilities to their individual situations. They can do this by clearly articulating corporate values, by specifying how these values are to be applied in overseas contexts, and by providing specific guidance, where possible, that helps managers to anticipate and respond to ethical dilemmas.

More and more multinational businesses are writing comprehensive codes of conduct that apply similarly in the United States and abroad. For example, the Caterpillar Tractor Co. issued a "Code of World Wide Business Conduct" whose "purpose is to guide us, in a broad and ethical sense, in all aspects of our world-wide business activities. Of course, this code isn't an attempt to prescribe actions for every business encounter. It is an attempt to capture basic, general principles to be observed by Caterpillar people everywhere."[32] Other businesses have a code section pertaining to practices in foreign business environments. For example, General Dynamics has a section in its code entitled "International Business." It states that "our policy is to comply with all laws which apply in the countries where we do business. In countries where common practices might indicate acceptance of standards of conduct lower than those to which we aspire, we will follow our own Standards as outlined in this booklet."[33]

Many U.S. companies' codes of conduct provide specific guidance regarding bribes and payoffs in foreign countries. For example, United Technologies Corp. published a "policy clarification circular" as part of its ethics code. This circular states the following:

"In each area of the world where UTC does business there are generally accepted customs regarding the exchange of business gifts—both with respect to the type and value of the gift and with respect to the manner of protocol of exchange."

UTC policy generally permits giving (and receiving) business gifts which are customary business courtesies and are reasonable in value and frequency. This is a flexible standard and intended to accommodate the range of circumstances worldwide. However, the concepts underlying the standard ("customary," "courtesies," "reasonable value", and "reasonable frequency") must be viewed against objective standards. Each of these concepts in effect is a limitation—business gifts should be infrequent tokens of esteem.

A business gift is *never* permitted if it is:

- prohibited by law or regulation

- prohibited by more stringent UTC policies applicable to business relationships with U.S. Government employees . . . or applicable to UTC employees in purchasing functions

- prohibited by known policies of the employer of the intended recipient; or intended to improperly influence, or would have the appearance of improperly influencing, the recipient

Corporate policies are sometimes modified to fit the cultural context. For example, the ethics code of a large company operating in Korea prohibited the use of company funds for cash gifts to suppliers, the assumption being that a cash gift to a supplier would be a bribe. However, a manager at the Korean site who had developed a strong personal relationship with a supplier discovered that, at weddings and funerals in Korea, a rather large cash gift was expected of all invited guests. Rather than break the company code, the manager took up a collection among the staff so that he could meet this cultural obligation. When the company discovered this, they changed the rule to allow for this type of gift as long as it was documented.

In addition to providing guidance through a code, one U.S. executive who talked with us about these issues emphasized the importance of explaining to your overseas business partners *why* you're required to behave in a particular way. Make it clear that this behavior is required by your home culture and your company's code of conduct and request their respect and their cooperation.

Finally, organizations must take care to match their reward systems to ethical goals. If ethical conduct is the goal, the organization must make it clear that the expatriate manager will not be punished, either explicitly or implicitly, for upholding the organization's ethical standards even if it costs the organization business. Because it's difficult, if not impossible to monitor expatriate managers or representatives' behavior from afar, organizations tend to focus on outcomes (the bottom line) to evaluate the expatriate's performance. For example, they set sales or production goals and evaluate performance in light of goal achievement. However, if the organization focuses only on outcomes, with no attention to how those outcomes are achieved, the expatriate manager is likely to do the same, and ethical goals are more likely to be compromised. On the other hand, if the organization recognizes the potential ethical dilemmas to be faced by the expatriate manager in trying to do business in a particular culture, they will be more likely to openly acknowledge that lost business is a possibility, and to reward the manager for conducting business within ethical guidelines.

How Different Are Ethical Standards in Different Cultures?

One way to answer this question is to think of four categories. First, are universal values that all human societies share. Second, we can think of comparable values that are similar, but open to cultural interpretation. Third, are values in tension. And fourth, we find values that are completely incompatible.[34]

Universal standards. Certain ethical standards are universally accepted. For example, the prescriptions, "thou shalt not kill" and "thou shalt not steal" are universal. Furthermore, the golden rule, "do unto others as you would have them do unto you," appears in the teachings of every major religion from Judaism to Buddhism:

Buddhism: "Hurt not others in ways that you yourself would find hurtful."

Christianity: "Whatsoever you wish that men would do to you, do so to them, for this is the law and the prophets."

Confucianism: Tsze-Kung asked, saying, "Is there one word which may serve as a rule of practice for all one's life? The Master said: "Is not reciprocity such a word? What you do not want done to yourself, do not do to others."

Hinduism: This is the sum of duty: Do naught to others which would cause pain if done to you.

Judaism: What is hateful to you, do not to your fellow man. This is the entire Law: all the rest is commentary.

Islam: No one of you is a believer until he desires for his brother that which he desires for himself.[35]

Also, research on cognitive moral development suggests that Kohlberg's stages of moral development (see Chapter 5) are universal. People follow similar developmental patterns in all cultures.[36] On this basis, we might argue that there is a ~~farily~~ fairly strong common ground for international business ethics.

Comparable values.   But, when it comes to interpretation and practice, the situation becomes more complex and ambiguous. For example, honesty is valued in most cultures, but the meaning of honesty may differ across cultures. The notion of "caveat emptor" (buyer beware) is considered dishonest, and therefore wrong in the United States, but it may simply be considered good business in Hong Kong.

In general, U.S. executives see the United States, Canada, and Northern Europe as being comparable with regard to ethical business practice because Canada and Northern Europe are culturally most similar to the United States, sharing comparable values. They view Southern Europe as presenting greater ethical challenges because of fewer comparable values, and developing countries, particularly those with autocratic governments, as presenting the greatest challenges because these cultures and their values are so different.[37]

Values in tension.   Nepotism examplifies values in tension. Many U.S. firms have rules against nepotism because they believe that hiring and supervising one's family members presents an inappropriate conflict of interest. However, in cultures that have a deeper tradition of extended family and clan loyalty, nepotism is not only approved, it is expected.

Incompatible values.   Finally, Donaldson offers child labor as an example of incompatible values. When Levi Strauss's CEO spoke to the Conference Board's ethics conference in 1994, he outlined the company's global sourcing guidelines. These guidelines were adopted in 1991 to ensure that produ:ts were being produced in a manner consistent with the corporation's values. The first guideline bans the use of child labor. Others limit working hours, mandate safe working conditions and environmental responsibility. Haas reported that the company had terminated relationships with five percent and requested change in 25% of its sourcing operations because of guideline violations.

David Vogel (1992) argues that a substantial "ethics gap" exists between the United States and the rest of the developed world. The level of public, business, and academic interest in business ethics is much higher in the United States than in any other capitalist country. Vogel attributes the greater importance Americans place on business ethics to a number of sources including:

1. **The Legal and Regulatory Environment**—In the United States there are more laws and regulations governing business behavior, and these are more strictly enforced. For example, making campaign contributions from company funds and providing gifts to foreign government officials to secure contracts are illegal in the United States but are not illegal in other capitalist countries. Furthermore, an aggressive U.S. press is more likely to expose business misconduct. Finally, tougher criminal penalties are being imposed on corporations and their managers. By contrast, although enforcement activity has increased in Britain, it is still infrequent. In France, fines are rare. Similarly, in Japan, fines remain small and arrests are rare.

2. Public Expectations—In the United States, the public is much more concerned with the ethical conduct of business when compared to the European and Japanese publics. This is evidenced by the greater interest of American investors in "social investment" mutual funds, more attention to published rankings of corporations on their social responsibility, and the number of consumer boycotts of companies because of their social policies.

3. Business Values—Despite its diversity, American culture owes a great deal to the Protestant work ethic, and the expectation that business managers will behave morally—doing "'God's work' by creating wealth."[38] This expectation is shared by much of the public and by many business executives themselves. Despite Americans' cynicism toward business ethics, there is significantly more cynicism in Europe and Japan. In Europe "the moral status of capitalism has traditionally been problematic,"[39] making capitalism and the pursuit of profit morally questionable. In Japan, because behavior such as under-the-table favors is an accepted part of the culture, many do not even perceive it as wrong.

4. Emphasis on the Individual Versus the Corporation—American culture also emphasizes the importance of the individual. Therefore, in the United States, the individual business person is expected to make ethical decisions based on his or her own values or moral compass, within established codes or rules. As a result, American firms are more likely to provide avenues for individuals to express their ethical concerns through ethics offices and ombudspersons. And, the American legal system is offering increasing protection for whistleblowers who expose the misconduct of their organizations. By contrast, in Japan a whistleblower is more likely to be viewed as a traitor than a hero and few European countries have passed laws protecting whistleblowers[40]

Finally, American business persons are more likely to believe that their rules and procedures regarding business conduct should be applied universally. For example, "the U.S. is the only nation that restricts its firms from making payments to secure contracts or other benefits outside its borders."[41] U.S. firms, more than those in other nations, are frequently criticized for exporting products that do not meet their own country's health and safety standards.

Many fundamental differences remain in the way business ethics is treated, even in the world's industrial nations. Recent developments suggest increasing interest in business ethics in other countries, and increasing similarities across countries in terms of the enactment of environmental and sexual harassment legislation and the prosecution of insider trading. For example, in Great Britain, a new British quarterly periodical, *The Business Ethics Review*, is being launched, university centers are being established, reports on British business practice are beginning to identify business ethics as important, and a number of organizations and interest groups are raising the business ethics issue.[42]

THE ORGANIZATION IN A GLOBAL BUSINESS ENVIRONMENT

Thus far, we have focused primarily on the difficulties faced by the individual who is attempting to do business ethically in a foreign environment. With discussion of the Foreign Corrupt Practices Act, we began to focus more on the organization's perspective on global business practice. In this section we will continue to focus on international business ethics from the broader organizational perspective.

Although more and more small businesses are venturing into the global market-place, large multinational corporations still represent much of international business, and the ethical expectations of them are often greater because of their size and visibility. These corporations face business ethics environments that vary widely from country to country. International law is often not particularly helpful, and it is often unclear whether a particular country's legal system has regulatory authority over global transactions.[43] Therefore, a firm's own ethical standards become an important guide for its workers. Multinational corporations also face questions of legitimacy that may cause them to consider whether they should even involve themselves in a foreign culture. If they do decide to do business in a particular foreign environment, what are their responsibilities, since laws and expectations can vary greatly from one culture to another?

Doing Business in a Foreign Country

American businesses are aggressively pursuing foreign markets. They face increased competition in the global marketplace, requiring them to become cost effective in a variety of ways, including manufacturing goods abroad or buying from foreign suppliers who can often produce goods more cheaply.

The challenge to legitimacy. Numerous ethical challenges accompany these forays into the international business environment. For example, in some environments, the very legitimacy of the company may be challenged. Particularly in developing countries, the company's motives may be questioned as:

- managerial lifestyles are perceived as overly materialistic
- labor-saving technology conflicts with the perceived need for jobs
- paying market wages is viewed as exploitation
- expanding locally is perceived as furthering control and dependence[44]

Furthermore, differences in the sociopolitical environment raise a host of other ethical questions. Should American companies invest in, or do business in, countries that practice racial discrimination, pollute the environment, or violate the human rights of their citizens? Does doing business in these countries or with these organizations tarnish a company's ethical reputation simply by association? Is it all right to do business in the country as long as the company avoids engaging in the unethical practices itself? Furthermore, is it allright to do business in a country if the company creates and sticks to its own standards with regard to issues such as racial discrimination, pollution, or safety? For example, should a company that manufactures childrens' sleepwear be required to meet U.S. safety (fire hazard) standards when selling this product in countries that do not have such strict standards? Some U.S. firms have clearly taken their ethical standards abroad. For Alcoa Aluminum, worker safety is a top priority. As they put it, they simply don't want to hurt anyone. This commitment to worker safety applies equally to foreign operations where Alcoa safety standards and practices often surpass host country expectations. When a fatality occurs at an Alcoa operation anywhere in the world, the CEO shows up to find out why.

The case of South Africa. The question of whether to do business in South Africa, a country that has dismantled its longstanding policies of racial segregation and apartheid, has been a prominent ethical issue for multinational businesses for many years. Some U.S. firms chose to stay out of South Africa completely, many feeling pressured to do so by institutional investors such as pension funds that prohibited investment in companies doing business in South Africa. Others elected to do business there while adhering to "The Sullivan Principles", a list of standards for U.S. multinationals doing business in South Africa, drafted by Leon Sullivan, an African-American minister. These principles called for integration of the races in work facilities, equal and fair employment practices, equal pay for equal work, training programs to prepare non-whites for higher level jobs, the movement of non-whites into those jobs, and contribution to the quality of employees' life outside of work.[45]

Nestle and infant formula. Once engaged in business in a foreign country, companies must also consider whether practices that are perfectly acceptable at home, are appropriate in the foreign environment. This is perhaps best exemplified in the now-classic case of marketing infant formula in developing countries, particularly in the 1970s and early 1980s. The Swiss conglomerate, Nestle, was singled out among companies who were engaging in a number of practices to encourage new mothers in these countries to give up breastfeeding and switch to formula.[46]

In addition to more routine advertising that inaccurately suggested that bottle fed babies would be more healthy, companies used so-called "milk nurses" to promote their products in maternity wards. These women, although dressed as nurses, were actually sales representatives who received a commission for selling formula.

Unfortunately, the switch to formula posed a serious health risk to the infants for three reasons. First, the formula must be mixed with water, which is contaminated in many of these areas. Therefore, infants fed the formula were at high risk for infections and diarrhea. Second, mothers in these areas often cannot afford to continue buying formula. Therefore, they dilute it or substitute cheaper products that contribute to health problems, including malnourished babies. Finally, and perhaps most important, women who give up breast feeding cannot simply change their minds and return to it. After a short time, their own milk production diminishes and they are no longer able to feed their babies themselves. They are forced to rely on formula. In response to organized protests and boycotts from numerous activist groups, the company finally agreed to alter its marketing practices.

Although some might argue that the marketing practices just described would be questionable even at home, they would not seriously compromise babies' health as they do in the developing country. Thus the very same practice could be considered ethical in one setting but highly unethical in another.

Reebok's human rights initiatives.   The Reebok corporation, manufacturer of athletic shoes, has made human rights an integral part of its corporate strategy. Its formal world-wide code extends its coverage to workers employed by third parties, mostly in Asian factories. Regular on-site visits are conducted by independent auditors and include inspections of facilities and interviews with employees. Reebok will terminate its relationship with factories that are found to be in violation of the code.

Development of a Transcultural Corporate Ethic

Some movement toward "a transcultural corporate ethic"[47] has occurred as a result of intergovernmental agreements reached during the last half of this century. These combine to set out normative guidelines for the business conduct of multinational corporations. The guidelines that emerge from these six agreements cover the areas of employment practices and policies, consumer protection, environmental protection, political payments and involvement, and basic human rights and fundamental freedoms, and are based on four principles:

1. *The inviolability of national sovereignty*—multinationals are expected to respect the "host country's economic and social development and its cultural and historical traditions."[48]

2. *Social equity*—pay scales are expected to insure equity between genders, as well as racial and ethnic groups.

3. *Market integrity in business transactions*—restrictions on political payments and bribes assume that these "inject non-market considerations into business transactions."[49]

4. *Human rights and fundamental freedoms*—this principle is based on belief in the inherent worth and dignity of every individual and equality of rights of all human beings. However, this principle often competes with other principles, especially the first, national sovereignty. For example, South Africa's apartheid system was based on the denial of human rights to its black citizens, and women are denied rights in many cultures and government systems.

An important question remains. Do these agreements actually influence multinationals to behave differently? Although multinational corporations are not explicit parties to these intergovernmental agreements they are not directly bound by them. However, they are indirectly affected to the extent that countries enact laws requiring companies to comply. The agreements may also be contributing to a more informal type of compliance as they contribute to the development of accepted cross-cultural moral standards. The more multinationals become aware of these standards, the more likely they will be to comply.

In the absence of binding agreements, Richard DeGeorge[50] has proposed seven moral guidelines designed specifically to help multinational corporations (MNCs) make more ethical business decisions.

1. MNCs should do no intentional direct harm.

2. MNCs should produce more good than bad for the host country.

3. MNCs should contribute to the host country's development.

4. MNCs should respect employees' human rights.

5. MNCs should pay their fair share of taxes.

6. MNCs should respect the local culture to the extent that it does not violate moral norms.

7. MNCs should work with the local government to develop and enforce just institutions such as taxes, and health and safety standards.[51]

CONCLUSION

From the individual's perspective, a foreign assignment is full of ethical challenges. Training and guidance, along with openness and flexibility, can go a long way toward preparing the expatriate manager to survive with integrity and sanity intact—perhaps even to enjoy the international business experience. From the organization's perspective, the expanding interest in business ethics abroad and the development of international guidelines to guide business behavior across cultural boundaries will help to level the playing field and contribute to making the international business experience a richer and more satisfying one for all concerned.

DISCUSSION QUESTIONS

1. If you were going on your first overseas business assignment, what would you do to be sure that you were prepared to deal with ethical dilemmas you would face? What questions would you ask your superiors in preparation for the trip?

2. Your firm is expanding globally and is sending executives overseas for the first time. What will you do to be sure these individuals are prepared to deal with the ethical dilemmas they will face?

3. Imagine that someone from another culture asked you to provide information about business ethics when dealing with American managers. What would you say?

4. Talk with someone from another culture. Ask for information that would be helpful to you if you had to do business in their culture. What did you learn that you didn't know before? How might you behave differently because of what you know?

5. Discuss the following statement from the chapter—"Women succeed [overseas] because they are seen as foreigners who happen to be women, not as women who happen to be foreigners." Can you think of other groups to whom this statment might apply?

6. Imagine yourself in a situation where you had to bribe someone or lose the deal? How would you think about it? What do you think you would do? Why?

7. Is the development of a transcultural corporate ethic just a form of U.S. interference in other cultures?

CASE

The Gift

You're an account executive with a multinational financial firm, and one of your biggest accounts is that of a shipping magnate in Greece. Several months after you've arranged very complex financing to build a new fleet of oil tankers for this customer, he asks if you and your wife would attend the christening of the first tanker. You, of course, agree to attend—it would be an insult to him if you didn't. When you arrive, he asks your wife to break the traditional champagne bottle over the bow of the tanker. Two weeks after the christening, your wife receives a package from your customer. In it is a gold bracelet with her initials and the date of the christening in diamonds. To return the gift would insult your customer, but accepting it would clearly violate your company's policy? What should you do?

Case-Based Questions

1. What kind of an ethical issue is this?

2. Why would it be against corporate policy to accept such a gift? Do you agree with the policy? Why or why not?

3. Put yourself in the "shoes" of each of the parties? How might they think about the issue?

4. Imagine that you are the corporate vice-president in charge of business ethics and conduct for your firm. Would you be willing to change this policy? Why or why not?

NOTES

[1]Black, J.S. & Mendenhall, M. 1990. Cross-cultural training effectiveness: A review and a theoretical framework for future research. *Academy of Management Review*, 15 (1): 113–136.

[2]Adler, N. 1992. *International dimensions of organizational behavior*. Boston: PWS Kent Publishing Co.

[3]Black, J.S. & Mendenhall, M. 1990. Cross-cultural training effectiveness: A review and a theoretical framework for future research. *Academy of Management Review*, 15 (1): 113–136.

[4]Hofstede, G. 1980. *Culture's consequences: International differences in work-related values*. Beverly Hills: Sage Publications.

[5]Triandis, H.C., Brislin, R. & Hui, C.H. 1988. Cross-cultural training across the individualism-collectivism divide. *International Journal of Intercultural Relations*, 12: 269–289.

[6]Albert, R.D. 1986. Conceptual framework for the development and evaluation of cross-cultural orientation programs. *International Journal of Intercultural Relations*, 10: 197–213.

[7]Adler, N. 1992. *International dimensions of organizational behavior*. Boston: PWS Kent Publishing Co.

[8]Simon, P. 1980. *The tongue-tied American: Confronting the foreign language crisis*. New York: Continuum Publishing.

[9]Triandis, H.C., Brislin, R. & Hui, C.H. 1988. Cross-cultural training across the individualism-collectivism divide. *International Journal of Intercultural Relations*, 12: 269–289.

[10]Triandis, H.C. 1984. A theoretical framework for the more efficient construction of culture assimilators. *International Journal of Intercultural Relations*. 8: 301–330.

[11]Albert, R.D. 1986. Conceptual framework for the development and evaluation of cross-cultural orientation programs. *International Journal of Intercultural Relations*, 10: 197–213.

[12]Jelinek, M. & Adler, N.J. 1988. Women: world class managers for global competition, *Academy of Management Executive*, 2 (1): 11–19.

[13]Adler, N. 1992. *International dimensions of organizational behavior*. Boston: PWS Kent Publishing Co.

[14]Adler, N.J. & Graham, J.L. 1989. Cross–cultural interaction: The international comparison fallacy? *Journal of International Business Studies*, Fall: 515–537.

[15]Albert, R.D. 1986. Conceptual framework for the development and evaluation of cross-cultural orientation programs. *International Journal of Intercultural Relations*, 10: 197–213.

[16]Ibid.

[17]Donaldson, T. 1992. When in Rome, do . . . what? International business and cultural relativism. In *The ethics of business in a global economy*. P.M. Minus, ed. Boston: Kluwer, 67–78.

[18]Adler, N. 1992. *International dimensions of organizational behavior*. Boston: PWS Kent Publishing Co.

[19]Ibid.

[20]Ibid.

[22]Fadiman, J. A. 1986. A traveler's guide to gifts and bribes. *Harvard Business Review*, July/August: 122–134.

[23]Longenecker, J.G., McKinney, J.A., & Moore, C.W. 1988. The ethical issue of international bribery: A study of attitudes among U.S. business professionals. *Journal of Business Ethics*, 7: 341–346.

[24]Tong, H. M. & Welling, P. 1981. What American business managers should know and do about international bribery. *Baylor Business Review*, November–December: 8.

[25]U.S. Government Accounting Office. 1981. Report to Congress, impact of Foreign Corrupt Practices Act on U.S. Business, March 4.

[26]Carroll, A. 1989. *Business and society; Ethics and stakeholder management*. Cincinnati: Southwestern Publishing.

[27]Behrman, J. 1988. *Essays on ethics in business and the professions*. Englewood Cliffs, NJ: Prentice-Hall.

Grosse, R. & Kujawa, D. 1992. *International Business*. Boston: Irwin.

Singer, A. W. 1991. Ethics; Are standards lower overseas? *Across the Board*, September: 31–34.

[28]Behrman, J. 1988. *Essays on ethics in business and the professions*. Englewood Cliffs, NJ: Prentice-Hall.

[29]Carroll, A. 1989. *Business and society; Ethics and stakeholder management*. Cincinnati: Southwestern Publishing.

[30]Donaldson, T. 1992. When in Rome, do . . . what? International business and cultural relativism. In *The ethics of business in a global economy*. P.M. Minus, ed. Boston: Kluwer, 67–78.

[31]Ibid.

[32]Code of worldwide business conduct. 1985. In *The Corporate Social Challenge: Cases and Commentaries*. F. D. Sturdivant, ed. Homewood, IL: Irwin, 159–169.

[33]General dynamics standards of business ethics and conduct. 1985. August: 17.

Carroll, A. 1989. *Business and society; Ethics and stakeholder management*. Cincinnati: Southwestern Publishing.

[34]Donaldson, T. 1994. Address to the Conference Board Meeting on Ethics, New York.

[35]Barach, J.A. 1985. The ethics of hardball. *California Management Review*, 27: 2.

[36]Snarey, J. R. 1985. Cross-cultural universality of social-moral development: A critical review of Kohlbergian research. *Psychological Bulletin*, 97: 202–232.

[37]Singer, A. W. 1991. Ethics; Are standards lower overseas? *Across the Board*, September: 31–34.

[38]Vogel, D. 1992. The globalization of business ethics: Why America remains distinctive. *California Management Review*, Fall: 30–48.

[39]Ibid.

[40]Ibid.

[41]Ibid.

[42]Mahoney, J. 1990. An international look at business ethics: Britain. *Journal of Business Ethics*, 9: 545–550.

[43]Dunfee, T. & Holland, R.C. 1993. Viable ethical standards for global corporations: A glimpse of what might emerge. Unpublished paper. Philadelphia: Wharton School.

[44]Carroll, A. 1989. *Business and society; Ethics and stakeholder management.* Cincinnati: Southwestern Publishing.

[45]Ibid.

[46]Post, J.E. 1985. Assessing the Nestle boycott: Corporate accountability and human rights. *California Management Review*, Winter: 115–116.

[47]Frederick, W.C. 1991. The moral authority of transnational corporate codes. *Journal of Business Ethics.* 10: 165–177.

[48]Ibid.

[49]Ibid, 168.

[50]DeGeorge, R. 1992. Ethics and Worse. *Financial Times*, July 3: 12.

[51]Hoffman, W.M., Lange, A.E., & Fedo, D., eds. 1986. *Ethics and the multinational enterprise.* Lanham, MD: University Press of America.

CHAPTER TWELVE

Advice from Executives

INTRODUCTION

IN ORDER TO get that "Straight Talk" we promised in Chapter 1, and to support our distinctly managerial focus, we went to the experts—executives who manage ethics every day. We interviewed two CEOs, one former and two current ethics officers (vice-president level) of large firms, a retired corporate vice president of public relations, and a world renowned college football coach. We asked them what advice they would share with our readers—managers and students—about managing for ethical conduct. In this chapter, we tell you who they are and what they said.

Who They Are (in alphabetical order)

Harry Birkenruth, Chief Executive Officer, Rogers Corp.

Kent Druyvesteyn, former Staff Vice President, Ethics, General Dynamics Corp. and now Associate Professor of Management, Lindenwood College, St. Charles, Missouri.

Lawrence G. Foster, retired in 1990 as Corporate Vice President of Public Relations for Johnson & Johnson. He has been honored for the important role he played in managing the Tylenol crisis, which is a classic example of good business ethics.

Joseph Paterno, head football coach, The Pennsylvania State University. Coach Paterno is world renowned, not only for winning football games, but for managing his football organization in a highly principled manner. Some of the quotes attributed to Coach Paterno are taken from his book, *Paterno by the Book* (New York: Random House, 1989).

Shirley Peterson, Vice President, Ethics and Business Conduct, Northrop Corp.

Vin Sarni, retired Chairman and Chief Executive Officer, PPG Industries, Inc.

Carl Skooglund, Vice President and Ethics Director, Texas Instruments Corp.

What They Said

A number of themes emerged from our interviews with these executives. Here are the themes and what these executives had to say.

WHAT IS BUSINESS ETHICS AND WHY IS IT IMPORTANT?

These executives were clear about what business ethics is and what it means to them and their companies. Business ethics is about building relationships of trust between people and organizations, an absolutely essential ingredient to conducting business successfully especially in the long term.

Carl Skooglund

Ethics is the ground rules of how we are going to relate to other people - the expectations and understandings that define how we are going to deal with others. And by others we mean customers, suppliers, governments, communities, but most of all, one another. When you think about ethics in that context, ethics can be taught because we sure can teach what our expectations and understandings ought to be.

We try to explain to people why ethics has a positive benefit. It is far more than just keeping you out of trouble, or mitigating your sentences with a judge. There are very positive even competitive reasons to be ethical. If you walk into a relationship and somebody says, "I know you, I know your track record, I can trust you," that's important. Two years ago, in a survey that we sent out to employees, I received an anonymous comment from somebody who said, "A reputation for ethics which is unreproachable is a silent partner in all business negotiations." I agree and it works in all personal and business relationships.

An unethical company is very difficult to do business with. You can't trust them. You're never sure if a commitment's a commitment. At TI, our customers have told us that they can be sure of one thing: once TI commits, we're going to break our tail to make it happen. That's an easy company to do business with.

Harry Birkenruth

I would never knowingly work with people whose integrity I questioned. It is damn tough to do things that are solid and useful if you deal with people you can't trust. That's true of customers, suppliers, employees, joint venture partners, anybody. Since most business is transacted on the basis of trust, if you end up dealing with people you can't trust, you've got problems.

Joe Paterno

(In his book, Paterno discussed his early years as head football coach): "I was caught up with racing like hell down the wrong road. The road was called Success. It was called Winning. It was called Don't Lose, No Matter What. I didn't yet know that there was a different route with different scenery called Excellence."[1]

(the following is from the interview)

It makes good sense to be ethical—to be honest. If there's a rule, I insist that we adhere to the rule. If my people say, "Hey the other guy is breaking the rule, I say in the short run, it may hurt us, but in the long run we'll be way ahead of them." It may mean we have to work a little harder. Instead of calling on 10 players to recruit five, we may have to call on 15 or 20. We may have to get up to meet at seven in the morning. It's certainly doable because we're doing it. I don't care if it's in football or in business. You've got to have enough guts and enough confidence in your ability to do it right.

There's a difference between success and excellence in the sense that it's easy to make money. It's easy to win. You can manipulate, cut corners. But, I think you have to have a standard that you believe in and stay with it. We're in it for the long run. This isn't a get-rich-quick kind of operation. If we were in business, we wouldn't play games with the company to get the stock up in the next three years. We'd be in it for the long haul. And, we'd be a better company. Once you establish that, the stockholders or the fans love you.

Vin Sarni

We are going to live by our ethics code. It will keep us out of trouble, we'll be doing the right thing, and in the long run it will pay off for us. That's been our experience. It is not enough to simply say that our conduct is lawful. The law is the floor. Compliance with it will be the absolute minimum with respect to the PPG associate, no matter where he or she works. Our ethics go beyond the legal code. They require us to behave in a manner which is not only lawful, but also morally acceptable to all of the constituencies with whom we have dealings, and that's what we believe. That's not just waving the flag. We live that. And, I personally believe that we have a competitive advantage from being that way.

BUILD A REPUTATION FOR INTEGRITY—AVOID PROBLEMS BEFORE THEY BEGIN

Organizations can avoid many ethical problems by recruiting the right people to join the organization and by building a reputation that precedes the organization's representatives wherever they go. Coach Joe Paterno was most outspoken on this topic. He claimed that the Penn State football program avoids lots of problems faced by other college sports organizations by being absolutely clear up front about its commitment to values and doing things "by the book," as he shows in the following quote.

> I think our reputation eliminates most problems before we start. Because we do have a reputation. If a kid is looking for some kind of a deal, he generally won't fool around with us. But, I remember one kid whose Dad openly said, " He can't live on that. He's gotta have more money than that." I said, "That's all we can do." He said, "Well somebody will give it to us." I wished the kid luck and walked out of the house. I also set tough standards with our alumni. I send them information about what they can do and can't do. We create an atmosphere with everyone that says, we do it right.

In Ethics Programs, Avoid the Word "Ethics"—At Least at First

A number of the executives we interviewed, particularly the ethics officers, were sensitive to the negativity often attached to the word "ethics." Employees seem to get defensive when they hear the word. They think to themselves, "Why are you here talking to me about ethics? Mine are fine." Savvy executives have learned to use the word ethics carefully or not at all in their organizations. The words "integrity" and "values" are popular substitutes.

Shirley Peterson

Words can be stumbling blocks to line managers. In my first two years on the job, I learned to be careful about using the word ethics. I realized it was a charged word. "You're gonna tell me that my ethics isn't ok? What is this? I don't want anything to do with that"—until everyone understood more what ethos means, and that values are a set of guiding principles. That's what ethics is all about—guiding principles or shared values that we want to live by.

Kent Druyvesteyn

The word "ethics" is an emotional word. It's not a neutral word. In fact, I would say that it prompts a uniformly negative response. I've always thought of ethics as being about good conduct, and yet when you use the word ethics in a societal or cultural context, it inevitably swings around to bad conduct. And so when you first stand up and say, "Hi, I'm here to talk about ethics," don't expect people to cheer. Don't expect people to say, "Oh I'm really glad, I can't wait to talk about ethics. I just love ethics." No, the response is going to be largely negative and defensive. They're not happy to see you. People are going to ask, "Why are you talking to ME about ethics?" Using the word ethics unfortunately implies that somebody has a deficiency. So, I would urge you not to use that word at least until you can make clear what you mean by it.

ASSUME THAT PEOPLE ARE BASICALLY GOOD AND AIM YOUR ETHICS PROGRAMS AT THE GOOD PEOPLE

A number of the executives we interviewed argued the importance of beginning with a key assumption—that most employees want to do the right thing. They also believe that ethics programs and initiatives should be proactively aimed at this majority of good people who are basically good, but who want and need guidance. Ethics programs should not be just a reaction to wrongdoers.

Kent Druyvesteyn

It has to do with how you view your employees—as people who know the difference between right and wrong and want to do what's right. The purpose of our program is to help employees. We're not here to catch them, condemn them, judge them. We're not here to replace missing virtues. We're not here to straighten crooked characters. We're not here to make moral philosophers. We would like to provide some rules of the road, some guidelines to follow in daily business relationships. And, we also want to give employees our assurance that, if they have questions and concerns that can't be resolved through normal channels (their supervisor or boss's boss), then we are an emergency channel they can use. We are here to provide assistance to people who know the difference between right and wrong and who want to do what's right. This process is to help well-intentioned employees do their job better.

I know that there are scumballs out there. I know that there are people who I have to be wary of and be on my guard against. But most of the people I interact with day by day are not like that. If they were, you may as well hang it up because life would be wretched under those circumstances. Society couldn't operate. Families would fall apart. It is impossible to conceive of any type of social structure if people didn't know the differences between right and wrong, and if they generally didn't wish to act upon these differences. There's a common-sense reason why people act upon this sense of right and wrong. It's because their reputation is tied to it—it's how others judge them. And, their self esteem is also tied to it—how they feel about themselves.

So, the purpose of setting up rules and regulations in organizations is not to take a group of people who are all villains and make them into moral saints. If that's the mission, it's doomed to failure. How in the world could a company be so presumptuous to believe that it could do that? Churches have failed to do that. That's not what we're up to. We're not a church. We're not philosophers. We're not theologians. We're business people. We know that in running an organization, it's useful to be consistent and to behave in a controlled manner. Our experience has indicated that employees are very grateful for having some signposts. You send an employee out onto the road of life, and the employee comes back and says, "But, there aren't any signs—even at the intersections—it's just a free-for-all, a jungle out there—no one knows what the rules of the road are." It is in the interest of the business to help establish what those rules are so that employees know what is expected of them.

Carl Skooglund

We aren't just here to catch somebody doing something. We purposefully say that we are not a policing organization and we are not an investigative agency. We don't go around trying to find people doing things wrong. If I can find people doing things right, that's great, because I can use that as an example of the kind of conduct we want, the kind of company that we want to be. I think the positive message is very, very important.

MOST PEOPLE PREFER BEING PART OF AN ETHICAL ORGANIZATION

Our interviewees also agreed that, given a choice, most people would prefer being part of an ethical organization—one that they can be proud to be associated with. But, they were also aware that many students who are getting ready to enter the business world are cynical. They've read about the scandals. They've watched TV and seen the movies. That view needs to be balanced by organizations that are supporting ethical business conduct.

Carl Skooglund

When we bring college recruits to Texas Instruments, I am normally a lunch speaker. I have never seen an audience more alert, wide-eyed, and receptive because they're really apprehensive. They think they're getting into a jungle. I tell them that I am not up here to tell you that there isn't wrongdoing going on. Anybody who reads the paper knows that there is. But there are an awful lot of companies that are working very hard to establish support networks for employees. But I tell them, when they go out on that interview, they have the right to ask the company, "What happens if my boss asks me to do something that I know is wrong? What should I do? What would you expect me to do?" You have a right to ask about the company's philosophy.

I quote Helen Hayes. She was quoted on the radio and I almost wrecked the car copying it down. She made a statement that applies to anybody who is a parent, who is a teacher, who is a manager, who is a supervisor, who is a spouse, anybody who is in a position of trust. She said, "When they call you a star, you are obligated to conduct yourself above reproach. People give you their hearts and their trust, and you have no right to let them down."

I close with, "Look, there are going to be decisions you have to make. There are going to be times when things will be given to you. There are going to be times when things will be taken away—perhaps even your job. But throughout your professional life, there is one thing that nobody can ever take away from you unless you make the decision to let them take it away from you, and that is your integrity." They are receptive to that. And, I think any company that doesn't deliver that message right up front is missing a big opportunity.

Kent Druyvesteyn

We've found that employees appreciate working in a place where they believe the standards of the company match their standards. Note that I didn't say it the other way around. Employees want and need to know that the standards of the organization match their standards.

Joe Paterno

It's not like the kids who come here don't want what we're selling—they want what we're selling.

DEVELOP CLEAR GUIDING PRINCIPLES

Our interviewees also agreed about the importance of providing clear, guiding principles. Employees need and want guidance from the organization about what is expected of them. Once those expectations are made clear, the organization must stick to them because employees will expect the organization to act on its commitments. Anything less will be seen as hypocrisy.

Lawrence G. Foster

I believe that the best approach to ethical conduct in a business organization is to have a codified set of principles that clearly state what is expected of individuals. At Johnson & Johnson, this is the corporate credo. It was written in 1943 by Robert Wood Johnson, Chairman and CEO and son of the company founder, and it's practiced diligently to this day. We are assuming that a company goes out of its way to hire management people who have a sound, basic integrity. Beginning with that, a set of written principles helps everyone understand what is expected of them. It becomes a yardstick by which business conduct is measured - by management, by the other employees of the corporation, and by the outside constituencies as well— public, stockholders, customers, press, etc.

Robert Wood Johnson felt very strongly that the credo was not just a flag waving, do-good document, but rather a very intelligent, albeit demanding, way to manage a business. The first responsibility is to customers, and this triggers many decisions, many of them difficult and sometimes costly.

Carl Skooglund

It's important to clearly define for people what your ethical expectations are up front. You can't expect people to behave in a certain way unless you clearly define it. The question is: what do you expect from representatives of your company?

Shirley Peterson

Without clarity about guiding principles, your attempt to build a quality life of your own, or quality in the organization is hampered. You have to have your values clearly established and written down. You have to have a vision of what it is you want to be in the long haul . . . and most importantly, goals and strategies to achieve it.

Values or guiding principles have to be woven into the fabric of all corporate systems—in hiring practices, in succession planning, in pay for performance and appraisal, and the education of management on how to manage their people. If those values aren't woven into all of the systems, you're going to have values conflicts that will cause more problems than you had before values were articulated.

If management is going to publish a statement of guiding principles, they really need to be reminded of the danger zone they're getting into. The danger zone is not quite understanding what the commitment is because once they've gone to that effort to put that all in writing, now the employees have something to stick right in their face. What is this? We value people? We treat one another with respect? We recognize contribution to diversity and we have few black or female line managers out there?

SEND MESSAGES THROUGH RULES, REWARDS, AND SANCTIONS

Although our interviewees agreed that most people are good and want to do the right thing, they also agreed that misconduct is a fact of organizational life. When rules are broken, the individual (no matter who it is) must be disciplined swiftly and surely. Discipline sends a clear message that top management means what it says. Managers should also "reward noble failure." If a person fails, but for the right reasons, the individual should not be punished, but rewarded.

Joe Paterno

If I have trouble getting the value of rules out of my system, maybe it's because I'm a man of a game. Without strict rules—*strict* rules—games can't be played.

The players know what the penalties are. They have a pretty good idea of what's going to happen to them if they break the rules. If you're not pretty specific, they'll misinterpret. So, we try to be specific and talk it out as a coaching staff before we present it to the squad. If I tell the players we have a rule, we have to enforce it and apply it to everyone. You can't say this is the rule and it's for everybody but your top quarterback. It has to be for everybody.

If we had an alum who did some of the kinds of things that have been done in the Texas area, he'd be gone. We wouldn't even let him buy a ticket. And our alumni know that. So that creates an atmosphere. Our alumni now brag about it. They understand that we're not afraid to be different.

Vin Sarni

Anyone who transgresses our ethics code will leave our employ. That's without question. We have cases where we did that. It's very hard to do. It's never pleasant. But, you have to lead by example and if you're going to rationalize the event, it won't work.

Carl Skooglund

It's very important that you send a signal that you are going to discipline people for unethical conduct. And you have to be sure that you are disciplining high enough in the organization. But when you move up in the organization, you use different criteria. Somebody at a lower organizational level may do something that's wrong, but then you need to ask if they knew it was wrong. If they didn't know it was wrong, then you ask, why didn't they know it was wrong? Is it because the manager didn't meet his or her responsibility to communicate and train them properly? So the manager may need to be disciplined. If you don't discipline you aren't sending the signal that you're serious. We don't publish what we do, but the word gets out quickly. That kind of news spreads like wildfire.

Leaders of an organization also have to continually stress their concern over the means that are used to attain the ends. I heard one person say, "Reward noble failure." If someone has made an effort and for whatever reason it didn't work, or maybe they had to walk away from a profit opportunity because it didn't taste or sound or feel right - recognize that effort. It sends a good signal.

THE IMPORTANCE OF LEADERSHIP

For most of the executives we talked with, leadership was the most important ingredient in a solid ethical culture. The top leader is probably the most important individual, but leaders at all levels serve as important role models for employees—in terms of what they do and what they fail to do. If ethics is to be perceived as important, the organization's line leadership must set an example. Finally, the image of a "coach" is an increasingly popular metaphor for manager. If Joe Paterno is correct, real coaches have a significant moral influence on the team.

Joe Paterno

"I wish I had known in those early days what I think I know today about coaching. I don't mean about techniques and play selection and strategies. I mean about coaching in its first and highest sense. A coach, above all other duties, is a teacher. Coaches have the same obligation as all teachers, except that we may have more moral and life-shaping influence over our players than anyone else outside of their families."[2]

I think you have to demand ethical conduct. Number one, you don't say, "Well we're gonna try." You go in with the idea that you have certain convictions, certain beliefs, morals, and that they make good sense over the long run. Ethics and honesty are investments. I've been in "business" for 43 years in the same store, dealing with the same clientele, and we're only as good as our reputation. It would be very difficult for me to come out and say some of the things I've said in the book and elsewhere if I didn't act that way. I've always believed that you could be successful playing by the rules, and by being considerate and sensitive to kids' needs. If you're honest and you bring people in around you who believe in what you're doing, then a powerful force is created.

Vin Sarni

Our system is no great revolutionary invention. It follows what we try to do in our company all the time. And that is first: lead by example. Second: if it's worth doing, do it now. And third: if it's really important to you, get involved. And that's the whole story. We lead by example. We are very, very concerned about the integrity of our company, and so the leadership group is constantly talking about it. We're hands on. We established the ethics committee here. The chairman is the head of it and he is the *Chief Ethics Officer.*

Carl Skooglund

Leadership makes all the difference in the world because the leaders' actions come across very clearly to people in the organization. Even more important, the leader's actions tend to be reflected all the way down the line. If the order of the day is to make the forecast at all costs, that message is going to filter down.

I've seen leaders who said that personal integrity was the most important thing. And I don't doubt for a minute that they meant what they said. But at the same time, they put incredible pressure for performance on their organization, to the point that you could be publicly slaughtered if you weren't meeting an objective. Pressure to make the goals, that's what counted. But, at the same time, the leaders were saying and believed that personal integrity, doing it right, was the most important thing. Hey gang, you can't have it both ways—performance at all costs AND personal integrity.

Kent Druyvesteyn

It's a leader's responsibility to define the rules of the road. As a leader, you have to determine the rules and you have to communicate them. I also believe strongly that leaders are responsible for enforcement and not some other department.

Anyone in a line management position, from first-line supervisor up, is in a special leadership position. Their actions are judged by all employees. They are also judged by what they avoid doing. Often, a person in a leadership position is found wanting, not because they act a certain way but because they fail to act. That's what the Tailhook incident was all about—a failure of leadership. Not because the leadership was there; most of the leaders weren't even at the convention. But, they knew about it and didn't do something about it.

There's an anecdote that illustrates why people in leadership positions should do ethics training as opposed to having specialists do it. Early on, at General Dynamics, we declared that our ethics training workshops were to be small and interactive, and that they were to be led by managers. And, we heard some complaints from managers who said, "We don't know anything about this." They thought we were going to have them teach Aristotle and Kant, but that's not what we were trying to do. We also had people in training say, "We can't have people in management do this. There won't be any quality control."

At that point I said, "Let's consider what it is we're trying to do here. What we are trying to do is raise awareness, to increase knowledge of company standards and stimulate commitment to those standards. That's the most important thing." Here's an analogy I'd like you to consider. You have some small children and you decide that you want to teach them about sex. There are a number of ways that you could do this. You could hire an expert—someone who knows all about sex, who knows the right words to use, who knows all the latest terminology, who is pedagogically very skilled. You could hire this person to come into your home, sit down in your living room with your children, and teach them about sex. I mean, isn't that good management technique—to delegate it to someone? On the other hand, you could do it yourself. You may have limitations. You don't know everything. You might be embarrassed or tongue tied. In the end though, who do you think would be more effective? To have the expert do it or for you to do it yourself? I have never had a person say that the expert would be more effective.

When you're talking about conduct, you're really talking about an attitude, a commitment which is best communicated by leaders. That's one of the things that people in leadership need to do. They get to set the tone by the example of their own conduct. We could have had all the workshops in the world. We could have even had Jesus and Moses and Mohammed and Buddha come and speak at our workshops. But, if after all of that, someone in a leadership position then behaved in a way which was contrary to the standards, that instance of misconduct by a person in a leadership position would teach more than all the experts in the world.

Lawrence G. Foster

If you look at the experiences of major corporations that have been tested in crisis or ethical situations, you will find that the performance of the CEO was critical. Those CEOs who assumed leadership promptly and made the right decisions brought their companies through quite successfully, while those who vacillated paid a heavy price.

Shirley Peterson

It's the CEO who makes the difference. To create the first draft of our values statement, we took the top twelve people in the corporation away, locked the door, and threw the key away for a couple of days, and just hammered out what they perceived the values should be. It was always a buyoff by the top people before we started running anything down through the system. We put it up the flagpole and let them shoot holes through it. They've got to own it.

MORE ON WHAT LEADERS SHOULD DO

Kent Druyvesteyn

Draw the Lines. As a leader, there are some things that you get to do. You get to decide what the policies, procedures, and practices of the organization are. It's hard to draw those lines sometimes, but you should establish what the lines are and then you ought to tell others about them.

Communicate Your Commitment. The second thing that you can do is to stand up publicly and declare your commitment. By saying it out loud, you're doing more than communicating the rules. You're communicating your belief that those rules are important.

Create a Few Guidelines and Enforce Them. If you have a 1001 rules, you're doomed for failure. There's no way you can police all that. You ought to have three or four general guidelines and then you can have specific rules for people in specific areas.

This is sometimes very difficult. But if you don't enforce the rules, then what you've said will appear hollow. Everybody's going to look at you and think you're a hypocrite. Enforcement is one way employees are going to judge your commitment. Because you have to enforce the rules, you should think about what it is you're going to say you stand for.

Treat Employees Fairly. Many people in the organization view you with some suspicion and distrust. So, they have a litmus test for whether or not you mean what you say about bribes, about improper political contributions, about doing business in an international environment and the requirements of the Foreign Corrupt Practices Act. The way employees judge whether or not you mean what you say is by how THEY are treated. Now, if you're a leader you might say that's not fair. What does how I treat employees with regard to pay, benefits, working conditions, job promotion opportunities and performance evaluation—what does all that have to do with bribes, kickbacks, and political contributions? From the employee's point of view, that is how they judge the leader's commitment to honesty and fair play.

Joe Paterno

Coach Paterno recounted several key incidents in his career as head football coach where he had to stick to his principles and stand up for what was right. Here's a powerful one that made an impression on us.

Stand Up for What You Believe at Critical Moments. The Miami game was a turning point for me in other ways, too, and less happy ones. Late that night, as we waited to board our charter plane, Jim O'Hara and I strolled around the terminal replaying the joys of our victory when I saw something that stopped our conversation cold. I looked again and sure enough two of our best players were standing at a not-too-visible spot of the airport bar, each fingering a glass of beer . . . "You're in trouble," I told them. "You know that you're never to be seen standing at a bar." Naturally they protested that they were having only one, that they were coming down after the great game, that nobody around here knew them. "Never means never," I said. Nobody on the squad could possibly have the faintest doubt about my rule: We don't want a Penn State football player to drink in a public place . . . He throws a bad light on the entire team, putting every member under suspicion. Furthermore, . . . football players are public figures, watched and talked about. Also they're role models. I reminded the two guys of the one loophole in my rule: You can sit down with your folks privately and have a glass of wine. You can even have a couple of beers on a Saturday night—in private, with personal friends. That won't make you victims of hearsay. But if I see you standing at a public bar, you're in trouble.

So now, these two kids had forced the decision on me. One of them had previously got himself in a minor jam with the police. It made a mention in the paper. "You're gone," I said. That meant for good. Off the team. To the other I said, "This is the first trouble I know about. You get one more chance, but you're suspended for the next two games." On Monday evening the captains . . . came to see me. The whole squad was meeting at that moment, they said, and had sent the captains to tell me that they felt the penalties were too harsh. They wanted me to take the first guy back and lift the suspension on the second—and they wanted to return to the meeting with my changed decision.

There are moments in the life of a manager when his ability to maintain control teeters on a hair. He can only manage with the consent of the managed, unless he's a prison warden. On the other hand, he can only manage by unambiguous assertion of authority. Those are opposites, in a sense. If the manager, who sometimes has to choose in a split second, chooses the wrong one of those two, his effectiveness is finished.

"Go back to your meeting and I'll be there myself in five minutes," I said.

The sentence was harsh, I said to myself, but the rule they had broken was perfectly clear, defensible, and necessary. The morale and support of the entire squad hung in the air. If I backed off, the message was clear as a bell: I'm afraid of you guys. Ignore this rule. Ignore any rule that itches as much as this one does. And if there's a rule that itches less, try me on that, too.

Five minutes later, that squad room was a tableau of sullen, hard faces. I looked around, eye to eye, then talked. "A rule that protects us all was broken. The decision I made was the best one for all of us. I have no choice but to stand with it." Faces stayed frozen, waiting. I couldn't read them. "If anybody here can't live with it, go. Right now. If you stay, you do it my way, the right way, living by the rules. If you decide to stay and do it that way, we'll have a great football team. I'm going to walk out of here right now. A minute later I'm coming back in. Whoever's here, that's who we're going to play with."

As I walked bravely out of there, imitating John Wayne the best I could, my knees were shaking. In the promised minute, I returned. Every frozen face that was there during my first visit was still there, although still frozen.[3]

COMMUNICATE, COMMUNICATE, COMMUNICATE

Our interviewees all spoke about the importance of candor and communication—both the quality and the sheer amount of communication about ethics in the organization. People need to hear about it frequently and they need to hear both the positive and the negative. They need to hear about ethics from their leader, and their concerns about ethics need to be taken seriously.

Shirley Peterson

On this whole business of what makes good ethics process—I don't think we've even talked about the most significant thing of all, and that is a built-in fear of speaking up. That's fundamental to all of this—honest talking and honest listening. First of all, generally we're all poor listeners. Employees are reluctant to tell it like it is—to be candid and honest with the boss. I think an ethics process is doomed if it doesn't deal with how to get people to ask questions and if it doesn't create an environment where managers are going to listen to their people.

Carl Skooglund

This is probably the most important thing—to set up an environment of candor in your organization. Open up the communication lines. Make sure people feel that they can discuss their opinions, their ideas and their thoughts. But most of all, set up an environment where people feel that they can sincerely bring up and resolve problems without being embarrassed or without fear of retribution.

Now, employees are going to come to you with little problems, and then they may come to you with really big problems. But, the first time you blow your stack, or jump down somebody's throat at a point where they really don't deserve it, you've probably capped the level of problem that you're ever going to hear. All I can say is, sometimes you need to do a lot of lip biting. The first time you shoot the messenger who brings you bad news, you have taken the first step towards squelching the ethics of the environment. Easy words for me to say, but I tell our managers: open up those communication lines and let people discuss their problems.

Kent Druyvesteyn

We publish regular articles in the company newsletter. There's a big poster prominently displayed. And, we have reported back on the kinds of questions and concerns that are raised to us. For example, a year ago, we sent out a little pamphlet called "The First Six Years." It went over the Chairman's signature and it was inserted into everyone's paycheck. It was mainly a numerical summary of what has happened, but its intent was to communicate that this is something to which we are committed, this is something which works. Just look at how many people have called when they have questions and concerns. We didn't want to make it the cornerstone of this publication but we had to show the results in terms of sanctions. We see a lot of other results but employees are very concerned about the correction of poor conduct in the workplace. They don't like to work in places where people get away with things—not just sloppy work, but misconduct. So, we also gave data on the number of sanctions, what it was that people got sanctioned for, and at what level in the organization the sanction was imposed because there is a widespread belief that these are police operations and only little people get hurt. Our data shows that about 70 percent of the sanctions are imposed on people in management, supervisory, or professional positions, so we publish that data.

Joe Paterno

When I'm coaching well, when I really have a good rapport, kids will come in and say, "Coach, why are you doing that?" When I don't do a good job, I get so caught up in some other things, that I don't spend enough time with the "employees." I don't get enough feedback from them about what's happening. They're not comfortable with me. They don't know me well enough to come and say, "I've got something on my mind. Can I talk it out with you or have you ever thought about doing this, coach?"

I meet with seven kids once a week at breakfast. A freshman, two sophomores, two juniors, two seniors and we talk. How are things going? Do you have any problems? I try to head off something before it happens. I think that's important.

USING BREAKTHROUGHS AND SUCCESS STORIES

Recall from Chapter 9 that organizational stories become a key part of that culture. Some managers have learned to consciously take advantage of real events that can become stories that reflect the organization's values.

Shirley Peterson

Two years ago, when we removed two high-level managers at one of our divisions because they did not live the values, that was a breakthrough. You look for breakthroughs that can demonstrate to the workforce the company's intent to live the values.

We also brokered a success story about a middle manager who stopped a shipment of Boeing 747 main fuselages from a plant in Hawthorne. It passed all specifications to be shipped, but he had set his quality standards so high that he stopped the shipment because of one little thing that wasn't that high standard he wanted. We told that story in one of our little newsletters and it was like a brushfire. It shows how thirsty people are for success stories. I'd get into a meeting at some division—a leadership conference—and they'd say, "Tell us more about that story of the guy over at Hawthorne—he stopped a shipment to Seattle?" These stories are very powerful. We now use these success stories in our Ethics Refresher Seminars with great success. These people become role models!

DEALING WITH CYNICISM

Cynicism is rampant in our society. People who are committed to ethics in their organizations frequently run headlong into it. People don't believe that they're for real. However, a commitment to ethics means rising above cynicism, having the courage of your convictions, and correcting injustice when you see it.

Joe Paterno

I don't care what cynical people say. I don't really pay attention. These are small people who are not willing to see that they don't have the confidence or courage to do it the right way. And when they see someone doing it the right way, deep down they feel guilty. They'd rather say that it can't be done that way, that everybody cheats. I hear that all the time. "Fine," I say. "You think what you want." I know what I do. People around me know. You've got to just run your organization. You can't worry about what these cynical people say.

Vin Sarni

I think that some cynicism possibly is justified. But I say to people like that—do something about it! That's the great thing in American business: individuals can do something. We are talking about the very structure that allows you to correct some injustices you see. The ethics protocol in our company and many companies does that.

ETHICS AND QUALITY

Several of our interviewees made the link between ethics and quality. They see a program that supports ethics as integral to programs that are designed to improve and maintain quality in the organization.

Shirley Peterson

I see a lot of merit in placing the ethics office in a very close synergistic relationship to the quality initiative. Ethics can help nurture a quality culture—where employees are encouraged to think, speak up, and improve key processes. It gets back to this business of what employees really want. This is about the crosswalk between ethics and quality and productivity and job satisfaction. I believe inherently people want to do the right thing and they want to do a better job.

Ethical leadership, vision, shared values, and goals that flow down to every employee are the keys to profitability. Our biggest challenge is to see that ethics is integral to the whole scheme of business success because it relates to the way you manage people and the culture of the company.

ETHICS AND DOWNSIZING

Over and over again, we heard this refrain. Organizations that have ethics hotlines find that the preponderance of their calls, inquiries, and reports have to do with the perception that people are being treated unfairly. And, executives find that their most common ethical dilemmas deal with people issues—whom to hire, discipline, fire, etc. Recently, the downsizing process has captured the ethical attention of top managers.

Kent Druyvesteyn

If you have had the courage to stand up and say out loud that treating people with dignity and respect is an important part of your organization and culture—that your organization is committed to fair play and to treating people honestly—then when you get into a downsizing or layoff mode, a great deal of pressure is created. Employees judge your commitment to all of those values. So, it puts a great deal of strain on the company's commitment to people. At the moment they receive their layoff notice, employees will personalize it. They'll look to the company and say, "Well what about these fairness issues?" So what do you do about it? I think that you can still maintain that commitment to the organization's values by the way you treat people in the layoff mode. You continue to treat them with dignity and respect which means you give them advance notice, as much as you possibly can. You provide assistance, if you can, to get placement elsewhere. You do whatever you can: giving information, help, answers to questions. Employees are not, by and large, unreasonable in their expectations. I know there are some who say, "You promised lifetime employment." But employees aren't stupid. They know that life doesn't have these permanent promises. And so if management thinks that they have to address that sense of global unfairness, they're missing the most important thing. When people go down to the benefits office, they're looking for answers. When the person down there says, "Well I don't know how this is going to affect you," then the employee says, "I thought they said they were going to treat us with dignity and respect and here in this moment when we're down, they can't even give us answers to questions that they ought to know the answers to."

Harry Birkenruth

Because we come from a small-town kind of environment and we are a New England company, we have a lot of people working for us who are related or who have small-town relationships with their close friends. We know each other personally. So many of the ethical issues we deal with relate to how we deal with people. My biggest personal ethical dilemmas recently have been associated with the downsizing process and its impact on people. For example, how do you deal with having to let people go when other members of the family work for the company? How do you deal with letting an excellent person go who has worked for the company for 20 years, but there just isn't a job for that person? I recently had a situation like that. We were in a downsizing process and a fella who had been with us for 20 years was the obvious person to go. There just wasn't a slot for him. He had done a tremendous amount for the company over the years, and he'll have a hard time moving. I might have dealt with it differently, but it would have been a major morale issue for others in the department. Younger people who were more deserving of staying would have seen it as, "Well, we talk a good game about merit, but when we really get down to it, we don't walk the talk, particularly for people Harry knows very well. So we let him go. However, I think a lot about that fella. And of course we're trying to help him. That's what I call an ethical dilemma.

WITH GLOBALIZATION COMES THE NEED FOR MORE FORMALIZED ETHICS PROGRAMS

Many organizations that haven't thought about ethics programs before are doing so now because of their involvement in the global marketplace. If people need guidance at home, organizations find that they need it even more when they are asked to do business in a foreign culture.

Vin Sarni

For a long time we had no formal ethics programs. But we did have a cultural heritage that emphasized that integrity is one of the greatest assets that a company could have, and to have a high level you must deal ethically in all that you do. So, the more formal program was a reemphasis of something that was here but not as visible. And, one of the things that I feel that creates a need to make this more visible, more proactive approach was our globalization.

As we globalized, and we saw different cultures and social mores and even legal differences, it became very clear that our people needed guidance, and needed help, and we needed to understand better what they were really faced with every day. So I think that the globalization issue really highlighted the need for some structure and some proactive guidance which we didn't have before.

CONCLUSION

We think this chapter is so valuable because it gave us the opportunity to share the thoughts of high level managers who live and breathe ethics every day. For some (e.g., ethics vice presidents) ethics is an explicit part of their daily work. For others (e.g., CEOs and football coaches), it is implicit in everything they do. It is a part of every decision, every quality initiative, and every downsizing effort.

When we analyzed the interview transcripts, we were surprised at how neatly their comments fell into categories and how much they seemed to agree about what's important. These executives are not cynical. They believe that ethics is essential to business—that good business is built on honest relationships and on a reputation for integrity and trust. They assume that most people are basically good and that they prefer to work for an ethical organization. They also believe that these same people welcome guidance and the organization's development and communication of a strong set of values. And, they believe that people want to see good conduct rewarded and misconduct punished. Finally, they have found that moral leadership and open communication are essential building blocks of an ethical organization.

DISCUSSION QUESTIONS

1. What does business ethics mean to these executives? What does it mean to you?

2. Based upon what you read, do you think these executives would actually give up business in order to avoid dealing with an unethical business partner? Would you?

3. Think of organizations you are familiar with that have a reputation for integrity. Where does this reputation come from? How is it maintained?

4. Why is the word "ethics" so highly charged? Are there other words that you prefer? Why or why not?

5. What are your assumptions about human beings? Do you believe that people are basically good and need support or are they bad and need to be controlled? Where do these assumptions come from?

6. Would you prefer working for an ethical organization? Why or why not? What has been your experience along those lines?

7. If you were to develop five guiding principles for an organization that you were going to run (or for the organization you're in), what would they be?

8. Think of a situation where you noticed that someone was rewarded for doing the right thing, or for doing the wrong thing. What was your reaction? How about a situation where someone was punished for misconduct. What was your reaction?

9. Think of leaders who have influenced you. How did they behave? What was the effect of their behavior on you?

NOTES

[1]Paterno, J. 1989. *Paterno: By the book.* New York: Random House, 95.

[2]Ibid., 81.

[3]Ibid., 115–117.

Appendix

.

APPENDIX

Integrative Case: Manville Corporation

(Case copyright ©1992 by Richard T. Dailey and Scott G. Hibbard. The generous cooperation of the Manville Corporation is gratefully acknowledged. This case was written as a basis for class discussion rather than to illustrate effective or ineffective management policies.)

INTRODUCTION

John McKinney, CEO of the Manville Corporation, one of the most profitable companies in the history of American business, had just heard a recommendation from his staff that the company file for reorganization under Chapter XI of the Federal Bankruptcy Code. "When I was told of that," Mr. McKinney said, "I went through the roof. I did not think that was right." The company was solvent, in fact profitable, but was required by accounting convention to book a $2 billion contingent liability against its $2.2 billion of assets. The welfare of 28,000 employees was at stake. Though Manville faced 17,000 asbestos-related health claims, of the 4,000 that had gone to trial the company had won half. According to Earl Parker, Chief Legal Counsel for the Manville Corporation, this allowed Manville to settle the remaining cases at reasonable figures. In Mr. McKinney's mind, there was no reason Manville could not continue as it had. It was August 20, 1982.

Asbestos

Asbestos is a grayish-white fibrous mineral that is strong, flexible, and heat resistant. It has been used in over 3,000 applications, but is best known as a fire retardant. Asbestos products include asbestos cement roofing tiles, corrugated siding, wallboard, sewing materials, pipe insulations, acoustical insulations, fabric applications, and asbestos-lined hand-held hair dryers. The mineral has been so widely used in numerous applications in public buildings and private dwellings that virtually everyone has had some exposure to asbestos.

311

But the worst exposures have occurred in the workplace, where asbestos has caused disabling and often fatal disease. Workers who produced asbestos products or installed asbestos insulation—without adequate filtration or ventilation systems—were exposed to particularly high concentrations of the asbestos fiber.

Ingested or inhaled asbestos causes mechanical injury to moving tissue, particularly to the lungs, where the constant motion of the lungs during air and oxygen exchange facilitates penetration of these fibers, cutting and damaging the lung tissue in the process. The microscopic fibers are not dissolved or expelled from the body, and are nearly impossible to totally filter from the air. Exposure to these fibers can result in asbestosis, lung cancer, or gastrointestinal cancer.

Asbestosis is a non-malignant progressive and irreversible scarring, thickening, and calcification of the lungs and their linings that makes breathing increasingly difficult—causing shortness of breath and fatigue from climbing even a single flight of stairs. The incidence of asbestosis appears to be directly related to the duration and intensity of exposure to the asbestos fiber. In his 1962-63 epidemiological studies of workers in the asbestos industry, Dr. Irving J. Selikoff, Director of Environmental Sciences at New York's Mount Sinai School of Medicine, found that almost 87 percent of the workers who consistently had been exposed to asbestos in the workplace developed asbestosis, and between 7 percent and 10 percent of asbestos workers died from asbestosis.

The studies conducted by Dr. Selikoff and his associates indicated that asbestos workers had seven times greater risk of developing lung cancer, and three times greater risk of developing gastrointestinal cancer, than did workers in other industries. His studies also concluded that the degree of fibrosis developed (scarring of the lung tissue) was directly correlated with the length of exposure to asbestos. Dr. Selikoff's studies were funded by the Manville Corporation.

Legal History

Manville faced its first lawsuit in 1968, fourteen years before the bankruptcy recommendation. By 1973 there had been thirteen cases. The case load did not become alarming until the later half of the 1970s, when several hundred claims were being filed each month. Dick Van Walsh, who managed asbestos cases for Manville, saw the number of cases as being on "some sort of bell-shaped curve," but he did not know where the company was on that curve.

> At that point in time, given the numbers and the lack of real science, I couldn't tell whether we were on an accelerating part of the curve or on the decelerating part of the curve—I just had no way to know. . . As every year went by, more and more claims came in at a faster rate . . . and we weren't seeing a peak or change in the shape of the curve and so by the late [70s] . . . the real pressure hit about what is the problem and we'd better really get our hands around this one.

There was also a conception within Manville's management that the epidemiological reports supported a theory that the worst of the asbestos cases had been seen.

"We felt that we had already probably paid off or litigated with most of the people who were seriously ill," Mr. McKinney said. "There were only going to be a handful after that."

The magnitude of the issue was difficult to grasp because it was "a sort of creeping problem," Dick Van Walsh said, "not like an airplane crash. This one just kept building every year. And so the psychology of it took time for it to really hit home in a major way."

The "creeping" nature of the asbestos litigation issue began with product-liability law as defined by the *Clarence Borel* vs. *Fiberboard Paper Products Corporation et. al.* in 1973. The court ruled that Clarence Borel, an asbestos-insulation worker since 1936, could sue eleven asbestos manufacturers for failure to disclose the foreseeable risk involved in the use of their products. This opened the door for the increasing number of claims which soon followed. By August of 1982, 20,000 lawsuits had been filed against Manville. The company had paid $50 million in claims and settlements.

Insurance Companies

Manville's position was complicated by the nature of its insurance coverage. Whereas most asbestos manufacturers had one or two insurance carriers, Manville had a total of 27 past and present carriers dating back to the 1920s. This led to the "trigger of coverage" argument among insurance companies and between Manville and its insurance companies. As expressed by Earl Parker, Manville's Chief Legal Counsel:

> There was a dispute as to which policy of insurance could be called on to respond to the occurrence. Was it the policy of insurance in effect at the time the person manifested an asbestos-related disease? Or was it the policy in effect at the time that he was first exposed to the asbestos, or was it some combination of those? And that is referred to as exposure or manifestation theories, and some of the insurance companies were arguing for exposure, some for manifestation—of course, depending on where their particular coverage set.

To resolve the impasse between Manville and its carriers, legal proceedings were scheduled to be held in San Francisco. Because of the number of parties involved, Mr. McKinney noted that "they were even refurbishing an old theater to hold the trial in, because there wasn't a trial courtroom big enough to hold that many lawyers."

Meanwhile, the insurance companies had stopped paying claims. Because of this, and because of the increasing volume of claims, Manville adopted a tougher litigation strategy. They were accused of stonewalling, of refusing to settle cases in favor of litigation. Mr. Van Walsh said that

> that's not really true. . . . We realized that we had to make sure we didn't pay for anything that wasn't a real case. And the only way to do that was to make sure that you work a case very hard so that you get the right facts, right data, and can make the right judgements. . . . We got tougher in demanding good facts . . . we didn't

ever adopt a "hands-off," stonewall policy of "we're not going to pay claims, we're going to try to clog the court system."

The most Manville could litigate in any given year was about 100 cases, of which it was winning roughly half. Total costs of litigation equated to one-third defense costs, one-third plaintiff legal fees, and one-third plaintiff compensation. In the second quarter of 1982, average cost of case disposition was $40,000. "There are people who say that the litigation expense would have been much less . . . if the companies had not defended the cases," Mr. Parker said. ". . . but you can't lay down your arms and settle cases when the plaintiff's demands are a million or ten million dollars per case." Mr. Parker felt that those cases which it won in court "were responsible for our being able to settle the remaining cases at reasonable figures."

According to Mr. Parker, the insurance companies argued that asbestosis was not accidental, that it was the result of intended actions by Manville. Manville argued that "the state of the medical art was not such that the company knew or could have known that the product was hazardous at the time that it was put into the marketplace." Manville also countercharged that those workers who would not wear respirators after being instructed to do so were guilty of contributory negligence. In those cases where the plaintiff smoked, the defense was able to call into question exposure to asbestos as the cause of the disease.

The U.S. Government

Much of the contention between Manville and its insurance carriers was based in the latency of asbestosis. Twenty to thirty years was needed for the disease to surface after exposure, the most common source of which was the shipyards of World War II. Because of its fire-resistant properties, asbestos was used extensively in the construction and refurbishing of warships. According to Bob Batson (who had primary responsibility of Manville's litigation against the United States), with the heavy use of asbestos-containing materials in ship construction, in a naval battle, "you essentially could be on fire, fight fire, and keep fighting."

The crisis atmosphere of the war demanded that ships be turned out as quickly as possible, with some shipyards turning out a ship a day. To do this, shortcuts were taken, in spite of the fact that information was available to the government which indicated that serious health risks to shipbuilders may be involved. Mr. Batson made reference to court testimony by Dr. Leonard Goldwater, head of medical programs for occupational medicine at the Navy shipyard in Brooklyn during WW II:

> . . . 75,000 workers in the shipyard and Goldwater testified . . . they knew they were at risk . . . they knew there was a number of industrial hygiene measures that could be taken to protect shipyard workers. The fact was, up until October of 1943 we were losing the war because we couldn't build ships fast enough. They were sinking faster then we could build them. So when you talk about the relative risk here and the importance for building ships and getting them out, they were willing to take the kind of risks that were involved.

. . . you talk to some workers who worked in these facilities during the war and they describe some pretty serious conditions. They talk about working double shifts, working conditions where the ventilation was in disrepair.

Roughly half of the claims filed against Manville were from shipyard exposure during WWII. During the war, the U.S. Government imposed mandatory wartime contracts on asbestos manufacturers to supply asbestos-containing materials to shipyards. Much of the specified fiber was from South Africa, which the government would purchase, transport, and sell to manufacturers at a profit. The asbestos-materials manufacturers would then make the required materials as specified by the government, which the government would purchase for use in its shipyards. As a result, Mr. Parker said, " . . . there was a very deep involvement of the government as a commercial party in this asbestos manufacturing experience and as an employer of the people." Because of this, and because the government had control of the materials and the workplace, in Manville's view the government should share the burden of asbestos-related health claims resulting from shipyard exposure. Earl Parker summed up Manville's perspective:

> The predominant argument by the government is that the government is sovereign and cannot be sued in a situation. People often quote that the "king can do no wrong," but the second part of the formula which often goes unquoted is "because the king sees that all wrongs are made right." And we were asking in this case that the sovereign government come in and make right a wrong that had been committed against these people. And, as I said before, the companies were not asking to be absolved but only for some participation, financial participation by the government in the compensation and for the creation of a more efficient means of compensating people rather than continuing the, what we thought was a very wasteful, tort litigation scenario.

Proposed Legislation

The Asbestos Health Hazards Compensation Act was introduced in the U.S. House of Representatives by Representative Millicent Fenwick in 1977, and in the U.S. Senate by Senator Gary Hart in 1980 and in 1981. This legislation would have barred victims from filing lawsuits under the tort system and would have administered claims through Workers' Compensation, and in so doing would have established a Workers' Compensation fund to help compensate asbestos victims. Both bills were sharply attacked by congressmen and asbestosis litigation attorneys as corporate bail-outs for the asbestos industry. Both bills were killed in committee.

Manville's Burden

In Mr. Batson's view, the issue was one of "relative knowledge"—that the government knew relatively more about asbestos health hazards than did anyone else. However, "Manville and others in the industry had already been tried and convicted essentially before information about the government came out. . . . "

Referring to those cases that Manville did lose, Mr. Parker surmised that, "you could say that the courts found that the company did know, or should have known, or had reason to know that the product was unsafe at the time." Mr. Batson, manager of Manville's asbestos litigation, concurred by saying that because the government was fully aware of the health risk, in a relative sense it was safe to assume that Manville was also.

Through the litigation process, documents surfaced which supported a conspiracy between Manville and Raybestos-Manhattan, another asbestos-materials manufacturer. Correspondence between the President of Raybestos and the General Counsel of Manville indicated that not only did both companies know of the hazardous nature of asbestos but they conspired to cover-up that knowledge. This became the basis for punitive damage awards against Manville depending, according to Mr. Parker, on which parts of the evidence a jury chose to believe.

Product liability law had developed from "buyer beware" to negligence to strict liability. The Borel case was the catalyst in bringing strict product liability to bear in the asbestos issue. The over-exposure which occurred in shipyards through WWII and up to the Korean War, and the long latency period of the disease, were the other elements which, in Mr. Parker's view, caused the financial crisis for Manville. This was exacerbated by inconsistent enforcement of health and exposure regulations within Manville itself. According to Mr. Parker,

> There were instances in the Manville record where managers of local facilities did not observe the policies the corporation had set forth, and I think you can link back to the corporation a failure to insist and enforce those policies in every location. There were instances where people were diagnosed as having asbestos-related disease and were not advised of that diagnosis and were not protected or removed from a dusty occupation. So there were many, many individual and corporate failings which contributed. . . . But I think I feel comfortable in saying that the, at least the financial, liability of Manville and the other asbestos companies was a result of over-exposure and the long latency period and the development of product liability law in the United States.

Manville's Culture

When John McKinney was faced with the decision of whether to file for bankruptcy, the Manville Corporation was ranked 181st on the Fortune 500 list of industrial firms. It was highly centralized and operated from a new corporate campus which it had built outside of Denver. To some it appeared to have a huge image of itself, much like a strutting peacock. For much of its history Manville was big, and it was insulated. Mr. McKinney said:

> . . . in 1960 probably 80 percent of the profits from the company came from asbestos. And by '77 or so it was down, but what had happened was you had a whole generation of people who grew up in the company not paying any attention to expenses. Nobody cared. I remember a guy who was head of the asbestos fiber division and coordinating the proposed projects; you know, spend so many million dollars

on a plant and his attitude was, "go ahead, we spill more than that every day at the mine." . . . [for] a long time they never borrowed any money, they had never issued any equity, the big deal at the end of every year was to see how many reserves you could set up to depress earnings. . . . I think the lowest cash-on-hand that the company would have during the yearly cycle was about $50 million, this was when the sales were something like $500 million.

There was a sense of family at Manville. It was difficult to get fired. During the depression the company (then Johns Manville) had no layoffs. In periods of deflation the company deflated salaries rather than cut back on the number of employees. The company instituted a 40-hour week prior to the Wagner Act. A strong sense of personal loyalty to the company was common among employees, with many buying company stock for their pension plans.

Tom Stephens, who became Manville's CEO subsequent to Mr. McKinney's retirement, saw the early Manville culture as having been largely derived from the wealth associated with controlling 70 percent of the world supply of a basic commodity.

So you had a culture built up that [with] almost anything that you did, you could still be successful. And so one of the keys to success is "don't screw up." It's not "go out and do something positive." It becomes a negative. Don't make a mistake. So you build up a culture where you're pretty insulated from the realities of the world.

As a result, Mr. Stephens felt that "too much of the asbestos problem was treated as an accounting entry." He also felt that the blame rested with society as much as with Manville:

Manville as a company really wasn't that different from society in general. They were not a bunch of green monsters that were sitting around a board table at Manville. They were probably some of the more capable people in American industry in those days. But they were a product of the society that they lived in.

Part of the Manville culture involved a code of ethics. To Mr. McKinney's recollection, documents requiring annual signatures were those concerning honesty in general business dealings, i.e., testimony which basically had to do with "not cheating," and "the thou shalt nots with respect to the things that could get you into any trust violation." Manville would not allow its employees to bribe foreign or domestic officials even when it was customary to do so. "We never were able to sell asbestos cement pipe in the city of New York because we wouldn't pay anybody off. We never sold any in Chicago because we wouldn't pay anybody off."

In Mr. Stephens' perspective, though Manville was in many respects exemplary in its ethical conduct, its system was not without fault:

We were way out ahead of most in terms of statements on ethics and employee safety and all that sort of thing. But it still had happened, and why? And the bottom line is the breakdown in getting from those statements of corporate ethics to the actual practices on the plant floor. Having a code of ethics written down is a nice start and you ought to have that. But what you really have to change is the mentality and the culture and the instincts of an organization and that's much more a function of actions in leadership than it is having something on the bookshelf. . . .

Plaintiff Compensation

To more effectively deal with the asbestos health claims, Manville attempted to work with other members of the industry in order to develop a common defense that could settle rather than litigate claims. In so doing, expenditures which were considered by Manville to be wasteful, such as legal fees (defense as well as plaintiff fees) and expert witness fees could be minimized. This would theoretically allow the claimants to receive, on the average, more compensation per claim at less total expense. In the mind of Chief Legal Counsel Earl Parker, by so doing, less money would be diverted from those most in need. Strict litigation allowed contingency fees as high as 40 percent.

By the early 1980s, it became clear to Manville's management that the claims process could not be managed on a tort system. Manville had been in litigation with its insurance carriers since 1980, and by mid 1982 cases were being filed at a rate of 500 per month. There were a great many more lawsuits than the system was designed to handle.

When Manville settled cases, however, it believed that in many instances it paid people who suffered no significant impairment and therefore deserved no payment. As Mr. Stephens saw it,

> . . . there are people out there that would take all of you they could get. There are people out there that have filed claims that have no physical impairment whatsoever. There are people out there that are in absolute miserable pain and dying. There are people that are not even sick yet.

Some cases were settled for as little as $100, and some were litigated for as much as $1,000,000. Neither approach appeared to Manville to be particularly fair to all involved or expeditious. Mr. McKinney said:

> . . . even settling a case for $7,000, you can't even open a file in the lawyer's office for $7,000. . . . in the second quarter of 1982 we litigated all cases and settled none. As a result of this our average cost of case disposition went from something like $15,000 a case up to $40,000 a case.

Mr. McKinney wondered if a modified compensation system in which Manville could make awards similar to the most generous federal Worker's Compensation scheme, could be devised. Perhaps in this way a larger percentage of the settlements would go directly to the claimants.

Legal Fees

Manville was well aware that roughly one-third of the awarded payments went to plaintiff legal costs. Mr. McKinney felt that, of the total amount that Manville could expect to pay out over a period of time, "the lawyers are going to pick up 30 to 40 percent of it and that's scandalous. You can justify a contingent fee for one or two cases but you can't for a thousand because you had already been paid for the same work. You do the work on the law one time."

Manville was also concerned that the number of cases being filed was not following the expected bell-shaped pattern. That is, the number of asbestosis victims was expected to increase consistent with the maturation of the latency period of the disease. As the latency period reached expiration the number of asbestosis cases should decline. "But," Mr. Parker said,

> the relationship between asbestosis and the number of cases filed in court, or claims filed, is not following that pattern. And I think, in part, that's because the lawyers responsible for handling these cases have brought cases for compensation on evidence of minimal exposure to asbestos and not symptom cases where there has been significant impairment or any impairment.

In addition, Manville saw itself being sued by workers who had received federal Workers' Compensation. By law, any compensation collected from other sources subsequent to receipt of Workers' Compensation benefits had to be paid to the government, less legal fees. "So they didn't gain a thing by going for it but their lawyer picked up 40 percent," Mr. McKinney said.

On the other hand, Marianna Smith, a former law school faculty member and former executive of the Trial Lawyers Association, pointed out that Manville did not make it easy for the plaintiffs' bar to prepare their cases:

> One of the things that happens in our legal system is that if you try one case against a manufacturer and produce documents and they're authenticated by the defendant, then typically you could walk into the next court room and that same manufacturer will say, "yes, I'll stipulate that I authenticated these in the last trial." Manville took the position that every case was the first case. So a plaintiff's lawyer spent . . . God knows how much time trying the same case over and over and over again.

She added, "These kind of things get people's dander up."

FASB Rule 5

The Financial Accounting Standards Board (FASB) is a board of accountants which sets standards and rules for the accounting profession. Rule 5, "Accounting for Contingent Liabilities," stipulates that, when a company has incurred contingent liabilities of an indeterminate amount, and those liabilities can be expressed in a range of low to high, then that company must book a reserve in the amount of the low end of that range. If that figure exceeds the assets of the company, then that company should file for bankruptcy.

In 1981, Manville commissioned a study by an independent firm to determine the expected number of claims to be filed against Manville. Conducted by Epidemiology Resources, Inc., the study predicted a minimum of 52,000 cases, a number which many in Manville were not comfortable with. According to Dick Van Walsh, General Counsel at Manville following Mr. Parker's retirement,

> You know when I say good science I mean as good on a scientific or epidemiological approach as we can get as to how many claims are going to exist out in the future. It had never been done, nobody had ever done that kind of study. And not only how many disease claims might there be, but then how many of those people might actually bring a lawsuit.

At $40,000 per case Manville was required to book a reserve to cover a contingent liability of $2 billion. Manville's assets amounted to $2.2 billion. The argument was advanced by senior Manville management that the reserve would essentially wipe-out Manville's net worth, thereby crippling its operations, and that bankruptcy was appropriate under circumstances such as these.

CEO McKinney did not want to hear this. He and other staff felt that the projected number of cases was too high. To test the validity of the commissioned report, Mr. McKinney ordered that a separate group of epidemiologists and biostatisticians be retained to test the methodology of the first study. To Mr. McKinney's disappointment, the second study verified the first. The voices calling for bankruptcy strengthened. And Mr. McKinney, having been a patent attorney for 20 years, knew the study could not be challenged, "despite the fact that we thought they were wrong by at least double." The difficulty lay in not only defining an unknown population, but predicting their behavior.

Mr. McKinney heard from his staff that if the company were to file for reorganization under Chapter XI of the bankruptcy code, the claimants would then be on the same level as all other creditors. Punitive damage awards would be eliminated which would allow for more equitable settlements of more claims. Exorbitant legal fees would be reduced. Claimants would not need to go through lengthy litigation, and could in fact expect their claims to be settled within 90 days after initiating the claim process. Plus, no better methodology or process had surfaced to handle the volume of claims generated by the asbestos health issue.

The question Mr. McKinney, CEO of one of the largest industrial firms in the world, had to answer was: how could existing and future claims be serviced without destroying a major company? Among his concerns were the welfare of Manville's employees and shareholders, that Manville Corporation remained profitable and no one had ever taken a profitable company into bankruptcy, that bankruptcy would be based on a potential contingent liability which no one knew for sure was real or accurate, and one which Mr. McKinney felt was inflated.

If Manville filed for bankruptcy, Mr. McKinney was concerned that the company would be perceived as evading its corporate responsibility, and that it would be the largest bankruptcy ever filed. He also had to wrestle with the reality that declaring bankruptcy went against every grain in his body.

DISCUSSION QUESTIONS

1. Identify the relevant facts.

2. Identify the pertinent ethical issues/points of ethical conflict.

3. Identify the relevant affected parties. Who are the stakeholders?

4. Identify relevant obligations to each stakeholder group.

5. Identify and evaluate the possible consequences of alternative courses of action.

6. Who are the responsible parties? Manville? the government? individuals?

7. Identify the relevant community standards that should have guided a person of integrity at the time.

8. How did Manville's culture affect its behavior?

9. Recommend programs and policies that would better insure worker safety.

10. Identify arguments for and against bankruptcy that might have been made at the time.

Index